FAST
FORWARD

Scott B. MacDonald
and Georges A. Fauriol

FAST FORWARD

Latin America on the Edge of the 21st Century

TRANSACTION PUBLISHERS
New Brunswick (U.S.A.) and London (U.K.)

Copyright © 1997 by Transaction Publishers,
New Brunswick, New Jersey 08903

All rights reserved under International and Pan-American Copyright Conventions. No part of this book may be reproduced or transmitted in any form or by any means, electronic or mechanical, including photocopy, recording, or any information storage and retrieval system, without prior permission in writing from the publisher. All inquiries should be addressed to Transaction Publishers, Rutgers—The State University, New Brunswick, New Jersey 08903.

This book is printed on acid-free paper that meets the American National Standard for Permanence of Paper for Printed Library Materials.

Library of Congress Catalog Number: 96–54513
ISBN: 1–56000–207–7
Printed in the United States of America

Library of Congress Cataloging-in-Publication Data

MacDonald, Scott B.
    Fast forward : Latin America on the edge of the twenty-first
century / Scott B. MacDonald and Georges A. Fauriol.
        p.   cm.
Includes bibliographical references and index.
ISBN 1-56000-207-7 (alk. paper)
1. Latin America—Economic conditions—1982–   2. Latin America—
Economic policy. 3. Latin AmericaPolitics and government—1980–
I. Fauriol, Georges A. II. Title.
HC125.M23   1997   96-54513
                                                                    CIP

Contents

Acknowledgments

The authors wish to thank the following for their assistance in finally completing this book, which took longer than initially expected because of the many changes facing Latin America, international markets, and the authors. While the authors assume complete responsibility for the accuracy of the book and stand by its conclusions, there are others who helped stir the creative pot. Special thanks go to Paul Luke at Morgan Grenfell for providing editorial comments on the entire manuscript, especially the chapters on Argentina, Brazil, and Chile. His time and effort as well as friendship are greatly appreciated. We also thank Allen Rodriguez at the Inter-American Development Bank for reading earlier drafts on the entire book; Professor David Scott Palmer at Boston University's political science department for his comments on the Peru chapter; Professor Albert L. Gastmann, now retired from Trinity College in Hartford, for comments on the entire book at various stages; Juan Villanueva at CS First Boston's Emerging Markets Fixed Income research department for reading and commenting on the manuscript in its later stages; and Uwe Bott at Moody's Investor Services for various chapters.

We also appreciated the exchange of ideas on the book and Latin America with Robert Windorf at Merrill Lynch Asset Management; Professor Jane Hughes at Brandeis University on Argentina, Brazil, and Venezuela; Bruce Zagaris of the Washington, D.C. law firm of Cameron & Hornbostel on Latin America; and Rensselaer W. Lee III of Global Advisors on Colombia.

The final version of the manuscript was completed in record time through the editorial efforts of Stori Davis, a Canadian research intern, until recently with the Americas Program at the Center for Strategic and International Studies in Washington, D.C.. The organizational support of Diane Arguimbau, Special Assistant to Georges Fauriol at CSIS, eased last minute requirements from the publisher.

Scott B. MacDonald wishes to thank his wife, Kateri, for her patience and support in completing the present work, his son, Alistair, and his daughter, Estelle, for making life that much more enjoyable. Special thanks are also reserved for his mother, Anita MacDonald, who has always been there.

Georges Fauriol adds his own note of appreciation to Janet Owens who has helped place this book and other endeavors in useful perspective.

The views expressed here are solely those of the authors and do not necessarily reflect those of the institutions for which the authors are employed.

Introduction

In March 1995, one financial advisor cautioned his readers: "Do not—I repeat, do NOT—sell any of your Latin American stocks, bonds or mutual funds. Chances are, you would be making exactly the same mistake as those hapless investors who dumped their holdings on October 19, 1987. In the long run, your Latin investments will provide handsome returns because that part of the world is steering away from inflation and adopting free enterprise. As a result, solid economic growth is virtually guaranteed."[1] Despite Latin America's economically depressed 1980s and the wake-up call of the 1994—95 Mexican peso crisis, financial markets and much of the business community remain relatively upbeat about the future of Latin America. In July 1995, only months after Mexico had been regarded on the critical list, the Mexican government issued a $1 billion bond, which U.S. investors lined up to purchase. Three questions flow from this outlook: first, is the optimism about the region deserved?; second, who is leading the economic-development parade?; and finally, where is the parade going?

Open the business section of any major newspaper and look at the stocks, and an interesting discovery can be made. Tucked in between the blue-chip stocks of IBM, General Electric, and NYNEX are a plethora of Latin American stocks representing the major telephone and telecommunication networks of Argentina, Chile, and Mexico, utilities in Bolivia and Chile, major banks, and a number of mutual funds covering the entire region. These are not penny stocks, but commercial paper traded on the New York Stock Exchange with a relatively high value and the ability to hold their own in tough interna-

1

tional markets. It would have been difficult to foresee major investment houses and brokers selling shares of Latin American funds and
companies in the early and mid 1980s. But in the 1990s, this is the
case and, despite the 1994—95 Mexican peso crisis, this trend is likely
to continue.

Over the next decade a number of countries in the region will be
severely challenged (for example Mexico and Venezuela), but a systemic repeat of the 1980s is not likely. However, while there have
been considerable changes in the region's economies, and Latin
America's position in the world has been considerably upgraded, the
region's transformation is not yet complete. Domestically, socioeconomic imbalances remain significant and large segments of populations are not quickly benefiting from recent economic reforms—worse,
some are arguing that in the short-term severe dislocations are more
likely. There is no doubt that poverty and dysfunctional public sector
institutions remain an Achilles' heel in any scenario of Latin America's
future.

Nonetheless, Latin America is gradually becoming less economically *dependent* on the core industrial countries. There is a trend toward *interdependence*, both within the region and with nonregional
trade partners. This is evident by the sizeable and growing number of
Latin American stocks now traded daily on the New York Stock Exchange, the NASDAQ, and the American Stock Exchange. The bonds
of Latin American governments and corporations also show up in the
portfolios of major insurance companies and state pension organizations. Conversely, U.S trade and investment patterns in Latin American economies have made the region a prime growth area along with
the Asia/Pacific area.

For the U.S. consumer, anecdotal evidence is slowly materializing:
almost half the orange juice consumed in the United States comes
from Brazil, Colombia is a prime source of flowers, and the raspberries in the local grocery store that you are eyeing come from Chile or
Guatemala. The shrimp put on the grill could come from Ecuador or
Panama, and the wine to complement dinner could be produced in
Argentina or Chile. Brand names like Corona, Dos Equis, and Concha
y Toro are gradually becoming part of the North American consumer
consciousness. Few North Americans are aware that the Mexican glass
conglomerate, Vitro, controls over a quarter of the U.S. glass market;
just as few Europeans know that another Mexican industrial giant,

Cemex, has bought substantial interests in Spain's construction sector.

The interdependence between Latin America and North America (the United States and Canada in this instance) was also mirrored in the U.S.-led effort to support Mexico in early 1995 when the peso came under attack by international currency traders. Mexico is a major trade partner of the United States and a key location for U.S. overseas investment. Although the same relationship does not exist between Canada and Mexico, the latter is growing in significance as a trade and investment partner. Moreover, the 1993 passage of the North American Free Trade Agreement makes events in Mexico City more keenly felt in Washington, D.C. and Ottawa than any time prior. Simply stated, Mexico's troubles are eventually those of the United States and Canada either through mutual security concerns (such as the drug trade), lost markets, or complications with foreign exchange rates, let alone illegal immigration flows.

What Do These Signs Suggest?

Latin America's role in the post-cold war world order is being shaped by economic dynamism, more effective diplomacy, and a cultural explosion. The region in all its complexity is undergoing significant structural changes and many of the current economic- and political-reform programs are providing the foundations of a hemispheric revival that, if successful, will carry into the next century. Latin America is emerging from the "lost decade" of the 1980s to a renaissance in the 1990s, in which its 466 million people are, through their democratic process, increasingly articulating their view of the way things should be in the international political and economic system. Although the renaissance is more pronounced in some countries than others (and perhaps bypassed in a few), Latin America as a whole has in recent years demonstrated a more coherent collective will of itself.

This does not presage the end of U.S. leadership in the Western Hemisphere. It simply points to a more mature regional interaction, a greater pace of cooperation in the Western Hemisphere, and a new equation in the international system. These trends were, to some degree, codified at the Summit of the Americas in late 1994. Held in Miami, this conclave of the leaders of the Americas save one, Fidel Castro, drew out an optimistic future of domestic economic growth, trade expansionism, and more equitable social distribution. The notion of a hemispheric free-trade area by the year 2005 became the corner-stone of the aspirations of senior government and business community leaders, trade negotiators, and international organization bureaucra-cies.

The striking feature of these developments may not be the ambi-tious free-trade area envisioned for the next century as much as the sea-change in individual and governmental attitudes that has occurred since the mid-1980s and the dark days of Latin America's debt crisis. The region's profound and painful economic reforms have been undergirded by a renewal in democratic leadership. The societal con-sensus this has engendered in most Latin American societies has be-come the key building block for maintaining a dramatic renaissance in the hemisphere. The implications of this renaissance are being ab-sorbed by the region's local community organizations and business leaders, both large and small, as well as increasingly by the global investment community. For their part, government leaders are forging the kinds of regional political interaction and cooperation that made the Miami Summit possible.

Latin America's Fast-Forward Process

The last decade has been a time of almost bewildering transforma-tions—the end of the Communist bloc and the Soviet Union, a militar-ily spectacular and victorious allied war against an Iraq that had in-vaded Kuwait, and long and deep recessions followed by recoveries in the United States, Japan, Canada, Australia, and Europe. Parts of Af-rica and Asia, such as Rwanda, Somalia, Liberia, and Afghanistan have spun out of control; and large parts of the former Soviet bloc are racked with myriad new problems ranging from bankruptcy, the smug-gling of plutonium, scandals in recently re-activated financial sectors, and the resurgence of undemocratic political forces.

Latin America is a region also undergoing considerable changes. Most U.S. citizens were forced to come to grips with this new reality during the national debate for the ratification of the North American Free Trade Agreement (NAFTA). Ultimately, NAFTA passed, but the perceptions of Mexico and Latin America generated by the debate were not always encouraging. In effect, the debate touched upon the role of the United States in a new international system which involves closer relations with its neighbors, one of which is Latin America.

Some of these debates resurfaced when international attention briefly focused on Mexico in the aftermath of its disastrous peso devaluation in December 1994 and the currency crisis that followed. There was considerable suspicion that not much had changed and that the problems of one Latin American country were the same throughout the region. This is clearly not the case.

Latin America is undergoing an uneven economic and political renaissance. The southern cone countries of Argentina, Chile, and Uruguay are enjoying a more sustained economic recovery and have weathered the 1994—95 international currency crisis relatively well. The same cannot be said about Mexico and Venezuela, both of which were the source of high expectations, but have been disappointing and curiously problematic. The outlook for Colombia remains uncertain as long as the mismatch between the nation's economic potential, and political and security challenges continue. At the same time Peru, long on a downward economic spiral compounded by substantial political problems, appears to be moving on a course toward recovery. The same, perhaps, can be said of Latin America's largest economy, Brazil, long troubled with divisive politics. The Cardoso administration that came into office in early 1995 is seeking to bring a deeper and more sustained process of reform to the country. The verdict on Latin America's smaller economies, including Central America and the Caribbean region, remains uncertain, but is most certainly dependent on the sustainability of the hemisphere's renaissance.

Latin America's fast-forward process is therefore defined here as a structural transformation of local economies from state-dominant to more market-oriented growth strategies by promoting exports and allowing imports, the diversification of products and trade partners, fiscal responsibility, and the privatization of large-scale state holdings. It also entails an openness to foreign investment and membership in key international economic institutions, including the International Monetary Fund, the World Bank, Inter-American Development Bank, and the GATT which is now superseded by the new World Trade Organization.[2] Much of the fast-forward process reflects the "Washington Consensus," a phrase coined by the Institute of International Economics' John Williamson.

However, to trade and market liberalization, sound fiscal and monetary policies, and privatization, we add a second, more long-term round of reforms that encompass institution-building (or reinventing government to perform better at lower costs): judicial and law enforcement reforms, educational reforms, financial and consumer regulatory reforms, local government administrative and budgetary reforms, and substantial retirement pension and health care reforms. As Moisés Naim observes: "Opening the stock market to foreign investors or eliminating subsidies can be done with the stroke of a pen and can have immediate results. Building the equivalent of a Securities and Exchange Commission or organizing a well-targeted social program to compensate the poor for the loss of subsidies requires complex organizational efforts that take much longer to bear fruit."[3]

Key elements to the success or failure of Latin America's transformation are pragmatic, democratic, and responsible leadership, a degree of social equity, and higher educational levels. It is important to underscore the latter—changes in the global economy increasingly demand a more literate workforce capable of assimilating new technologies and harnessing them to drive the national or even regional development process. At the same time, failure to address social inequalities provides fertile ground for political turmoil that can derail the fast- forward process.

These considerations lead us to focus particular attention on the region's larger and more influential actors. Argentina, Brazil, Chile, Colombia, Mexico, Peru, and Venezuela are pivotal nations, shaping the definition of the changing regional environment. We have added Cuba to the equation. Its political and socioeconomic development lag is an aberration, and a point of continued U.S. strategic interest. Changes are on the horizon and Cuba's reintegration into the region's economic and political system will probably be a catalyst for a renewed Caribbean-Central American environment. Combined, this emerging Latin American renaissance has implications for the United States and for its European and Asia-Pacific partners and competitors, ranging across economic, political, and security interests.

Defining Latin America

Economists Eliana Cardoso and Ann Helwege capture Latin America's diversity in the following observation:

In Chichicastenango, Guatemala, the local people wear handloomed clothing bearing the traditional pattern of their home town. Women wear backstrap looms between tending fields and cooking meals. In Buenos Aires, Argentina, women race between supermarkets, nursery schools, their offices, and their psychoanalysts. Half of the population of Guatemala cannot read and write; Argentina's illiteracy is less than 5 percent. Both countries face debt crises, inflation, and unemployment, yet the differences in their economic bases are so profound as to make a mockery of efforts to address their problems in the same breath.[4]

We easily acknowledge the vast diversity that is encompassed in the term "Latin America." In a geographic sense, this book refers to the community of nations that begins with Mexico in the north and, heading south, includes Central America, the Caribbean, and South America. Latin Americans are largely Roman Catholic with a sizeable Protestant minority, and generally speak Spanish (Portuguese in Brazil). For its part, the Caribbean includes a large number of English-speaking nations, Haiti (Creole and French are also spoken), as well as countries with French and Dutch dependencies (areas not emphasized in this study). As a whole, this large region that begins at the U.S. border with Mexico accounts for over 466 million people and some of the developing world's most competitive economies (for example, Chile) and largest economies (Brazil, the 7th largest in GDP size in 1995, and Mexico, the 20th largest).

The World Bank defines Latin American and Caribbean countries as middle-income economies; only Haiti is regarded as low-income, placing it among the poorest countries in the world. This means that most of the region enjoys a higher standard of living than countries in Sub-Saharan Africa, South Asia, Central Asia, and is on a rough par with the newly developing Eastern European countries. Only four major Latin American countries—Argentina, Brazil, Venezuela, and Uruguay—qualify for the upper middle-income bracket, which makes them comparable in World Bank terms to South Africa and Greece. However, Latin America clearly lags behind the dynamic Asian economies, such as Hong Kong, South Korea, Singapore, and Taiwan.

The structure of Latin American economies varies considerably. Global commodity markets are important for a number of Latin American countries: coffee from Brazil, El Salvador, and Colombia; oil from Venezuela, Mexico, and Ecuador; and sugar from Cuba, Guyana, and the Dominican Republic. Yet, the days that even small commodity price fluctuations were earthquakes in local economies are largely over. Agriculture as a percentage of GDP has declined. Many of today's Latin economies are more broadly based on industry and services. This is not to say that Latin American nations have economies as

highly industrialized or service-oriented as Singapore's, but the overall trend since the 1960s has been to downsize agriculture and augment industry and services.

The contrast between the reality of Latin American economies and
politics and the perceptions of North Americans is a complicated matter. For many, a beleaguered Central America was the overwhelming
image of the past decade—with right-wing death squads in El Salvador and Guatemala, the Sandinistas and their leftist revolution in Nicaragua, and the outside involvement of the United States, Soviet Union,
and Cuba. The perception of Latin America in the 1980s was characterized by the external debt crisis, riots and demonstrations against
International Monetary Fund-imposed austerity programs, and grinding poverty. Added more recently to these largely unpleasant images
were the faces of drug kingpins and their cronies, from Pablo Escobar
in Colombia to General Manuel Noriega in Panama. The perceptions
are also defined by images of refugees and illegal immigrants stream-
ing into the United States, symbolic of Latin America's endemic crises
and adding a sense that U.S. taxpayers are being taken for a ride.
There is, in fact, a serious problem with these images; they confirm
the uncertainties regarding Latin America and the Caribbean, leading
to exaggerated claims by both critics and supporters of the region.
What these contrary perceptions and images suggest is that the U.S.-
Latin American relationship has yet to mature with the public at large.
Recent instances of this include the bitter national debate over the
ratification of the North American Free Trade Agreement in 1993, as
well as the dynamics of the 1996 U.S. presidential elections.

We see the Western Hemisphere as representing a dynamic group
of nations, beginning to shape their own destiny despite lingering
socioeconomic problems. Images of the future that are evoked are
governments continuing to move toward more open political systems,
citizens with a wider economic stake and mechanisms to control it,
busy stock exchanges, and the implementation and use of high technology to enhance national productivity leading to improved living
standards. The involvement of Chilean companies in the privatization
of Argentine companies, and the purchase by Mexican companies of
U.S. and European firms is another facet of this image. The same goes
for Brazilian engineering firms building highway interchanges in South
Florida or Argentine energy companies prospecting for oil and gas in
Central Asia. The outlook the authors wish to project is that Latin

America, in a broad sense, is a region on the move—in the fast-forward mode. There are no guarantees that "tomorrow will be a better day," but the possibility of a vigorous Latin America seeking a greater role in world affairs is already happening. The course this process is taking, as well as its implications, is at the heart of this book.

Notes

1. Richard E. Band, *Profitable Investing* (1995), p. 4.
2. See Jeffrey Sachs, "Consolidating Capitalism," *Foreign Policy* (Spring 1995): p. 51.
3. Moisés Naim, "Latin America the Morning After," *Foreign Affairs*, (July/August 1995): p. 54.
4. Eliana Cardoso and Ann Helwege, *Latin America's Economy: Diversity, Trends, and Conflicts* (Boston: The MIT Press, 1993), pp. 2–3.

ATLANTIC OCEAN

México
México City

Cuba Havana

Bahamas Nassau

Virgin Islands Charlotte Amalie
Anguilla Basseterre
St. Kitts-Nevis Basseterre
Belize Belmopan
Jamaica Kingston
Antigua St. Johns
Montserrat Plymouth
Haiti
Guadeloupe Basse-Terre
Port-au-Prince
Dominica Roseau
Guatemala Guatemala City
Dominican Republic
Martinique Fort-de-France
El Salvador San Salvador
Santo Domingo
St. Lucia Castries
Honduras Tegucigalpa
Puerto Rico San Juan
St. Vincent Kingstown
Nicaragua Managua
Barbados Bridgetown
Costa Rica San José
Grenada St. George's
Trinidad & Tobago Port-of-Spain
Panama Panama City

Guyana Georgetown
Venezuela
Suriname Paramaribo
Caracas
French Guiana Cayenne
Colombia
Bogotá

Ecuador Quito

Peru
Lima

Brazil Brasilia

Bolivia La Paz

PACIFIC OCEAN

Paraguay
Asunción

Chile Santiago

Argentina
Buenos Aires

Uruguay Montevideo

2

A Changing Latin America

Latin America is changing in the 1990s; in some countries the transformation is substantial and possibly a distinctive departure from the past. In a sense, the region has found the fast-forward button. In those countries there is an exciting, rapid pace of change, a societal consensus that the correct direction is being taken, and a major breakthrough in economic development appears within grasp. The trendsetters are Chile and Argentina. There are significant developments in Brazil. Uruguay, Bolivia, Peru, and a few Caribbean Basin countries are pursuing significant changes. Mexico's case is more complicated, too problematic for a brief assessment here. Colombia remains an enigma, sustaining generally sound macro-economic policies, but in a politico-security environment that is corroding the entire society.

What appeared to be an Asian phenomenon of take-off development is occurring in Latin American countries in the 1990s. The key elements of take-off development include self-sustaining economic growth, the transformation of the economic base from agricultural or primary commodities to industry and services, and an improvement in socioeconomic conditions beyond meeting basic human needs. Take-off development also places a greater emphasis on assimilating new technology that enhances the economy's overall performance and eventually opens the door to membership in the club of industrialized nations.

After an almost decade-long period of recession, many of Latin America's economies have returned to the growth track: stock markets are revitalized, functioning as a source of domestic and foreign funds, and flight capital is finding its way back into local investment. Other sources of external capital now available include Latin American mu-

11

tual funds which allow North American, European, and Japanese investors to participate in the economic renaissance. Most Latin American countries have elected governments, and the mood about the future is becoming increasingly positive, or at least more realistic. There is a subtle, yet fundamental transformation in how Latin Americans regard the world and their place in it.

The circumstances affecting the people from the Rio Grande in the north to Tierra del Fuego in the south in the late 1980s demanded that changes be made. These changes carried with them political and socioeconomic implications, and influenced how Latin America interacted with the international system, itself undergoing sweeping transformations. In the late 1990s, the potential exists that some Latin America countries will have sustained high rates of economic growth, an increased standard of living, and strengthened democratic governments. These developments also have concomitant foreign policy elements—Latin America will assume a greater role in shaping the international political and economic system, perhaps prematurely referred to as the "new world order."[1] For example, Mexico became the twenty-fifth member of the OECD (Organization for Economic Cooperation and Development) in May 1994, sometimes referred to as the "club of industrialized nations." More significantly, Latin policy initiative has played a key role in defining the Western Hemisphere's 1990s trade and economic momentum.

The Challenges to Latin American Growth

Latin America in the mid-1980s was at risk of becoming irrelevant in the international system—its economies, with few exceptions, had stagnated, reform seemed impossible, and the region as a whole appeared to be falling behind other parts of the world, most notably the dynamically-growing Asia/Pacific region. (For a more complete treatment of the Latin American debt crisis, see Appendix.) Although Latin American nations had undergone a democratic revolution in the 1980s, serious questions confronted the region: could the "new" democracies revitalize their economies?; just how "democratic" were these nations, considering societal imbalances in living standards and claims in some cases of electoral fraud?; and would Latin statesmen opt for the traditional populist approaches to their societies' problems, which were part of the cause for the malaise?

At the heart of answering these questions is one of the major riddles of development: can democratic governments (in their broadest definition) preside over an "economic take-off"? After all, the "economic miracles" of Singapore, South Korea, and Taiwan were not initially paralleled by political development that was deeply democratic in a liberal, Western sense. Neither were they political systems that were totalitarian, complete with thought police and concentration camps. Opposition groups were tolerated within certain limits; indeed elections were held and other parties were allowed a voice (not too loud) in the process. Not fully democratic in a Western liberal sense, not fully authoritarian or totalitarian, what were these states? Steven Schlossstein calls this form of political system "authoritarianism on the soft shell."[2]

The argument, simply put, is that soft-shell authoritarianism has provided a key political prop to adopting an outward-oriented export growth model that is complemented by massive incentives to increase private savings, an unswerving commitment to public education and infrastructure improvement, cultural homogeneity, and a consistent focus on value-added production. As Schlossstein notes: "Japan and the Little Dragons all figured out rather early on that the traditional system of import substitution had more limitations than benefits, so they turned to exports instead."[3] In the 1990s, South Korea and Taiwan have evolved into more open political systems, with the former actually having elected a president, Kim Young Sam, who was a former political dissident, while the latter held direct presidential elections in 1996.

Latin America has adopted many of those same orientations in the economic arena, especially the rejection of the import- substitution model that was a "deliberate effort to promote the emergence and expansion of domestic industries by replacing major imports such as textiles, shoes, household appliances, with locally produced substitutes."[4] The import-substitution model also depended on the imposition of protective tariffs and quotas to help promote local industry as well as external financing. Consumerism and the emergence of a postindustrial age in which access to new technology drove international and local markets, not to mention the developing world's external debt crisis, began to take away the attractiveness of this inward-looking model, especially when enhanced global communications made evident the superiority of foreign consumer goods.

Chile and Mexico in the 1980s and Argentina in the early 1990s, it can be argued, made much of the economic transition away from the import-substitution model with political systems somewhat similar to soft-shell authoritarianism. The question that hovers over the entire Latin American horizon is whether or not the economic breakthrough can be made by political systems that are more open and democratic. Among countries under consideration in this book, this is a major challenge to the governments in Chile and Argentina as well as those in Brazil, Colombia, and Venezuela. The verdict remains out and certainly the experience of Mexico in 1994–95 raises many questions concerning the difficulty such developments entail. No matter what is said and done, the process of development remains difficult.

By the late 1980s, something began to change in a number of countries. The basic assumptions of Latin American development were challenged by an increasingly broad segment of technocratic leadership in both public and private sectors. In fact, a sea-change of values and world views regarding economics and politics accompanied this process. Although Chile and Mexico were the pacesetters, implementing sweeping reform programs at earlier periods, the idea that the way things were done in the past was flawed and that another approach was needed began to permeate the region. In particular, the inward-looking economic nationalism that spawned import-substitution and protectionist barriers was dropped in favor of export-led growth models that were characterized by export promotion, two-way trade liberalization, tax reform aimed at creating incentives for foreign direct investment as well as flight capital repatriation, and trimming the state's role in the economy through privatization.

Like Chile and Mexico before them (as well as Bolivia's lesser-known success), important economic reforms were introduced in Venezuela, Colombia, and Argentina in the late 1980s and early 1990s. Efforts to convert heavily state-dominated economies into more free-market economies are now in motion (to varying degrees) in even the most politically and economically depressed countries, such as Peru, Nicaragua, and El Salvador. The way forward is not easy and is fraught with dangers as reflected by the February 1992 coup attempt in Venezuela, the April 1992 presidential coup of Alberto Fujimori, and Mexico's political and currency troubles in late 1994 and early 1995. Moreover, Venezuela clearly backslided on its efforts to restructure the economy in 1994 and 1995. Despite some economic reforms, Cuba stands out as an anachronism, looking backward to the glory of a revolution that never matched expectations.

Mexico deserves special mention in regard to the various political and economic difficulties facing developing countries in the 1990s. While the events of December 1994 cast a shadow over the entire fast-forward process in Latin America, suddenly it appeared that Mexico, a star pupil, was found wanting: an intended currency devaluation turned into a currency freefall that took the Mexican government much of 1995 to sort out. The critical issue was that Mexico, having achieved much in fiscal restraint, reduced inflation, and export generation, became vulnerable to an import consumer binge that resulted in ultimately unsustainable current account deficits. In a sense, as long as international investors were confident that Mexico could maintain its payments on its foreign-exchange obligations, it was a sound investment. However, the country's weak position with its external account and the policy decision to devalue by the new Zedillo administration opened the peso to attack from currency traders, who questioned the strength of Mexico's reform process.[6] Billions were spent in foreign exchange reserves defending the peso, which eventually caused Mexico to turn to support from Washington, D.C. and the multilateral lending institutions. Argentina's and Brazil's currencies also came under attack, but they managed to survive the onslaught with their foreign exchange reserves in a manageable position. Despite the battering of the Mexican peso and some questioning regarding the depth of Latin America's conversion to more market-oriented economics, the reform process will continue although governments will occasionally be tempted to turn to populist solutions in times of difficulty.

Defining the Post-Cold War Order

What is the post-cold war order and how will developing countries, such as those in Latin America, fare? Is it an international system that will be characterized by peaceful relations between nations, based on trade and commerce? The conclusion of U.S. political scientist and occasional Washington policy maker Joseph S. Nye in 1992 is worth noting: "In short the new world order has begun. It is messy, evolving, and not susceptible to simple formulation or manipulation."[7] In effect, it is the international system that commenced around November 1989, when the Berlin Wall came down, the nature of power became more multidimensional, and relations between countries and international and domestic actors more complex. Whether this is a "new world disorder," as some have come to call it, only begs the question.

The fall of the Berlin Wall was a dramatic symbol of the end of one world order and the birth of another, and an assessment of the underpinnings of that transformation resulted in a profound debate among mostly North American and European elites. Although overstated, Francis Fukuyama convincingly surmised in his "The End of History?" that "The triumph of the West, of the Western *idea*, was evident first of all in the total exhaustion of viable systemic alternatives to Western liberalism."[8] This did not occur overnight but ultimately the assessment was backed-up by the collapse of Soviet political influence (and strategic control) in Central and Eastern Europe. This saw a shift away from central planning, and adoption of market economics along with open elections in such countries as the Czech Republic, Hungary, the Slovak Republic, and Poland. This was followed by the reunification of Germany and the absorption of the former German Democratic Republic in 1990, and the failure of a hardliner military coup in the Soviet Union in August 1991.

But how has the purported "end of history" played in the non-European world? By the early 1990s the ideas of Western liberal democracy and capitalist economics were in the ascendence and their major competitors for much of the twentieth century, communism and socialist economics, had disappeared at an almost bewilderingly quick pace, leaving behind a historical residue of such countries as North Korea and Cuba. Even the People's Republic of China, which retains a tight and undemocratic political development structure, has adapted an economic system ("market socialism") that is a curious hybrid of free market capitalism and statist economic development programming. Islam, often portrayed as the next threat to Western liberalism, remains a house divided—capable of enormous disruptions, but not a systemic challenger with a working or readily copied approach to economic growth. In fact, many aspects of the hardline Islamic regimes, such as Iran and Sudan, may have some appeal socially or culturally but are not widely attractive as alternative economic development models.[9]

The idea of a coherent, let alone unified, nonaligned bloc of developing ("Third World") nations sharing a wealth-equalizing international agenda vis-à-vis the more developed West, is dead. This does not mean that the global tensions that undergirded this thinking no longer exist. But not only has the "Third World" changed, but so has the "First World." The broad range of countries sharing the dubious mantle of the Third World have limited common interests, especially when comparing South Korea and Uruguay at one end of the spectrum and Chad and Haiti at the other. A process of economic differentiation has transformed the Third World of the 1960s and 1970s, fractured it in the 1980s, and created several new "worlds" in the 1990s based less on ideological solidarity and more on economic realities.

What, then, is replacing the old cold war order? One early conceptualization was proposed by the Council on Foreign Affairs' Shafiqal Islam: "Future historians may choose 1989 as the year the cold war between capitalism and communism ended and the new conflict began within capitalism. They may argue that it was in 1989 that America and the West turned from containing the Soviet Union to containing Japan."[10] Indeed, some analysts argue that Japan, Europe, and the United States are heading toward a period of "Genghis Khan economics"—a no-holds-barred economic slugfest.[11] Even if somewhat exaggerated, these early assessments pointed to the emergence of a new international system dominated by an economic agenda. In effect, countries with competitive economies would have the edge in shaping a new world order.

Much of the post-cold war analyses thus stipulate a world evolving into three major trading blocs (American, Asian and European), divided into hierarchies of trade partners.[12] What was perceived to evolve from this environment may be particularly harsh. The global economy would be dominated by a *troika,* or triad, of developed countries following a democratic-capitalist economic model. The triad would focus on trading and, to some extent, investing in those areas of the developing world that—selectively—are economically rewarding. With that kind of definition, those nations with little to offer economically or providing higher than reasonable risks will be on the losing end of this process. Notes Jeffery T. Bergner, a former Senate Foreign Relations Committee staffer: "The world is not becoming more and more equal in all of its component parts. The rich and strong are getting richer and stronger."[13]

This was a world view shared by Jacques Attali, the eccentric former French head of the European Bank for Reconstruction and Development.[14] Attali's eurocentric vision is important to note for an American readership because of what it assumed about the United States and for what it suggested regarding the subject of this study, Latin America. Latin America and Sub-Saharan Africa would acquire (or reacquire) the status of spheres of influence. Warfare between nations then becomes something of the past. In a common reflection of European thought about the post-cold war order, the United States appears in steep decline and other forces, notably Europe and Japan, now must be taken into strategic consideration. If the lesson for the developing world is that it should be wary of Washington's declining influence, that was a misleading assessment of Europe's own strategic limitations. If off-base on the latter, Attali did allude to an important point: in the post-cold war era, developing regions of the world, such as Latin America, would now more than ever diversify their economic relationships in a process evolving toward increasing global maturity. In effect, in the long run, Latin America would escape the notion of simply being a "sphere of influence."

In contrast, a more visionary sweep of the future appears in the works of Alvin Toffler, who believes that the world will be divided between fast and slow economies, not between East and West or North and South. History is shaped by the creation of new civilizations and the engine of change is technology. Technological innovation and its impact on the flow of history, according to the Toffler, comes in waves: the First Wave was the agricultural revolution, which led to feudal-style social systems; the Second Wave was the industrial revolution, which gave birth to "mass society" and its competing socialist and capitalist versions; and the Third Wave, which is now in motion, is globally integrated, cybernetic, and information-driven.[15]

At the edge of the twenty-first century, the third wave of economic development (and with it the creation of a new civilization) is that of the symbolic or information-based economy, where less hard cash is traded and symbols of cash are instead used. As Toffler noted in *Powershift: Knowledge, Wealth, and Violence at the Edge of the 21st Century*: "The bar code on the pack of Marlboros, the computer in the Federal Express truck, the scanner at the Safeway checkout counter, the bank's automatic teller, the spread of extra-intelligent data networks across the planet, remotely operated robots, the informationalization of capital, all are preliminary steps in the formation of a 21st-century economy that will operate at nearly real-time speeds."[16]

Toffler's vision is that of a power shift based on technology: the ability of countries to create and assimilate technology will determine their place in the international pecking order—first-, second-, or third-wave civilizations. This clearly cuts across all nations, making those with the most educated populations and open societies potential trendsetters as fast economies. As Toffler notes: "The new system for making wealth consists of an expanding global network of markets, banks, production centers, and laboratories in instant communication with one another, constantly exchanging huge—and ever-increasing—flows of data, information and knowledge." He adds, with direct implications for both developed and developing nations: "This is the 'fast' economy of tomorrow. It is this accelerative, dynamic new wealth-machine that is the source of economic advance. As such, it is the source of great power as well. To be de-coupled from it is to be excluded from the future."[17]

The message is clear. For those countries that rely simply on cheap labor, strategic locations, and commodities, the danger of being left behind in the development process is increasingly serious. In a somewhat more optimistic vein, Toffler points to the possibility of certain developing nations using technology, knowledge, and wealth to graduate into the centers of modern development as presently represented by North America, Europe, and parts of Asia. If this possibility were to occur, it would gradually modify the stark vision of economic blocs held by so many.

A factor linked to Toffler's power shift is the rise of an instantaneous international economy and the enormous impact of twenty-four hour, global financial flows. The 1994–95 Mexican peso crisis and the ensuing "Tequila hangover" in which the currencies of countries as diverse as Brazil and Argentina, Sweden, Italy, Canada, Thailand, and Turkey all came under pressure, reflects the emergence of a new world with unmarked boundaries and open definitions of sovereignty. A new global actor has arrived: the money managers. International financial markets have become the domain, among others, of U.S. mutual and hedge-fund investors who controlled perhaps $2 trillion in assets.[18] The profit and loss horizon for many within this group is short, especially as technology has made it considerably easier to enter and exit markets. As William Glasgall and Bill Javetski noted of international currency markets: "In this new market, money moves faster than ever, raising the possibility that billions can flow in or out of an economy in seconds. So powerful has this force of money become that some observers now see the hot-money set becoming a sort of shadow world government—one that is irretrievably eroding the concept of the sovereign powers of a nation-state."[19]

International currency markets in a new world system play a central role in making certain there is an ongoing flow of funds for trade and investment. At the same time, these markets provide the opportunity to make profits based upon speculation. To a degree, what emerged from Mexico in December 1994 was that countries that failed to deal with their economic problems, such as current account imbalances, budget deficits, and high inflation, would eventually be disciplined by the market. Moreover, this behavior was manifested toward such developing countries as Mexico and Turkey, as well as developed countries like Italy, Sweden, and Canada. And discipline can be rapid. As financial journalist Gregory J. Millman noted:

> Like the vandals who conquered decadent Rome, the currency traders sweep away economic empires that have lost their power to resist. Time after time in country after country, when governments can't cope with the new financial realities, traders are the agents of creative destruction. Although investors have always had to take into consideration the quality of a government's management of its economy, traders now have an unprecedented degree of power to sweep the financial foundation out from under poorly managed, politically unstable or uneconomic governments before the bureaucrats even know what has happened.[20]

The hot money—power mavens function in a world constructed of information highways, constantly producing a flow of data. While there is perhaps some merit in letting market forces provide discipline to governments that have not been responsible in dealing with runaway budget deficits, there are also considerable dangers. In particular, the world of currency traders and related money managers operates in an environment sometimes based on rumors, not facts. A perceived event in one country can cost that country millions of dollars in defense of its national currency that has come under attack for no reason except a mistaken rumor that set off alarms with currency traders.

In the 1990s, Mexico, and to lesser extents, Argentina and Brazil have already felt the dangers associated with an instantaneous economy. In Mexico's case, the impact was devastatingly brutal and required outside assistance—hardly the clarion call for a new Latin America. Yet, Argentina managed to survive the onslaught of speculation against its currency and by moving quickly to shore up international support, many of the problems in Mexico were not repeated. In many respects, the Argentine reform process proved to be more durable than expected when put to the acid test. Whether lessons have been learned is unclear; as long as the economic (and political) management process remains fragile, Latin American countries run the danger of massive and damaging global financial pressures.

Latin America—A Passing Fancy?

The titles "Latin Financial Markets Are Sizzling" and "Latins Ride High" on the covers of magazines such as *The Economist* and *BusinessWeek* reflected the growing excitement about Latin America's prospects in the early 1990s.[21] As one editorial commented: "A market revolution is taking hold across Latin America, and companies are jumping into the action. From the icy Straits of Magellan to the meandering Rio Grande, governments are selling off their assets and dismantling fortresses of tariffs and red tape."[22] Is this current fancy for Latin America by business communities in North America, Europe, and Asia ephemeral, the "academic lite" analysis of busy journalists, corporate economists, and government officials? Or, asked in another fashion: is Latin America's economic and political restructuring real or will the fast-forward motion be followed by severe reverses, especially in the aftermath of Mexico's 1994–95 time of troubles?

While there is much to be excited about in Latin America in the 1990s, the danger of being too enthusiastic is that judgements may indeed prove ephemeral. Enthusiasm in investment circles ran strong for Latin America in 1993, only to weaken in early 1994, partially due to hikes in U.S. interest rates, and to be absolutely chilled in late 1994 and early 1995 because of Mexico. A year later it was cautiously rebounding, except in Mexico. Rediscovery of Latin America as a place for foreign investors carries with it, for example, a rush for new business based on weak data and little discrimination in some cases between countries or credits. Moreover, it is wrong to think that the problems facing Latin America—uneven income distribution, violent revolutionary movements, ecological disasters, and corruption—have all been swept away.[23] Even in two regional trendsetters, Chile and Argentina, poverty, pollution, and crime are serious concerns; in countries such as Mexico, Brazil, and Peru they are front and center of daily political life; and Venezuela has for some time appeared to be slipping down that slope. The fast-forward button, subsequently, is being hit by some countries, but the resulting pace change is different from case to case, and even within each country, with some sectors advancing more rapidly than others.

There are those that think that Latin America's current experiment with market economics is doomed to failure. With a decidedly leftist bent, James Petras, Morris Morley, and Steve Vieux, have continued to argue that Latin America's future will be marked by either a new round of military coups or, more likely, populist revolutions which will reject a capitalism that is forced upon them from the declining hegemony of the United States and its local allies.[24] The wave of democratization which took place in the 1980s, the authors contend, is doomed to failure because the elected governments have become aligned with "establishment forces," hence betraying the masses. That betrayal has come in the form of adopting neoliberal economic programs that are "coordinating the flow of billions [of dollars] to northern banks" and slashing state budgets and policies that are "the fruits of decades of popular mobilization and struggle."[25]

According to those who still cling to dependency theory, such as Petras et al, the 1990s are pivotal in Latin America because of the decline of United States leadership (due to the failure of capitalism in the north), which weakens Washington's ability to prop up its "semi-colonies" and thwart the revolutionary proclivity of the masses. As analyzed in later chapters in this study, there is no doubt that there will be major crises over the inequalities in income distribution, corruption, unmet expectations of voters, and the difficulties of economic change and their potential political fallout. But in this zero-sum view, Latin America is left with little to do for itself, and in a sense, the capabilities of Latin American societies to rejuvenate themselves are underestimated.

While these dark prognoses may be acknowledged, there is a difference between ideological posturing and careful assessments of the future. Clearly, the potential for failure remains a constant danger and should temper enthusiasm about a better Latin American future. In this context, a U.S. academic's cautionary note is well-taken: "Any analysis of the present period must take into account tensions between marketplace logic, reinforced by the demands of the world economy, and pressures to consolidate democratic institutions and expand popular participation beyond the arena of political policies."[26]

For our part, we believe that a well-defined departure from past economic modes is occurring and that a real chance exists for some countries of attaining a competitive level of development early in the twenty-first century. Many analysts believed that the prospects for Japan, Singapore, Hong Kong, Korea, and Taiwan in the early 1950s were dismal and that little in the way of reform could reshape their economies. Yet, as Jon Woronoff noted: "What has occurred in East Asia is a fascinating story in itself. Indeed, it has many elements of the ideal success story. Five countries started out at a pitifully low level of economic development, they overcame countless trials and hardships, and finally they managed to rise above most others."[27]

Latin America's level of development is not as low as those of the five Asian nations in the aftermath of the Second World War. A number of countries are beginning that climb to overcome "countless trials and hardships," and a select few will manage to rise above the majority. In some cases, there will be failures and disappointments, but the process of change that is occurring should not be ruled out as a passing fancy.

The change in thinking about development strategies in Latin America is significant, with some referring to it as a "sea change" because of its sweeping nature.[28] While the business community is actively responding to new opportunities in Latin America, other observers are expressing cautious optimism. Richard Feinberg, initially on President Bill Clinton's National Security Council and former president of the Inter-American Dialogue, commented in 1992 that, "caveats notwithstanding, the new optimism and self-confidence gripping much of Latin America is well-grounded in fundamentals. The region is now governed by better economic policies, smarter policymakers, and more consensual democratic policies."[29] Such optimism is merited despite the major uncertainties regionally. The analysis that follows in subsequent chapters reconfirms this.

Conclusion

In a shifting post-cold war environment, Latin America represents a key region where a remarkable adjustment is taking a more pragmatic track than the troubles of the 1980s would have suggested. The image of a region defined often as a pool of cheaper labor and raw materials, is also an active global economic participant, and a close and profitable partner of the United States. Obviously, considerable obstacles exist to the fulfillment of an economically viable politically stable Latin America, but in the 1990s, this is the path upon which a number of countries have embarked. In making difficult decisions of economic structural adjustment and political reforms, sweeping aside past inward-looking economic practices, establishing more democratic societies, and seeking a more international role, Latin America is finding the fast-forward button.

Notes

1. See, for example, Joseph S. Nye, Jr., "What New World Order?" *Foreign Affairs* 71, no. 2 (Spring 1992): pp. 83–113.
2. For a complete discussion of this, see Steven Schlossstein, *The End of the American Century* (New York: Congdon & Weed, Inc., 1989), pp. 119–46.
3. Steven Schlossstein, *Asia's New Little Dragons: The Dynamic Emergence of Indonesia, Thailand and Malaysia* (Chicago: Contemporary Books, 1991), p. 9.
4. Michael P. Todaro, *Economic Development in the Third World* (New York: Longman, Inc., 1981), p. 533.
5. For an assessment of Mexico's currency problems, see Jonathan E. Heath, *The Devaluation of the Mexican Peso in 1994, Economic Policy and Institutions,* (Washington, D.C.: CSIS, Policy Papers on the Americas, 1995).
6. Joseph S. Nye, Jr., "What New World Order?" *Foreign Affairs,*(Spring 1992): p. 96. For an excellent discussion of the end of the Cold War and its implications on the international system, see Young Whan Kihl, "Korea After the Cold War: An Introduction," in *Korea and the World: Beyond the Cold War,* Young Whan Kihl, ed. (Boulder, Colo.: Westview Press, 1994), pp. 2–4.
7. Francis Fukuyama, "The End of History?" *The National Interest,* No. 16 (Summer 1989): p. 3.
8. For literature on this topic, see John L. Esposito, *The Islamic Threat: Myth or Reality?* (New York: Oxford University Press, 1992); Robin Wright, "Islam, Democracy and the West?" *Foreign Affairs* (Summer 1992): pp. 131–45; The SOREF Symposium, "Islam and the U.S.: Challenges for the Nineties," *Proceedings of The Washington Institute* (April 27, 1992): pp. ??; Scott B. MacDonald, "European-Middle Eastern Relations: What Looms on the Horizon," *Middle East Insight* (July/August 1991): pp. 38–41; and Edward Shirley, "Is Iran's Present Algeria's Future?" *Foreign Affairs* (May/June 1995): pp. 28–45.
9. Shafiqal Islam, "Capitalism in Conflict," *Foreign Affairs: America and the World 1989/90,* p. 172.
10. Jean-Claude Casanova, "Déclin américain?" *L'Express,* (August 28, 1992): p. 15.
11. Lester Thurow, quoted in *The International Herald Tribune,* (January 31, 1989): p. 1. Thurow added an African appendage to the European sphere. Other examples of this thinking include Michael Silva and Bertil Sjogren, *Europe 1992 & The New World Power Game* (New York: John Wiley & Sons, 1990); and Peter Drucker, *The New Realities* (New York: Harper & Row Publishers, 1989).
12. Jeffery T. Bergner, *The New Superpowers: Germany, Japan and the U.S. and the New World Order* (New York: St. Martin's Press, 1991), pp. xix-xx.

13. See Jacques Attali, *Lignes d'horizon* (Paris: Fayard, 1990).
14. A summary of the views of Alvin and Heidi Toffler is presented in their book, *The Politics of the Third Wave* (Atlanta: Turner Publishing, 1995). For a review of that book, see Barbara Ehrenreich, "Surfing the Third Wave," *The New York Times Book Review* (May 6, 1995): p. 9.
15. Alvin Toffler, *Powershift: Knowledge, Wealth, and Violence at the Edge of the 21st Century* (New York: Bantam Books, 1991), p. 390.
16. Ibid., p. 391.
17. Glasgal and Jaetski, "Hot Money," p. 47.
18. Ibid., p. 48.
19. Gregory J. Millman, *The Vandals' Crown: How Rebel Currency Traders Overthrew the World's Central Banks* (New York: The Free Press, 1995), pp. xii-xiii.
20. See "The Debt Crisis R.I.P.," *The Economist* (September 12, 1992): pp. 15–16.
21. Stephen Baker, Elizabeth Weiner, Geri Smith, Ann Charters, and Ken Jacobson, "Latin America: The Big Move to Free Markets," *Businessweek* (June 15, 1992): p. 51.
22. Nathanial C. Nash, "Latin Economic Speedup Leaves Poor in the Dust," *New York Times* (September 5, 1994): pp. A1, A14.
23. See James Petras and Morris Morley, *U.S. Hegemony Under Siege: Class, Politics, and Development in Latin America* (New York: Verso, 1990); and James Petras and Steven Vieux, "Myths and Realities: Latin America's Free Markets," *Monthly Review* (May 1992), vol. 44: pp. 9–20.
24. Petras and Vieux, "Myths and Realities," p. 19.
25. William C. Smith, "Neoliberal Economic Reforms and new Democracies in Latin America," *North-South Issues* (May 1992): p. 1.
26. Jon Woronoff, *Asia's 'Miracle' Economies* (Armonk, N.Y.: M.E. Sharpe, Inc., 1986), p. 19.
27. See Pedro Aspe, Andres Bianchi, and Domingo Cavallo, *Sea Changes in Latin America* (Washington, D.C.: Group of Thirty, 1992).
28. Richard E. Feinberg, "Latin America: Back on the Screen," *International Economic Insights*, (July/August 1992), p. 2.

3

The Trendsetters I: Chile

The daily tempo of commerce in Chile is carried out to the beat of international trade and investment. In 1995, Chile's trade with the rest of the world reached almost 45 percent of GDP, making it one of the most open economies in the developing world. Trade and investment in trade have been the motors of Chile's startling growth performance. By 1995 with a real GDP expansion of 8.4 percent, the country had enjoyed eleven years of uninterrupted growth, with an average annual rate of 7 percent for the last eight years, while unemployment has declined from 14 percent in the mid-1980s to about 5.5 percent in 1995.

As for foreign investment, stock market capitalization of over $40 billion is impressive for a country of Chile's size and almost exceeds gross domestic product. In the early 1990s, the Santiago Bolsa de Valores was one of the most active stock markets in the world. International investors had the choice of five closed-end funds specializing in Chilean stocks, four quoted in London and one in New York. No other stock market in the world the size of Chile's can boast that number of specialist closed-end funds. Foreign direct investment is plentiful. Joint venture programs with New Zealanders, Finns, and the Spanish produce fruits, copper, and wine that wind up in foreign markets all over the world.

What has been most impressive about Chile is that, when the autocratic rule of General Augusto Pinochet Ugarte gave way to a renewed experiment with parliamentary democracy in 1990, the new rulers did not feel bound to bury the economic programs of the old regime. Indeed, the program has been deepened and extended. At the same time, the power of General Pinochet, who remained as a key official in the armed forces, has gradually declined and the authority of the civilian head of state has gradually increased. Prospects for relatively harmonious civil-military relations during the rest of the decade are positive.

Chile's economic story was one the few Latin American success stories in the 1980s. While Argentina, Brazil, and Peru ended the decade in crisis, Chile's economy was vibrant, inflation was under 30 percent, and relations with the international financial markets were exemplary. Chile reached the mid-1990s with a strong economy and a popularly elected government. Some analysts still feel the glow of Chile's success has a malevolent hue that emanates from the figure of General Pinochet, who dominated this South American nation of 13 million people. Others, on the other hand, argue with equal intensity that Chile's rapid advancement to a higher level of development owes much to Pinochet's economic legacy. Either way, there can be no doubt that Chile is the most likely of all Latin American countries to generate Asia-like economic expansion into the next millennium.

The Foundations of Modern Chile

Chile's history, since the early days of Spanish colonization, is one of overcoming the isolation borne of its location at the end of the South American continent. This geographic isolation is made more complete by the Andes mountains that separate the country from Argentina to the east, and by the northern desert that is a natural barrier to easy communication with Peru and Bolivia. Despite this isolation, Chile evolved as part of the international economy, known primarily for its exports of silver and copper. By 1870, Chile controlled around 25 percent of the world's copper market. Following Chile's acquisition of northern territory (a result of the War of the Pacific successfully waged against Bolivia and Chile's former ally, Peru [1879–83]), there was also a boom in nitrates. The nitrate boom, stimulated by heavy foreign demand as a major ingredient in fertilizers and explosives, brought in foreign investment. European companies were preponderant in Chile. The nitrate trade lasted until World War I, but thereafter fell away dramatically with the introduction of synthetic nitrates. Copper slowly gained in importance, functioning as the foundation for the Chilean economy into the 1990s.

Chile's political development was largely constitutional and, in a limited conservative sense, democratic, especially after the initial turmoil of the independence period in the early nineteenth century. The evolution of the Chilean economy had three major corresponding political implications. The first was that the expansion of mining stimulated societal and, thereby political, transformations. While the country's traditional landowners would continue to hold political sway into the early twentieth century (some argue later), two new elements emerged as part of the ruling elite—the northern mine owners and merchants in rapidly expanding urban areas. Chile's towns and cities assumed political and economic importance as the country's population became increasingly urbanized: in 1850 only 6 percent of the Chilean population was living in urban areas, by 1900 the figure had climbed to 20 percent, rising to between 25 and 30 percent until the 1930s.[1] To a large degree, this urbanization was fueled by immigration. From 1890 to 1930, Chile's population rose 50 percent as a result of massive European immigration. In Chile's relatively compact society, these new groups created a significant challenge. However, there were family linkages between the established landowners and the immigrants. Landowners frequently had relatives in the new upper (and lower) sectors of the economy.[2]

The second political implication was the creation of a working class. As Chile's mining industry went from one ore to another, there was an ongoing need for skilled labor. A result of European immigration was also the rise of unionization. This occurred first in the nitrate fields of the north. The geographic isolation of the mining areas, in a sense, encouraged the growth of working-class cooperation as an antedote to the anomie created by isolation. The second trend was related: the importation of new ideas of worker-management relations and questions about the ownership of the means of production. Some of the new members of Chile's working-class came from European countries where the ideas of Karl Marx had already begun to take shape, and were in the process of giving birth to Communist parties.

The third trend was the training of the Chilean military and its evolution in the national polity. While the training the Chilean armed forces received from the officers of the Imperial German Army instilled a strong sense of professionalism, an equally strong strain of anticommunism was ingrained. As Chilean author and politician Genero Arriagada noted: "The viscerally anticommunist tradition of the Chilean army had begun long before the Russian Revolution in 1917 . . . anticommunism in Chile developed at the beginning of the twentieth century as a result of the conflict between two major European influences: Prussian militarism brought by the officers of the Imperial German Army hired to train Chilean soldiers versus the socialist ideas of the Second International, which at the time opposed war, armies, the concept of the nation-state, and the idea of the Fatherland."[3] It was no mistake then that Bolshevik and communist ideas were condemned in the *Memorial del Ejercito de Chile* fifteen years prior to foundation of the Chilean Communist Party in 1922. Moreover, the military's anticommunism and growing labor militancy often brought these forces into conflict, especially as the army was frequently deployed to put down strikes, often with considerable consequences as in the Iquique massacre of 1907 when (depending on the account) between five hundred and two thousand workers were killed.[4] The military-labor friction would remain a factor through the twentieth century and play a major role in the 1970–73 period.

For future developments, two key dates can be regarded as crucial to Chile's development and how the nation was shaped in the late twentieth century. As Chilean political scientist Manuel Antonio Garreton has noted: "The most significant turning points were the promulgation of the Constitution of 1925 and the economic crisis of 1929. The latter gave rise to what has been termed the 'inward-looking' model of development, which was driven by the process of import-substitution."[5]

The liberal 1925 constitution was the work of President Arturo Alessandri, who won the presidency in 1920 on a platform of radical social and political change. This led to a revolution of rising expectations among the poor and middle classes, a revolution that was thwarted by the world economic slump of 1929. After a short-lived military dictatorship to quell the upheaval that was created by the economic crisis, democracy was reinforced: first under Alessandri and then under a Popular Front coalition that elected the radical Aguirre Cerda to the presidency in December 1938. Under Cerda's administration, a State Development Corporation (CORFO) was established to plan and direct an industrialization process aimed at substituting imported consumer goods with locally produced items.[6] The *raison d'être* of CORFO was that with the compressed capacity of Chile to pay for imports in the aftermath of the nitrate industry's collapse and the Great Depression, the country should not rely on imported consumer goods. These would therefore be substituted by local industry. Domestic Chilean industry would be promoted by a mixture of protectionism, subsidies, price controls, access to credit, and state investment.

In the political sphere, the so-called compromise state emerged, which was "oriented by an overall logic of dependent capitalist development." The compromise state meant that no single class was able to dominate the country's politics, with each class being obliged to "adopt a strategy of accommodation and to permanently incorporate new groups into sociopolitical life in order to guarantee the stability of the political system."[7] The Chilean political economy that evolved was characterized by the import-substitution model and a "democratic" game of juggling the right, center, and left.

Chile's development up to 1970 was characterized by a political system divided among several ideologies. The right consisted of local business interests part of which were linked to foreign, largely U.S., industrial concerns involved in the copper sector, a strongly anticommunist military, and a middle class of a liberal democratic bent. The center included much of the middle class, a few elements of the industrial class, and moderate groups in the working class. It was represented initially by the Radical Party (Partido Radical) and, by the 1960s, the Christian Democrats (Partido Demócrata Cristiano). The left consisted mainly of working-class citizens, supported by middle-class intellectuals largely orbiting the universities. Its main political groups were the Communists and Socialists.

When Eduardo Frei won the presidency in 1964, the Christian Democrats carried much of the future hope for Chilean democracy that appeared polarized between the right and the left. As Valenzuela and Valenzuela (1985) noted: "the Christian Democrats claimed to be a new and cohesive ideological center, intent on breaking the political stalemate. They argued that their reformist strategy would lead to genuine economic and social progress and that it represented a viable third way between the right and Marxist left."[8] However, the Christian Democrats proved rigid in approaching the political game, failing to develop interparty alliances that would have maintained the working of the compromise state. Instead the foundations for the post-1970 period were laid. As the Christian Democrats sought to modernize Chilean capitalism and give it a human face, they refused alliances and incurred resistance. At the same time, the country's society was undergoing sweeping transformations: the peasants were increasingly incorporated into the nation's social and political life, and the urban poor were organized for political involvement. As the 1960s advanced, Chilean society became more politicized, especially given the influence of external events such as the Cuban revolution. Chile's political life became more radical, with an increasingly vocal and aggressive left questioning the legitimacy of the capitalist system. In return, the Chilean right was equally vocal about the "chaotic" and "demagogic" nature of extended political participation and state intervention.[9]

The Allende Years

By the 1969 congressional and 1970 presidential elections, the centrifugal tendencies in Chilean political life meant that the Christian Democrats could no longer maintain their hold on political power. In a three way contest, Salvador Allende and the broad leftist coalition, the Popular Unity or Unidad Popular (UP), won the day. Allende became president with 36.2 percent of the vote, overcoming the conservative candidate (34.9 percent) and the Christian Democrat (27.8 percent).

The Allende government was immediately confronted with a number of problems. First and foremost, the UP coalition was a loose-knit alliance, ranging from moderate Socialists and social democrats to hardline Communists and even more radical revolutionaries. The campaign platform was based on a transition to socialism while preserving Chile's democratic system, though the consensus as to implementation was lacking. While the Allende administration nationalized the copper mines, incurring U.S. displeasure, the radical elements of the UP felt the transformation to socialism was not advancing quickly enough. Also, radical elements favored a more fundamental agrarian reform than the one introduced by Allende. Initially, diverging views were contained, but by 1972 it became evident that the UP was facing immense internal strife and external pressure.

The Allende government's major operational problem was its economic policies. Initially, wage increases and new worker benefits helped stimulate domestic demand and made 1971 a year of dynamic growth. The measures to benefit the workers, partially through a forced reallocation of national wealth, also helped maintain political support for the UP government, which won 50 percent of the vote in the 1971 municipal elections. However, what was politically advantageous in the short term was economically problematic in the medium term. Chile was hit hard by rising inflation in 1972 (up to 164 percent) and reduced access to international credit. Unable to produce enough consumer goods for the new wave of local consumers, imports made up the difference. This situation soon led to a foreign exchange outflow. To make matters worse, Chile was hit by a savage blow from its international terms of trade. A sharp rise in the international price of oil, of which Chile was a net importer, coincided with a record fall in the price of the country's main export, copper.

The final problem facing Allende was the hostility his Marxist experiment incurred from the right, especially the military. Initially shocked by Allende's victory, the right regrouped and by 1972 the UP lost a number of by-elections. More importantly, the Christian Democrats joined the active opposition. By late 1972, Allende's ministers were congressionally censored and efforts were made to limit the powers of the chief executive. Additionally, the right and center resorted to effective extra-parliamentary tactics, calling supporters out into the streets to demonstrate opposition to Allende. The government tried to respond with its own popular rallies, but the revolt of the middle classes—typified by the saucepan-beating demonstrations of housewives protesting higher prices—was difficult to assuage. Industrial disputes proliferated. In an embarrassing volte-face, Allende had to incorporate members of the military into the government, which enabled him to quell the strikes of October 1972. The armed forces were soon wooed by political parties from the right and the left. Considering the military's traditional anticommunist tendencies, this situation alarmed an increasing number of senior officers who were also concerned about possible contamination of the ranks with communism and the emergence of leftist paramilitary groups.

The polarization of Chile's political life continued through 1973. The March 1973 election deprived the Allende government of control in both houses of Congress, but the right failed to garner a two-thirds majority capable of impeaching the president. Throughout the year the economy deteriorated to a background of grumblings within the military, a dramatic upswing of political violence, the arming of leftist groups, and the clandestine involvement of the U.S. Central Intelligence Agency to foment anti-Allende sentiment. On 11 September 1973, the military decided to end the slide into civil war, launching what was to become a brutal and deadly coup that decapitated the

Chilean left. Allende is reported to have committed suicide and a number of his closest supporters were killed in a fierce battle for the presidential palace. Suspected leftist sympathizers were rounded up in a nation-wide sweep and many were killed. Sporadic resistance to the right-wing coup resulted in some military casualties. With the crushing of leftist resistance, a new era in the country's political and economic development commenced.[10]

The General's Shadow

When General Augusto Pinochet came to power in 1973 the country's economy was deeply troubled and the threat of civil war hovered on the horizon. By the end of his tenure as the nation's chief executive, Pinochet left an economy that was the envy of most of Latin America and a political system that had voted him out of office and replaced him with a democratically elected leader. Although his shadow continued to fall over the country from his post as commander in chief of the armed forces, Chile passed from one stage of development to another. How did the general transform Chile in the 1973–88 period?

Chile under military rule underwent four broad, overarching phases: (1) the consolidation of power, 1973–76, which was marked by the rise of General Pinochet as the undisputed national leader; (2) a period of political neutralization overshadowed by economic reforms inspired by the "Chicago Boys" from 1976–82 and the institutionalization of Pinochet's "revolution"; (3) an economic crash and political awakening, 1982–84; and (4) an economic revitalization and political opening, 1984–88. A core element throughout military government was the steady, some would say ruthless modernization of the economy. In this, the Pinochet years were highly successful. Where the Pinochet government was not successful, at least from its perspective, was in the depoliticalization of the country. These two factors clearly must be considered in understanding Pinochet's rule as well as the rebirth of Chilean democracy and the country's ongoing economic trendsetting in the 1990s.

When the military assumed power in 1973 there was no certainty that it would be able to retain power. It was believed by many, including those on the left, that supporters of the Allende government were well-armed and would spring into action against the armed forces.

Apprehension about an all-out civil, war coupled with the military's almost doctrinal belief that communism was an all-encompassing alien threat, explain the ruthless and precise nature of the armed forces' assault on the Chilean left. The added neo-Gaullist perception that civilian politicians were to blame for the nation's troubles carried over into an active policy of neutering even the centrist and rightist political parties, some of which supported the coup. In a sense, the military perceived that too much political mobilization and the compromise state led to a systemic paralysis that brought the country to the brink economically and politically.

While a campaign of repression and neutralization of representative organizations characterized the political front, Pinochet increasingly gained power within the *junta*. He was quick to recognize that the new regime required an economic policy and, to a limited extent, civilian partners. This brought the Pinochet regime to incorporate the services of a team of technocrats who would provide it with an ideological component and economic game plan which went beyond the military's simple object of ousting Allende. In later years, Pinochet likened himself to General MacArthur who created an apolitical, technocratic, capitalist basis for the Japanese economic miracle, borne out of the ashes of the Second World War. The technocratic team earned the nickname the Chicago Boys because many of its members were graduates of The University of Chicago and were students of U.S. monetarist economist Milton Friedman.

The Chicago Boys provided the blueprint for Chile's revolution. This entailed a complete societal transformation and an adoption of an outward-oriented economic strategy, which meant that Chilean capitalism would be restructured from its protected import-substitution mode. As Chilean political scientist Manuel Antonio Garreton noted: "This time, the project of capitalist transformation came from the technocratic sector, which relied upon all the coercive resources of the state. It was a model of outward development characterized by an unrestricted opening of the economy, a reduction in the role of the state, a replacement of the latter by the private sector of the economy, and the expansion of market mechanisms."[11]

One of the first acts of the military government was to reprivatize what the Allende government had nationalized. From 1974–78, farms, companies, and banks were returned to the private sector. However, ownership of the newly reconstituted private sector remained concentrated in a few hands, largely through large conglomerates that encompassed industry and finance. Government acquiescence in the face of this immense concentration was ultimately to prove, however, a near-fatal error.

After several years of economic dislocation, with real GDP falling by 13 percent in 1975, Chile appeared to regain its momentum in 1976 when real GDP growth was 3.5 percent. This was a modest forerunner of what was to come: from 1977 to 1980, real GDP growth averaged an impressive 8.55 percent. Chile was off and running and the Chicago Boys were riding high. It was publicly debated that Chile was rapidly moving to a higher level of economic development; indeed closing the gap between itself and the lower tier of industrialized nations. Moreover, the Chilean "miracle" was creating a new export-oriented entrepreneurial class that identified with the changes. Chile was also regarded as a place that was open to, and safe for, foreign investment. Foreign banks extended credit to Chilean banks and companies in an ever upward moving spiral.

The seeming success of the Chicago Boys' economic program encouraged Pinochet to provide a formal structure for his "revolution." The 1973–75 period was notable for the destruction of the country's democratic institutions and its replacement by a personalized authoritarian rule. Yet, Pinochet and his closest supporters still felt the need to create a "legitimate" and constitutional form of government. Additionally, the opposition of the Catholic Church, which formed the Vicariate of Solidarity in 1976, and international pressure helped push Pinochet into holding a plebiscite in 1978. The choice was simple: voters could either vote "yes" or "no" in defense of his authority to create a new institutional order. It was no surprise that the government won the contest, claiming a 75 percent victory. This was followed by another plebiscite in 1980. As Arturo Valenzuela noted: "Convened at the height of the economic boom, that election had no safeguards for participation by the opposition, in contrast with the 1988 referendum. According to the government, 67 percent of the voters approved the new charter, which included transitory articles to maintain Pinochet's authority through the 1988 plebiscite, when his mandate could be renewed for another eight years."[12]

The structure of the Chicago Boys' economic experiment had two near-fatal flaws. The first was that it was based on a monetary model, which leaned toward maintaining a strong currency. The second was that it proved to be less than successful in generating a level of domestic savings adequate to sustain the high level of economic growth that had been generated, necessitating a high level of reliance on foreign capital. Additionally, Chile remained very dependent on copper: in 1981 that commodity accounted for 44 percent of exports. This combination of factors was soon to have a negative impact on Chile.

Chile entered 1981 with an overvalued currency. The pegging of the peso to the U.S. dollar, at a time when Chilean prices and wages were growing much more strongly than in the United States, destroyed the competitiveness of nontraditional exports. The high exchange rate, which coincided with radical import liberalization sucked in consumer goods at an alarming rate. This situation was aggravated by a large drop in copper prices, which flattened exports by close to $1 billion, and created a severe balance-of-payments crisis. Other contributing factors were a global recession and a hike in interest rates on Chile's now sizeable external debt. As the means of payment were reduced, the amount of payments went up. Although Chile managed a 5.5 percent growth rate in 1981, the Chicago Boys' experiment was revealed as highly imperfect when, in 1982, the economy contracted by a devastating 14 percent. The country was unable to pay its external debt and the highly indebted private sector, which had borrowed externally through the banking sector which it owned, was swept by a wave of interrelated bankruptcies.

The economic crash brought Chile into the third period of military rule. The Pinochet government was confronted by an imploding economy, which posed serious questions about the regime's ideological approach. What was highly ironic was that the government that professed free-market capitalism was forced to assume control of large sectors of the national economy in order to avoid a complete collapse, notably the intervention by the central bank of many of the country's leading commercial banks to prevent total financial collapse. What was particularly difficult for the government to swallow was that for any return to international credit-worthiness, the private sector's external debt, which accounted for 84 percent of the total foreign debt, had to be assumed by the state.[13] Yet, the Pinochet regime had little choice. For example, if the regime were to let the insolvent banks fall, a ripple factor would have worsened an already near-depression situation. As a World Bank study noted: "it would have caused a chain of bankruptcies in two thirds of the banking system and large segments of borrowers, and it would have undermined the confidence on the financial system."[14]

State intervention in the economy was broad and would have significant ramifications for the country's future. In 1983, business failures reached unprecedented numbers and the foundation of the Chilean economy—the large scale conglomerates—began to go under. The conglomerates had severe credit problems and could not roll over their loans. The state's assumption of the liabilities of the main commercial banks gave it control of around 80 percent of the once private financial system, and indirect control of companies that were deeply indebted to them.

The 1981–83 economic crisis also stimulated a political awakening that eventually culminated in the 1988 plebiscite. The Pinochet government, despite its ability to retain power, remained vulnerable to its lack of legitimacy in the eyes of many Chileans. While the economy had boomed, the issue of regime legitimacy was not as pressing. However, this changed when the country was struck by a depression in 1982–83. A renewed public interest in the political arena included concerns about human rights' abuses and the need for better distribution of income throughout Chilean society. In May 1983 a protest movement emerged when the Confederation of Copper Workers called for a nationwide strike. By August, Chile was rocked by anti-Pinochet demonstrations. The governmental response was a tough crackdown with multiple deaths and numerous arrests. Also, however, there was a greater willingness than in 1974–75 to protect the basic human needs of the poor. A U. N. study argued that Chile was much more successful than bigger countries, like Brazil and Mexico, in protecting basic needs in the adjustment process prompted by the external debt crisis.

The 1983 demonstrations revived interservice tensions within the Pinochet regime. While the army was staunchly pro-Pinochet and had few qualms about being heavy-handed in dealing with dissent, the air force and navy sought to discreetly distance themselves from this policy line. These two branches of the military establishment, as well as a number of army officers, had misgivings about the considerable power wielded by the secret police. In the mid-1970s Chile's National Intelligence Agency (then called DINA) was active in "disappearing" members of the opposition. DINA was implicated in three spectacular overseas assassination attempts, the most infamous being the fatal bombing of Allende's ambassador to the United States, Orlando Letelier in September 1976 in Washington, D.C. The Chilean government denied involvement in these acts, but from the beginning many fingers pointed to DINA and its leader, the sinister General Manuel Cantreras Sepulveda.

Although DINA was reconstituted into the National Information Center (Central Nacional de Informaciones) and Cantreras was shunted aside, air force and navy officers remained ill at ease with reliance on the secret police. Moreover, the Pinochet regime's odious image overseas ostracized Chile's military from its traditional international links and some of the interchange of ideas concerning new tactics and technology was missed.

While air force and navy misgivings existed, the armed forces were partially held together by the failure of Chile's moderate politicians to provide a unified front. Additionally, an ultraleft opposition emerged, the Frente Manuel Rodriguez (Manuel Rodriguez Front or FMR), which had ties to the Chilean Communist Party and Cuba. The FMR had few reservations about using force against the state: in early 1984 it made its presence known with a bombing campaign. The most spectacular attack came on 1 April 1984, when a round of explosions severed electricity to two-thirds of the country.

In the aftermath of the economic crisis, the Chilean political arena re-awoke in 1984. Despite the inability of the old line political parties to unify, opposition to the regime grew. Days of national protest were organized in March, April, May, September, and October. In November 1984, the cabinet resigned and Pinochet imposed a new round of crackdowns and imposed a state of siege. Many Chilean analysts predicted that the general would soon be forced out of power either by other members of the military or by a massive popular protest.

Pinochet, however, was able to survive the economic crisis and the political awakening. It soon became evident that the general would leave office on his own schedule and according to his own set of rules. This was demonstrated in September 1984 when the machinery for the transition to democracy was introduced, which encompassed draft legislation governing voter registration and the legalization of political parties. Although a step was taken to institute a return to democracy, the date for the plebiscite when the Chilean population would vote yes or no for such a transition would not be until 1988 or 1989. Moreover, Pinochet let it be known that he would serve his full term, which lasted until March 1989.

While dark clouds of doom hung over Chile's political life in 1983 and 1984, the economic managers of Pinochet regime's scrambled to adjust to changing circumstances. To a large number of Chileans, the Chicago Boys' neoliberal economic experiment was a disaster, especially as unemployment climbed to 30 percent by the end of 1983. Members of the working and lower-middle classes felt the Chicago Boys' approach was biased against them, while many capitalists, who disliked foreign competition in their home market, joined the ranks of detractors. For the private sector in general, the neoliberal approach had proven to be another round of unpredictable economic activity.

The task of getting the economy back on track was hindered by the termination of foreign credit from international banks. Chile was on its own. What evolved from the 1983–84 period was a more pragmatic neoliberal economic ideology. This meant greater flexibility in meeting the needs of particular sectors, reflationary measures (such as fiscal deficits of around 4 percent of the GDP), and subsidies, including a special employment program. Additionally, credit policies were tailored to meet the needs of specific sectors. For example, in the agricultural sector the government created minimum guaranteed prices (called preference price bands) for wheat, oilseeds, and sugar beet with the intention of alleviating the uncertainties which highly volatile international prices had brought for producers.[15] Along similar lines, the government in 1983 increased the general level of import tariffs from 10 to 20 percent.

The incentive for the Pinochet regime to adopt a mildly reflationary program was that an economic recovery would help return the country to political stability. In the short term, this meant the reduction of unemployment, renewed support from the business community, and an undermining of the opposition's attack on the regime. This, in turn, would allow the long-term plan of transforming Chile into an export-oriented capitalist society to continue.

Recovery and Transformation, 1985–88

Chile's economic recovery began in 1984 when the real GDP growth rate was 5.9 percent. Although the economy slowed to 2 percent growth in 1985, the groundwork was laid for a new and better-founded boom. The 1985–88 period was the beginning of Chile's most dynamic period of economic expansion: real GDP rate expanded by an average of

6.3 percent in the 1986–88 period, while unemployment fell from 30 percent in 1983 to 12.7 percent by 1988.[16]

Chile's economic planners embarked upon a diversification program of exports and markets. The heavy dependence on copper had been made painfully evident in 1982. The desire was to break Chile's traditional dependence on one export and introduce new products which would buffer the economy when copper prices fell. Although it was acknowledged that copper would remain the country's major export, agricultural, livestock and ocean products, and manufactured goods were given special attention. The new products would be aimed at the export market by new entrepreneurial groups which meant a reduced role for the traditional conglomerates that had dominated the country's economic life. At the same time, the opening up of the domestic market, a process which had been temporarily interrupted during the crisis years of 1982–83, was revived.

One of the innovative forces behind what was becoming a structural transformation of the Chilean economy was the Fundacion Chile. This organization was founded in 1976 by the Chilean government and the U.S. firm, ITT Corporation, a firm that was deemed to have colluded in the overthrow of Allende. The Fundacion's mission was to facilitate transfer of new technologies and production systems to augment the development process. Fundacion Chile's agro-industry programs were an influential factor in the expansion of the nation's fruit and vegetable exports.

A variety of new products were introduced to Chilean consumers and in many cases the export market, often with the assistance of the Fundacion. Some of these new products included sauces and purees for desserts, fruit pulp for yogurt, prepared cocktails, and wine coolers. The combination of enhanced quality-control services, new and improved products, and ongoing assimilation of new technology helped Chile's diversification effort to leap forward, broadening and deepening the export base. Instead of relying solely on copper Chile, by the late 1980s, had become an international force with its grapes, raspberries, apples, salmon, and wines.

Chile's wines have traditionally been of excellent quality, but not widely known beyond Latin America. Awareness of Chilean wines was meager in North America and Europe. Beginning in the early 1980s Chilean vintners began to penetrate the U.S. market at the lower end of the quality and price scale. By the mid-1980s, Chilean brands

like Concho y Toro and Vina San Pedro (Gato Blanco and Gato Negro) were becoming standard items in many U.S. and European stores.
By the late 1980s, the Chilean wine sector had also witnessed an
upswing both in joint ventures (as with Californian vintners) and foreign investments (as with Spanish investors).

In the period between 1985 and 1988, the export earnings of the
agricultural, livestock and ocean products sectors grew from $515
million to $930 million.[17] Nor were fruits, vegetables, salmon, and
wine alone in their overseas appeal: the Chilean manufacturing export
earnings rose from $1.168 billion to $2.273 billion during the same
period. Diversification efforts did not mean that copper was ignored.
While fruits, vegetables, and manufactured goods were taking off, the
copper industry enjoyed a period of sustained growth. Assisted by
foreign investment from Finnish, Japanese, British, Australian, and
U.S. firms and buoyed by relatively high international prices, copper
maintained its lead role. Copper exports rose from $1.8 billion in 1985
to $3.4 billion in 1988, retaining its position of around half of the
export earnings.

TABLE 3.1
Total Chilean Exports, 1985–1988 and Percentage of Copper
(in U.S.$ millions)

	1985	1986	1987	1988
Total Exports	3,804	4,199	5,224	7,052
Copper in $	1,789	1,757	2,235	3,416
Copper (%)	47.0	41.8	42.8	48.4

(Source: Banco Central de Chile, *Statistical Synthesis of Chile 1985–1989*, p. 35)

The scope of Chile's export achievement was noted by Chilean economist J. Lavin, who wrote in 1988: "While in 1971 we exported 412
different products to 58 countries, the mark 'Made in Chile' is now
printed on 1,343 products in 112 countries. Between 1973 and the end
of 1986 the number of exporting companies increased thirteen times,
the growth that took place during the two last years being especially
significant, when 798 companies entered the export process."[18]

Chile's export diversification reduced the proportion of its exports
going to the U.S. market and, with the exception of Brazil, to other
Latin American countries. Exports to Japan, other Pacific Basin nations (including Australia and New Zealand), and a number of European countries increased. Market penetration occurred despite the

Pinochet regime's less than savory international reputation for its human rights' abuses. This was partially because of the good quality of Chilean products as well as the comparative price advantage. The appropriate blend of technology, marketing and determination made Chile one of Latin America's foremost exporting powers by 1988. In many respects its developmental path was similar to that of Singapore, Korea, and Taiwan—an emphasis on exports, the introduction, assimilation and implementation of new technology to enhance export-oriented product lines, and a political system that was relatively authoritarian.

While export reform was a core element of the new Chile, other measures were taken to restructure the economy. As part of the ideological viewpoint that the Chilean state needed to reduce its role as a market presence, investor, and planner and designer of the country's developmental and industrial strategy, privatization was highly regarded. Before departing from office, the Pinochet regime presided over one of the world's most radical privatization programs, including 33 state-run enterprises in the period between 1985 and 1990. The attraction of privatization, which was embarked upon afresh in 1984, was that it (1) got the government out of an area in which it had no role; (2) added to public-sector revenues; and (3) provided a means of external debt reduction.

Chile's total external debt in 1985 was $20.5 billion, the bulk of which the public sector was directly or indirectly responsible for, largely because its creditors obliged it to assume responsibility, via guarantees, of private-sector debts. Chile was assisted by the International Monetary Fund (IMF) with an SDR-extended fund facility of $750 million in 1985, and also signed an agreement with its creditor banks to stretch out over 12 years $6 billion of principal due at the end of 1987. The private bank deal also came with a $785 million, ten-year new money credit to help cover the balance-of-payments deficit in 1985 and 1986. An additional source of outside credit was a World Bank loan of $250 million for structural adjustments in 1985 and 1986. Yet, Chilean planners were aware that these measures only kept the financial wolf of insolvency at the door—they did not provide an immediate means of debt reduction. Other measures were needed, hence the turn to privatization and debt-to-equity conversions.

Chile began its debt-conversion program in May 1985, partly as a means of stimulating foreign direct investment in the privatization of state enterprises. The debt-conversion program was founded on the purchase of Chilean external debt papers at a discount on the burgeoning secondary market for developing country debt and swapped into certain currency instruments at a lower discount. These could then be used to swap into the equity of local companies, including privatized entities, or used to repay indebtedness to Chilean banks.

The Chilean government had found an ingenious means of external debt reduction through the debt-equity mechanism. Chilean debt was reduced without recourse to international reserves at a substantial discount to face value. New investment was simultaneously increased from what it would otherwise have been. The debt-conversion program complemented the privatization process. Privatization also, of course, carried a political content. It was decided that in this round of privatization, ownership of the means of production would be "democratized." This meant that the old-line conglomerates would not be given back their companies, maintaining a dominant position in the private sector's evolution. Rather, other elements of the population would be brought into the capitalist system through investment, creating a system of "popular capitalism."

One of the major items the Pinochet government had implemented was the creation of savings programs, such as a mandatory pension-fund savings scheme. By the mid-1980s, pension funds emerged as major investors in the economy. They provided capital for investment and, through a pension-fund company, many Chileans became owners in shares of companies. As economist Patricio Meller noted: "In this reprivatization a different set of divestiture procedures was used: 'popular capitalism', stock exchange and bidding among prequalified buyers. All of these transactions (except those for 'popular capitalism' programs) required 100 percent cash down payments. Dissemination of ownership was a clear objective."[19]

Chile's privatization program included most of the country's public utilities, such as the telephone, telecommunications, and electricity companies, and the national airline. By 1988, the sales of state-owned companies reached $1.1 billion, part of which came from foreign investors.[20] At the same time, the debt-equity program, including the purchase of shares of privatized state firms, reached $5.6 billion of debt retirement by 1988. By the end of 1989, over half of the medium- and long-term debt owed by Chile in 1985 had been expired by the debt-conversion program. Although the country's total debt did not decline *pari passu*, falling from $20.5 billion in 1985 to $18.7 billion in 1988, this was largely because of new loans (as from the World Bank) to finance investment, not consumption.

The growing confidence in Chile by foreign investors in the 1985–88 period contributed to the country's economic success. According to the Chilean Central Bank, actual direct foreign investment in 1985 stood at a modest $137 million, led by the mining sector. By 1988 that figure rose to $787 million, though still led by mining, the services sector was close behind. The stock market was one major attraction, as the Santiago Bolsa de Valores went from a capitalization of $2.8 billion in 1985 to $6.85 billion in 1988.[21]

By 1988, Chile had advanced considerably from 1973. While export-sector expansion and diversification, and debt-equity and privatization programs were clearly dynamic, advances in the high-technology area were equally significant, especially in positioning the country for the next round of economic competition. Consider some of the following points of achievement in 1988:

- Chile's banking system entered the age of high technology, having a total of 9.6 million bank transactions conducted yearly through 180 automated teller machines.
- Chile was the first Latin American nation to connect to the SWIFT system, which permits electronic fund transfers among member banks around the world in four seconds.
- Mobile phones had entered the country through Cidcom, a local Chilean company.
- Chile's telex network was the most advanced in Latin America with 6,500 telex machines and four rival private companies, Telex Chile, VTR Telecomunicaciones, Texcom and ITT Comunicaciones Mundiales.
- Fax machines were also making their entrance into the local market (having entered in 1986).
- Between 1970 and 1987, the number of telephones in service doubled, led by the modernization of the Companía de Teléfonos de Chile.
- Chile had created a number of multinational companies that were increasingly active in other Latin American markets, such as SONDA (Sociedad Nacional de Procesamiento de Datos), Hipermercados Jumbo (with a store in Argentina), Madeco, SA (a telecomunications and cable firm), and Lord Cochrane publishing house.
- Atari computer sales began in 1980. In 1983, 800 units were sold; 30,000 in 1986.
- Chile's fishmeal industry was one of the most competitive in the world, having made substantial use of new technology.

Although General Pinochet had many detractors, most recognized that by 1988 he had presided over a structural and attitudinal transformation of his country. Unlike Chile's neighbors in Latin America, hyperinflation was never experienced, unemployment was not on the rise, and the economy was not afflicted by flight capital. Instead, foreign capital was pouring in, most sectors of the economy were enjoying rapid expansion at home and abroad, and even the level of per capita income was creeping upwards. The political issue of whether or not Pinochet would have another term had yet to be resolved. Although the political awakening that commenced in 1983 and 1984 had slowed somewhat in 1985 and 1986, it resumed in 1987 as the country geared up for the 1988 plebiscite which offered the potential that the general would perhaps find the exit ramp and democratic government would return to Chile.

The General Finds the Exit Ramp

By 1 January 1988 Pinochet had presided over a remarkable economic transformation and had ruled longer than any other Chilean political leader. Yet, there were clouds on the horizon. The economic success story did not reach all elements of Chilean society and discontent simmered in the shantytowns that surround Santiago. The old line political parties, such as the Socialists, Communists, and Christian Democrats, had not faded away and were now clamoring about the 1988 plebiscite which was promised in the 1980 constitution. Although the regime had clamped down on the Manuel Rodriguez Patriotic Front, the organization continued to be active. Together with the armed wing of the Movimiento de Izquierda Revolucionaria (MIR), they were responsible during 1983–86 for 3,326 dynamiting cases, 1,889 acts of sabotage, 649 armed assaults, and 162 kidnappings or assassination attempts.[22] The front also conducted a near-miss assassination attempt on General Pinochet in September 1986. By 1988, these radical leftist organizations were still active.

Furthermore, the United States was pushing hard for the Chilean government to return the country to the democratic fold, which meant it preferred Pinochet to exit the political stage. U.S. officials were active in providing funds for activities to promote a fair election, while the U.S. Congress was forcing the administration to be less supportive of lending to Chile by the multilateral agencies, particularly the World Bank. As part of the U.S. effort to expedite democratic rule, the National Endowment for Democracy appropriated $1 million to finance opinion polls, media consultants, and the parallel vote count. The U.S. push for an open plebiscite eventually incurred claims by the Pinochet government of "foreign intervention" and the U.S. ambassador was snubbed by the Chilean president.

Pinochet, however, had no plans of leaving easily. Though bound by the 1980 constitution, he decided to actively campaign for the *"sí"* vote in the plebiscite, which was to be held in October 1988. If the *"sí"* vote carried the day, Pinochet would be given the opportunity to serve another presidential term of eight years. If the *"no"* vote won, competitive elections for president and members of parliament were to be scheduled the following year. To guarantee that the "transition" to a new Chile was entrenched to the end of the century, the 1980 constitution provided that the individuals serving as the armed forces' commanders in chief and director general of the National Police at the end of the transition period were to remain in their posts until 1997.

The country prepared for the plebiscite through early 1988 and into the summer. Convinced that Philippine dictator Ferdinand Marcos' ultimate overthrow was in some part due to the fraudulent way in which he conducted the 1986 elections, Pinochet and his advisors wanted a clean election in Chile. The general strongly felt that he would win and did not want charges of fraud to discredit his victory. There were two key reasons he thought he would win in a fair contest. According to U.S. journalist Pamela Constable and Georgetown University Professor Arturo Valenzuela: "His aides constantly reassured him that 'decent' Chileans appreciated his long sacrifice, and the enthusiasm of the crowds at orchestrated rallies seemed to prove it. Pinochet was also contemptuous of his opponents, whom he viewed as a motley crew of demagogues unable to compete with his solid record."[23]

While the nation's vote was indeed divided in mid-1988 over whether or not to give Pinochet the *"sí"* vote, the opposition finally managed to form a broad front of sixteen parties, the Command for the *No*, in August 1988. With 92 percent of the voting-age population registered to vote by the August 30 cut-off, the Command for the No emerged as a tough new challenge for Pinochet. The General took to the campaign trail, lecturing the population that a yes vote was for order and progress and a no vote for chaos, communism, and a return to 1973.

For their part, the Command for the *No* presented a sharp alternative to Pinochet's message of a clear-cut choice between the new Chile of rapid economic development and prosperity, and the tormented past of the Allende years. Provided access to television for the first time in years, the opposition parties carefully crafted messages that carried the theme that there were abuses under military rule and that not everyone was part of the new order that had emerged. Equally important, the Christian Democrats, elements of the Socialist parties, and moderate centrists indicated that the Pinochet government's economic reforms had indeed brought the country a considerable distance forward and not everything was negative or would have to be undone. In fact, much of the capitalistic path would be continued, but with greater social concern for those elements of the nation that had been hard hit by the changes.

On 5 October 1988 Chile went to the polls. A majority of 54.7 percent voted no compared to 43 percent voting yes, setting in motion a return to democratic government. Pinochet was forced onto the exit ramp because he had seriously underestimated his opponents and the population's desire for change, had overestimated the population's fears of communism, and had failed to grasp that there were elements of society that did not feel a part of the new Chile.[24] On the other hand, his ability to win the vote of over 40 percent of the electorate after a fifteen-year reign and a protracted period of international opprobrium, was in a sense a victory, albeit Pyrrhic.

Despite predictions that the center-left political alliance that had favored the yes vote would dissipate in the 1989 elections, it held together. In two elections, one for parliament and the other for the presidency (on 14 December 1988), the right surrendered power at the ballot box, despite the government's pump-priming the economy. The center-left coalition dominated by Christian Democrats and Socialists won 72 of 120 seats in the Chamber of Deputies, and 22 of 38 contested seats in the Senate. The right maintained a narrow majority in the Senate due to electoral formulae that allowed the government to appoint nine senators. In the contest for the presidency, Christian Democratic leader, Patrico Aylwin won 55.2 percent of the vote over his nearest opponent, former Pinochet government finance minister Hernan Buchi, who gained 29.4 percent of the vote, and a far right independent candidate, millionaire Francisco Javier Errazuriz, with 15.4 percent of the vote. The combined vote of Buchi and Errazuriz mirrored that of Pinochet in the 1988 plebiscite.

Sustaining Political and Economic Liberalization

When the moderate President Aylwin entered office in March 1990 ending seventeen years of military dictatorship, he inherited an economy that had expanded by the rapid rates of 7.4 percent in 1988 and 11.5 percent in 1989. Exports were continuing to rise (reaching $8.1 billion in 1989) and the government enjoyed a budget surplus. For his part, Aylwin was ill-disposed to overturning the broad promarket parameters of Pinochet's economic policies. He therefore returned to meet the higher social-spending commitments made during his election campaign by allowing the fiscal deficit to balloon. Thus the social program was financed by reversing Pinochet's 1989 value-added tax (VAT) rate cuts and by increasing corporate taxation, albeit to leave corporate taxes well below international levels. His dedication to sound finance was in a sense helped by one of Pinochet's parting shots, which made the central bank independent. The newly independent central bank, under Andres Bianchi, was quick to tighten monetary policy in 1990, which had been relaxed by Pinochet in an effort to support the presidential candidacy of Hernan Buchi.

Nevertheless, Chile's coalition was successful in continuing the country's forward economic motion, registering real GDP growth in 1991 of 5.4 percent. Indeed, the government was successful in reducing inflation from 27.3 percent in 1990 to 18 percent in 1991, and 13 percent in 1992. Additionally, the Aylwin government concluded two deals, one with its international banks and the other with the United States to reduce the total external debt. The deal with the international commercial banks also included a return to the voluntary credit market for Chile, indicating that it was no longer perceived as a troubled developing world debtor, a fact continued in 1992 by Chile's elevation to "investment grade" by some of the international bond-rating agencies.

With these results the financial press broached the possibility that Chile was indeed becoming a Newly Industrializing Country (NIC) along the lines of South Korea, Singapore, and Taiwan and was in the process of fulfilling its Pacific Basin, as opposed to Latin American, destiny. In fact, one Chilean commentator noted as early as 1988: "Defying geography and the plans made by dozens of economists, who in the sixties, dreamed of Chile being integrated with Peru, Bolivia, Ecuador and other Andean nations, the country today is more like Australia and New Zealand than like any of its Latin American neighbors."[25]

Chile's claim to a Pacific destiny is increasingly evident in international investment literature, a status enhanced by the rating firm Standard & Poor's designation of BBB in 1992, making the southern cone country investment grade for the first time. Further upgrades have followed: Standard & Poor's moved Chile to BBB+ in 1993 and A- in 1995, and Moody's Investor Services assigned it an investment grade rating of Baa2 in 1994 and upgraded to Baa1 in 1995. Both ratings placed Chile in a peer group that included the Czech Republic (Baa1/ A), Israel (A3/A-), and China (A3/BBB), and a higher level than all other Latin American countries, Greece, Hungary, Poland, the Slovak Republic, and South Africa.[26] According to Emelio Bassini, president of the Latin America Fund and Chile Fund, Chile is already the "sixth Pacific Tiger," joining the ranks of South Korea, Hong Kong, Thailand, Taiwan, and Singapore. Chile's growth of 10.3 percent in 1992 was higher than any of the Asian Tigers, except China, although the pace was to slow down in 1993–96.[27]

The claim to honorary "Tigership" is sustained by several factors that Chile shares with the Asian tigers: high real GDP growth, a large trade surplus, diversified export base, low unemployment, relatively low inflation, declining external debt, and a balanced budget.[28] Chile's standing as a Pacific Tiger is reinforced by a high-performance stock market. Equally significant is that Chile has moved away from the past of populism-communism and protectionism, thereby plugging into the post-cold war era and the interrelated nature of economic development in the last decade of the twentieth century. The huge inflow of foreign capital into the economy in 1991 and 1992, putting upward pressure on the peso and helping to boost growth has left the central bank with the luxury of having to raise interest rates to prevent growth reaching double digits. This is a problem which many of Chile's neighbors would love to have and confirms Chile's attraction as a member of the new world order. According to the IMF, foreign direct investment in Chile in 1991 was $563 million and $737 million in 1992.[29]

Foreign investors continued to regard Chile positively through the crisis with the Mexican peso in December 1994 and early 1995. Despite the bearishness of foreign investors toward Latin America in general in early 1995, and a fall in the sale of shares of Chilean companies traded on U.S. stock exchanges (through American depository receipts or ADRs), Chile actually witnessed an increase in foreign direct investment. According to Chile's Foreign Investment Committee, foreign-investment approvals in the first quarter of 1995 rose 16 percent to $1.005 billion from $866.6 million a year prior.[30]

The Challenge

There remain, however, lingering problems that may slow Chile's ascent to permanent Tiger status. While the outgoing Pinochet regime bequeathed its civilian successor a largely robust macroeconomic situation, it also left its civilian successor a government with a number of problems including stubbornly high inflation, and lingering questions about the country's "social debt," i.e. the need to rechannel funds further to broaden health-care benefits and education.

Chile's future economic policy is going to be a major factor in whether or not a consensus is maintained in the civilian elite. As journalist Malcolm Coad noted in 1991, with relevance in the mid-1990s: "Few wish to risk the stability which distinguishes Chile from its neighbors or its dynamic new export sector. But these successes were achieved through neglecting the internal market and a brutal depression of living standards."[31] According to Coad, those living below the poverty line grew to 40 percent under the Pinochet regime and incomes of 80 percent of the population declined by up to 40 percent. According to World Bank data in the mid-1990s, the top 20 percent of Chile's society account for around 60 percent of national consumption, one of the most dramatic discrepancies in Latin America.[32] Although some of these imbalances were being reduced in the last years of the Pinochet government and have been further addressed under Aylwin and Frei, they continue to represent potential landmines for the returned civilian political forces.

The Aylwin administration addressed the problems with a package of tax increases, a higher minimum wage ($100 a month) and increases in pensions, family allowances, and other benefits. Most of this has been paid for by tax increases. Some of the benefits of economic growth became evident during the Aylwin government: between 1987 and 1992, the number of Chileans living below the poverty level declined from 44 to 33 percent.[33]

Eduardo Frei's election to the presidency in December 1993 maintained the government's policy of improving the human condition.

The government's priorities to raise investment in education to 7 percent of GDP from 5 percent and to alleviate poverty reflect an awareness that meeting basic human needs is important in the development process.[34] At the same time, the Frei government did not turn to new taxes to finance social spendings, pushing instead ahead with a new round of privatizations. In mid-1994, a new list of state-owned or partially state-owned companies, including Edelnor, the northern power utility, and Lan Chile, the state airline, was drawn up. Although initially there was concern that the Frei administration would be more populist than its predecessor, it has maintained a commitment to tight fiscal policy. The goals of improving social conditions are to be achieved by government avoidance of large-expenditure projects that can be done by the private sector.

Another point of concern for post-Pinochet administrations is the need to maintain Chile's competitive edge in economic innovation, which has been a key factor in the country's economic success. This means an ongoing ability of the nation's business community to tap into and assimilate technological changes in the rest of the world, the ability of the work force to respond to these changes on the training and skills front, and the awareness and flexibility of the government to create and maintain an environment conducive to these developments. Essentially, this means that in the future greater spending will have to be allocated for education and job training. The inclusion of those elements of Chilean society that have not fully shared the nation's dynamic growth could potentially became a force that could derail the Chilean craft from its growth track.

While inflation and unemployment represent socioeconomic challenges, a number of delicate political problems face the government. This includes the residual influence of Pinochet and the military in the nation's political affairs, and the difficulties of maintaining a broad consensus on development strategies within the ruling coalition of Christian Democrats and Socialists and their center-left allies, the Party for Democracy. Governmental fragility stems from the Party for Democracy's charges that the Socialists are allowing the Christian Democrats to "hegemonize" the coalition. Although the 1992 municipal elections, the nation's first ever, had the potential to be a point of tension between the various coalition members, the contest reaffirmed the political status quo—the coalition of parties supporting then President Aylwin won a majority of the votes. President Frei has maintained the center-left Party for Democracy's unity, though he asserted greater presidential authority in 1994 and 1995 instead of allowing greater party autonomy. At the same time, none of the members of the ruling coalition have demonstrated an interest in leaving the ranks of the government.

Another potentially problematic area is Chile's continued dependence on the copper industry. Although the economy has been diversified, and mining only accounts for 7 percent of the GDP, copper accounted for roughly 35 percent of total exports in 1993. In recent years, copper prices have been relatively high and foreign investment has actively helped raise copper exports by boosting production. While it is likely that improved and more efficient means of production will help maintain Chile's comparative advantage in the copper market, a radical downturn in this commodity's price could have a negative impact on the economy.

While there are many current and potential problems facing Chile, elements of the country are creating the foundation for the next economic wave. Chile is on the path to developing its own high technology companies capable of taking the country to the next notch in the economic game. Without the expertise capable of helping the country tune in, assimilate, and apply new breakthrough technology, Chile could run the risk of stagnating at a time when the international competition is intensifying in Latin America as well as globally. Part of Chile's drive to achieve a dynamic Pacific destiny of becoming an NIC, is the development of its computer industry. In 1990 Chilean computer and software sales grew approximately 15 percent in real terms, recording total sales of $200 million.[35] The two major Chilean corporations in the field, Sonda and Cientec, S.A., reported a 43 percent increase in sales. Sales have continued to be strong through the mid-1990s.

Sonda was created in 1974 by an engineer, Andres Navarro with only ten employees and a sales volume of $500,000. By 1986, it had grown into one of Chile's cutting edge companies, employing 600 people, with offices in Peru and Argentina, and was South America's largest computer firm. Sonda's major breakthrough was with the development of software called STF, which specialized in on-line banking attention.[36] This product was sold in large volume in Argentina and Peru.

In 1990, Sonda's total sales were $50 million and profits were $7.5

million, making it still the leader in Chile. In that year it developed specific software for the forestry, lumber, fishery, mining, and banking sectors. In 1991, Sonda turned to the health-care sector. Additionally, the Chilean firm exported around $6.5 million of software to Argentina, Colombia, Indonesia, Mexico, Peru, and Venezuela. Chile's infomatic industry is not limited to national companies. The ranks of foreign companies include International Business Machines (IBM), Unisys, Data General, National Cash Register (NCR), Compaq, Acer, and Sun Microsystems. Even Apple Computers has an active representative, Apple Chile S.A.

Chilean companies are also willing to create strategic alliances with foreign firms, much in the same fashion exercised by Mexican and U.S. firms. In 1992, Companía de Teléfonos de Chile (CTC) joined forces with its main shareholder, Spain's Telefonica SA, to expand its business to other Latin American countries. Accordingly, the joint venture announced its intention to bid in upcoming privatizations of state-owned telephone companies in Honduras, Panama, and Uruguay as well as compete for cellular concessions in Colombia, Ecuador, and Peru.[37]

The question returns: has Chile achieved a Pacific Tiger destiny? In many respects, Chile fits the profile of a Singapore and South Korea. However, there are certain differences that must be taken into consideration. Although Chile is the leader in Latin America in terms of investment as a percent of GNP at a little under 30 percent, it lags behind Thailand, China, Indonesia, Malaysia, and South Korea, all of which are closer to 40 percent of GNP. As *The Economist* (1995) noted, the average for East Asian economies was 35 percent compared to 22 percent of GNP for Latin America: "It is therefore hardly surprising that East Asia's growth rate has been roughly double that of Latin America in recent years."[38] Chile has clearly done much to encourage savings and investment, which has resulted in strong and self-sustaining growth for over a decade. However, if Chile's investment as a percent of GNP were higher, one might wonder if the Latin American country would be closer in terms of its level of development to South Korea or Singapore.

Chile decidedly has a Pacific destiny, but its status as a tiger is still tentative. Furthermore, the Pacific destiny will have to be increasingly balanced with an American destiny that provides greater interaction with its neighbors, especially as markets continue to integrate. While the United States and Japan are important trade partners, the regional pattern of trade places an emphasis on North America (the United States and Canada) which account for 19 percent of Chile's total exports, Pacific Asia with around 27 percent, and the European Community with 38 percent. Latin America accounted for only 12 percent of total Chilean exports. This, however, is beginning to change with Brazil emerging in the 1990s as a growing trade partner, especially in the area of imports.

In a world rapidly merging into a number of competing trade blocs, Chile initially remained apart, refusing to join either the Andean Pact or MERCOSUR, the common market between Argentina, Brazil, Paraguay, and Uruguay. Instead, Chile placed an emphasis on bilateral trade negotiations with Mexico, Argentina, Brazil, Venezuela, Colombia, and the United States to open markets. Chilean hopes were that framework agreements will become trade accords, which will permit new markets for Chilean goods (especially those with value added). By the mid-1990s, Chile placed its bets and began discussions with both MERCOSUR and NAFTA.[39]

At a meeting of the Western Hemisphere's leaders in Miami in December 1994, the United States renewed its promise to make Chile the next member of NAFTA, expanding membership beyond itself and Canada and Mexico. Such membership would reinforce Chile's tiger status. However, Chilean membership into NAFTA has been anticipated since the Bush administration stated in 1992 that Chile, with the most advanced economy in Latin America, would be the next country admitted into the trade group.[40] Inclusion into NAFTA would be a positive development for Chile, but considering the Byzantine political nature of Washington, in particular its reaching an internal consensus on trade matters, NAFTA membership is likely to take its time. In fact, the very concept of Chile's accession to NAFTA assumes a consensus on regional trade policy which is not completely shared by Brazil and a revitalized MERCOSUR group.

In tandem with the waiting game over NAFTA, Chile's hope of joining MERCOSUR became more likely and made considerable economic sense since it includes its two largest trade and significant investment partners, Argentina and Brazil. To this end, formal negotiations for free trade with its neighbors (rather than from a customs union) were begun in 1995 and brought to fruition in June 1996. MERCOSUR's attraction was clearly augmented by the slow pace of negotiations with the United States. Another key factor is that the preferential tariffs enjoyed by Chile in MERCOSUR countries under the aegis of the Latin American Integration Association (ALADI), officially expired at the end of 1994. Chile has indicated that it wants an accord that extends the trade preferences indefinitely, and advances towards free trade through a schedule of tariff reductions lasting between six and ten years.[41] A win-win strategy, developing closer trade relations with MERCOSUR, allows Chile to integrate itself more closely with two of the largest economies of Latin America—Argentina and Brazil.

Conclusion

Chile is clearly a pacesetter in Latin America's development race. Its ability to broaden the base of the economy, to diversify exports and markets, and to deepen the reform process to encompass financial liberalization and privatization are guideposts to other nations in Latin America, Africa, Eastern Europe, and the newly marketizing republics of the former Soviet Union. While Chile's progress is substantial and should be applauded, considerable new challenges exist related to the new, higher level of development. These include the outcome of free-trade agreements in the Americas, and the differing options facing Chile between an expanded NAFTA and a MERCOSUR-led South American market. Domestically, there remain residual uncertainties regarding the final disposition of the role of the military, and that of General Pinochet in particular. Yet, Chile appears posed to reach the next rung of development, enjoying both capitalism and democracy, which may place it ahead of some of the Pacific Tigers and make it more like a younger version of a Portugal, New Zealand, and Spain. The latter countries have achieved considerable success in their economic development, while maintaining or reactivating their democratic form of government. Chile has both democratic and capitalist traditions, which should provide for the further development of an economically progressive, yet equitable society into the early twenty-first century.

Notes

1. Thomas E. Skidmore and Peter H. Smith, *Modern Latin America* (New York: Oxford University Press, 1989), p. 112.

2. Ibid.
3. Genero Arriagada, *Pinochet: The Politics of Power* (Boston, Mass.: Unwin Hyman, 1988), pp. 86–87.
4. J. Samuel Valenzuela and Arturo Valenzuela, "Chile and the Breakdown of Democracy," in *Latin American Politics and Development*, ed. Howard J. Wiarda, (Boulder, Colo.: Westview Press, 1985), p. 222.
5. Garreton, Manuel Antonio. *The Chilean Political Process* (Boston: Unwin Hyman, 1989).
6. Valenzuela and Valenzuela, "Chile," p. 224.
7. Manuel Antonio Garreton, *The Chilean Political Process* (Boston, Mass.: Unwin Hyman, 1989), p. 4.
8. Valenzuela and Valenzuela, "Chile," p. 232.
9. Garreton, *The Chilean Political Process*, p. 13.
10. The literature on the Allende years and the regime's downfall is extensive. See Nathaniel Davis, *The Last Two Years of Salvador Allende* (Ithaca, N.Y.: Cornell University Press, 1985); Paul E. Sigmund, *The Overthrow of Allende and the Politics of Chile, 1964–1976* (Pittsburgh, Pa.: Pittsburgh University Press, 1977); James R. Whelan, *Out of the Ashes: The Life, Death and Transfiguration of Democracy in Chile 1833–1988* (Washington, D.C.: Regnery Gateway, 1989); and Mark Falcoff, *Modern Chile, 1970–1989: A Critical History* (New Brunswick, N.J.: Transaction Books, 1989).
11. Manuel Antonio Gerreton, "Chile: In Search of Lost Democracy," in *Latin American Political Economy: Financial Crisis and Political Change*, eds. Jonathan Hartlyn and Samuel A. Morley (Boulder, Colo.: Westview Press, 1986), p. 206.
12. Paul W. Drake and Ivan Jaksic, "Introduction: Transformation and Transition in Chile, 1982–1990," in *The Struggle for Democracy in Chile, 1982–1990*, eds. Paul W. Drake and Ivan Jaksic, (Lincoln, Neb.: University of Nebraska Press, 1991), p. 5.
13. Ricardo French-Davis, "El Problema de la deuda externa y la apertura financiera en Chile," *Coleccion Estudios CIEPLAN* no. 11 (December 1980): pp. 121–22.
14. Felipe Morris with Mark Dorfman, Jose Pedro Ortiz, and Maria Claudia Franco, *Latin America's Banking Systems in the 1980s: A Cross-Country Comparison* (Washington, D.C.: World Bank Discussion Papers, 1990), p. 81.
15. Stephany Griffith-Jones, *Chile to 1991: The End of an Era?* special report no. 1073 (London: Economist Intelligence Unit, 1987), p. 30.
16. Banco Central de Chile, *Statistical Synthesis of Chile, 1985–1989* (Santiago: Banco Central de Chile, 1990), p. 12.
17. Ibid., p. 35.
18. J. Lavin, *Chile: A Quiet Revolution* (Santiago: Empresa Editora Zig-Zag, 1988), p. 51. The title in Spanish is *Chile, Revolucion Silenciosa*.
19. Patricio Meller, "Chile," in *Latin American Adjustment: How much has happened?* ed. John Williamson, (Washington, D.C.: Institute for International Economics, 1990), p. 81.
20. See M. Marcel, "Privatizacion y finanzas publicas: el caso de Chile, 1985–1988," *Coleccion Estudios CIEPLAN* no. 26 (June 1989): pp. 5–60.
21. International Finance Corporation, *Emerging Stock Markets Factbook 1991* (Washington, D.C.: International Finance Corporation, 1991), p. 119.
22. Milan Marinovic, "Hipotesis del terrorismo," *Cuadernos de Cienca Politica* (University of Chile), cited in *Que Pasa* (September 1987): p. 17. Also cited in *A Nation of Enemies: Chile Under Pinochet*, Pamela Constable and Arturo Valenzuela, (New York: W.W. Norton, 1991), p. 265.

23. Constable and Valenzuela, *A Nation of Enemies*, pp. 304–5.
24. Ibid, 310.
25. Lavin, *Chile: A Quiet Revolution*, pp. 20–21.
26. Scott B. MacDonald and Kathleen Stephonse, *Chile: A Country Profile, DLJ Credit Research,* (February 1996) p. 2.
27. China's real GDP in 1992 was 12 percent, followed by Malaysia at 8.5 percent, Thailand at 7.5 percent, Taiwan at 6.7 percent, Singapore at 5.6 percent, and Indonesia and Hong Kong at 5.5 percent. "Economic Indicators, Selected Asian Countries," *Far Eastern Economic Review* (March 18, 1993): pp. 56–57.
28. Emelio Bassini, "The Chile Fund," *Smith Barney: A Look at the ROC Taiwan Fund and the Chile Fund*, vol. 2, no. 7 (December 1991): p. 7.
29. International Monetary Fund, *International Financial Statistics September 1994* (Washington, D.C.: IMF, 1994), p. 160.
30. Philip Sanders, "Foreign Investment in Chile Rises 16% to $1 Bln in First Qtr," *Bloomberg* (May 2, 1995).
31. Malcolm Coad, "Special Report/Chile: Andean Exception," *South* (September/October 1991): p. 46.
32. World Bank, *World Development Report 1995* (New York: Oxford University Press, 1995), p. 221.
33. David C. Walters, "Good News in Chile: Economy is Growing, Unemployment Down," *Christian Science Monitor* (February 2, 1994): p. 6.
34. David Pilling, "Chile Resumes Its Grand Sell-Off," *Financial Times* (September 9, 1994): p. 5.
35. "Briefs," *Times of the Americas* (May 1, 1991): p. 14.
36. Lavin, *Chile: The Quiet Revolution*, p. 139.
37. "Chile's Telecom Firms Prospect Latin Markets," *Latin American Information Services Americas Trade & Finance* (September 1992): p. 8.
38. "Emerging Market Indicators," *The Economist* (May 6, 1995): p. 106.
39. MERCOSUR is a customs union with the key features of a common external tariff. NAFTA is a free-trade agreement, based on lowered tariff barriers among the three member countries—Canada, Mexico, and the United States. In practice, Chile could not entertain membership in both groups since the obligations of each organization conflict. Chile's discussion with MERCOSUR therefore entailed only *free trade*, a process motivated greatly by a Brazilian interest in generating a South American counterweight to U.S. influence in NAFTA.
40. Calvin Sims, "Chile Fears a Delay in Trade-Bloc Entry," *New York Times* (May 5, 1995): p. D4.
41. "The Economist Intelligence Unit," *Chile 4th Quarter 1994* (October 21, 1994): p. 13.

4

The Trendsetters II: Argentina

Argentina is a pivotal country in the Latin American developmental process. Since the late 1980s, it is attempting to reshape itself economically with a political system far more open and transparent than when Chile was attempting a similar transformation in the 1970s. If democratic-capitalism faltered in Argentina, a dark cloud would immediately loom on the horizon of the region. Yet, Argentina began the decade of the 1990s with an economy racked by hyperinflation, a steep recession, and cut off from international capital markets. Popular antipathy to both traditional political parties—Radicals and Peronists—was running high and the conventional academic wisdom was that neither was capable of diverting Argentina from the road to ruin. The overall assessment of Argentina's future was grim. So much had gone wrong and many Argentines were despairing that their society had no way out of what was becoming a developmental cul-de-sac of seemingly endless shock-treatment programs and bitter, disappointing results.

By the mid-1990s Argentina was on the rise again. The economy, though contracting by 3.5 percent in 1995, and growing anemically in 1996 had enjoyed considerable growth in the 1991–94 period at an average of over 6 percent per annum, inflation cooled to an amazing 3.9 percent in 1994 and 1.6 percent in 1995, exports reached $20.8 billion in 1995, and key debt ratios (debt-to-GDP and debt-to-exports) continued to decline. Relations with the country's external creditors had been normalized earlier in the decade and President Carlos Menem won a second term in the May 1995 elections. Argentina's public sector, long since the Achille's heel of the national economy, was largely restructured. Equally significant, Argentina weathered the so-called "Tequila" effect from the Mexican peso crisis and related ripple effects on Argentine financial markets.

In the 1990s there are signs that, out of the rubble of past reform efforts, fundamental structural changes are taking shape in Argentina that hold promise for a sounder path of development. Is Argentina poised for an economic renaissance? Is the country reaching the "fast-forward" stage of development? This South American country of 32 million people is certainly in the process of change. The long decline of Argentine society that commenced in the 1940s and 1950s and deepened in the 1960s, 1970s, and 1980s, has been arrested and, argu-ably reversed. It would appear that Argentina has overcome what Paul Lewis, in *The Crisis of Argentine Capitalism*, called the "permanent stalemate,"—a situation in which the country's vast, interventionist, pluralistic, bureaucratic system with an ever-expanding appetite for revenue and credit must be reformed by the same agents that led it to voracious consumption, profligate spending, and complicated red tape that ruins the nation's credit and currency.[1] While this does not insure that Argentina is the next South Korea or Taiwan, the Latin American country stands a reasonable chance of emerging in the early twenty-first century as a member of the more advanced economies of the world.

The Argentine Experience

Argentina's historical experience was strongly influenced by an up-per class largely of European descent that emerged from the colonial period. First came the Spaniards, who founded Buenos Aires and pushed settlement outward into the fertile *pampas*. While the colony, and then country, attracted new waves of European settlers, the native popula-tion was largely eliminated. By its independence in 1816, Argentine society was largely formed around the metropolis of Buenos Aires, the primary port through which the produce of the *pampas* was shipped to foreign markets.

Argentina's economic development during much of the nineteenth and early twentieth centuries was characterized by heavy involvement in international trade, largely in commodities such as beef and grains. Argentine society was initially characterized by a small, yet dominant landowning elite and a large politically inarticulate mass. Ongoing immigration in the mid- and late nineteenth century, however, created a middle class that was increasingly aggressive in the nation's politics. At the same time, the economy followed an outward-oriented development strategy, which through the agro-export sector's backward and forward linkages, helped stimulate local industrialization.[2] A considerable amount of British foreign investment helped develop the country's industrial and communications infrastructure, in particular in Buenos Aires as the region's major port. By the last quarter of the nineteenth century Argentina was highly integrated in the world economy.

One of the active political forces that had its beginnings in the late nineteenth and early twentieth centuries and is still active is the Radical Civic Union (UCR). Founded in 1890 and dominated in its beginning stages by Hipólito Yrigoyen, the Radicals favored an armed route to power, leading popular revolts in 1890, 1893, and 1905. The failure of these revolts and the new election law of 1911, which provided for universal and compulsory male suffrage, a secret ballot, permanent voter registration, and minority representation in Congress, however, brought the Radicals into the electoral process. Within a short period of time, the Conservatives, who had dominated the nation's politics for several decades, were ousted and Yrigoyen became the first Radical president.

Although the Radicals held sway for 14 years, they made no major transformations in economic policy, a situation that allowed the conservative landowning elite, and those linked to foreign trade, to maintain a substantial degree of political clout. Part of the problem was the lack of a comprehensive Radical program. In a sense, the Radicals lost their revolutionary zeal: their chief objective became to win recognition of the right of the middle class to participate fully in the socioeconomic and political life of the nation, or at least recognition of its right to a share of the spoils of office.[3] The Radical weakness in developing a stronger ideological foundation would help maintain the party's identification as a middle-class party, leaving the working class largely untouched and a ready foundation for populist politicians in the post-1930 period.

The Radicals were not the only party failing to capture the allegiance of the emerging working class. Argentina's Socialist party was established in 1890 and never fully developed into a full-fledged mass movement. While the Argentine right was able to mobilize considerable resources linked to the economy and, at times, the military, the left was weak and often divided. The socialists appeared unable to mobilize what should have been their key constituency—labor. As one scholar noted: "The failure of socialism and the success of populism are connected: the weakness of socialism in Argentina, and in Latin America in general, opened the way for populist politicians to galvanize the unintegrated masses into a forceful political movement. In Argentina, this correlation is especially pronounced: the failure of democratic socialism before 1930 left vacant a political space that Colonel Juan Domingo Perón successfully exploited in the wake of the 1943 coup d'état."[4]

The Radicals' failure to create a new national program of any significance, a lengthy tenure in office, and the growing senility of President Yrigoyen during his second term coincided with the global depression in the late 1920s. By 1930, these forces collided with Conservative resistance to relinquish any more power, which would have been likely considering the rapid expansion of voter participation—most of which favored the Radicals. The liberal democratic institutions, which had brought Argentina a period of considerable political stability and helped attain a level of economic development comparable with that of southern Europe, were regarded by the Conservatives as dangerous. Popular disillusionment with the second Radical Yrigoyen government and the Conservative sympathies of the military set the stage for a 1930 coup. The significance of the coup was that it marked a departure from the path of liberal democratic government (as it was), relative political stability, and a gradual improvement in the standard of living to an extended period of economic stagnation and political instability.

The 1930 coup unleashed political forces in Argentina that were detrimental to national unity and well-balanced economic progress. As Snow commented: "The social, economic, and political elite that governed Argentina between 1862 and 1916 was dedicated to national development. Such was decidedly not true of the elite in power following the 1930 coup. The government did lead the country out of depression and restore a degree of prosperity; however, it also saw to it that this prosperity was distributed even more inequitably than before. Argentina was run almost exclusively for the benefit of the landed aristocracy."[5] From 1930 forward, changes in the political regime were linked to recurrent attempts to mobilize nationalist-populist coalitions and the reaction of conservative military and business sectors.[6]

Within two years of the military coup, the Conservatives were back in power. With their narrow base of support and resistance to power-sharing, they found it hard to contend with large new groups of political participants, many of whom were recent immigrants from the politically charged Europe of the 1930s. The emergence of an urban working class, in particular, was a development that the Conservatives failed to address in the period of congressional dominance that lasted to 1940. The Radicals, with a majority in Congress that year, quickly sought to make the Conservative presidency unworkable. By 1943, Argentine "democracy" had become gridlocked and had lost much of its legitimacy in the eyes of the people.

Argentina Under Perón

The breakdown in Argentine democracy came when leaders in the military launched a coup in 1943. Assuming the role of keeper of the national conscience, the new *junta* was soon dominated by Colonel Juan Domingo Perón. Unlike much of the Argentine political elite and most of his fellow officers, Perón astutely comprehended the importance of the working class as an untapped and unchannelled political force. Through his position as secretary of labor, the colonel soon campaigned for, and received, working-class support. What followed were a number of improvements in the working class standard of living: wages were raised substantially; existing ameliorative labor legislation was enforced for the first time; new trade unions were formed and existing unions allied to Perón were allowed to expand; and, in general, labor power, as guided by Perón, was soon active in making inroads into the nation's power structure.

Perón, during the three years leading up to the 1946 elections, created a strong base of support and outmaneuvered his rivals within the armed forces. Creating the Argentine Labor Party, he contested and comfortably won the February 1946 presidential elections. As head of state, Perón continued his "revolution" of reconfiguring Argentine society to share the national wealth between all social strata. This meant that the process of unionization continued, wages and benefits increased, and a modern social security system was established.[7] A hybrid of Marxist and capitalist extremes, Perón instituted a form of corporatist structure that politicized national life and attempted to regulate the relative influence of key sectors of Argentine society.

Perón's rule clearly was not democratic. An avowed admirer of Italian and Spanish fascism, the Argentine leader used the working class as the regime's pillar of support, but did not allow it to participate in ruling the country. As Snow noted: "Although honestly elected in 1946 and reelected in 1951, Perón moved steadily in the direction of authoritarian rule. Freedom of the press was virtually destroyed, the judiciary was purged as were the universities, and opposition leaders were harassed, exiled, or imprisoned."[8] By 1955, he had alienated the Catholic Church, and important elements of the military. Moreover, Perón's strident nationalism in the 1940s meant that Argentina entered the postwar period relatively isolated from financial aid and direct investment. When agrarian prices fell in the 1950s, international reserves came under considerable pressure, impelling the Peronista regime in 1951–52 to adopt highly orthodox stabilization packages to reduce external account deficits and regain credibility with the international financial community.[9] In September 1955, the military intervened, ousting Perón who was soon off in exile.

The Argentine military coup did not end the political turmoil that had come to characterize the country. Argentina remained badly polarized and factions within the armed forces fought a brief quasi civil war in 1962. The country staggered into elections called in 1963. Arturo Illia, the leader of the People's Radical Civic Union (UCRP) won, but only with one-fourth of the vote. President Illia's short-lived administration was characterized by a lack of direction and ended in yet another military coup in 1966. The Argentine economy, rocked by ongoing political crises, was in difficult straits and many Argentines harbored serious doubts about the ability of civilian politicians to manage the nation's affairs.

Dissatisfaction with most of the civilian political elite, the ongoing "threat" of Peronism, and the failure of democratic experimentation, led the military to consider corporatist ideas of governing society and managing the economy. Military authorities in Argentina were motivated to purge their society of populist forces and to rationalize their capitalist economies.[10] In neighboring Brazil the military had likewise assumed control of the political process, creating what was to become a military presidency that lasted until 1985. Looking north to events in Brazil and sharing the same frustrations with civilian ineptitude, the Argentine military closed Congress, dissolved the nation's political parties, and invested considerable power in the hands of a retired general, Juan Carlos Onganía.

The Onganía regime sought to lead an Argentine "revolution" in which the armed forces were to function as the disinterested and impartial guardians of the state and nation. The prior failures of the democratic government had "created propitious conditions for a subtle and aggressive Marxist penetration of all areas of national life . . . that place[d] the Nation in danger of falling before the advance of collectivist totalitarianism."[11]

Argentina's problems, however, were beyond the ability of General Onganía and his military and civilian colleagues to resolve. Although the military understood that the country's political structure was incapable of adequately responding to all the demands made on it and that a fundamental restructuring was required, they too lacked unity. The lack of internal consensus was evident throughout Argentine society, extending beyond the military to include industrialists, exporters, and union leaders.[12] Union leaders, in particular, presided over a bitter factionalization between reformists and revolutionary tendencies. The lack of societal consensus, in fact a furthering of societal divisions, meant that seven years of military rule came and went with very little changed beneath the surface of national life—except efforts to depoliticize the working class probably reinforced support for the Peronista movement.

The failure of the Onganía regime was starkly brought home on 29 May 1969, when a major uprising occurred in the city of Córdoba. The *Cordobazo*, as it was later called, lasted for roughly a week, was largely spontaneous, and resulted in the introduction of troops to suppress the rioting citizenry. Although the rest of the country did not ignite into an *Argentinazo*, the rebellion of one of the country's major cities greatly weakened Onganía. He was forced out in June 1970 and eventually General Alejandro Lanusse took command, seeking to stop the wave of violence that swept the country in the late 1960s and early 1970s. That violence was caused by Peronista and Marxist terrorist groups attacking military and business figures and, in some cases, fellow Peronistas. In this atmosphere of political decay, the military opted out of politics and allowed national elections in March 1973. The victor was the Peronista candidate Hector Campora who gained 49.6 percent of the vote, well ahead of his competitors.

Campora's administration was short-lived as he and his vice president resigned, causing new elections in which Juan Perón himself ran as a candidate. Juan Perón soon returned from exile, won the election, and resumed his role as president of Argentina. While there was initial euphoria within the Peronista movement over the turn of events, the left and right wings were badly split. Under Campora, the left wing gained ground, especially within the youth movement. Under Perón, the right gained ground in the labor sector and the universities. Events were further complicated by Peron's unexpected death on 1 July 1974, following which he was replaced by his widow, Maria Estela Martinez de Perón (Isabel).

Isabel's reign was short. Not prepared to be Argentina's chief executive, she was soon confronted by a dramatic resurgence of political violence and outright hostility from the armed forces. On the economic front, the oil price hike of 1973–74 forced import costs to rise from $1.98 billion in 1973 to $3.2 billion in 1974, drastically slashing Argentina's trade surplus.[13] Skyrocketing fuel prices, moreover, stimulated inflation, already on the rise because of a widening government budget deficit. Isabel's administration also suffered from its rampant corruption. To those anti-Peronistas in the armed forces, it appeared that "democratic experimentation" had once again put Argentine society in a situation that was rapidly spinning out of control. In 1976, Isabel was removed from power and a new hardline authoritarian regime was formed around General Jorge Videla.

A worsening political and security environment led the new Videla administration to launch the "dirty war." The military's campaign to suppress terrorist groups within three years gutted many radical organizations and restored order. The cost, however, was high as thousands of individuals were subjected to arbitrary arrest, imprisonment, and torture. Many people, picked up by security forces, simply disappeared, never to be heard from and were presumed dead. Internationally, Argentina became well-known for its major human rights' abuses.

While the Videla regime was relatively successful (though brutal) in dealing with terrorism, the economy continued to be highly problematic. The objective of achieving a sustained economic recovery was not within grasp. Although exports increased, Argentina's economic growth was fueled by heavy foreign borrowing. The exchange rate for the peso went from 80 to the U.S. dollar in 1974 to 260,000 in 1982.[14] Moreover, the military regime's minister of finance, Martinez de Hoz (1976–80) favored an open economy over the import-substitution model. Seeking to uproot previous efforts of import-substitution, de Hoz's years represented one of the most radical efforts in Latin

America at the time to dismantle the regulatory apparatus of state-led import-substitution industrialization models.[15] Argentina went far to lift controls on both capital movements and trade. Yet, the effort failed.

At no stage did de Hoz succeed in eliminating the public sector deficit. This undermined the *tabilita* exchange rate systems which adjusted the exchange rate in a way that reflected forecast (full) inflation, rather than actual (high) inflation. As the limitations of this policy became more apparent and capital flight accelerated, increasing concessions were made to the financial and industrial elite whose power, at least in theory, de Hoz's open-economy reforms were supposed to dilute.

Despite the problematic nature of Argentina's political economy, the country was able to tap international capital markets. Between the end of 1975 and the end of 1980, external debt expanded by 236 percent. Where did all the money go that fuelled the rise in external debt from $3.2 billion to $18.9 billion? As Lewis commented: "What did the Argentines do with the loans they got? Many of them imported luxury goods, took vacations, or bought dollars and deposited them overseas. Private business firms took advantage of the government's deregulation to contract debts whose interest charges were lower than those prevailing locally."[16]

The military regime, under Roberto Viola, limped into 1981 discredited at home for its failure on the economic front, and tainted at home and abroad for the excesses of the dirty war. In an effort to regain national support, the military sought to capture the Falkland Islands (Islas Malvinas) from the British. Initially successful in unifying the nation behind the regime, the rapid defeat that followed and the hyperinflating economy forced the military to withdraw from power. National elections were held on 30 October 1983, which were won by Radical Raùl Alfonsín much to his surprise, with 52 percent of the vote. The Peronista candidate, Italo Luder won only 40 percent of the vote.

Argentina as a Failure: Alfonsín Struggles

By the early 1980s Argentina was a quintessential example of a country that had squandered its resources, failed to fulfill the economic aspirations of its people, and marginalized itself internationally. It had a wealth of mineral resources, including hydrocarbons and fertile soil, and a strategic location in the Southern Atlantic, but the record of the country's leadership in harnessing what the country could offer had been woeful. Despite the euphoria surrounding the return of democracy in 1983, the new government was not immune to economic troubles.

President Alfonsín and his Radical Party government inherited a country recovering from the Falklands/Malvinas conflict, an economy in crisis, and a powerful and antagonistic labor movement largely identifying with the Radicals' traditional political opponents, the Peronistas.[17] The Alfonsín administration's early programs collided in 1984 with the labor unions and soon the two forces were enjoined in a bitter struggle. Alfonsín sought to override labor opposition through government intervention in union elections and an initiative to reform labor laws. When this failed, he tried to organize a social pact between the government and unions. That too failed. Finally came the Austral Plan in June 1985, which froze both prices and wages, and in theory, committed government to a balanced budget and no recourse to the printing press.

The Austral Plan was initially successful, which helped the incumbent Radicals win the November 1985 congressional elections. However, prices drifted upward in 1986 and by the September 1987 gubernatorial elections the Austral Plan was a failure, as deficit spending, lack of progress on economic reform, and a burgeoning internal debt combined to derail efforts to curb inflation. In 1987, the Argentines stopped paying the external debt. Local financial markets were seriously perturbed about reserve loss and the austral depreciated rapidly. To maintain the integrity of the government's public-debt issues, the Central Bank had to overcome concern about its debt-service capacity. The Bank made an early payment of a coupon or BONEX—large U.S. dollar-denominated government bonds—to vouch safe its commitment to honoring its liabilities.

Another attempt at reform came with the Plan Primavera, which was launched in August 1988, but soon failed. As for the impact of the economy's deterioration on the Radical party in the 1989 presidential contest, Argentine economist Juan Carlos de Pablo noted: "In 1989, a victim of hyperinflation, Alfonsin's candidate was also defeated in the presidential election."[18]

As Argentina entered the 1990s, its economy could only be described as in crisis. Real gross domestic product contracted by 2.7

percent in 1988, by 4.5 percent in 1989, and 0.5 percent in 1990. Inflation had shifted gears to hyperinflation, reaching 4,924 percent (per annum) by the end of 1989, before slowing to 1,344 percent in 1990. The only bright spot was the achievement of a current account surplus of $1.8 billion in 1990, breaking a string of deficits. As Jane Hughes commented in 1990: "The list of failures in Latin America's debt management is . . . topped by Argentina, a spectacular failure by any standards. Argentina has emerged as 1989's most intractable debt problem, with little hope for resolution in sight."[19]

One outcome of Argentina's stagnation, hyperinflation, and real negative interest rates was flight capital. According to Argentine government estimates, flight capital had risen over $30 billion as of 1991, but it could well have been between $40–50 billion. Uruguay became a key offshore finance center in South America, largely due to the economic crises of its neighbors, Argentina and Brazil. Bank secrecy laws opened the doors to millions of Argentine accounts in the finance houses across the Rio de la Plata. The practice of having an account in Montevideo was evidently not limited to the wealthy, many in the middle classes have sought to save their income in a safe haven. This situation was reinforced by the weak enforcement capabilities of the Argentine tax authorities, who placed an emphasis on taxing financial intermediation, trade, and agriculture. Moreover, Argentina long maintained the rule that income legally generated offshore was not subject to Argentine regulations, a de facto incentive to capital flight.

Enter Carlos Menem

When Carlos Menem won the presidential elections in May 1989 and his Peronista party captured a majority in Congress, there were few hopeful prospects. Granted, the transfer of power from one civilian president to another was a step forward in symbolizing the consolidation of democracy: since the return of democracy in 1983, the Alfonsín administration had been challenged by three military coup attempts as well as one armed rebellion by leftist guerrillas. However, Menem as a candidate presented a picture of a Peronista populist, who appeared likely to revert to spending to solve the economic crisis and to further the splintering of the country's political life.

The reality of Menemism has been very different. Confronted with a grave economic crisis, dim prospects of outside assistance, and a "bad boy" reputation on the external debt question, Argentina looked as though it was heading in the same direction as Peru under President Alan García—towards almost complete international isolation from creditors and a near-systemic collapse. Yet these worries were not borne out by events. Upon taking office in 1989, the Menem government understood that the country was hemorrhaging capital (international reserves had fallen under $1 billion as of June 1989) and moved quickly to remedy the situation. A radical economic reform program was implemented that has continued, with modifications, to the present. While there have been problems, important transformations have commenced.

The key areas of reform include an overhaul of the tax structure, privatization, trade liberalization, financial market reform, and fiscal control. Other elements of the reform program include the elimination of price controls and government approval for new foreign investment. These measures have gone a considerable distance to remove any legal distinctions between domestic and foreign capital. Interchangability between the Argentine rechristened "peso" and foreign currency has also been encouraged. In early 1992, the government estimated most of the difference between bank reserve requirements on peso and foreign currency deposits. This situation allowed Argentines to hold foreign-currency checking accounts in Argentina. Although reform programs in the 1980s repeatedly sought many of the objectives set out by Menem, they ultimately lacked the necessary political will. The Menem administration has demonstrated a greater will to stay the course; even opening up parts of the economy like the oil industry—hitherto a nationalist taboo—to foreign investors.

One of the most controversial planks of Menem's economic reform has been privatization. Unpopular with the labor unions, the privatization of much of the state-owned economic sector is a key element to structural change and debt reduction. It also seeks to improve economic productivity through better management and cost-efficiency as public enterprises have produced a negative return on capital in every year since the early 1950s. The two largest privatizations have been ENTEL, the telephone company, and Aerolíneas Argentinas, the state airline. Majority stakes in both were sold for a combination of cash and external debt. The telephone company sale generated more than $200 million in cash and $5 billion in debt cancellation through debt-to-equity conversions, while the airline deal produced $260 million in cash and $2 billion in debt cancellation.[20] As Argentina's then financial representative in Washington, D.C. Daniel Marx noted: "A portion of the cash and debt paid in these privatizations was provided by domestic companies and is a tangible demonstration of renewed confidence among domestic investors."[21]

While the privatization of telephone and airline companies was the source of considerable international attention, the Menem administration has pressed hard on other fronts. Argentina's secondary oil and natural gas fields were privatized, putting an end to nearly twenty-six years of state monopoly over hydrocarbon exploration and exploitation.[22] By mid-1991, sixty-nine oil fields were sold. Other areas that were privatized include concessions to manage a railway line, 10,000 kilometers of highways, and a zoo. The state's interests in the electricity sector, gas, water, munitions, and hotels have also been put up for sale. These interests alone are thought to be worth about $20 billion to the state. Privatizations continued in 1993, with the government willing to sell 40 percent of the jewel in the Argentine crown—the state oil and gas company, Yacimientos Petroliferos Fiscales (YPF) -that was valued at $7–8 billion.[23] Another 30 percent stake would be privatized at a later date, leaving the government with 30 percent ownership and employees with 10 percent. Significantly, YPF's partial privatization was accompanied by a complete corporate restructuring and employee downsizing from over 51,000 on 30 December 1990 to 7,500 on 31 December 1993.[24]

Privatization has helped cut the fiscal deficit, one of the major problems that dogged previous governments, both civilian and military. Along these lines, the Menem government recorded a public sector surplus of over $4 billion in the second half of 1991 and first half of 1992, of which half came from privatizations. As for the primary fiscal balance, the Argentine government's performance in the past has not been exemplary. To address the problem of profligate state spending, the Menem government has pursued a policy of employment reduction and has revised the public-sector salary structure, along with introducing effective budgeting and expenditure controls. A three-year plan was put into effect in January 1991 to cut 122,000 central government jobs, which was estimated ultimately to save $1.5 billion.[25] In January 1991, the government released 21,000 contractual workers, which was followed over the next several months by the release of thousands of permanent employees.

The Menem government has also reexamined its tax policies and launched a new program to enhance the efficiency of the tax structure, and reduce the tax disincentives to investment. The emphasis is now much more on indirect taxation—VAT (Value Added Tax) now stands at 16 percent and exceptions have been reduced and rates of direct taxation are being cut. A special tax program was implemented in 1991 which limits taxes on repatriated funds to 1–2 percent flat. Additionally, special emergency taxes on bank deposits and withdrawals, and on the net transfer of securities, have been eliminated. Other efforts on the tax front include toughening laws for noncompliance with tax payments with a recourse to close firms, and to monitor closely the 1,000 largest taxpayers.

Although some slippages have occurred in the program, the overall thrust of structural adjustment is continuing. The team of Economy Minister Domingo Cavallo that launched a new round of comprehensive reforms in April 1991 reflected determination to adhere to the economy's transformation. Under the April program, the Austral (later rechristened the peso) was made fully convertible at 10,000 per U.S. dollar and the monetary base was linked to the level of international reserves. At the same time, almost all nontariff import barriers were dismantled and the maximum tariff was reduced from 50 to 22 percent, with an average tariff of about 9 percent.[26] Moreover, indexation was abolished and export surcharges removed.

Despite concerns about exchange rate competitiveness, Argentina appears to be sticking to its difficult course. Although much discussion of Argentina relates to its macroeconomic achievements, supply-side successes have multiplied. In particular, Argentina has made progress in diversifying its export base to nontraditional goods. One example of this process is within the agricultural sector. As *The Financial Times'* John Barham noted: "Argentina is better known for its fertile pampas of swaying wheat that stretch beyond the horizon than for its delicious nectarines, strawberries, kiwis, avocados, passion fruit, artichokes, or asparagus."[27] After several years of experimentation, the nontraditional agricultural products have begun to come into their own: in 1991 fruit and vegetable exports rose 10 percent to $270 million, after a 14 percent increase the previous year. They accounted for around 12 percent of Argentina's agricultural export in the early 1990s.

Although Argentina has entered the fruit and vegetable markets later than its neighbor, Chile (which did so in the 1980s), the larger country possesses a number of advantages which could be converted into profits: first and foremost, it has more land than Chile; second, Argentina is closer to European markets; and third, its soil and largely predictable climate of warm summers and cold winters make it one of the most efficient producers of agricultural goods in the world. One of the challenges for Argentina in the 1990s will be to capitalize on these advantages. This means dealing with microeconomic bottlenecks, such as an inefficient and expensive electricity distribution system, unmodernized ports, and an outmoded transportation network. It also means catching up with the Chileans in packaging and marketing techniques.

The 1995 Elections

The elections in May 1995 were highly significant for Argentina as President Menem was allowed to run for a second consecutive term. Menem's Peronista party won important provincial elections in September 1991, and congressional elections in October 1993, 1994, and 1995 were dominated first by Menem's initiative to change the constitution, and second by his campaign. In November 1993, an agreement was reached between Menem and Alfonsín (as leader of the Radicals) about the basic tenets of constitutional reform required for the former to legally seek reelection. A constituent assembly, elected in April 1994, established the constitutional changes to include lifting the previous restriction on the reelection of incumbent presidents, reducing the president's term in office from six to four years, and allowing direct voting for the president with a second round if there is no clear winner in the first round.

Argentina's national elections were held on 14 May 1995. Voters cast their ballots for president as well as 130 seats in the 267–seat Chamber of Deputies, one-third of federal senators, and 14 provinces held local gubernatorial races. The Peronista ticket was headed by Menem and Carlos Ruckauf, a lawyer-politician who served as minister of labor in the government of President Isabel Perón (1974–76) and subsequently as Menem's ambassador to Italy. Ruckauf also served as a member of the Argentine Chamber of Deputies, and prior to the 1995 election, as minister of the interior. The Peronista campaign centered on the continuation of the economic reform process and emphasized the stability that the first Menem administration brought Argentina. Argentina in the mid-1990s had monetary stability, and international confidence in the country had largely returned.

One of the two competitors to Menem and the Peronistas was the Radical presidential candidate Horacio Massaccessi, governor of the province of Río Negro and his vice presidential candidate, Antonio Hernández, a law professor. Although the Radicals were the traditional party of the Argentine middle class and formed the major opposition to Menem within the formal political system, they lost some degree of popularity over Alfonsín's agreement to change the constitution to allow for two consecutive terms for incumbent presidents.

The other major contender to Menem was a former Peronista governor and then a senator, José Octavio Bordón, who headed the ticket for FREPASO (Front for a Country in Solidarity). The vice presidential candidate was Carlos Alvarez, a former Peronista congressman. FREPASO was a coalition of ex-Peronistas, ex-Radicals, Christian Democrats, the Intransigent Party, Socialist Unity, and a number of other smaller leftist groups. While the Radicals' appeal declined during the course of the campaign, Bordón and FREPASO emerged as the major challenge to Menem.

Both FREPASO and the Radicals found running against Menem and the Peronista government difficult. However, Bordón was able to chip away in opinion polls against Menem over social issues and the government's past problems with scandals. As U.S. political analyst William Perry noted: "The reforms carried out by Menem and his no-nonsense finance minister, Domingo Cavallo, have entailed considerable hardship for the population. Moreover, significant sections of the electorate habitually dislike the Peronists, disapprove of the wrenching liberalization measures, or distrust the moral probity of Menem and his entourage."[28] Although Bordón appeared to gain significant momentum late in the campaign and managed to eclipse the Radicals in the final tally, he failed to make significant headway against Menem.

The results of the May 1995 elections were a solid endorsement for Menem and the Peronistas. The president won a second term, gaining close to 50 percent of the vote compared to a little under 20 percent for Bordón and a disappointing 17 percent for the Radical candidate.[29] The Peronistas also won a solid majority of the seats in both the Congress and Senate.

Although the Radicals and FREPASO were left-of-center during the campaign, both parties indicated that within a broad framework they would maintain the Menem administration's economic policies though they would soften certain of the more harsh aspects of structural adjustment. Concerns were raised in the aftermath of Menem's strong victory that would weaken Argentine democracy. Natalio Botana, a political scientist at the Di Tella Institute commented: "This drive toward supremacy by Menem is detrimental in a modern democracy because it weakens the system of parties, as it places men above institutions."[30] At the same time, other analysts regarded FREPASO's strong showing to be positive as it possibly indicated the emergence of a new party capable of replacing the Radicals as a new and more effective opposition. Yet, by 1996 there were clear signs that the pull of the 1999 presidential succession was already being felt, with FREPASO's fragile political coalition one of its early casualties. The Radical victory in the Buenos Aires mayor race in 1996 comfirmed continuing shifts.

Caution Points

In the medium term, optimism about Argentina must be tempered by an acknowledgement of a number of caution points. While there is a large constituency who favor the continued transformation of the Argentine economy, supporters for the old order continue to manifest disenchantment with the reform process. The negative side effects of the structural-adjustment process of cutting wages have clearly caused a deterioration in the living standard of many working-class Argentines. Spontaneous riots and looting, as in the case of the city of Rosario in May 1989 and February 1990, illustrate the problem as did the high rates of unemployment during the economic slowdown in 1995.

There remain doubts, too, about the viability of the fiscal program (in particular, when taking into account provincial budgets) and the current level of the exchange rate (especially in the aftermath of Mexico's peso crisis in early 1995). The problem of external debt lingers despite a Brady Plan debt- reduction accord between Argentina and its commercial banks in 1992. The following sections in this chapter concentrate on seven areas of concern: the need to deepen democracy, the labor unions, the military, corruption, the fiscal program, the exchange rate, and the external debt question. The basic conclusion is that, while each of these concerns should give pause to excessively optimistic views about Argentina's future, the positive omens are weightier.

Deepening Democracy

One of the major issues facing Argentina in the future is whether the democratic process can be deepened. The accomplishment of Alfonsín passing the presidential sash to Menem should not be understated, but if the democratic-capitalist model is to meet the population's demands, Argentine political institutions may have to become more responsive. There is general agreement that the constitution, which dates back into the last century, needs to be overhauled. However, the apparent desire of Menem to be allowed to stand for a further presidential term could militate against a clear-headed consideration of the shape of Argentina's democratic institutions. The fact that Menem and Alfonsín were able to reach an agreement about the process for reelection, and that amendments to the constitution were made by an elective body, bodes well for the democratic idea of compromise in Argentina.

Concerns have also been raised about a down grading in the balance-of-power between the chief executive, the Supreme Court, and Congress. Menem has often bypassed Congress by using executive orders, while placing progovernment judges in the judicial system. While this outmaneuvering of possible opposition from these bodies has allowed Menem to pursue his economic program often unhindered, it also raises questions about the dangers of weakening checks and balances. It also underscores what political scientist Guillermo O'Donnell noted in 1991—that Argentina, like many other democracies in Latin America, is not a representative democracy, but rather a "delegative," democracy where, once elected, a politician rules as he or she sees fit.[31] This situation can also open the door to abuses, such as corruption. Menem's second term (1995–99) is likely to test these considerations.

Labor Union Power

Discontented elements in the labor unions are important challenges to Argentina's reform process, though their influence appears to have markedly declined by the mid-1990s. Argentina's trade unions have traditionally been highly politicized and active in representing its memberships' concerns as perceived by the leadership. Moreover, the labor movement has had few qualms about using its political clout to oppose measures as President Alfonsín had the misfortune to experience.

Although the unions are largely of Peronista tendencies, they have found themselves generally at odds with the Menem government. While the officially recognized Confederación General del Trabajo (CGT)-San Martín grudgingly gave support to Menem's early policies, the CGT de Azopardo, which represented a large number of public-sector employees, strongly opposed plans for privatization and liberalization.[32] As the reform process gained momentum in 1990 and 1991, labor union resistance also gained momentum.

In July 1991, the country's three major union leaders, Luis Barrionuevo, Saul Ubaldini, and Lorenzo Miguel, formed an alliance against the Menem government. These labor leaders were not without encouragement, as Ubaldini had ties to former Colonel Mohamed Ali Seineldin, who led a four-day army rebellion in December 1988. The colonel, in turn, was a friend of Menem's estranged wife, Zulema Yoma de Menem, who is an old-line Peronista of the populist bent and has publicly criticized the economic reforms. Argentine sociologist Juan E. Corradi notes: "there are popular sectors in Argentina that continue to tolerate the vices of Peronism, that feel represented by populist and authoritarian leaders, and that even see in the abhorrence of union bosses among democratic and progressive sectors . . . a confirmation of their proletarian authenticity.[33]

But while Argentina's labor unions remain one of the major forces that is the most open in its opposition to change, it is questionable that the rank and file of these organizations have firmly entrenched beliefs that economic reforms are all negative. The hard core old-line Peronista union leadership has suffered from the collapse of the Eastern bloc due to the discrediting of the state-dominated economic model. A string of opinion polls has indicated that grassroots labor is not against important structural reform, including privatization. Reformists within the Peronist party are succeeding in marginalizing the old union leadership which, in turn, has led to a bifurcation of the CGT (the main labor union) into two groups, one "modern," the other "traditional."

The head of the traditional wing of the CGT, Saul Ubaldini, a scourge of President Alfonsín, has been sufficiently neutered by President Menem to the point that he failed to win the Peronista candidacy in his home state and so ran for election in September 1991 under his own banner. He achieved only 2 percent of the vote. After the September election Menem lost little time announcing a ban of all political strikes.

Notwithstanding this neutering of much of the union leadership, it would be erroneous to ignore the residual power of labor. In November 1992, the administration was clearly rattled by the success, albeit hardly thoroughgoing, of the one-day general strike called by the unions. The leadership has proven adroit at marshalling support from aggrieved sectors of the middle class for its campaigns on partisan issues, such as pensions, more education, and health spending. In 1992, there was much talk in the press about a "black deal" between the unions and the government, though Finance Minister Cavallo insisted he had given no concessions to the labor movement.[34]

Two supply-side reform requirements—an overhaul of the pension system and labor-market reform—have been much delayed by Menem's insistence that the unions be granted an important say in the whole process. Whatever the results, it is likely that they will involve much greater union involvement than Cavallo would have desired. The announcement of a $1.5 billion social-spending package by Menem in January 1993, while apparently consistent with the ambitious fiscal targets of the new extended program agreed upon with the IMF in 1992, demonstrate that Menem is sensitive to claims that his government is aware of Argentina's social deficit, in particular, the objectively woeful condition of state pensioners.

The Military

A traditional but now considerably weakened source of opposition to the government is the military. Although the armed forces and Peronistas have in the past been at odds, Menem as candidate, and later in office as president, advocated reconciliation and political balance. A difficult decision to make, he more or less closed the era of investigations of military officers linked to human rights' abuses during the "dirty war" in the 1970s. When dealing with the military budget, Menem cancelled or constrained new technology projects and acquisitions; but he attempted to provide the armed forces with a new and expanded overseas peacekeeping mission (under UN auspices) and sought to bring them back into the fold of being a "normal" branch of government. This policy of working with the armed forces as opposed to working against them partially explains his ability to survive at least one coup attempt and perhaps neutralize the desire within the ranks for more in the future.

Menem's decision to make a contribution, albeit a small one, to the anti-Iraq coalition during the 1991 Gulf War was welcomed by the Argentine military. It provided the armed forces an opportunity to demonstrate that they could play a positive role in international relations, especially as they were on the winning side. In a sense, a small amount of pride in the armed forces was regained, an important development considering the legacy of defeat in the Falkland/Malvinas conflict. It also reflected Menem's belief that his country's future lies in an alliance with the industrialized democracies and not as a nonaligned power.

Menem's ability to guide the military to a more apolitical role was mirrored in the September 1991 elections. In particular, the relatively poor showing of one of Argentina's Falkland/Malvinas veterans, retired colonel Also Rico in Buenos Aires Province, attested to a lower political profile for the military and, perhaps by extension, ex-military men. Although the 1992 military coup attempts in Venezuela demonstrated the danger of ignoring the military undercurrent that is always present in Latin American politics, the process of normalizing relations with the armed forces in Argentina appears to be proceeding successfully. It was significant that during the 1995 elections the military was not a factor—except in the public confessions of former military officers about their experiences in the "dirty war."

Corruption

Another point of concern is corruption. While Menem and Economy Minister Cavallo have accomplished much in terms of macroeconomic reform, corruption in Argentine society could pose serious problems in attracting foreign investment and in the functioning of the economy. There have been efforts to deal with the issue and a number of officials have been sacked. In December 1992, a cabinet reshuffle was widely interpreted as removing ministers with impeccable credentials from the government because of the issue of corruption.

One of the most public cases involved the Swift-Armour meat packing company which, in 1994–95, complained to the U.S. government about an Argentine official who asked for a bribe in return for permission to import machinery. The then U.S. ambassador, Terence Todman, sent two ministers a letter of complaint, which was leaked to the Argentine press. Menem's brother-in-law soon resigned as a presidential advisor. Other members of Zulema Yoma de Menem's family had been fingered for their involvement in smuggling, drug-money laundering, and bribery. Although most of Zulema's family left the government in 1991, actual criminal proceedings were slow to get started. A more recent case (1995–96) that drew attention involved IBM, a non-existent Argentine corporate entity, and the Argentine government.

Corruption, therefore, lingers as a worrying issue. In this context, however, the measures announced by President Menem later in October 1991 are significant. He attacked the "cobweb" of rules, regulations, and restrictive practices that had long been a feature of Argentine economic life and a root cause of corruption. Dozens of government agencies were closed and bureaucratic controls lifted. The desired effect was to reduce corruption and encourage greater integration of economic activity into the formal tax system. Yet, despite these efforts, allegations of corruption within the government continue to circulate.

Fiscal Progress

One of the Achilles' heels for Argentine governments has been fiscal policy. As a World Bank report suggested, the five stabilization programs in the 1984–89 period were killed by largely insufficient adjustment in the public sector.[35] Whenever fiscal policy failed to stimulate revenue-raising through taxation, and government spending remained out of balance with revenues, inflation returned and went to higher levels than before the policy was enacted. The key to controlling inflation, as the Menem administration has done thus far, is reducing the government deficit.

Pressures remain, however, that could derail the process. Once most major privatizations are completed, the fiscal balance that is essential to the longevity of covertibility will not be propped up by one-off asset sales. While the elasticity of the tax system has undoubtedly improved, there were doubts that fiscal balance would be possible if GDP growth fell much below the 4 percent level of 1993. Many economists expected growth to tail off below the high level of 1992, in which case the validity of the "4 percent" hypothesis would be tested. Argentina's rapid growth in 1993 and 1994 did not test that, but the slowdown in 1995 clearly put the fiscal situation under greater pressure. It remains to be seen whether over the long run the Argentine government can raise the sufficient revenues to generate an underlying operating surplus. However, the additional investment in staffing the tax collection agency bodes well for a much-improved level of collection. New measures have also been discussed concerning fiscal adjustments in the provinces though this is likely to be tested in the second Memen administration.

Currency Valuation

Currency valuation has been another point of concern for the Menem government. Throughout the 1980s, the value of Argentina's currency almost consistently lost ground against other currencies, especially the dollar. In 1990 and early 1991, the fall of the Austral was steep, leading to the near-dollarization of the economy. This obviously had a negative societal impact, as many Argentines found themselves rushing to pay bills as quickly as possible to avoid a deterioration in the value of their paychecks. In addition, this hurt productivity. For many Argentines, the sense that things had wobbled out of control was most evident in the value of the currency.

Since April 1991, the government has committed to defend the national currency at a rate of one peso to the U.S. dollar. In 1992, complaints by industrialists about the level of the currency multiplied. The government refused to concede that the currency was overvalued, contending that producers should try to trim costs rather than complain about the exchange rate. In October 1992, the authorities attempted to improve the cost structure of the export sector by introducing some protectionist measures. Nevertheless, in November 1992, on the eve of the one-day general strike, rumors abounded that Menem would dispense with the service of Cavallo, leading the markets to buy over $330 million that month alone. The central bank reacted swiftly to this stiff test to convertibility and allowed local interest rates to rise and announced a deeper dollarization of the economy (for example, foreign-exchange check accounts). These efforts had the desired effect.

In December 1992, the Central Bank bought $1.5 billion as the markets began to accept the authorities' resolve. However, as 1993 progressed, many Argentines assumed at the time that a dismantling of the convertibility plan was a question of "when" rather than "if." The $1.5 billion trade deficit recorded in 1992 underscored worries about the sustainability of the current account imbalance ($7.1 billion in 1992 with a deficit of $6 billion projected for 1993).[36] Delays in pension and labor reforms inflamed concerns about the shortage of savings in the country (and hence the need for foreign borrowings and external deficits) and the uncompetitiveness of Argentine wage rates (which were more than twice the level of Brazil in U.S. dollar terms in 1992).

Despite considerable pressure to devalue in late 1994 and early 1995, Argentina maintained currency parity. One of the reasons Argentina survived the "Tequila hangover" effect was the prompt action of the government. In particular, the Menem government was able to implement a successful $7.5 billion financial package with the support of the International Monetary Fund, multilateral credit agencies, and commercial banks, which clearly helped shore up a bank system hard-hit by an outflow of currency.

External Debt

No discussion about Argentina's future would be complete without some mention of the external debt burden. The external debt issue continues to be a lingering concern, though prospects have improved because of an agreement between Argentina and its commercial bank credits to conduct the Brady Plan debt-reduction program, which was completed in the second quarter of 1993.

Argentina's record as a debtor in the 1980s was not admirable. Several agreements with the commercial banks were signed and quickly discarded. Menem's election did not initially portend any change from the past track record. However, the Peronista administration pursued the issue with a certain sense of purpose that ultimately surprised many analysts. First, Argentina worked down the size of its external debt through debt-for-privatization and other market mechanisms of debt reduction. Second, Argentina made small interest payments to the banks (roughly $60 million a month in early 1992). Although this amount was small in relation to the amount owed, it indicated that there was a willingness to recognize the need to resolve the problem.

Also, given that most banks in North America and Europe carry provisions of 70 to 100 percent of the loan, the yield on unprovisioned exposure produced by $60 million was relatively high. Finally, Argentina's willingness to swallow tough economic reforms paved the way for the International Monetary Fund to approve a one-year standby loan of $1.04 billion in July 1991 to Argentina, which also unlocked $325 million from the World Bank. There followed another (extended facility) program with the IMF in 1992. These moves were essential in helping Argentina move toward a Brady deal, given that the multilateral organizations were sources of enhancement for Brady bonds.

Argentina's total external debt at the end of 1993 was $76 billion, equal to 23 percent of GDP, a lower ratio than in Mexico and in Venezuela. Foreign exchange reserves reflected the country's dynamic growth in the early 1990s, providing comfortable international reserves. The Mexican peso crisis, however, threatened Argentina as currency speculators attacked the currency. Although Argentina was able to quickly cobble together international support which helped replenish its foreign exchange reserves, the threat of currency speculation remained an ongoing concern throughout 1995, indicating that for the many significant transformations in the southern cone country, certain weaknesses remain and demand constant attention from the authorities.

An Argentine Renaissance?

While the "feel" for change being articulated now in Argentina is not a quantitative measure, a few economic indicators provide a rough idea of the evolution. After several years of contraction, real GDP rose 8.5 percent in 1991 and over 9 percent in 1992. Unemployment fell from 18.5 percent in 1989 to an estimated 7 percent in 1992, while inflation also declined from over 3,000 percent to under 18 percent in the same period. Another positive set of trends is evident in financial matters: in 1991, the Buenos Aires *bolsa* rose nearly 500 percent and in 1992 Argentine borrowers reentered the euromarkets, including three issues by the Republic of Argentina.

Enthusiasm about Argentina's reform process must be carefully balanced with the awareness that, while the finger is on the fast-forward button, obstacles exist. As Argentine economist Roberto Bouzas noted in 1992: " . . . stability is still precarious, and sustained economic growth is far from restored. Furthermore, the reform process has entailed large stabilization and social costs."[37] Those social costs are evident in the following: recent government figures indicate that over one-third of the population live in poverty and that real wages fell steadily in the 1989–91 period.[38]

Despite the magnitude of the problems that confronted Argentina in the early 1990s, it is possible that by the end of the decade the economy will prove itself transformed. The process of adjustment is clearly difficult and wrenching and unfortunately there is no overnight, rapid development model. However, Argentina is surrounded by Latin American neighbors that have rejected the old notions that long guided much of development economics. These include the view that the role of the state is to act as the manager of resource mobilization and allocation, and that the private sector, with its links to the outside world, is not necessarily acting in the best national interest. As Chile and Mexico are demonstrating, the notion of "Third Worldism," statism, and "Southern Solidarity" have given way to market-oriented strategies. Argentina under Menem appears to posses the political will needed to break through the bottlenecks and allow market forces to set the pace of growth. The Menem administration has grasped that there is a new world order and it is in this international system that Argentina must find its future.

Diplomatically, Menem's Argentina has worked hard to place itself firmly in the Western camp. The anti-U.S. rhetoric that had occasionally marked Argentine foreign policy statements since the 1940s have disappeared. This was made very evident in the decision to send two Argentine navy ships to the Persian Gulf to participate in the U.S.-led alliance against Iraq during 1990–91, and by Argentine support for the U.S. policy toward Haiti in 1994 and 1995. In a sense, Menem appears to be working to guarantee a positively charged international environment for the new Argentina emerging from the rubble of the old. This is especially the case with the United States and the European Community (including the United Kingdom with which diplomatic relations have resumed).

Conclusion

Argentina's development process has made considerable strides in the early 1990s. While there is room for satisfaction, the nation faces some continuing changes and considerable problems in the late-1990s.

After years of dismal rule, effective civilian rule has been restored to public applause, but the political cycle could yet again be ready for another turn. That political cycle can always include a slide backward, into a state and a political elite incapable of sustaining difficult economic and political reforms.

Argentina will remain one of Latin America's most pivotal nations—capable of maintaining a fast-forward mode of development. Yet, there are no guarantees that Argentina will sustain its present pace of development beyond the turn of the century. Moreover, much hinges on the health of the international economy to which the country is rapidly linking itself. As the 1990s progress, decisions made in Brasilia, Washington, Bonn, and Tokyo will have an impact in the Southern Cone, a factor that makes Argentina's voice in the process more pressing. Argentina's fast-forward option is creating a new world in which it must have a voice—to influence policy and enhance the international environment's reinforcement of the country's many sacrifices.

Notes

1. Paul Lewis, *The Crisis in Argentine Capitalism* (Chapel Hill: University of North Carolina, 1992), p. 494.
2. William C. Smith, *Authoritarianism and the Crisis of the Argentine Political Economy* (Stanford, Cal.: Stanford University Press, 1989), pp. 18–19.
3. Peter Snow, "Argentina; Politics in a Conflictual Society," in *Latin American Politics and Development*, eds. Howard J. Wiarda and Harvey F. Kline (Boulder, Colo.: Westview Press, 1989), p. 131.
4. Jeremy Adelman, "Socialism and Democracy in Argentina in the Age of the Second International," *Hispanic American Historical Review* 72, no. 2 (May 1992): p. 211. Adelman's essay indicates that the socialists' failure to create a mass-based party oriented along the lines of democratic socialism opened the door to populist politicians (especially Perón), and includes Gino Germani, *Estructura social de la Argentina: análisis estadístico* (Buenos Aires: Editorial Raigal, 1955); Samuel L. Baily, *Labor, Nationalism, and Politics in Argentina* (New Brunswick, N.J.: Rutgers University Press, 1967); Richard J. Walker, *The Socialist Party of Argentina, 1890–1930* (Austin: Institute of Latin American Studies, University of Texas, 1977); Ronaldo Munck, *Argentina: From Anarchism to Peronism* (London: Zed Books, 1987); and Isidoro Cheresky, "Sindicatos y fuerzas políticas en la Argentina pre-peronista," in *Historia del Movimiento obrero en América Latina* vol. 4, ed. Pablo González Casanova (Mexico City: Siglo Veintiuno, 1984), pp. 147–99. In a sense, the socialist party's failure was the cause of the next several decades of tumultuous political behavior in Argentina. This remains one of the great "ifs" in Argentine history; if democratic socialism had taken root, the course of history might have been much more akin to the political development of France or Italy. Considering the "if" nature of the debate, this point is likely to continue to be an ongoing source of discussion.

5. Snow, "Argentina," p. 132.
6. Robert R. Kaufman, "Stabilization and Adjustment in Argentina, Brazil and Mexico," in *Economic Crisis and Policy Change: The Politics of Adjustment in the Third World*, ed. Joan M. Nelson (Princeton, N.J.: University of Princeton Press, 1990), p. 66.
7. Snow, "Argentina," p. 133.
8. Ibid.
9. Kaufman, "Stabilization," p. 68.
10. Ibid., p. 69
11. "Acta de la Revolución Argentina," in *El onganiato: La espada y el hisopo* vol. 1, ed. Gregorio Selser (Buenos Aires: Carlos Sarmonta Editor, 1973), p. 300.
12. See Guillermo O'Donnell, *El Estado Burocratico Autoritario, 1966–73: Triunfos, Derrotas y Crisis* (Buenos Aires, Argentina: Editorial de Belgrano, 1982), pp. 229–308.
13. International Monetary Fund, *International Financial Statistics Year Book 1991* (Washington, D.C.: International Monetary Fund, 1991), p. 197.
14. Snow, "Argentina," p. 136.
15. Kaufman, "Stabilization," p. 70.
16. Lewis, *Argentine Capitalism*, p. 462.
17. Ian Roxborough, "Organized Labor: A Major Victim of the Debt Crisis," in *Debt and Democracy in Latin America*, eds. Barbara Stallings and Robert Kaufman (Boulder, Colo.: Westview Press, 1989), p. 8; and Aldo Ferrer, *Living Within Our Means: An Examination of the Argentine Economic Crisis* (Boulder, Colo.: Westview Press, 1985), p. 48.
18. Juan Carlos de Pablo, "Argentina," in *Latin American Adjustment: How Much Has Happened?*, ed. John Williamson (Washington, D.C.: Institute of International Economics, 1990), p. 113.
19. Jane Hughes, "Latin America," in *The Global Debt Crisis: Forecasting for the Future*, eds. Scott B. MacDonald, Margie Lindsey and David L. Crum (London: Pinter Publishers, 1990), p. 28.
20. See Daniel Marx, Testimony before the Senate Finance Subcommittee on Deficits, Debt Management and International Debt, Washington, D.C., June 12, 1991.
21. Ibid.
22. Gary Mead, "Argentina ending oil monopoly," *Financial Times* (July 12, 1990): p. 22. Salomon Brothers Emerging Markets Research, *Emerging Markets Biweekly* (April 21, 1993): p. 2.
24. Yacimientos Petroliferos Fiscales, *YPF Prospectus* (January 5, 1994): p. 4.
25. Barham, "Argentina to cut back bureaucrats," *Financial Times* (November 27, 1990): p. 22.
26. Paul Luke, *Developing Country Investment Review* (London), Chartered West LB, June 26, 1991.
27. Barham, "Passionfruit Grows on the Pampas," *Financial Times* (August 14, 1991): p. 20.
28. William Perry, *The 1995 Argentine Elections: Pre-Election Report #2* (Washington, D.C: Center for Strategic and International Studies, 1995) p. 1. Also see Mark Falcoff, *The 1995 Argentine Elections: Pre-Election Report #1* (Washington, D.C: Center for Strategic and International Studies, 1995).
29. Calvin Sims, "Menem's Victory in Argentina Seen as Endorsement of Free Market," *New York Times* (May 16, 1995): p. A13.
30. Ibid.

31. Luigi Manzetti, "Argentina: The Costs of Economic Restructuring," *North-South Focus* vol. II, no. 1 (1993): p. 5.
32. Smith, *Authoritarianism*, p. 305.
33. Juan E. Corradi, *The Fitful Society: Economy, Society, and Politics in Argentina* (Boulder, Colo.: Westview Press, 1985), p. 151.
34. The so-called black deal was allegedly a concession by the government to have the unions administer pension funds under the new social security reform. According to Luigi Manzetti: "This translated into an estimated $3 billion business, which for many Argentine union bosses, notorious for manipulating the health care funds they already control in their own interests, was too much to resist." See Manzetti, "Argentina," p. 5.
35. See World Bank, *Argentina: Reforms for Price Stability and Growth* (Washington, D.C.: World Bank, 1990).
36. See Paul Luke, *Dangerous Deficits: Current Account Trends in Argentina and Mexico*, Morgan Grenfell, (October 29, 1992).
37. Roberto Bouzas, "Beyond Stabilization and Reform: The Argentine Economy in the 1990s," in *In the Shadow of the Debt: Emerging Issues in Latin America* (New York: The Twentieth Century Fund Press, 1992), p. 83.
38. Manzetti, "Argentina," p. 3.

5

The Game Intensifies: Colombia

Colombia has two realities. One is of men with guns, conducting the lucrative, yet illicit business of drug-trafficking along with their sometimes allies in the local revolutionary movements, competing for profit and influence with right-wing paramilitary squads. The other reality is that of a Colombia following a path of prudent economic management and political liberalization, despite an almost relentless assault on the country's political institutions. While the former image is often distorted and overstated, it has had an impact on the latter. It is, therefore, no understatement to note that Colombians have not enjoyed long periods of relative social calm, but that the Colombian economy has demonstrated considerable dynamism and its political system a surprising resilience.

From 1980 to 1992, according to the World Bank, the Colombian economy expanded at an average annual growth rate of 3.7 percent, while national elections have been held on schedule and elective offices have been widened to include state and local governments.[1] Colombia, alone in Latin America, did not reschedule its external debt in the 1980s. It has one of the most diverse economies in the region, it has been rated by at least one major rating agency as investment grade (Chile being the only other exception to this in the region) and, in spite of tremendous political problems, the fast-forward button is being pushed.

Colombia in the 1990s teeters on the edge of moving forward or failing. Although privatization programs have been launched, trade regimes liberalized, and a broadening of elective offices has been implemented, serious questions linger about the extent of societal consensus over the direction of economic reforms and the nature of political responsibility exercised by national leaders. Politically, the corrosion of the narcotics trade is high among the nation's political leadership and cuts widely across the country's social fabric. Despite the durability of the political systems to survive authoritarian challenges, the danger of economic failure and ossification of the political system under the influence of international organized crime, personal greed, party politics, and corruption remain critical challenges in the 1990s and beyond. A Colombia unshackled from such security concerns would probably experience even more rapid development, benefit from greater foreign investment, and its citizens enjoy a more peaceful life that would allow them to concentrate on more productive pursuits. Colombia's leadership must also consider that while their nation remained ahead of the pack during the 1980s, that competitive edge is being dulled by the ongoing costly nature of security concerns and a Latin America that has, in many cases, adopted many of the same prudent economic management characteristics and then some.

Historical Background

Colombia emerged from the Spanish colonial period led by an upper class largely of European descent and, while it attracted new waves of European settlers, much of the native population was either eliminated or became small peripheral groups in society. A small segment of Colombia's population is of African descent, especially in Caribbean coastal areas where slaves were brought to work on sugarcane plantations or in the mines. Independence was achieved in 1819 and the newly sovereign state was initially part of a confederation that included present-day Venezuela, Ecuador, and Panama. That confederation collapsed by 1830 and Colombia and Venezuela went their own ways. Colombia eventually lost control of Panama when that country became independent in 1901.

Colombia's Modern Economy

Much of the North American public has nurtured an image of Colombia as a land painted in Miami Vice shades of violent pink and pastels. Cocaine and marijuana traffickers ply their wares in the United States, Canada, and the rest of the world, providing an image of a country run by smooth-talking men with pony tails, dressed in thousand dollar silk suits, and prone to violence when crossed. Speculation about the amount of money returning to the country from illicit cocaine exports has skewed the debate on Colombia's economic development. Much of Colombia's economic development has nothing to do with the illicit drug trade and many Colombians are as apprehensive of visiting New York City and Washington, D.C. as they are in dealing with the daily *narcotraficante* threat.

The Colombian economy and political system that now exist are the products of an evolution beginning in the same historical womb as Venezuela. Although Colombia and Venezuela share historical roots and are both regarded as democratic-capitalist in the 1990s, their experiences to that point are radically different. Colombia emerged from a larger federation that originally spanned Ecuador, Venezuela, and Panama, all of which parted company by 1901. Beginning in the 1840s, two political parties, the Partido Social Conservador (Conservative Party) and the Partido Liberal Colombiano (Liberal Party) became institutionalized as focal points of Colombia's political life. The Conservatives were largely rural, agriculturally based, and favored a role for the Catholic church in society. The Liberals were more secular-minded, largely urban, and trade and commerce oriented. Despite their differences both political parties were conservative in terms of economic management, while their institutionalization as the central points of the political economy made it difficult for a strongman to come to the fore.

Colombia has a relatively distinctive path of development in the twentieth century, in sharp contrast to other Latin American countries because it has not had populist macroeconomic policies. Political groups with a populist agenda have never won the presidency nor have been able to obtain important minorities in the Congress.[2] This has meant that while elements of the import-substitution model were adopted—notably foreign exchange controls, protectionist trade measures, and state ownership of certain sectors—economic management has remained conservative. Expensive spending binges to feed personal or regime popularity simply did not occur to the same level as elsewhere in the region. As Colombia evolved as a nation, it remained divided into fairly autonomous and economically independent regions. The emergence of a national market did not occur until the 1930s, a process largely facilitated by the advent of large-scale cultivation and export of coffee and other agricultural goods.

In the early twentieth century, the industrial sector began to emerge around oil and manufacturing. As in the rest of Latin America, the advent of industrialization created new political groups who sought a voice at the economic table. Political reforms in the late nineteenth and early twentieth centuries gradually expanded the political base of the Liberals and Conservatives, creating increasingly national parties and weakening local party bosses. At the same time, Colombia's press maintained a strong tradition of independence, helping insure an out-of-government auditing of the government's economic decisions.[3]

The two-party political system that dominated Colombia's development came under profound pressure in the late 1940s. The 1946 elections were tension-filled as considerable rhetoric was used, especially from the Conservative party leader, Laureano Gómez, who led a self-proclaimed mission to save Colombian society from "heresy" and "communism," and to preserve traditional Hispanic and Catholic values.[4] Behind the candidacy of Mariano Ospina Pérez and inspired by Gómez's rhetoric, the Conservatives entered the contest unified and ready to compete. The Liberals were split between the official party candidate Gabriel Turbay and the highly charismatic populist Jorge Eliécer Gaitàn. Ospina became the next president, but the bitterness of the campaign lingered. When Gaitàn was assassinated on April 9, 1948 by what appeared to be a disgruntled job seeker, the city of Bogotá erupted into a massive riot. Referred to as the *bogotazo*, this marked the commencement of a period in Colombian history known as *la violencia*. A new round of interparty warfare gripped the country, with Liberal guerrilla bands explicitly seeking to overthrow the Conservative government and, in some cases, to conduct a social revolution.[5]

The widespread nature of political violence, the increasing use of the military to crush the Liberal insurrection, and the declaration of a state of siege that closed the Liberal- dominated Congress in November 1949, weakened the two-party political system. The Liberals withdrew from the election in November 1949, handing the presidency over to Gómez, whose position was weakened by personal illness. The ultimate outcome was a military coup on the part of General Gustavo Rojas Pinilla, the commander in chief of the armed forces, on June 13, 1953. The Rojas regime lasted until 1957, when he was driven from power by the resurgent Conservatives and Liberals.

The highly destructive nature of *la violencia* and the brief military regime effectively brought the two parties together to form the National Front. There were four overarching characteristics of the National Front that were to guide the country into the 1980s: first, in subsequent elections there was to be an equal division (parity) between the two parties and only those parties, in all legislative bodies ranging from municipal councils to the national congress;[6] second, all appointed positions (apart from the military and the small civil service) were to be similarly distributed between the parties, again at all levels of the government; third, the presidency must alternate between the two parties every four years; and fourth, nonprocedural measures must be approved within all elective bodies by a two-thirds vote (which implied support for legislation from portions of both parties). This system was to last until 1974 when the political system was opened to all parties.

Under the National Front, Colombia's political system was not fully democratic in the representative sense, as in the United States, Canada, or France. As veteran political scientist John Martz noted: "Colombia has been a limited or qualified democracy in which even the constitutional rules of the game have restricted popular participation and the unhindered interplay of competing forces and interests. This has been consistent with a deep-seated experience of elitist control over the political process readily traced back to the early years of the republic."[7] Although this system would unravel under a number of pressures in the late 1980s and early 1990s, the National Front clearly left an imprint on the country's political culture.

Although the National Front system changed through the years, it became the mainstay of the political system for a lengthy period of time. This provided a degree of stability, especially as *la violencia* was gradually brought under control despite the emergence of Marxist guerrillas. Economic policy under the National Front was largely conservative, maintaining a balance between the market and the intervention of the state. While much of the economy was left to the private sector, the government extended and maintained control of such infrastructural facilities as roads, railroads, telecommunications, and electric utilities. Moreover, the state was deeply involved in the development of energy resources, including hydrocarbons, coal, and hydroelectric power.[8] The government was also active in the promotion of the country's major export, coffee, and assisted the agricultural sector to diversify into other areas, such as flowers. Foreign participation was welcome under the guise of joint ventures, though sectors like coffee remained largely in Colombian hands.

Colombia's state played a significant role in the economy. In sharp contrast to neighboring Venezuela where the government pump-primed the economy, first with oil revenues and later with foreign loans, the government in Colombia opted against such policies. Miguel Urrutia, a Colombian economist, has noted: "Since within the political class there has been sufficient economic literacy for the spread of the belief that there is some relationship between money supply and fiscal deficits and inflation, neither local politicians or the head of the state are willing to risk the wrath of the public by supporting expansionist fiscal or monetary policies in order to obtain the doubtful political gains generated by faster growth or less unemployment, if the possible cost is inflation."[9]

The Colombian economy expanded by 5.7 percent in the 1965–80 period.[10] Not a major oil producer, but with domestic capacity, Colombia weathered the oil shocks in the mid-1970s. While other countries had a stronger clip of growth, such as Ecuador (at 8.7 percent) and Brazil (at 9 percent), Colombia entered the 1980s in a better position and was not forced to reschedule its external debt. While Colombia had borrowed, it had not borrowed well beyond its means of repayment. From the 1980–85 period, growth slowed to an average annual rate of 2.5 percent, during which it avoided the massive contractions that pummelled other Latin American economies. In 1982, the depth of the recession, the Colombian economy slowed to 0.9 percent—compared to -13.6 percent in Chile, -0.6 percent in Mexico, or -4.3 percent in Bolivia. Furthermore, Colombia's conservative economic management kept inflation relatively low, never reaching over 30 percent throughout the 1980s; something that could not be said of Argentina, Brazil, Bolivia, and neighboring Peru and Venezuela. In the 1986–89 period the economy recovered with an annual average growth rate of 4.5 percent.

Although the coffee boom in 1986 helped move the economy out of the recession, export diversification policy found new sources of export revenues in mining, hydrocarbons, and other nontraditional goods such as flowers and textiles. In 1986, coffee accounted for over half of the country's exports; in 1990, petroleum and derivatives accounted for 27.6 percent, followed by coffee with 19.8 percent and coal at 7.7 percent, gold 5.5 percent, and nontraditional goods at 37.6 percent.[11] The steady expansion in exports was largely to the United States, but

Germany, Japan, The Netherlands, and Venezuela were also important markets.

A Self-Sustaining Economic Growth Model?

Colombia survived the 1980s without rescheduling its external debt, overcoming a steep recession at the beginning of the decade, and sustaining a positive growth rate. Although estimates of growth were forced downward in 1990 to 2.5 percent, Colombia appears to be the exception to the rule in Latin America. In many respects, it has achieved self-sustaining economic growth. Is Colombia a model for other countries in Latin America searching for the fast-forward button? The answer is no—Colombia's economic path is unique and cannot easily be recast and imposed elsewhere. At the same time, there is perhaps greater hope for Colombia maintaining a fast-forward motion than in neighboring Venezuela.

The strength in Colombia's economy in the 1990s is that export growth is a key factor in maintaining growth, the government's fiscal accounts are in good shape, and the country's political elite has a consensus that ongoing economic reform is necessary for their country to compete in international markets. While these trends were already in motion during the Barco administration in the late 1980s, the reform process gained considerable momentum under the Gaviría administration and continued under Ernesto Samper Pizano, who assumed the presidency on 7 August 1994. Gaviría launched five major areas of reform (the Apertura program), that sought to improve Colombia's international competitiveness:
- eliminating import quotas and reducing effective tariffs from 44 percent in 1989 to 11.6 percent in 1992;
- removing foreign investment controls;
- increasing independence for the central bank;
- privatizing state enterprises and financial institutions;
- and reducing restrictive labor practices.

The Colombian government did implement a number of the reforms. Previously required authorizations for imports were abolished and nontariff barriers to trade were dismantled for 97 percent of all imports.[12] Furthermore, tariff scales were cut from 44 percent in 1989 to 11.6 percent in 1991 with the exception of automobiles, while the import surcharge was reduced from 10 percent to 5 percent. Although Colombia still has certain protectionist barriers in place, there has been a considerable dismantling of the old trade regime.

One of the major areas cited by Colombian businessmen as an impediment to expanding trade was the foreign exchange control system that was initially put in place in 1967.[13] To prevent capital flight, Colombian authorities restricted the holding of hard currency to the Central Bank, which then functioned as the intermediary between Colombian businesses and the outside world. This system led to many abuses and a number of large Colombian firms established offshore shell corporations in such places as the Cayman Islands, Channel Islands, and Luxembourg, where they could easily maintain dollar accounts for business. Foreign exchange controls, therefore, guaranteed that billions of dollars remained outside of the country. The Gaviría administration with Law 9 of 1991, moved to rectify the situation: foreign exchange transactions were simplified and decentralized, and financial institutions and registered foreign exchange brokers were empowered to function as intermediaries in the foreign exchange market. In a major step from the past, Colombians were finally allowed to hold foreign currency which they are free to deposit abroad or to convert into Colombian pesos.[14]

Relaxing foreign-exchange rules has helped raise Colombia's foreign-exchange reserves. These rose from $4.21 billion in 1990 to $8.6 billion in 1994. This also helped stimulate direct foreign investment in the Colombian economy, which increased from $159 million in 1988 to $1.7 billion in 1993 and around $3.5 billion in 1994.[15] While these positive trends are often proclaimed to be drug profits returning from overseas, it would be erroneous to portray all of them as being derived from illicit sources.

The Gaviría government also tackled the difficult and sensitive issue of privatization of state-owned enterprises. The scope of the program was not as large as in other parts of Latin America due to the fact that state ownership of the economy was not as extensive as it was elsewhere. Moreover, Ecopetrol (Empresa Colombiana de Petroleos) and Corbacol (Carbones de Colombia), the state firms responsible for the oil and coal sectors, were not for sale. The privatization program targeted six banks nationalized in the early 1980s, investments held by the Instituto de Fomento Industrial (a government holding company with shares in 22 firms), and companies in the telecommunications (such as Empresa de Teléfonos de Bogotá), electricity/gas, military, and port sectors.[16]

Although opposition to privatization existed and slowed the process, evidenced by a court battle instigated by dock workers and the 1992 strike in the telecommunications sector, some advances were made. In particular, three cellular telephone concessions were sold to private investors for $624 million. U.S. communications firms McCaw Cellular Communications and LCC Inc. were minority shareholders and held operations in the Bogotá area.[17] In 1994, it was announced that the government planned to sell its share of CARBOCAL, the world's largest open-pit coal mine.

The opening of the Colombian economy and the sale of state-owned enterprises was reinforced by improvements in foreign investment laws. In particular, regulations pertaining to portfolio and direct investment were relaxed: in 1991 legislation was passed that provided equal treatment of domestic and foreign investors. Additionally, the Foreign Investment Statute of Colombia eliminated the requirement of receiving prior approval from the National Planning Department for almost all foreign investments. Moreover, financial reforms improved the accessibility of Colombian company shares on the bolsa in most industries except for a select few: national defense and security, and toxic waste management companies.

Labor reform was enacted in 1990 when the Colombian Congress reformed labor regulations. In particular, rules pertaining to severance pay were modified, making employers contribute to a severance fund that reduced the retroactive nature of severance liability under the previous law.

The Gaviría administration continued the reform process in 1992 and 1993. The government announced plans to construct three types of duty-free zones—industrial, technological, and tourist—to help stimulate the economies of five areas of the country while increasing exports. These zones were earmarked for Cartagena, Pozos Colorados, the Morrosquillo Gulf in the department of Sucre, Ladrilleros on the Pacific, and an area of the Colombian Amazon that was not identified.

Ernesto Samper, who narrowly defeated Andrés Pastrana by less than 2 percent in a second round vote in June 1994, succeeded President Gaviría in August 1994.[18] Samper campaigned as a progressive who understood the pressing need to solve Colombia's social problems, while his opponents portrayed the Liberal candidate as an old-fashioned "tax and spend" populist.[19] The elections were largely peaceful, punctuated by only a few isolated guerrilla attacks on polling stations—none of which were fatal. In sharp contrast to the 1990 elections, none of the candidates for president were assassinated.

While indicating that the economic reform policies would generally continue, President Samper and his Liberal Party administration promised a softening of the economic reform program and an increase in social investment through the use of revenues generated by the Cusiana oil fields. In particular, the new administration pledged to augment the construction of low- income housing and improve the national infrastructure.[20] Other priorities included further integration of Colombia into the international community, the promotion of exports, and ongoing efforts against the drug trade.

The Coca and Guerrilla Equations: Tough Hurdles

Any assessment of Colombia's economic future cannot ignore the issue of the drug trade.[21] Indeed, the illicit trade in cocaine, marijuana, and, most recently, heroin, has made Colombia infamous in many law enforcement agencies around the world as a major source of illegal drugs. It was also a factor in the 1994 presidential election when allegations were made that a Cali cartel leader agreed to donate $3.75 million to Samper's campaign—a charge that was immediately denied.[22] The issue of the Samper campaign's alleged involvement in taking drug money would not disappear as reflected by the charges in 1995 against Fernando Botero Zea, Samper's former campaign manager and appointed defense minister. By 1996, the matter had mushroomed to include members of the cabinet, as well as multiple finger-pointing across Colombia's political landscape. Not only was Samper under siege, but also Colombia's relationship with the United States. In a psychological blow in 1996, Washington refused to "certify" Colombia under the annual U.S. International Drug Cooperation Review.

Yet, the view that the drug trade is *the* Colombian economy misses the fact that the legal Colombian economy is dynamic and can be regarded as significant. What is the overall impact of the illicit drug trade on Colombia? Is it a hidden sector of the economy that provides the country with a twisted advantage vis-à-vis the rest of Latin America?

Estimates of the amount of money raised by the illicit drug trade vary considerably as do considerations of the impact of the trade on Colombia's economy. At the low end of the scale, some analysts argue that only around $200–300 million of drug money returns annually to

Colombia and the impact on the domestic economy is not entirely positive. According to Miguel Urrutia, a Colombian economist, the *narcotraficantes* have a tendency to launder their profits through contraband, sometimes in the form of high-cost luxury goods such as fast cars, large haciendas, and sports teams.[23] At the higher end of the scale, estimates range from $2 to $4 billion of drug money returns to the country. According to estimates from the Banco de la Republica (the central bank), the amount of drug money returning to the country could have ranged from $600 to $800 million in 1989.[24] This amount of money, it is contended, keeps the wolf of fiscal bankruptcy outside the door, allowed Colombia to avoid rescheduling its external debt in the 1980s, and has greatly pushed along economic expansion even when the rest of Latin America slowed considerably as in the early 1980s. The truth is probably somewhere in the middle.

The negatives of the drug trade on the economy are measurable. While there is little doubt that narco-dollars flow back into the country, the power and influence of the drug *capos* is ultimately disruptive. Drug money purchases of contraband goods undermine local industries; the violent nature of the cartels contributes to the country's political turmoil and scares away foreign investment; the drug trade's smuggling element complicates the shipping and passage through customs of Colombian exports in many key markets; and the corrupting influence of traffickers on the political system erodes public confidence in the government. According to Colombia's then finance minister, Rudolf Hommes, foreign investment in Colombia would be 25 percent higher if murders and kidnappings by the guerrillas and drug traffickers did not exist; yet, it is estimated that $1 billion is already being spent annually fighting the drug war.[25]

Ultimately, drug money and its investment must be considered as a highly volatile source of funds not tied to licit markets and economies, vulnerable to international law enforcement measures, and nontaxable for the Colombian government. The Colombian government's war on drugs represents an ongoing high security cost to the state, diverting funds that could be well-utilized for infrastructural and educational improvements. For example, although late in admitting it, the drug trade is contributing to a growing problem of local consumption, and in remote regions of the country has contributed to the disruption of Amerindian society.

Another negative impact of the drug trade is the devastating assault it has conducted against the legal system. From the mid-1980s to November 1991, a total of 235 judges were murdered by drug traffickers and paramilitary death squads, including several supreme court justices, an attorney general, and a minister of justice.[26] Pay for judges is poor, protection easy to penetrate, and facilities lacking. According to one source, judges receive 400,000 new cases a year and are able to process only 70,000; one in 1,000 crimes is punished.[27] The weakening of the judicial system either through *plato* (silver) or *pluma* (lead)— bribery or assassination, is an ongoing and serious problem. As Carlos Arrieta et al. noted: "A public employee is a person who cannot resist the pressure exerted by drug traffickers. The economic power of the traders of illegal drugs, compared with low salaries of state employees, breaks down any attempt at control."[28] All of these factors contribute to the deterioration of the investment environment and constantly threaten a breakdown of law and order in the country.

While the drug trade casts a shadow over Colombia, it would be erroneous to leave the impression that blows have not been struck against the drug capos. The Medellín cartel, which actively sought to disrupt Colombian society by an all-out campaign of violence against the state, has been broken, with at least two of the major leaders, Pablo Escobar and José Rodríguez Gacha ending their lives in a hail of gunfire. In 1995, efforts against the Cali cartel resulted in the arrest in June of Gilberto Rodríguez Orejeula, one of that group's alleged leaders.[29] Yet, skeptical observers—in the U.S. Congress and among U.S. law enforcement agencies—continue to question the over-all viability of Colombia's anti-drug efforts.

While the drug trade usually captures the headlines in North America and Europe, Colombia has another hurdle—its various guerrilla movements, which field around 8,000 guerrillas. Leftist guerrillas, such as the Revolutionary Armed Forces of Colombia (FARC) and National Liberation Army (ELN), have continued to target foreign investors for kidnappings and assassinations, while the country's oil industry is repeatedly attacked. The latter offers a soft target due to the nature of pipelines stretching for miles. The Cano-Limon oil pipelines have been a particular favorite of guerrilla bombings. *Semena* magazine, Colombia's leading newsweekly, asserts that the FARC and ELN extort at least $200 million annually from rural businesses, levy taxes on coal and gold production, and provide paid guard services to cocaine and heroin laboratories.[30] The link to the drug trade is significant in the 1990s because it is lucrative, imposes no ideological conditions, and can replace the former suppliers of economic resources for terrorists, namely the Soviet Union and the Eastern bloc, which have disappeared with the end of the Cold War.[31]

Colombia's guerrilla movements emerged in the 1960s and 1970s, in part spinoffs of the Cuban Revolution and the exclusive nature of the National Front's political system to anyone outside of the Conservative and Liberal parties. Although thousands of guerrillas have been brought back into the formal political system by negotiations, established parties, and won seats in congress, a certain hardcore movement refuses to surrender their goal of radically transforming Colombian society into a Marxist-Leninist state. Ongoing attacks by far right paramilitary groups, sometimes working with local military forces against union leaders, leftist politicians, and intellectuals, reinforce the guerrillas' penchant to seek a violent solution.

To address some of the guerrillas' grievances as well as to open the political system, the Gaviría administration moved to rewrite the 1886 Colombian constitution and make it more democratic and inclusive. The Gaviría government felt that restructuring Colombia's economy and opening the political system to those elements who felt excluded, like the guerrillas, was a critical task. Gaviría strongly believed that the political system as it stood was not representative of all Colombians.

A special election was held in December 1990 to form a 73 seat constituent assembly. With a strong showing from the Alianza Democrática-M-19 (the party of former guerrillas in M-19) and the traditional parties, the laborious process of penning a new charter for the country commenced. By July 1991 Colombia had a new constitution. This provided the legal framework for much of the economic reform process. On the political front, decentralizing political power, embarked upon in the late 1980s, extended the direct vote of governors and mayors to the regions and municipalities, positions previously appointed by the president.[32] It was felt that a more open economy and political system would undermine the cause of the remaining guerrilla forces in the field.

Evidence to the contrary came in November 1992 when leftist guerrillas stepped up their attacks on the government. In one round, 30 bombs were detonated across Colombia, killing at least nine people and wounding sixty. Targets included public buildings or banks in

Bogotá, Medellín, Cucta, Armenia, Pereira, Turbo, and other cities. This was soon followed by a raid in which twenty-six policemen guarding oil drills in the countryside were killed.

The government's response was to declare a national state of emergency for 90 days. Under this writ Gaviría prohibited radio and television from interviewing guerrillas and drug traffickers, foreign companies would lose their contracts with the government and be prohibited from doing business in Colombia if they were proven to have paid ransoms, and security was increased for members of the armed forces and police. Responding to the situation, Gaviría stated: "One cannot make peace with those who have abandoned the ideal of revolution for a juicy bank account based in kidnapping, drug trafficking, extortion and murder."[33] In many respects, Colombia's guerrilla movements had become business concerns in their own right, integrating illicit activities with licit, in a parallel fashion to the drug traffickers with whom they are ideologically far apart.

Despite the more mercenary aspects of the guerrilla movements, the Samper administration indicated in 1995 that it was prepared to negotiate and would not discuss such issues as drug trafficking and kidnapping that would condemn the talks before they even started. Moreover, some analysts believe that the guerrilla groups, such as FARC, would prefer to lay down their arms, if the country's political system, dominated by the Liberals and Conservatives, could make a space for them in Colombia's political life. Alfredo Molano, a sociologist and specialist on Colombia's guerrilla conflicts noted: "What the guerrillas want is a true opposition party and that respect for their level of influence be guaranteed."[34] The path to the emergence of a new recognized political party, representative of the guerrillas, will clearly be a difficult goal to reach, considering the lucrative illicit businesses that will have to be sacrificed and the probable opposition of the more entrenched conservative groups in Colombia, some of which have access to paramilitary squads willing and able to kill leftist politicians.

The combination of the drug trade and guerrilla activity continue to hinder Colombia's ability to fully benefit from foreign investment as well as from developing its substantial oil potential in the 1990s. Insecurity remains a major problem. This has resulted in the practice of quiet affiliation with local Colombian firms, appointing local managers to avoid risks, and holding shareholders meetings outside of the country. In 1992, security organizations reported more than 500 kidnappings by common criminals or guerrillas.[35] As one company official declared in March 1992 of the security situation: "That continues to be the determining element in a foreign investment. Putting it on a scale, I would say that violence weighs 100 percent while the stability of the rules of the game, profitability or market conditions weigh in at about one half."[36] According to one estimate, if Colombia did not have the violence problem, its economy would be growing at rates of 8 to 9 percent annually.[37] Security concerns were echoed by a U.S. company, Political Risk Services, which noted in November 1991: "The new constitution gives more power to the Congress, but the biggest threat to the continuation of the leadership of President César Gaviria Trujillo is the possibility that he might be assassinated."[38] Fortunately, Gaviría survived and was able to pass the presidential sash to this successor in 1994.

Clearly, the violence related to the drug trade and guerrilla insurgencies are substantial obstacles that neutralize the best efforts of the government to open the economy and transform its structure. While a number of Latin American countries have managed to attract a considerable amount of foreign investment in the early 1990s, Colombia's share remains modest—relatively small compared to the billions of dollars pouring into Mexico, Chile, and Argentina. By the mid-1990s, there were even some suggestions that the combination of drugs and guerilla violence, coupled with the political paralysis of the Samper administration, was dampening further the business and foreign investment climate.

Colombia's Regional Integration Effort

Colombia in the late 1980s and early 1990s embarked upon policies that sought to promote regional economic integration. Although the creation of a free-trade area with Venezuela proved a disappointment in 1994 and 1995 due to problems in Caracas, other agreements are opening new trade opportunities. Even the agreement with Venezuela initially witnessed an increase in trade which would provide a stronger foundation for a time when the economy in the neighboring country recovers. Colombia has also been active in promoting a free-trade pact with Chile and working with the Andean Pact (Colombia, Venezuela, Ecuador, Bolivia, and Peru) and the G-3 (Colombia, Venezuela, and Mexico) to enhance trade relations. Further afield, Colombia maintains ongoing discussions with the United States on a wide number of trade issues and in February 1994 Gavíria made an official visit to Japan seeking major infrastructure investment required to exploit the recent petroleum discoveries.[39]

One of the major influences in moving Colombia to become more actively engaged in regional economic systems has been the creation of NAFTA. While this influence should not be overstated, neither should it be understated. Colombia's minister of foreign trade, Juan Carlos Calderon, commented in 1992 that NAFTA was positive "because when the process of integration is completed, the United States and Mexico will be able to concentrate more closely on the Initiative of the Americas."[40] The Colombian minister was also blunt in noting what the stakes were in not joining the economic integration movement: "If countries do not integrate, they will be left behind."[41]

Although the atmosphere has cooled somewhat since Samper replaced Gavíria and Clinton replaced Bush in the United States, the Miami Summit held in December 1994 held out some promise that momentum for regional economic advancement will be maintained. Yet with delays in Chile's chances of becoming the fourth member of NAFTA by the late 1990s, the entire regional integration process slowed down. Mexico's peso crisis in 1994 within two weeks of the Miami Summit set the schedule back. And perhaps most significantly, Colombia's hopes for regional integration have always run up against the political reality in Washington which has assigned to drug policy cooperation considerable salience.

Can Colombia Compete?

The process of opening the Colombian economy and developing greater integration raises questions about competitiveness. One result of the free-trade agreement with Venezuela was the purchase of Banco Tequedama in Colombia by Venezuela's Banco Construcción and the purchase of shares of Banco Ganadero by Venezuelan investors. Yet, not all Colombian firms are buy-out candidates. Briefly consider Bavaria, Colombia's large food conglomerate.

Anyone travelling to Colombia and has a thirst for a good beer is familar with the Bavaria brand name. The company was founded in 1930, is headquartered in Bogotá and has a near-monopoly over the production and distribution of beer in Colombia. Can Bavaria compete in world markets? Taking into account its holdings in Cervecerias del

Ecuador as well as its investment (22 percent) in a major Portuguese brewer, Central de Carvejas SA, the Bavaria group has an installed capacity of 34.6 mm hecoliters per year—a figure which puts the company as the fifth largest brewer in the world behind Anheuser Bush, Miller, Heineken, and Kirin.[42]

While Bavaria represents one of Colombia's competitive corporate giants (and there are others such as Cadenalco in retail and Cartón in forestry products) that is capable of competing internationally, other Colombian firms are known to foreign investors. One such corporation is Financiera Energetica Nacional (FEN), the government-owned energy sector financial institution, which issued dollar-denominated bonds in the U.S. market in 1994. FEN was established in 1982 to finance the electricity sector and was charged by the government in 1990 with supervising the sector's financial and operational reforms. With $1.7 billion in assets at the end of 1993, FEN is one of the country's largest financial institutions.[43] Significantly, the Colombian company has a BBB—from Standard & Poor's, which makes its investment grade one of the few in Latin America.

Another dimension of Colombia's ability to compete in international markets is its sizeable supplies of oil and gas. While hydrocarbons represent a double-edged sword in development as reflected by Venezuela's dependence on oil, Colombia thus far appears to be managing its oil wealth in a better fashion. What makes Colombia's hydrocarbon riches important is that, after Venezuela and Mexico, it is Latin America's largest oil exporter to the United States. That is a significant turnaround for a country that only a decade prior was a net importer. Considerable exploration was conducted in the early 1990s by the private sector which found Colombia more attractive after the government opted to bear more of the cost of oil exploration and development, while indicating that it was planning a series of tax breaks.[44] One of the largest projects in the oil boom is the $7 billion development of the Cusiana and Cupiagua fields. Undertaken by a consortium of foreign firms and Ecopetrol, these fields hold 2.1 billion barrels in proven oil and gas reserves, with a probable further 3.9 billion barrels waiting to be discovered.[45]

The surge in the hydrocarbon industry represents an opportunity for the Colombians. The ongoing guerrilla insurgencies are a threat to oil pipelines, while the so-called war tax of $1 a barrel on production to help the government fight the guerrillas has made Colombia questionable to some foreign investors. The Colombian government is reconsidering the war tax and has indicated that more funding will be channelled into social spending, a demand often made by leftist guerrillas. Furthermore, Colombia must also act to make certain that foreign investors continue to be interested in their market—without competitive inducements, many of the former Soviet republics in Central Asia, China, Vietnam, and Cuba are now open for foreign oil exploration. Consequently, Colombia's oil industry can help maintain a healthy pace of economic growth, but will have to be more pragmatically managed, taking into consideration an eventual settlement with guerrillas and rising international competition.

Conclusion

Colombia has opened the electoral process to a greater body of its citizenry and liberalized substantial sectors of the economy. A great strength to Colombia has been and continues to be its fiscal conservatism, which has contributed to its ability to stave off the worst excesses of the 1980s debt crisis and assisted the ensuing structural adjustment. Yet, Colombia's advances have been slowed by the ongoing domestic violence and corruption related to the narcotics trade, revolutionary movements, and right-wing paramilitary gangs. One offshoot of the drug trade could be an appreciation of Colombia's currency vis-à-vis the U.S. dollar, which could have negative implications for the competitiveness of Colombian exports. It should be remembered that part of Colombia's economic strategy carrying it forward into the next century is export-driven. Ultimately, failure to address the local violence/security problems will overshadow the positives of a leadership consensus on an export growth strategy, the abundance of natural resources (oil, coal, and timber), energy self-sufficiency, and a talented economic elite.

Notes

1. World Bank, *World Development Report 1994* (New York: Oxford University Press, 1994): p. 166.
2. Miguel Urrutia, "On the Absence of Economic Populism in Colombia," in *The Macroeconomics of Populism in Latin America*, eds. Rudiger Dornbusch and Sebastian Edwards (Chicago: University of Chicago Press, 1991), p. 370.
3. Ibid., p. 378.
4. Robert H. Dix, *The Politics of Colombia* (New York: Praeger, 1987), p. 35.
5. Ibid.

6. Ibid., pp. 41–42. The rest of this paragraph is based on this source.
7. John D. Martz, "Contemporary Colombian Politics: The Struggle Over Democraticization," in *The Colombian Economy: Issues of Trade and Development*, eds. Alvin Cohen and Frank Gunter (Boulder, Colo.: Westview Press, 1992), p. 22.
8. Ibid., p. 63.
9. Urritia, "Absence of Economic Populism," p. 379.
10. World Bank, *World Development Report 1988* (New York: Oxford University Press, 1988), p. 224.
11. Latin American Investment Securities Limited, *Colombia: A Look at the Stock Market and Economy* (March 1992): p. 14.
12. Latin American Investment Securities Limited, *Colombia*, p. 17.
13. For further information see Robert Grosse, "Colombia's Black Market in Foreign Exchange," *World Development*, vol. 20 (August 1992), pp. 1193–1207.
14. Latin American Securities, *Colombia*, p. 17. Law 9 of 1991 means that a Colombian resident may freely buy and sell income in foreign currency from services rendered, sales of goods and services to tourists, and donations that do not exceed $20,000. Also see Jorge Lara-Urbaneja, "New Rules," *Latin Finance* (May 1991): p. 61.
15. International Monetary Fund, *International Financial Statistics December 1994* (Washington, D.C.: International Monetary Fund, 1994), p. 172.
16. Latin American Securities Limited, *Colombia*, p. 17.
17. Lowell Fleischer and Eduardo Lora, *Colombian Policy in the Mid-1990s* (Washington, D.C.: The Center for Strategic and International Studies, 1994), p. 38.
18. For more information on the 1994 Colombian elections see Lowell Fleischer, *CSIS Western Hemisphere Election Study Series* (Washington, D.C.: The Center for Strategic and International Studies, 1994).
19. Fleischer and Lora, *Colombian Policy*, p. 7.
20. Suhas Ketkar, Walter Molano, and Dorothy Ellis, "Colombia: A Post-Inauguration Update," *CS First Boston Economist Department Update* (November 1994): p. 2.
21. For an excellent discussion on why Colombia became a major drug source country see Francisco E. Thoumi, "Why the Illegal Psychoactive Drugs Industry Grew in Colombia," *Journal of Interamerican Studies and World Affairs*, vol. 34, no. 3 (Fall 1992): pp. 37–64.
22. Fleischer, *Colombian Elections*, p. 5.
23. Miguel Urrutia, "Cost-Benefit Analysis of the Drug Trade for Colombia," a paper presented for the Project on Hemispheric Cooperation of Drug Abuse and Trafficking, Woodrow Wilson Center, Washington, D.C., April 1990. For further information on the drug trade in Colombia, see Scott B. MacDonald, *Dancing on a Volcano: The Latin American Drug Trade* (New York: Praeger, 1988); Scott B. MacDonald, *Mountain High, White Avalanche: Cocaine and Power in the Andean States and Panama* (New York: Praeger, 1989); and Rensselaer W. Lee III, *The White Labyrinth: Cocaine and Political Power* (New Brunswick, N.J.: Transaction Publishers, 1989).
24. See Hernando José Gómez, "Notas sobre el tamano del Narcotráfico y su impacto economico," *Revista Ecónomia Colombiana* (Bogotá) (February 1990). Also see Scott B. MacDonald, "Colombia," in *International Handbook on Drug Control*, eds. Scott B. MacDonald and Bruce Zagaris (Westport, Conn.: Greenwood Press, 1992): pp. 162–63.
25. U.S. Drug Enforcement Administration, *Colombian Economic Reform: The Im-*

pact on Drug Money Laundering Within the Colombian Economy (Washington, D.C.: Drug Enforcement Administration, September 1994), p. 7.

26. Ken Dermota, "Traffickers' Death Threats Shake Colombia's Tottering Judicial System," *Times of the Americas* (November 27, 1991): p. 4.

27. Tina Rosenberg, "Latin America's Magical Realism," *The Wilson Quarterly* (Autumn 1992): p. 66.

28. Quoted from Andrés Benavente Urbina, "Drug Traffic and State Stability," *North-South* (August–September): p. 35.

29. Joseph B. Treaster, "Arrest in Colombia Heartens U.S.," *New York Times* (June 12, 1995): p. A8.

30. James Brooke, "Guerrillas Are Imperiling Colombia's Oil Bonanza," *New York Times* (November 10, 1992): p. A3.

31. Benavente Urbina, "Drug Traffic and State Stability," p. 36.

32. See John Dogas, et al., *Los caminos de la descentralización: diversidad y retos de la transformación municipal* (Bogotá: Departamento de Cienca Políca, Universidad de Los Andes, 1992).

33. "Emergency Is Declared in Colombia," *Washington Post* (November 9, 1992): p. A16.

34. Howard LaFranchi, "Latin America's Longest Guerrilla War Tries a Short Cut," *Christian Science Monitor* (March 2, 1995): p. 7.

35. "Colombia Violence Scares Off Investors," *Times of the Americas* (March 18, 1992): p. B4.

36. Ibid.

37. Ibid.

38. *LDC Debt Report/Latin American Markets*, (November 11, 1991): p. 7.

39. Fleischer and Lora, *Colombian Policy*, p. 35.

40. Hector Hernandez M., "NAFTA Expected to Stimulate Foreign Trade," *El Espectador* (August 16, 1992) FBIS-LAT: and in (September 15, 1992): p. 27.

41. Ibid.

42. Latin American Investment Securities Limited, *Colombia*, p. 27.

43. Standard & Poor's, *Emerging Markets October 1994*, (, 1994): p. 86.

44. James Brooke, "Colombia Becoming an Oil Power in Spite of Itself," *New York Times* (March 20, 1995): p. D2.

45. Ibid.

6

Mexico: From Trendsetter to . . .

Mexico entered the 1990s as a major trendsetter in Latin America's economic renaissance. There was a mood of confidence about the country's reforms, mirrored by an inflow of capital, falling inflation (8 percent in 1993 and 1994), fiscal consolidation, and a Brady Plan debt deal which reduced Mexico's debt burden. Even Mexico's political environment appeared to open up slowly. Confidence in Mexico was reinforced by the passage of the North American Free Trade Agreement (NAFTA) in the three member countries. Mexico also joined the ranks of the Organization for Economic Cooperation and Development (OECD)—the first Latin American nation to do so. Economic data also appeared to sustain the claims of optimists: in 1992, Mexico's per capita income—measured at purchasing-power parity—was in the same range as that of the lower-income OECD countries, such as Greece, Portugal, and Turkey.[12] There was a feeling that Mexico had truly exited the lost decade of the 1980s and had discovered the path forward into "industrial country status." As one U.S. business guide to Mexico boldly gushed: "Mexico has emerged from the developmental Dark Ages and entered a new frontier."[3]

Such prognostications proved inaccurate. The ill-conceived December 1994 peso devaluation and the ensuing crisis in early 1995 brought back many of the old concerns about Mexico's political and economic systems. Symbolically, the traditional May Day rally and parade of the "official" union movement in Mexico City's Zocalo was cancelled in 1995 for the first time in modern Mexican history because of concerns that it could turn into a demonstration against the government's economic policies. Yet, despite certain similarities between 1982 and

1994—a current account crunch, buildup of short-term debt obligations, and turning to the United States for assistance—there have been significant structural changes in the Mexican economy. For starters, Mexico is now part of a dynamic North American community through NAFTA. In the 1990s, the Mexican economy is far less dependent on oil exports (manufacturing accounts for a much larger percentage of exports and GDP) and the economy is considerably more open. Additionally, the political system presiding over the national economy is gradually opening. Although this is a difficult process, Mexico's ability to move to a higher stage of development depends on political reform—without it, societal tensions are likely to increase and function as obstacles to economic objectives.

What went wrong in Mexico, once a star pupil of economic change in Latin America? Has the reform process been entirely derailed or was it ever on track? Without a doubt the changes occurring in Mexico in the short term are problematic, but in the long term they are likely to prove the reformers were moving in the right direction, albeit in a zig-zag fashion, not in a straight line—the way forward complicated by political issues such as resistance to political liberalization and corruption. If the reconfiguration of Mexico's socioeconomic system fails (which threatened to in December 1994), the implications of failure will stretch well beyond its borders into the United States and will add a negative tone to the developmental debate in the rest of the Americas.

The Path of History

Despite all of its problems, Mexico in the 1990s is a nation on the move. It has the eleventh largest population in the world, with more than 80 percent of its people under 40 years of age, and is the thirteenth largest in the world in terms of geographic size. Mexico is the planet's fifth largest oil producer and possesses the world's seventh largest oil reserves. Beyond its hydrocarbon resources, Mexico has an abundance of silver, lead, zinc, and copper. It is also a major agricultural producer and now ranks among the lower tier of the most industrialized countries. Multinational corporations, from Ford to Mitsui and British Telecom, actively ply Mexican markets alongside local private sector companies, such as Bimbo, Vitro, and Cementos de Mexico (Cemex). The reality of the 1990s is that Mexico is in the process of reshaping its economy. To appreciate the rites of passage that this country of almost 100 million people is undergoing, it is helpful to understand the distance travelled in terms of both historical evolution and perceptions.

Mexico's history is rich with the rise and fall of great peoples and personalities. Before the arrival of the Spaniards, Aztecs, Mayans, and Olmecs developed advanced civilizations based on astronomy, agricultural cultivation, and architecture, including the construction of the pyramids. The arrival of the Spanish in 1519 swept away much of the local Indian civilization, but the people endured providing an important element of the Mexican population throughout the centuries to follow. A long period of Spanish colonization eventually led to independence in 1821.

Mexico's birth as a nation was marked by a lengthy period of domestic political turmoil, foreign interventions (French and U.S.) and spurts of economic growth followed by difficult adjustments to changed international market conditions.[4] Although Mexico survived its early decades as a sovereign nation, it lost considerable territory to an aggressive United States and was dogged by adverse political conditions: Mexico had 50 governments in the thirty years to 1850. At midcentury the first of Mexico's modern social reformers appeared, led by Benito Juárez. Promoting modern forms of federalism and civil rule, Juárez rallied the republican cause in the 1860s in a bitter civil war that also featured European armies and princes. This turbulent tenure was followed by the rise of General Porfirio Díaz, who assumed the presidency in 1877 and dominated national politics until 1910. Still debated among historians of Mexico, Díaz shaped Mexico's modern economic structure, being responsible for centralizing administration and putting in place an industrial infrastructure that included a railway system of 12,000 miles, a communications network, and shipping ports.[5] Additionally, Mexico's banking system was established and capital (both local and foreign) flowed into agriculture, mining, and industry.

The "Porfiriato" was one of the most stable periods of Mexican history until the mid-twentieth century. However, as Mexico's economy robustly expanded, the gains were enjoyed largely by a small class at the top of the societal pyramid. An emerging middle class who favored a democratic form of government and a more equitable distribution of wealth soon collided with the Porfirian state. Francisco Madero eventually emerged as a leader of the liberal opposition, ultimately forcing Díaz off into exile. Madero was elected president in June 1911, but in 1913 he was assassinated and Mexico was engulfed in a bloody and bitter civil war that lasted in varying forms into the 1920s. The revolution was an extreme uprooting of Mexican society and, for a time, succeeded in the mobilization of large segments of the rural and Indian population into the political process.

By the early 1930s, a new Mexican polity reconfigured around what eventually emerged as the Institutional Revolutionary Party (Partido Revolucionario Institucional or PRI).[6] The presidency of Lázaro Cárdenas (1934–40) in retrospect stands as the high mark of the revolutionary phase of modern Mexican history and continues to frame part of the national debate over development in the 1990s. The legacy for the PRI was a commitment to: (1) strong Mexican nationalism; (2) a central role for government in economic management; (3) an elevation of the political role of labor, both in industry and agriculture; (4) a preference for agricultural development over industry; and (5) limits, if not outright suspicion, of foreign investment.

Cárdenas set to work to reconfigure Mexican politics in such a fashion that his vision of Mexico would take root and survive his tenure. Consequently, the PRI was consolidated into three broad sectors—labor, farmers, and white collar workers. Labor, in particular, made gains in the political front, especially with the creation of the first national labor confederation, the Confederacion de Trabajadores de Mexico (CTM). The military was politically defanged and made responsible to a civilian president who was elected for a 6 year nonreelective term. Cárdenas also greatly augmented the government's role in the economy. The railways were nationalized in 1937 and the oil industry was expropriated from U.S. and British owners in 1938.

The government's movement into the role of economic player also had its roots in the international environment in which the Cárdenas administration found itself in the mid-1930s. While Cárdenas' personal convictions were important, external factors cannot be overlooked. As Mexican historian Ramon Eduardo Ruíz commented: "The Great Depression, as it did everywhere else, invited government intervention to restore the economy; the Republic's maladies, its helmsmen believed, exceeded the therapeutic powers of the private sector. The failure to comply with the ideals of 1917, as the Six-Year Plan documented, required government action, a view shared by reformers unhappy with the capitalist model, who wanted to revive stipulations in

Article 27 for Mexican ownership of natural resources."[7] Hence, the nationalization of the oil industry.

During the presidencies of Manuel Avila Camacho (1940–46) and Miguel Alemán (1946–52), Mexico's political economy was dominated by the PRI, which in turn dominated the society through the state apparatus. Confrontation was often avoided through an active policy of co-optation into the official political system. Elections were held on schedule, but were not competitive with the PRI winning all federal, state, and almost all local contests. Mexico's political system had evolved into an authoritarian regime, characterized by limited pluralism in which the PRI determined who participated within the system and who had the right to organize and compete for power.[8] Economic growth occurred, but some of the gains made by the lower classes under Cárdenas were reversed and business groups sought to regain a degree of lost power.

A period of consolidation ensued under the presidencies of Adolfo Ruíz Cortines (1952–58), Adolfo Lopez Mateos (1958–64), Gustavo Díaz Ordáz (1964–70), and Luis Echeverría (1970–76). Mexico became one of the fastest growing economies in the world. From 1950 to 1981, the real GDP expanded at an average rate of 6.6 percent annually.[9] Although the population growth rate was a high average of 3.4 percent for the same period, real GDP per capita raced ahead by 3.2 percent yearly. Mexico's dynamic economic expansion, especially from 1950 to 1975 was also achieved in the absence of high inflation and a relatively stable exchange rate.

The "stabilizing development period" of 1955–70 was based on a strategy of state-led import substitution, combined with highly restrained credit and fiscal policies implemented by technocrats of Mexico's powerful Central Bank and Treasury.[10] This meant that from the mid-1950s Mexico began to increase nominal tariff levels and impose quantitative import restrictions and domestic price controls.[11] The lower wage earners, who had lost ground in the 1940s, caught up in the 1950s and made improvements in the 1960s and early 1970s.

During the stabilizing development period, four sets of tacit understandings guided the political economy.[12] First and foremost, macroeconomic policy authority would be centered within the treasury and Bank of Mexico, two institutions which gained a privileged place within the state apparatus. Secondly, in exchange for the creation of a "suitable investment climate," business groups would maintain a relatively low profile in national politics, depending on political access to informal contacts and consultations conducted through officially recognized associational organizations. Thirdly, in exchange for collaboration in the task of social control and electoral mobilization, the leadership of the CTM and other allied groups of unionized workers would be provided with the support of the state and expanding material resources to distribute to their members. Fourthly and finally, the state would deal with resource limitations by shifting spending priorities and attention away from social services and distributive programs aimed at the PRI's traditional peasant constituency toward the expanding urban underclass. This system worked well through the 1950s and 1960s.

The Descent

Mexico's success was not without serious underlying problems. In the late 1960s the structural problems inherent in the import-substitution strategy began to cause concern among policy planners. The growing imbalance in the nation's external accounts was particularly threatening: despite rapid import substitution and export growth that was large by Latin American standards, the growth of imports outstripped that of exports.[13] This was reflected by the deterioration in the current account balance of payments which went from a deficit of $261 million in 1961 to a little over $1 billion in 1970.[14] One factor was the increasing inability of agriculture to keep apace with the needs of a growing population, which meant that growing food imports contributed to a widening external account deficit.

Equally disturbing for the nation's governing elite was the political crisis of 1968 that coincided with Mexico's hosting of the Olympic Games. This political crisis undermined the core notion that the PRI represented a national consensus on the direction of the country. The stabilizing development mode of economic strategy, which had led to a boom in the 1960s, weakened the economic position of the lowest echelons of the peasantry and new groups of marginal and urban poor.[15] Both groups felt politically peripheralized. Elements of the middle class also felt excluded from the political process. As Roberto Newell and Luis Rubio commented: "The majority of middle-class members, intellectuals, students, and business people were altogether relegated to a nonparticipant role, one that simply did not fit with either their social or economic status or their aspirations."[16] The bloody crushing of student demonstrations in the summer of 1968 was politically embarrassing to the Díaz Ordaz government and revealed the regime's political decay. The crisis helped foster further discontent in Mexican society.[17]

When Luis Echeverría came into office in 1970, he sought to reverse what was a politically and economically deteriorating situation with his policy of "shared development." In contrast to the idea of the previous decade which was growth first and distribution later, shared development was a growth strategy that incorporated marginal groups into the process of development. This meant the new government gave priority to energy, agriculture, and public welfare, and relied to a large extent on public expenditures to achieve its goals.[18]

The Echeverría administration soon had considerable problems: substantial state-demand stimulus, egalitarian wage policies, and excessive monetary expansion. Collectively, these factors translated into a short spurt of rapid economic growth followed by high inflation and balance-of-payments problems. Failure to implement tax reform in 1972 only weakened the government's ability to deal with the widening range of problems. Additionally, the private sector was not enthralled with the shared development strategy that redistributed income away from profits and the pockets of the privileged elite. Capital soon began to seep out of the country to the United States, while the value of the peso plummeted after being set afloat in August 1976. By the end of his *sexenio*, Echeverría was confronted with a broad-based economic crisis and was forced into the distasteful act of signing an IMF stabilization agreement. At the same time, Echeverría's political reforms (which were not extensive) exacerbated the situation as they allowed more voices to be heard, but failed to concede any real power to groups outside of the PRI. In a sense, the growing forces outside of the PRI state were challenging the right of a centralized, small, and authoritarian bureaucracy to determine the direction of the country.[19]

Echeverría passed on to his successor José López Portillo (1976–82), a Mexican economy that was at its lowest point since the 1930s. López Portillo adopted "an alliance for production" approach that entailed an accord among the major social groups to stimulate production and encourage economic recovery, with an explicit sacrifice of workers' incomes. It was critical to pull the various sectors of the economy's leadership together. Relations between the private sector and Echevarría had been bitter in 1975, while the organized labor and business sectors were badly polarized by the crisis. These measures, however, failed to address the structural problems in the Mexican economy, which were partially defined as inefficient industry protected behind substantial trading barriers. Corruption in both the government and the labor unions also were factors that stalled initiatives and left the Mexican economy handicapped in international competition.

The structural problems confronting Mexico were observable in the external accounts. After an initial import contraction and an improvement on the current account deficit in 1977, the deficit widened substantially through the end of the decade. A complicating factor was the second oil price shock in 1979–80, which made oil-rich Mexico look more creditworthy to many international banks. Hence, many of the economic reforms that were needed to address structural inadequacies were postponed because of renewed access to outside credit. Both the international bankers and the Mexican government had a hand in pushing the country into the debt trap that was to mark the rest of the 1980s. As long as oil prices were high (which they were from 1977 to 1981), Mexico could continue to maintain a facade, partially paid for by foreign creditors.

The economic problems were further complicated by the disappearing consensus within the PRI. In the cabinet, two broad lines of thought conditioned the policies that emerged—the "liberal-rationalists" and the "nationalistic-populists." The former favored "the creation of an economically sound platform of sustainable growth, placing large emphasis on capital formation and the growth of productive employment, strong collaboration with the private sector, and a rapid growth in trade and other economic relationships with the rest of the world." The nationalistic-populists, in contrast "aimed to create a strong and independent Mexico with a dominant public sector, a subordinate private sector, and a broad popular alliance as strong and backing."[20] These two contending forces within López Portillo's cabinet reflected radically different philosophical ideas about the future of Mexico. As the president played one group against the other, Mexico zig-zagged through the end of the 1970s. Tough decisions were often carefully avoided to obscure the lack of unity, a situation briefly papered over by the oil bonanza.

The anti-Washington flavor of López Portillo's foreign policy undermined Mexico's position with North American creditors who were increasingly suspicious of their southern neighbor. Mexico City's perceived siding with the leftist forces in Central America as well as the maintenance of open ties to Castro's Cuba were used as flashpoints for U.S. conservative constituencies in any discussions about Mexico. Relations were also complicated by the rise of drug trafficking through Mexico.

A steep hike in interest rates in 1981 and 1982 and a deep recession in the United States, Mexico's major export market, meant that efforts to revitalize the Mexican economy soon faltered. When oil prices fell in 1982, the combination of heavy interest payments and a trade deficit left the country with a massive $16.1 billion current account deficit, which Mexico's foreign exchange reserves of $828 million could not match. Recognizing the myriad nature of these problems before year-end, the López Portillo administration was forced to seek a rescheduling of its external debt of $78 billion in August 1982.[21] In September, López Portillo, as a parting shot, announced he was nationalizing the banking system and imposing exchange controls. The reason for expanding the state's purview was that flight capital was bleeding the Mexican economy dry and the banks were a major force in facilitating that action. By nationalizing the bank sector and imposing exchange controls, the government would gain command of capital and terminate outflow. Mexico had entered the difficult decade of the 1980s.

The New Economic Direction

Mexico faced considerable gloom when Miguel de la Madrid assumed the presidential sash in 1982: the country was in a deep economic crisis, Mexico's international reputation as a creditworthy nation was low, and there were considerable questions about the PRI's legitimacy to govern the nation. To make matters worse, longstanding allegations of widespread corruption at the most senior levels of government began to emerge publicly. In fact, there have been claims that Echevarría's and López Portillo's "takes" involved billions of dollars. Although much of the blame for Mexico's economic crisis in 1982 was the result of the import-substitution strategies implemented over thirty years, the more immediate problem was macroeconomic mismanagement.[22]

Despite the dire national straits, President de la Madrid implemented many of the economic reforms that would help guide Mexico out of the mire. Throughout his tenure, de la Madrid confronted the daunting challenge of how to jumpstart the economy and reform it for long-term sustained growth, while maintaining the PRI's unquestioned political dominance. At the same time, de la Madrid and his leaning toward the liberal-rationalist wing of the PRI accelerated the polarization within the ruling party. This reconfiguration of the PRI, with the nationalistic-populists losing ground, also had reverberations in Mexican society, as an initially small segment of the middle class began to identify with what would be far-reaching, yet in the short-term, painful changes.

De la Madrid inherited a relatively closed economy and the magic of economic growth was elusive. As 1982 ended, the real GDP actually contracted by 0.6 percent. The debt crisis clearly was a major burden. The process of stabilization and structural adjustment that loomed ahead—the shift away from a dependence on oil exports to a more broad-based economy—would be difficult and would take several years. This was apparent in 1983, when the economy contracted by another 4.2 percent. At the same time, inflation rose to 27.9 percent in 1982 and to 59 percent in 1983.

The de la Madrid administration sought to adjust the economy to the constraints imposed by a sharply curtailed flow of external credit and by the burden of servicing the external debt. At the same time, Mexican policy makers were aware that the state's large role had to be either scaled down or abandoned. This required a reduction of the public sector and shifting the burden of providing many services to the private sector, which in turn would have to become more efficient and competitive as a foundation for sustained economic growth and financial stability. Efforts were also made to improve the administration of public-sector spending, augment public-sector income through tax reform and higher prices for public-sector goods and services, and reorganize the public administration to enhance efficiency.

Tax reform implemented by the de la Madrid administration (and continued under Salinas) was one of the most essential stabilization measures taken. Without fiscal stabilization there would be an ongoing general lack of confidence in public finance and interest rates would probably remain high. Undertaken as part of a larger package to bring the budget under control, tax reform had three components:

widening the tax base to include all economic activity in the Value Added Tax (VAT) (thus taxing the agriculture and transportation sectors previously excluded); simplifying the tax structure which made the system moderate as it relied on a few, broadly administered taxes (though tax rates were cut substantially, the widened base assured that there was no net loss of revenue); and enforcing tax laws through a focus on auditing current returns as opposed to returns from previous years.[23]

Implementing these policies was not easy due to residual resistance by those elements of society immediately affected, such as the bureaucracy and elements of the industrial class that benefitted from protectionism. However, Mexico had little choice—it could either continue to founder or could seek to undertake a difficult, yet necessary structural adjustment to a more open and competitive economy.

From 1983 to 1987 the Mexican government sold, liquidated, or transferred 130 state-owned firms, which assisted the de la Madrid administration in its reduction of the public-sector spending as a proportion of GDP from 32 percent in 1981 to 19 percent in 1987, excluding interest payments on foreign and domestic public-sector debt.[24] The de la Madrid administration also restructured laws concerning majority-owned foreign investment in pharmaceuticals, tourism, hydrocarbon technology, computers, and high technology, and brought Mexico into the General Agreement on Tariffs and Trade (GATT).

Although de la Madrid did not abandon Mexico's independent stance in international affairs, his administration was notable for toning down anti-U.S. rhetoric. The combination of market-oriented economic reforms, and a less-critical foreign policy in most cases, provided an improved environment for cooperation in a number of areas. This would be essential when de la Madrid passed the baton on to his handpicked successor, Carlos Salinas de Gortari in 1988.

De la Madrid ended his tenure with a sense of uncertainty. Despite his efforts to stabilize the economy and to begin structural adjustment, his administration had been dogged by problems: the 1985 earthquake that destroyed large sections of Mexico City, the 1986 oil price collapse, the 1987 stock market collapse, and the 1988 Hurricane Gilbert. The combination of these factors squeezed the Mexican economy and left the next administration to obtain a $3.5 billion bridging loan from the United States to address pressure on the external accounts.

Passing the Baton: From de la Madrid to Salinas

De la Madrid stabilization and structural adjustment reforms came close to sinking the chances of Salinas winning the presidential elections. While the PRI maintained control over the nation's political apparatus, the party threatened to fragment. De la Madrid's policies reduced the numbers of PRI faithful in the bureaucracy and many of those linked to the status quo, sometimes referred to as the *dinosaurios* (dinosaurs), resented the new world they were being dragged into. Additionally, as part of the burden of stabilization and structural adjustment fell on the workers, a number of PRI-affiliated labor unions were increasingly hostile to de la Madrid and the reform process. The working class was particularly hard hit by the rise in inflation, which reached a peak of 132 percent in 1987. Although de la Madrid had negotiated the Economic Solidarity Pact with labor and business in December 1987, the serious deterioration in real salaries created a wider pool of dissatisfied Mexicans who were ripe for an anti-PRI protest movement.

While elements of the labor movement and dissident members of the PRI in the bureaucracy would not have represented a serious challenge to Salinas' bid for the presidential sash, the emergence of the left-of-center Cuauhtémoc Cárdenas Solorzano as an opposition presidential candidate was an outright call to arms for those threatened by the changes. The son of Lázaro Cárdenas, Cuauhtémoc was a Priista associated with the *Corriente Democratica* (Democratic Current), but left when he felt elements of the party were not being adequately represented. In particular, he favored democratic reforms beyond the new electoral code of 1986—something that the party hierarchy found unsettling.

Taking dissident populist Priistas with him when he left the party to form the Democratic Front for National Reconstruction (Frente Democratico Nacional or FDN), Cárdenas soon forged an alliance of disgruntled government bureaucrats, dissident PRI-affiliated labor unions, scattered leftist groups, and some peasant groups. (Part of this coalition became the Partido de la Revolucion Democratica or PRD.) With this far-ranging alliance, Cárdenas mounted a substantial challenge almost overturning the reformist PRI's applecart.

Cárdenas represented a force to turn back the clock to the pre-1982 debt crisis, and, to some, back to the populist years of his father, Lázaro. As Mexican historian Ramón Eduardo Ruíz noted of the Cárdenas challenge: "Its appeal was a populist one, beyond parties, aimed directly at the people, demanding respect for the Constitution and promising to revive the spirit of social justice. Instead of austerity, Cárdenas talked about money for education, public health, and programs of benefit to campesinos and small farmers. For labor, he asked for just wages and unions free of *charros* (appointed bosses); the middle class, he pledged honest elections, independent political parties, democracy, and legislation to protect 'authentic' Mexican industry. Payments on the foreign debt, which he likened to a yoke on Mexico's neck, he thought misguided, calling for a postponement as well as a cancellation of part of it."[25] In terms of foreign policy, Cárdenas was strongly opposed to U.S. involvement in Central America and favored negotiations among the various political groups to resolve their own disputes.

For a people whipsawed by the debt crisis-induced austerity of de la Madrid, the call to tune out the outside world, in particular the United States and the commercial banks, and to spend money on Mexicans, sounded positive. Moreover, Cárdenas was a decidedly more interesting political personality than Salinas. The latter was regarded as a technocrat and supported ongoing structural adjustment, further changes and the unknown future that potentially threatened (or least the opposition played up) the Americanization, not the modernization of Mexico. Yet, Cárdenas represented a turning back of the clock: foreign investment was largely negative and technology transfer did not enter the equation, capital for the many egalitarian programs he promised did not exist in a readily accessible form, and the "just wages" he would obtain for Mexican labor would run up against the reality of international comparative advantages.

Over charges of electoral fraud, Salinas won the 1988 contest with an official 50.7 percent of the vote compared to Cárdenas' 31.1 percent and 17 percent for Manuel Clouthier, the candidate for the right-of-center PAN (National Action Party or Partido Accion Nacional). The PAN had been the major opposition to the PRI throughout most of the 1970s and 1980s. Despite the questions over whether or not Salinas won a clearcut electoral majority, it was the first time that the PRI "allowed" such a substantial opposition vote to become public, and opposition parties gained seats in both the federal and regional legislative bodies in substantial numbers for the first time. PRI maintained 260 seats in the Chamber of Deputies, compared to PAN's 101 seats and the FND's 138.

Salinas quickly consolidated his position by arresting the corrupt and powerful head of the petroleum workers union, Joaquín Hernandez "La Quina" Galicia, and indicting several wealthy business leaders who were "tainted" by the October 1987 stock market collapse for fraud. The former action served notice to establishment dissidents that their opposition would no longer be tolerated.[26] An underlying concern for Salinas and his close associates was public discontent with the PRI's corruption, especially the alleged pillaging of public funds conducted by former presidents Echeverría and López Portillo.

Salinas accelerated Mexico's economic restructuring. His administration soon made further reductions in public-sector spending, redirected public-sector spending to improve the country's industrial infrastructure (especially in the areas of electricity, oil, transportation, and agriculture), and continued tax reforms. Inflation was also brought under control by maintaining a tight monetary policy, falling from 114 percent in 1988 to 11.9 percent in 1992, and 8 percent in 1993.

There was also ongoing success in diversification of exports. One of the problems that had led to the external account crisis in the early 1980s was the overdependence on oil exports. In 1981, petroleum accounted for 75.5 percent of all exports; by 1989 it had fallen to 34 percent.[27] Other exports, including coffee, shrimp, automobiles, electronic parts, and textiles rapidly expanded in significance making up the difference.

TABLE 6.1
Mexico's Exports and Percentage of Oil Exports, 1982–1991

Year	Total Exports (in US$ billions)	Percentage of Oil Exports
1982	21.2	76.5
1983	22.3	69.2
1984	24.2	67.5
1985	21.7	66.6
1986	16.0	38.4
1987	20.7	40.1
1988	20.6	32.0
1989	22.8	34.1
1990	26.8	36.0
1991	27.4	32.1

Source: International Monetary Fund, *International Financial Statistics Yearbook 1991* (Washington, D.C.: International Monetary Fund, 1991), p. 523. 1991 estimate from Chartered WL *Developing Country Investment Review*, Spring 1992, (London), p. 24.

Some analysts have argued that Mexico's diversification was partially or largely a function of price rather than a movement away from dependence on oil exports, and that it would be a "terrible misunderstanding" of Mexico's "progress" to overstress diversification.[28] Such a view precludes gains in nonoil export sectors, especially manufacturing and agriculture. According to the OECD, manufacturing accounted for 59.2 percent of Mexico's total exports in 1991, while the structure of production was dominated by services (59.7 percent), followed by industry of which 23 percent was manufacturing.[29] The following table reflects the growth of nonoil exports.

TABLE 6.2
External Sector Exports (% of growth)

	1986	1987	1988	1989	1990	1991
Exports	3.2	10.1	5.8	2.5	3.5	5.1
Nonoil Exports	41.0	23.7	15.2	7.5	12.0	12.8

Source: Nora Lustig, *Mexico: The Remaking of the Economy* (Washington, D.C.: Brookings, 1992), pp. 40–41.

Privatization has been one of the cornerstones of the Salinas administration. During the de la Madrid administration, 653 state-operated firms were sold, leaving Salinas with 502 companies.[30] In a December 1988 *Wall Street Journal* interview, Salinas signaled that his administration would continue the privatization program and was willing to sell any remaining firms that did "not represent a strategic responsibility for the Mexican state."[31] Teléfonos de Mexico (Telmex), the state-owned telephone company, was sold in 1990 and shares quickly gained in value on the New York and Tokyo stock exchanges. This was followed by the sale in 1991 of some of Mexico's largest banks, including Banamex and Bancomer. Even some highway construction was privatized. In November 1991, Salinas sent a constitutional amendment to Congress which would allow individual ownership of *ejido* lands owned by the state and farmed collectively.

The economic reform measures of de la Madrid and the acceleration of the process under Salinas made Mexico the ideal first country to settle its external commercial bank debt with a "Brady Plan" deal. Mexico also benefitted from its strategic proximity to the United States and that country's security concerns vis-à-vis its southern neighbor. Despite the reform efforts of the early and mid-1980s, Mexico's external debt remained significant. In 1988, it stood at a daunting $107.5

billion and the debt service was close to 30 percent of all exports of goods and services. Mexico's debt-for-equity program helped reduce the burden, but it still remained high. Moreover, Mexican authorities grew concerned that the debt-for-equity program would help fuel inflation, which was 132 percent in 1987 and 114 percent in 1988. While an innovative Mexican bond deal was done in February and March 1988 by J.P. Morgan, it failed to bring about the needed and hoped for large-scale debt reduction.[32] Another option was needed—the Brady Plan.

The Brady Plan was announced in March 1988 by then U.S. secretary of the treasury, Nicholas Brady. It sought to provide debt reduction for those countries that made significant progress with structural adjustment and reforming the economy. The Brady Plan was the successor of the Baker Plan, which had guided U.S. debt policy throughout the 1980s and relied on new lending to help heavily indebted developing countries that were following free-market reform programs to grow out of the debt trap. The Brady Plan, in contrast, helped heavily indebted countries to line up funds with the IMF, World Bank, the Inter-American Development Bank, and other donors to buy back the country's debt at a discount.

Negotiations to settle Mexico's external commercial bank debt began shortly after the Bush administration entered office in late 1988. After a lengthy period of discussions, an agreement was hammered out between Mexico and its 450 commercial banks in 1990. Under this agreement, the commercial banks agreed to receive Mexican government bonds in return for reducing Mexican debt principle and interest. The Mexican bonds were backed by $3.5 billion that were used to purchase U.S. Treasury zero-coupon bonds and by an additional $3.5 billion held as a guarantee of eighteen months of interest payments by Mexico. The accord's significance was that by converting almost half of Mexico's floating interest-rate debt to fixed-rate securities, the Latin country's vulnerability to future interest rate shocks would be reduced and the net credit transfer—net borrowing minus interest payments—would be reduced from an average of 5.75 percent of GDP in 1982 through 1988 to around 2 percent annually.[33]

Although the actual size of debt reduction disappointed some, Mexico's Brady Plan deal was a trendsetter for other countries that followed, including Argentina, Brazil, Venezuela, Poland, the Philippines, and Nigeria. More importantly, the deal helped Mexico's balance-of-payments and provided greater confidence in Mexico among investors and creditors. This was crucial for Mexico as its companies began to reenter international capital markets in 1991 after a long absence.

Although the Salinas administration's success in getting a Brady Plan deal for external debt enhanced Mexico's attractiveness to foreign investors, the process of opening the country to outside investment was well under way before the December 1990 commercial bank accord. The de la Madrid administration saw the merit in opening up the country to greater outside investment. Hence, he began the process and his successor accelerated it.

Foreign direct investment (this does not include portfolio investment) was an area of success for the Salinas administration. It was recognized that foreign investment could provide the means of employment, help finance development, stimulate technological enrichment of Mexican industry and agriculture, and open doors to foreign markets. Mexico, in the 1970s, had been characterized by heavy regulation vis-à-vis foreign direct investment (FDI), which was due to the import- substitution model's protectionist nature. With the external debt crisis of the early 1980s, the policy environment changed: while Mexico had enjoyed easy access to international capital markets in the late 1970s during the oil boom, in 1982 credit evaporated.

Mexico was forced to adjust to new realities. To stimulate diversification away from oil dependency, FDI became more attractive as a means to develop tourism and industry. During the last years of the de la Madrid administration greater flexibility was given to majority ownership of Mexican firms by foreign companies. One avenue for this was the debt-for-equity conversion program. This allowed holders of Mexican commercial bank debt to exchange that debt for local equity holdings. The program gave foreign firms access to ownership in selected sectors of the economy. In the early years of the debt-to-equity program, not all sectors were open to foreign ownership and the desire was to channel foreign investors into areas that did not threaten Mexican national interests. The Salinas administration, however, gradually widened the area under the purview of debt-for-equity conversions. Table 6.3 reflects the development of the program in the mid-1980s to early 1990s.

TABLE 6.3
Debt-to-Equity Conversion, 1986—First Quarter 1991
(in millions of U.S. dollars)

Year	Total
1986	413
1987	1,680
1988	1,056*
1989	532
1990	435
1991	—

* Does not include an estimated $6–8 billion related to prepayment at a discount of private sector debt since the August 1987 signing of an agreement to restructure foreign-exchange risk coverage trust-fund debt. Source: International Monetary Fund, *"Private Market Financing for Developing Countries,"* cited in *IMF Survey,* February 3, 1992, p. 41.

The need for capital to finance the new Mexico rising from the debt debacle was greater than what could be offered through debt-for-equity conversions. Moreover, it was acknowledged that a considerable pool of Mexican flight capital, estimated between $25 to $80 billion, remained in overseas accounts.[34] Consequently, in the late 1980s the Salinas administration overhauled old laws and introduced new ones concerning FDI in Mexico as part of a broader reform program. The results were impressive: while FDI ranged between $700–900 million in the 1970s and stood at around $2–2.5 billion through the 1982–88 period, FDI inflows gained momentum in 1989 and 1990, posting $4.5 billion in 1990. The privatization begun in 1990 of the Mexican government telephone company, Teléfonos de Mexico, S.A. (Telmex), demonstrated that foreign investors had growing confidence in the new Mexico. FDI inflows in 1991 were a record $9.8 billion. Under the new FDI code enacted by the Salinas administration, the gauge of foreign investment expanded beyond tourism into manufacturing and other services, such as telecommunications and commercial activities. The stock market, having been rediscovered in the late 1980s, served as an increasingly significant entry point for foreign capital wishing to invest in the Mexican economy.

To the Salinas administration, debt-for-equity offered some relief from the debt burden, but other, less inflationary options beckoned, such as Mexico City's *Bolsa de Valores* or the stock market. The Bolsa is electronic, plugged into the world economy and becoming an integral part of the country's domestic resources to locally raise capital. In 1981, it had a market capitalization of $10.1 billion; by September 1991, that figure stood at an impressive $76.3 billion, with considerable growth occurring since the beginning of the year.[35] In many regards, it is symbolic of the new Mexico being forged. A 1992 *Euromoney* report captured the significance of the stock market: "Companies are rushing to take advantage of cheap equity capital after a year in which the Mexican stock market has been one of the world's top performers. The Mexican Market Index began in 1991 at around the 600 point level, and had broken through 1,300 points by November, putting the market on a prospective price/earnings (p/e) ratio of around 12."[36]

Backed by the success of the stock market to generate capital, the Salinas government moved to privatization of Mexico's banking sector in 1991. While other sectors were privatized earlier, the decision to move ahead with the country's eighteen commercial banks carried political baggage, considering their nationalization in 1982. From mid-1991 to March 1992, the Mexican government launched into privatizing twelve banks in competitive auctions for $10 billion (a relatively high price considering the assets being sold), largely to Mexican buyers due to laws that prevented majority ownership by foreigners. Mexicans were concerned that their banks lacked the necessary sophistication to compete with foreign banks—many Mexican banks were inefficient, used outmoded technology and had excessive personnel.

The modernization of the Mexican financial system echoed within the government. In March 1992, the Finance Secretariat (SHCP or *Hacienda*) formally assumed the responsibilities of the Budget Secretariat (SPP), which left the former the sole branch of the federal government responsible for financial planning, supervision, budgetary control, governmental accounting, and the National Statistics Institute (INEGI). The merger of the two secretariats caused the elimination of one cabinet-level position, seven director generals, a principal administrative officer, and around 200 middle-management positions.[37] More significantly, the merger of the two departments streamlined government operations and the decision-making process. It also greatly enhanced the authority of the Finance Secretary, overturning the decision of López Portillo in 1977 to divide budget and finance activities, in part to weaken those bureaucracies.

Another area of financial reform was the enhanced autonomy of the Bank of Mexico, the country's central bank. Advanced to the Mexican

Congress in May 1993, the law provided that the Bank of Mexico receive new authority to protect its policies from politically motivated manipulation, and future presidential administrations and their Treasury secretaries.[38] In many respects, the Bank of Mexico began to function more along the lines of the U.S. Federal Reserve Board.

Another area that demonstrated considerable expansion in the 1980s and early 1990s was the *maquiladoras*. These in-bond manufacturing plants assemble components imported tax-free for reexport, largely to the U.S. market. Using low labor costs and easy access to the United States, the major activities of *maquiladoras* include the automotive industry, electrical and electronic goods assembly, and textiles. Most of the components for this sector are from the U.S., but Japan and South Korea are also important suppliers. Although this type of company is concentrated along the U.S.-Mexican border, *maquiladora* operations were opened in Oaxaca and Yucatan. The success of the program is partially measured by the following statistics: by the end of 1989 there were 1,795 companies in the program, compared with 588 at the end of 1984; employees numbered 437,000 in 1989 compared to 225,000 in 1984; and total net *maquiladora* exports rose from $851 million in 1982 to $3.1 in 1989.[39] Despite the turmoil following the 1994 peso devaluation, this sector continued to be an important Mexican platform for exports.

Agricultural Reform

The Mexican government also addressed agricultural reform. In the early 1990s, the farm sector was characterized by a lack of capital and shrinking farm size. While the country's farm sector accounted for 30 percent of the population, it constituted only 8 percent of GDP. The World Bank in 1991 estimated that 11 million of 27 million rural Mexicans live in extreme poverty and noted that "lagging rural and agricultural development" were at the root of the problem.[40] Hence, the Salinas government focused on agriculture as a sector in need of reform.

Reforming Mexican agriculture is a highly political issue. From the beginning of the Mexican Revolution, ownership of land was important to the rural population. The PRI's power in the countryside was founded on its control over distribution of land. Land disputes were settled by the agrarian reform ministry, which meant the PRI. While the status quo gave the PRI control over the rural population, making them a base of support, the difficult conditions in the countryside and the lack of efficiency in cultivation cannot have been missed by even casual observers. It was no mistake that many of those fleeing to the United States came from the poor southern and rural parts of Mexico.

Under the laws derived from the revolution, every Mexican was granted the right to land and a system of *ejido* or communal farms was created. These provided a place where the farmers managed their state-owned plots of land, but shared capital expenditures and equipment. In the early 1990s, *ejido* farms accounted for close to half of all Mexican farms. The paradox of the system was noted by journalist Damian Fraser: "The *ejido* system, and the commitment to land reform, has provided land for millions of Mexicans. But it discouraged private investment in agriculture and the creation of larger, more efficient farms."[41] A major problem was that *ejido* farmers were prohibited from selling, renting, and mortgaging their land. Lacking collateral, the *ejido* farmers were consistently confronted with an inability to raise capital, a situation worsened by the external debt crisis in the 1980s.

The Salinas government announced in November 1991, and implemented in early 1992, reforms in the agricultural sector that were meant to rectify the situation. Simply stated, the *ejido* system as a constitutional right to own land was eliminated. *Ejido* farmers went from being land-users to land-owners, a significant transformation. While the state role was trimmed from being a distributor of land, private sector farmers gained new powers: those that created limited companies would be permitted to cultivate up to 2,500 hectares of irrigated land. Prior to 1992, they could farm only up to 100 hectares.

The government's motivation was twofold: first, it was hoped that the reforms would attract new investment and technology to Mexican agriculture and reduce poverty in the countryside; and second, by ending the *ejido* system the PRI embarked upon a political gamble of loosening its direct control over many rural areas.[42] At the same time, it is calculated that the prosperity that will be introduced will also help the PRI maintain its political support. The economic reform of creating a more efficient agricultural sector, therefore, dovetails with reforming the political system by removing one political control, while providing the means for an improved standard of living in an area long troubled. There are no guarantees that this policy will succeed, but if it does, a new class of farmers will find they also have a stake in the process of change that is shaping Mexico at the edge of the twenty-first century.

The Trade Gambit: The North American Free Trade Agreement

A key to graduating Mexico to the next level of development was the North American Free Trade Agreement or NAFTA. While de la Madrid pushed Mexico into the GATT, Salinas moved in October 1989 to create the foundations for a new partnership with the United States and ultimately, Canada. The Mexican president and President George Bush committed their governments to carry out negotiations to improve the bilateral commercial environment. This followed a trip to Europe, in which Salinas witnessed the tremendous developmental challenge facing Central and Eastern European countries. Mexico's needs were given limited attention and Salinas' agenda for a trade deal with the United States assumed a new urgency. In 1990, Presidents Salinas and Bush further committed their countries to negotiate a free-trade agreement. Canada soon joined the process, throwing open the possibility of creating a North American free-trade area.

Official negotiations for NAFTA began in June 1991, with the goal of creating a North American free-trade market of more than 360 million consumers and producers, and an annual output of more than $6 trillion.[43] The Free Trade Agreement (FTA) sought to eliminate restrictions on the flow of goods, services, and investment among the three countries.

Mexico's interest in a free-trade agreement with the United States and Canada was derived from Salinas' vision of it as an opportunity to attract foreign direct investment and, perhaps more significantly, as a means of gaining access to better technology and generating employment. There was also the growing concern in Mexico City about the emergence of trade blocs that threatened to exclude Mexican goods in foreign markets. Mexico's inclusion in its own trade bloc would provide it a steady market with two of its largest trade partners. And through a trade bloc of its own, Mexico would have greater strength in dealing with other trade blocs such as the European Union, and the Association for Southeast Nations (ASEAN). The fact that Canada and the United States had earlier (in 1989) concluded an FTA, indicated that such an accord could be achieved—the danger of not participating was to be left on the outside looking in.[44]

Selling NAFTA to the U.S. public was not an easy process.[45] It became a volatile issue in the 1992 presidential and congressional elections, and was one of the Clinton administration's first major foreign-policy tests in 1993. Opposition to the NAFTA concept also emerged in Canada and Mexico. In the United States and Canada, concerns were vocalized about the "threat" of jobs being lost to Mexico, which offers lower wages vis-à-vis U.S. and Canadian companies. Environmentalists were critical that polluting companies would seek to escape tighter regulation in Canada and the U.S. for the less sophisticated regulation and supervision in Mexico.[46] Concerns were also vocalized about political corruption in Mexico, the growing influence and links to the country's political establishment of the drug trade, and the weakness of the judicial system. Furthermore, a number of issues have remained outstanding in trilateral negotiations, such as opening up Mexico's financial sector to foreign companies. In particular, Mexico has been reluctant to open its banking sector to foreign banking interests at least until Mexican banks are strong enough to compete on an equal footing with their Canadian and U.S. competitors.

In Mexico, opposition to the NAFTA was motivated by a number of concerns, some of which mirrored those north of the border. Concerns were vocalized that by embracing North America, Mexico would soon be entirely dominated by the United States—economically, politically, and culturally. One of the leading opposition voices to NAFTA was Cárdenas, who criticized Salinas for "surrendering Mexico's sovereignty," in his eagerness to sign an agreement with the United States and Canada. The left-of-center leader also thought "political conditionality" should be attached to any NAFTA deal.[47] The thinking about political conditionality was taken from the European Union's handling of Greece's, Portugal's and Spain's memberships. The EU would not accept those countries until they had democratic governments. Mexican political analysts, like Jorge Castañeda, believed that a similar measure should be applied to Mexico to help advance their country's political liberalization.

Despite hard political lobbying against NAFTA in the United States, the agreement eventually passed in Congress late in 1993 by a surprisingly comfortable margin. It appeared that the concerns summarized by MIT economic professor Rudiger Dornbusch carried the day: "If you are concerned about good jobs at good wages, freer trade with

Mexico will deliver just that; more good jobs for Americans as Mexico prospers and becomes a major market for American goods in the way Spain did for the European Community. If you are interested in better living standards in Mexico, freer trade will deliver that too: Mexicans would become more confident as their country is integrated into a North American institutional setting that makes slipping back into populism and chaos very unlikely. And if you are interested in political opening in Mexico, ask yourself whether there is a better way than free trade and economic integration to swamp Mexico with the democratic American way?"[48]

A New Revolution?

Mexico's economic revolution in the late 1980s and 1990s was predicated on the notion that a more open, competitive Mexico was the only way to modernize the nation. While foreign investment was part of this shift, there was a growing awareness that technology could be tapped and used to make Mexico more competitive vis-à-vis other developing countries and even the industrialized countries, like the United States and Canada. As President Salinas stated at Harvard University on 10 April 1991: "The change in attitude and the need for a new outlook are based on sound reasoning. One reason is the demand by Mexicans for opportunities that will enable them to raise their standard of living after years of stagnation and inflation. The other is the conviction that the changes in the world make it imperative for countries that seek to endure in the coming century to improve their ability to compete, seek new forms of association and carry out the internal changes that will allow them to participate in the globalization of the economy."[49] In a sense, Salinas recognized that without the assimilation of new technology, Mexico would become a "slow" technology economy, destined to fall further behind the developed community of nations.

Elements of Mexico's political leadership recognized the necessity of shifting from a traditional mistrust of the North and other outside influences, to joining the North and using that opportunity to break from the past. Mexico's acceptance of the high-technology challenge and assuming the burden of transforming Mexican society is observable in the increasing utilization of computers, turning to the stock market as a high-technology option to further stimulate and channel

foreign investment and raise local capital, and developing new strategic alliances (or purchases). This acceptance reflects a new thinking
and process of conducting business in the 1990s. Anyone with a broader
grasp of world affairs can readily observe such links occurring in other
parts of the world, as in the case of Spanish and Portuguese companies
developing strategic alliances with German, French, and British firms.
Economic integration, strategic alliances, and the rapid assimilation of
new technology are reflections of a changing world order, but one that
offers a differentiation between those countries that pick up the game
and those that do not. Elements of Mexican society appear to have
picked up the new game.

The shift to cross-border alliance building and mergers between
U.S. and Mexican companies has already commenced. One of the best
known is Vitro's ownership of Anchor Glass. The Monterrey-based
glass manufacturer purchased Anchor Glass, a Florida-based manufacturer of soft drink containers, in 1989. Anchor Glass also has long-
term contracts with U.S. beer refiner Anheuser-Busch for beer containers. Through the Anchor purchase and others (Latchford Glass),
Vitro emerged as a significant force in the United States controlling 27
percent of the glass container market by 1991.[50] As a result of financial difficulties in 1994 and 1995, due in part to rising competition
within the U.S. market, Anchor Glass was supported by its Mexican
parent, which infused $50 million equity into the company in 1995
and provided additional liquidity in the form of a $20 million letter of
credit.[51]

Vitro demonstrates that despite the troubles in Mexico's economy,
a Mexican company can compete on a global basis. Vitro is one of the
three largest glass container manufactures in the world and the largest
publicly traded industrial firm in Mexico. It has a strategic alliance
with luggage manufacturer Samsonite in the United States, and is busy
expanding into the rest of Latin America. The Mexican firm owns
glass facilities in Guatemala, Costa Rica, and Peru. In 1995, it purchased Vidrio Lux, Bolivia's largest glass producer (with around 70
percent of the local market).[52]

Vitro is not alone in the quest to create alliances or expand operations over national borders. Breadmaker Grupo Bimbo works with
McDonald's; the retailer, Cifra has signed up with the Wal-Mart chain
of department stores; and Grupo Nacional Provincial, Mexico's largest
insurance company, entered a strategic alliance with Liberty Mutual

Insurance Company of Boston. Cifra is Mexico's leading retail chain and has a lucrative concentration in Mexico City. The alliance with Wal-Mart has clearly given the Mexican firm a comparative advantage over many of its local competitors. Partially because of its growing international savvy and linkages, Cifra gained special attention on the Mexican stock exchange. Along with Grupo Bimbo and Cifra, Grupo Carso has joint ventures with a number of U.S. firms, and Coors has an equity stake in Mexican brewer Femsa.[53]

Cemex is another Mexican company, like Vitro, that has expanded overseas. It owns cement and concrete distribution firms in Texas and California, including its consolidated company Sunbelt Industries, as well as operations in Spain. Other Mexican companies with U.S. ownership include Banomex with the California Commerce Bank (bought in 1978); Bancomer with Grossmont Bank (in 1982); the Chihuahua Group took control of M Bank in El Paso, Texas (in 1990); and Transportacion Maritima Mexicana, a private merchant marine line, bought a rail line and loading facility in Texas.

Mexico's advances also include plugging into technology. Although considerable problems exist and should not be casually shrugged off, Mexico is becoming part of the information age. One example is telecommunications. One of the hottest stocks on the New York Stock Exchange in 1991 was Telmex. The reason for this is because the company, now privatized, has aggressively pursued the improvement of Mexico's telecommunications system. Telmex's expansion program is to digitalize 50 percent of telephone exchanges and 65 percent of the long-distance networks by the end of 1996. Other plans include extending phone service to all villages and towns of more than 500 people.

Although many phone users in Mexico still have reason to complain about service, the country's telecommunications network is expanding daily and in a relative sense, it is far better than in many other countries. New lines are constantly being installed and Telmex is seeking to improve customer service. One example of doing so has been to install monitoring devices that will allow the company to gauge the progress of quality improvement more closely.[54] Telmex has also developed alliances with Southwestern Bell and France's Cable and Radio to improve its access to technology and ability to compete, especially as it looses its monopoly on long-distance communications in 1996.

Another example of Mexico's plunge into the high technology game was in November 1991. SERTEL, Mexico's computer reservation system, entered into an agreement with SABRE, the American Airlines travel information service, to market SABRE under the service name ALON.[55] The arrangement would observe SABRE, tailoring information for the Mexican traveller, while SERTEL would market the system. Additionally, the two companies agreed to eliminate the language, data transmission, and other obstacles that have hindered Mexican travellers in the past. SERTEL's chief executive officer, Alex Heida noted, "This contract is an example of Mexico's commitment to upgrading its data communications infrastructure."[56]

Mexico's travel industry sits on the verge of sweeping transformations in the 1990s. Currently, the majority of Mexican travel agencies do not utilize computer reservation systems. SERTEL is expected to be on the cutting edge of those transformations. Established in the 1970s by the Mexican government, the travel company was privatized in 1990 and has assumed the role of plugging Mexico's tourist industry into the informatic age. At the same time, the SERTEL-SABRE alliance is not alone in the Mexican market. WORLDSPAN, the merged computer- reservations system of Delta Airlines, Trans World Airlines, and Northwest, is also actively plying the Latin American country's market.

Mexico's financial services (despite the setbacks in 1994 and 1995) are also plugging into new technology. Badly in need of updated computer application, many Mexican banks are scrambling to implement new, automated forms of banking. The awareness that technological modernization is critically needed if Mexican banks are to compete with foreign institutions has prompted a quest for strategic alliances. For example, Banamex, the country's largest bank, acquired credit-card processing technology from Banc One of Columbus, Ohio, in preparation for the creation of a bank-card processing firm to serve Mexican and Latin American banks.[57]

The Revolution Incomplete: The 1994 Christmas Crisis

President Ernesto Zedillo was not intended to be the PRI's candidate in 1994. In March, Luis Donaldo Colosio, Salinas' choice for successor, was gunned down at a rally in Tijuana. In the ensuing chaos, Zedillo, then the campaign press secretary and a former minister for education, emerged as the candidate. In a tough campaign, complete with debate with the two other major presidential candidates (Cárdenas and Manual Clothier of the PAN), Zedillo managed to hold his own and go on to win the election in August 1994. Although there were claims of fraud, the election was regarded as relatively clean. The new president entered office on 1 December 1994, inheriting a badly fragmented political party; an economy in need of correction, in particular, the area of the current account; a population in dire need of growth and an improvement in their daily life; a simmering insurrection in Chiapas; and growing foreign-investor nervousness with political and economic trends in Mexico.

Mexico's effort of converting a developing country into an industrial one ran into trouble in December 1994 and took many by surprise despite early warnings by some. Those included Moody's Investors Service, which refused to raise the country an investment grade rating, and Washington-based Christopher Whalen, a consultant to a number of major international firms working in Mexico. As early as April 1993, Whalen's publication, *The Mexican Report* noted: "In 1993 Mexico faces much the same choice it has faced over more than a century of relying on international capital markets to finance purchases of foreign goods and services: devalue the currency or borrow further from abroad."[58] Simply stated, as the following table indicates, Mexico's widening current account balance-of-payments deficit needed to be financed either by borrowing abroad or making exports more competitive through monetary means.

However, the Mexican government postponed the devaluation in 1993 (and through most of 1994) due to concerns that such an action would undermine the campaign for NAFTA ratification, or more broadly, its claims to being an industrialized country. There were also fears of jeopardizing chances to become investment grade by either Moody's or Standard & Poor's—key to maintaining foreign-investor confidence and lowering the cost of funds raised in international markets. Moreover, Mexico's major international investment banks were careful about what their analysts wrote concerning Mexico because of concerns about harming prospects for either gaining or maintaining the Mexican government's business.

TABLE 6.4
Mexico's External Accounts, 1989–1994

	1989	1990	1991	1992	1993	1994
Current Acct.						
Bal. (US $bn)	–6.1	–7.5	14.9	–24.8	–23.4	–29.5
For Ex. Re. ($bn)	6.5	10.1	17.9	19.4	25.4	6.3

Source: International Monetary Fund, *International Economic Update, May 1995*
(Washington, D.C.: International Monetary Fund, 1995), p. 92.

On 20 December 20, the newly-inaugurated Zedillo administration announced its decision to move ahead with the devaluation of the peso. Heavy losses in international reserves were mounting, reflecting eroding foreign-investor confidence in the face of a massive current account deficit and a year of political crises. As Jonathan Heath noted: "The government had planned a soft-landing approach to correct the problem based on an increase in foreign direct investment, the obtaining of an investment grade so as to lower the country risk perception, and an eventual increase in export growth over import growth."[59]

What initially began as a widening of the exchange rate intervention band which had been in place since 1991, ended in a near currency freefall. Sailing into uncharted waters, the Zedillo administration observed an outflow of foreign capital and days later allowed the exchange rate to float. The result was that before the announcement of a recovery plan in March 1995, the peso's value plummeted by around 54 percent. As December 1994 passed into January 1995, Mexico was a country potentially teetering on the brink of running out of foreign exchange reserves with a substantial build-up of payouts looming on the horizon in the form of *tesobonos*, short-term Mexican government bonds denominated in pesos but payable in dollars. At the end of 1994, the government had $29 billion worth of outstanding *tesobonos* coming due in the upcoming months. With a large current account deficit to service and an overall balance-of- payments shifting against Mexico, foreign investors were clearly nervous about Mexico's ability to pay its obligations. By February, the United States brokered a rescue plan that ultimately encompassed $20 billion in loans and loan guarantees, and close to $30 billion in loans from the IMF and other organizations.

In March 1995, the Zedillo administration implemented a new economic program, emphasizing tight monetary and credit policies to reign in inflation which had shot upwards in early 1994, and a reduction in the current account deficit. Interest rates rose sky-high, which negatively impacted a banking sector already troubled by weak loan quality portfolios. The government, therefore, also stepped up to deal with a banking system that by May 1995 was hard-hit by the peso crisis: thousands of bank clients defaulted on corporate loans, auto-financing deals, and mortgages, with over $10 billion in uncollectible loans.[60] Throughout 1995, a number of Mexican banks threatened to fail and required government intervention to remain afloat.

Mexico's ability to survive the 1994 crisis was due to its ability to draw upon international support and the underpinning resilience of the Mexican economy. Clearly 1994 was not a replay of 1982. Significant strides had been made in restructuring and retooling the Mexican economy: since the mid-1980s the budget deficit was reduced from 9 percent of GDP to a balance; domestic markets were opened to foreign competition; foreign investors were welcomed; and a substantial privatization program was implemented. All of this helped Mexico make a significant turnaround in external accounts. As Columbia University's Michael Adler noted: "There was a massive reduction in the current account deficit, from $28 billion in 1994 to $654 million in 1995, which reduced the rate of the increase in Mexico's total external debt from 8 percent to almost zero percent."[61]

Yet an important area has been lagging—political reform. That lacuna aggravated other problems, namely current account vulnerability and the fickleness of international capital. This is evident in comparing Spain and Portugal and their membership in the European Union in 1986 with Mexico joining NAFTA—a debate used by members of the Mexican government to defend their policies of allowing sizeable current account deficits. It was argued that Mexico's current account deficits were actually a reflection of growing economic strength: Mexico had enough foreign investment to pay off the import bonanza. As journalist Peter Passell noted: "After all, Spain and Portugal ran far larger current account deficits after they joined the European Community and investors rushed to take advantage of their newly certified status."[62]

Mexico's status, and the status of Spain and Portugal at these historical junctures were radically different. The Iberian countries attracted considerable foreign direct investment during the early 1980s and less portfolio investment. Moreover, the technology did not exist then for rapid inflows and outflows that characterized portfolio capital flows in the 1990s that so traumatized Mexico. Another key factor was that the Iberian countries had emerged from authoritarian regimes (Spain, Franco, and Portugal, Salazar/Caetano) and were regarded as democratically elected governments. The ability of leaders in Lisbon and Madrid to claim political legitimacy from the population was central to supporting foreign investor confidence.

Mexico in contrast, it can be argued, is having a hard time disregarding its authoritarian past. In 1994 there were several political blows to investor confidence—the Chiapas uprising in January, the assassination of the PRI's presidential candidate Luis Donaldo Colosio and kidnapping of wealthy businessman Alfredo Harp in March, the assassination of political official José Francisco Ruíz Massieu in September, and revelations throughout the year about the penetration of drug trafficking organizations in the Mexican government. Additionally, Mario Ruíz Massieu, the Deputy Attorney General, resigned in November, making accusations of a PRI cover-up in Colosio's assassination.[63] He was subsequently arrested in the United States with suspiciously large amounts of money.

In late 1995, the overlapping investigations of the Colosio and Massieu assassinations almost appeared to converge with the arrest of Raul Salinas, the former president's somewhat extravagant brother. This triggered sharp public tension between the Zedillo government and former president Salinas, who ultimately left Mexico in public disgrace—without yet being formally linked to the assassinations. This situation and others indicated that there were ongoing divisions within the PRI's political structure, while the Zedillo government continued to have problems with its weak level of public credibility as well as an expanding political opposition on both the right and the left.[64]

The Critical Hinge of Political Reform

Mexico's political development is the critical hinge upon which the country will move. In 1979, Peter H. Smith characterized the political system as "an unquestionably 'authoritarian' regime—a regime that is characterized by 'limited pluralism' . . . and one that is identifiably and analytically distinct from democratic or totalitarian types of rule."[65] Since then, Mexico's political system has evolved, becoming more open yet maintaining certain authoritarian tendencies. As the PRI's consensus unravelled in the late 1980s, three tendencies emerged.

Cárdenas and the Corriente Democratica felt the pace of political reform should be quicker and was more important than economic reform; they departed to take their place to the left of the PRI. The more conservative status quo faction of the PRI, the *dinosaurios* did not want any surrender of power and influence, and opposed all changes; they remained and form a group to the right within the PRI.

This left Salinas and the liberal-rationalists, who favored a gradual political opening, which was complemented by economic reforms. Zedillo is probably the inheritor of this group, though he may be more politically liberal. In time, popular capitalism would have a widespread base of support from the population and the experiment with free-market economics would finally carry the country up to the next notch of development. Though never stated publicly, at times the appearance was that once a sustainable form of economic growth was reached, the Mexican people would be given full political liberty. The observation of Sidney Weintraub and M. Delal Baer is most fitting: "Electoral democracy eventually came back to Chile, and it is making inroads in South Korea and Taiwan; and it is also coming, in fits and starts, to Mexico."[66]

Although the Mexican political system is still criticized for not being fully democratic, there has been a hesitant opening. In the 1976 presidential elections, the PRI candidate won 87 percent of the vote and in 1982 de la Madrid won 68 percent, but in 1988 Salinas officially garnered a little over 50 percent and Ernesto Zedillo was roughly the same in 1994. Prior to 1988, all governors in Mexico, the majority in all state assemblies, and a majority of municipal presidencies in all states were PRI. Changes in the electoral legislation under de la Madrid and then Salinas made a degree of political pluralism possible. This was reflected in the July 1989 gubernatorial election in Baja California Norte in which the PRI lost to PAN for the first time since 1929.

It would be wrong, however, to argue that Mexico's political system has reached a state of viable openness. The challenge lies not only with the inner factions of the PRI-led political process, but also to some degree with the opposition itself. For example, there remains opposition to the sequence of economic reform over political opening, with its integration into North America and capitalist approach.

Mexican historian Ramón Eduardo Ruíz provides some insights to those in the opposition camp. Sympathetic to Lárenzo Cárdenas and his son, Cuauthémoc, he regards industrialization and the links with the United States detrimental to Mexico's interests. His view of the round of industrialization that commenced in the 1940s and continued through the 1970s is telling: "With industrialization, the dream of a bucolic, agrarian, and self-sufficient Mexico flew out the window. Instead of a 'socialist paradise,' Mexico would be capitalistic, offering freedom for private enterprise and the laws of supply and demand. The 'trickle-down' theory held sway."[67] To Ruíz, the Mexico that de la Madrid, Salinas, and Zedillo are trying to create will end in failure, perhaps launching a new revolution: "Washington's largesse, which Salinas described as a glowing victory for Mexico, won the hearts of his visible supporters, among them the three hundred or so wealthiest families, the Catholic hierarchy, much of the middle class, United States officials, and investors in accord with the government's drive to privatize the economy. The hyperbole of Salinas received enthusiastic endorsements from big business and industry, one sure sign of who benefitted from the financial accords. That applause too, reminded one of the days of Don Porfirio, whose policies incurred the wrath of the rebels of 1910."[68]

Is Mexico marching into another bloody revolution because the PRI has become a late twentieth-century version of the Porfiriato? The answer is probably not. However, political reform is essential for Mexico to move out of its economic difficulties in the mid-1990s. Jonathan Heath cautioned in mid-1995: "Mexico needs to conclude its reforms and modernization efforts, with political reform on the front burner. Unless a more democratic political system can be implemented, future devaluations and crises cannot be avoided."[69] Moreover, attention is also needed in social policies—the heavy weight of another adjustment to pull Mexico through the 1994–95 economic crisis has fallen on a population already dealing with several years of tough structural reforms.

While there is a relative consensus that political reform is necessary in Mexico, the pace and direction of Mexico's economic integration with the outside world also carries potential problems. While some concerns are related to the desire not to surrender protectionism and xenophobia, the opening of the Mexican economy and its integration to the larger world beyond does carry potential danger zones that need to be advanced upon with caution. Sylvia Maxfield noted: "Similarities among Mexico, Argentina, Chile, and Brazil suggest that international financial integration tends to divert national financial resources away from long-term investment in national industry. In all cases we see a rise in short-term financial activity that profits financiers and their industrial associates at the expense of small and medium-sized entrepreneurs and the nation's industrial base."[70] The danger is that the gains become too concentrated in the hands of a few, perhaps those close to the government, leading to charges of "crony capitalism" and corruption.

Mexico's reform process is not occurring without social pain. While poverty is found in urban settings, it is more concentrated in rural areas and the more industrial north enjoys a higher standard of living than the south. It was estimated in 1984 that between 10–19 percent of the population lived in extreme poverty.[71] Although updated data is sparse, the sharp and protracted cuts in social expenditure after 1982 hurt a sizeable segment of the population.[72] The OECD noted in 1992 that the population below the poverty line was characterized by low educational levels (either no school at all or only a few years of primary school); no social security coverage; and the worst health conditions in the total population in terms of higher infant mortality and shorter life expectancy.[73] The same group occupied housing with no water, sewerage, or electricity, while food accounts were close to 60 percent of these households' monetary expenditures. The continuing disparity between the wealthy and poor in Mexico has the potential to fuel social unrest. Moreover, poverty of a large segment of the population does little to create a sizeable internal market for Mexican goods.

Clearly, a healthy and productive population would offer more to Mexico's economic advance in the late twentieth century. The Mexican government is seeking to deal with some of these problems through its social pacts and target programs (aimed at certain groups), but the 1994–95 economic crisis greatly curtailed the government's ability to deal more comprehensively with the country's pressing social issues. Consequently, social pressures are likely to remain an ongoing political concern for Mexico into the next century.

Conclusion

Mexico in the 1990s is at a pivotal position. In many respects, it has made significant, if not revolutionary changes. Yet, considerable problems remain, the key ones being political and will take time to be solved. These include further opening the political system and dealing with corruption. The process of change remains difficult—the short-term challenges of the balance-of-payments, the peso's viability in the aftermath of December 1994 debacle—and the political reform proves that. If these challenges are successfully overcome, Mexico's long-term prospects are truly dynamic. If not, Mexico risks slipping into a deeper political crisis and many of the gains of the past will be negated. In a regional context, the implications for the United States—in the form of trade flows, immigration movements, and law enforcement pressures—would be profound. Yet, the sheer weight of the Mexican nation in U.S. strategic calculations of the early twenty-first century suggests front-rank attention by decision makers in both countries—and therefore, a relative sense of optimism in the long run.

Notes

1. Organization for Economic Cooperation and Development, *OECD Economic Survey: Mexico* (Paris: OECD, 1992).
2. Jay and Maggie Jessup, *Doing Business in Mexico* (Rocklin, Cal.: Prima Publishing Company, 1993), p. 14.
3. One of the problems the new country faced was how to manage its external debt. See Jan Bazant, *Historia de la deuda exterior de Mexico (1823–1946)* (Mexico City: El Colegio de Mexico, 1968). Worthwhile in its treatment of the French intervention see Luis Garfias M., *La intervencion francesa en Mexico: La historia de la expedicion militar francesa enviada por Napoleon III para establecer el Segundo Imperio Mexicano* (Mexico City: Panorama Editorial, S.A., 1980, and for a general treatment of the convoluted diplomacy and politics of European intervention in Mexico, see Jasper Ridley, *Maximilian and Juarez* (New York: Ticknor & Fields, 1992). On the earlier war with the United States, see John Edward Weems, *To Conquer a Peace: The War Between the United States and Mexico* (College Station: Texas A & M University Press, 1974.
4. For treatment of the Porfiriato see Fernando Rosenzweig, *Historia moderna de Mexico: El Porfiriato, La Vida Economica* (Mexico City: Hermes, 1965); and Roger D. Hansen, *The Politics of Mexican Development* (Baltimore, M.D.: The Johns Hopkins University Press, 1971).
5. For a history of the PRI's early stages and other political parties see Jesus Anlen, *Origen y evolucion de los Partidos Politicos en Mexico* (Mexico City: Texts Universitarios, 1973).
6. Ramon Eduardo Ruiz, *Triumphs and Tragedy: A History of the Mexican People* (New York: W.W. Norton and Company, 1992), p. 396.
7. Peter Smith, *Labyrinths of Power: Political Recruitment in Twentieth-Century Mexico* (Princeton, N.J.: University of Princeton Press, 1979), pp. 3–4.
8. Timothy Heyman and Pablo Riveroll, *Mexico: Emerging from the Lost Decade* (London: Baring Securities, 1991), p. 34.
9. See John K. Thompson, *Inflation, Financial Markets and Economic Development: The Experience of Mexico* (Greenwich, Conn.: Jai Press, 1972); and Alejo

Fco. Javier, "La Politica Fiscal en el Desarrollo Economico de Mexico," in *La Sociedad Mexicana: Presente y Futuro*, ed. Miguel S. Wionczek (Mexico City: Fondo de Cultura Economica, 1974).

10. Eliot Kalter, "The Mexican Strategy to Achieve Sustainable Economic Growth," in *Mexico: The Strategy to Achieve Sustained Economic Growth*, eds. Claudio Loser and Eliot Kalter (Washington, D.C.: International Monetary Fund, 1992), p. 3.

11. Robert R. Kaufman, "Stabilization and Adjustment in Argentina, Brazil and Mexico," in *Economic Crisis and Policy Choice: The Politics of Adjustment in the Third World*, ed. Joan M. Nelson (Princeton, N.J.: Princeton University Press, 1990), p. 92.

12. Jose Ayala and Clemente Ruiz Duran, "Development and Crisis in Mexico: A Structuralist Approach," in *Latin American Political Economy: Financial Crisis and Political Change*, eds. Jonathan Hartlyn and Samuel A. Morley (Boulder, Colo.: Westview Press, 1986), p. 243.

13. International Monetary Fund, *International Financial Statistics Yearbook 1991* (Washington, D.C.: International Monetary Fund, 1991), p. 532.

14. Roberto G. Newell and Luis F. Rubio, *Mexico's Dilemma: The Political Origins of Economic Crisis* (Boulder, Colo.: Westview, 1984), p. 110.

15. Ibid.

16. See Ramon Ramirez, *El movimiento estudiantil de Mexico: julio-diciembre de 1968*, 2 vols. (Mexico, D.F.: Ediciones Era, 1969).

17. Ayala and Duran, "Development and Crisis," p. 245.

18. Newell and Rubio, *Mexico's Dilemma*, p. 201.

19. Ibid., p. 208. Newell and Rubio are hardly alone in breaking down Mexico's political elite into nationalistic-populists and liberal-rationalists. Yale professor Sylvia Maxfield takes a similar track, arguing that Mexican financial politics have been characterized by a strong division between a banker's alliance, backed by a central government (mainly the Central Bank and Treasury Department) intent on fostering private markets to stimulate national development, and a national populist coalition concerned with controlling the nature of that development. See Sylvia Maxfield, *Governing Capital: International Finance and Mexican Politics* (Ithaca, N.Y.: Cornell University Press, 1990).

20. One of the best accounts of Mexico's 1982 financial crisis is in Joseph Kraft, *The Mexican Rescue* (New York: Group of Thirty, 1984).

21. Nora Lustig, *Mexico: The Remaking of an Economy* (Washington, D.C.: The Brookings Institution, 1992), p. 3.

22. Rudiger Dornbush, "Mexico's Economic Success Story: Lessons for Brazil," *Harvard International Review* (Fall 1991): p. 44.

23. Inter-American Development Bank, *Economic and Social Progress in Latin America: 1987 Report* (Washington, D.C.: Inter-American Development Bank, 1987), p. 345.

24. Ruiz, *Triumphs and Tragedies*, pp. 478–79.

25. One view of the clamp down on corruption was that it was actually an effort to instill order in the regime's ranks. Christopher Whalen notes of the arrest of Galicia: "No one disputes that the Petroleum Workers Union chieftain was corrupt, but La Quiana's arrest in 1989 for murder and weapons possession actually was a sham manufactured by the Mexican police. The true goal was to restore discipline among the recalcitrant oil workers, who bankrolled the successful but stolen presidential race a year before of Cuauhtémoc Cárdenas, the son of Mexico's revered nationalist leader, Lázaro Cárdenas." Christopher Whalen, "Bordering on

Repression," *The Washington Post* (December 27, 1992): p. C1.

26. International Monetary Fund, *International Financial Statistics Yearbook 1991*, p. 523.
27. Comments made to one of the authors in interview of an analyst of a U.S.-based bond rating firm in May 1993.
28. OECD, *Economic Survey: Mexico*, p. 9.
29. *Mexico Journal*, November 7, 1988, p. 11.
30. Quoted from Roderic A. Camp, "Mexico," in *Latin America and Caribbean Contemporary Record Vol. VII: 1987–1988*, eds. James M. Malloy and Eduardo A. Gamarra (New York: Holmes and Meier Publishers, 1990), p. B308.
31. For details see Robert A. Bennet, "Billions Are in Play Today in Mexico's Bond Sale," *New York Times* (February 26, 1988): p. D5; and Peter Truell, "Mexico Stands on Familar Ground at Forefront of Foreign-Debt Crisis," *Wall Street Journal* (December 31, 1987): p. 4.
32. Alan Stoga, "Beyond Coexistence: The United States and Mexico," *CSIS Policy Papers on the Americas* vol. II, report no. 6 (May 10, 1991): p. 13.
33. The $25 billion figure is that of the Mexican government and the $80 billion came from a study conducted by Morgan Trust in 1988. In 1990, Rudiger Dornbush suggested that the figure could be as high as $200 billion. See Roberto Salinas, "Privatization in Mexico: Good, But Not Enough," *The Heritage Foundation Backgrounder* (November 15, 1990): p. ; and Sergio Sarmiento, "Hacer como ellos," *AmericaEconomica* (December 1991): p. 66.
34. International Finance Corporation, *Emerging Stock Markets Factbook 1991* (Washington, D.C.: International Finance Corporation, 1991), p. 135; and International Finance Corporation, *Quarterly Review of Emerging Markets, Third Quarter 1991*, (Washington, D.C.:International Finance Corporation), p. 90.
35. "Mexico, No Turning Back," *Euromoney Supplement* (January 1992): p. 29.
36. Luis Acevedo Pesquera, "SHCP's Organigram Gets Modernized," *El Financiero Internacional* (March 9, 1992): p. 4.
37. LDC Debt Report, "Bank Autonomy Plan Nudges Mexico Toward First World," *LDC Debt Report* (May 24, 1993): p. 1.
38. Timothy Heyman and Pablo Riveroll, *Mexico: Emerging from the Lost Decade* (Mexico, D.F.: Baring Securities, 1991), p. 80.
39. Damian Fraser, "Salinas sows seeds for economic benefits," *Financial Times* (March 6, 1992): p. 26.
40. Ibid.
41. As Wayne Cornelius noted of *ejido* reform: "Salinas-initiated amendments to Mexico's constitution permit the privatization of the *ejido* (communally held) land and mandate changes in the governance of *ejido* communities. Those reforms could unleash new forces of pluralism and political competition in the countryside. The end of tight control over land transfers by *ejido caciques* (political bosses) tied to the ruling party opens up new opportunities for opposition parties to expand their support in rural communities that traditionally have been the most reliable sources of PRI votes, many of them fraudulently obtained." Quoted from Wayne Cornelius, "Mexico's Delayed Democratization," *Foreign Policy* (Summer 1994): p. 57.
42. U.S. Department of State, "North American Free Trade Agreement," *U.S. Department of State Dispatch* (February 17, 1992): p. 110.
43. Stoga, "Beyond Coexistence," p. 19.
44. A balanced account of the political debate over NAFTA in the United States is found in George W. Grayson, *The North American Free Trade Agreement, Re-*

gional Community and the New World Order (Lantham, MD.: University Press of America, 1995). Placing the issues in an economic policy context, see *The NAFTA Debate, Grappling with Unconventional Trade Issues*, eds. M. Delal Baer and Sidney Weintraub (Boulder, Colo.: Lynne Rienner, 1994). The debate concerning NAFTA still continues and is likely to do so for several more years. For two diverging views see two letters to the editor, Wayne A. Cornelius, "NAFTA Costs Mexico More Job Losses Than U.S.," A24; and Jerome Levinson, "Long-Shaky Peso," *New York Times* (October 17, 1995): p. A25.

45. The National Democratic Committee in 1991 argued against NAFTA noting "an unrestricted U.S.-Mexico free trade agreement would be a disaster for workers in both countries. It would destroy jobs in the United States, while perpetuating exploitation of workers and inflicting widespread damage of the environment of Mexico. The beneficiaries would be multinational corporations and large banks . . . ." Quoted in Rudiger Dornbusch, "If Mexico Prospers, So Will We," *Wall Street Journal* (April 11, 1991): p. 29.

46. John Ross, "Activists Face Free Trade Together," *El Financiero International* (March 9, 1992): p. 11.

47. Ibid.

48. Address by the president of Mexico, Carlos Salinas de Gortari,at the Annual Meeting of the American Society of Newspaper Editors, Harvard University, April 10, 1991, p. 2.

49. Sarmiento, "Hacer como ellos," p. 66.

50. Bloomberg, "Anchor Glass Sr. Notes Cut to B2 from Ba3 by Moody's," Bloomberg (September 27, 1995).

51. Bloomberg, "Mexico's Vitro Acquires Bolivian Glass Maker Vidrio Lux," Bloomberg (October 2, 1995).

52. Euromoney, "Just Waiting for the Signatures," *Euromoney Supplement* (January 1992): p. 35.

53. Stephanie Georges, *Telefonos de Mexico–Have You Ever Seen the Rain?* (New York: Solomon Brothers, 1991), p. 3.

54. Mickey Torres, "SABRE gains access to Mexican market," *Times of the Americas* (November 27, 1991): p. B4.

55. Ibid.

56. "Newscan: Business Briefs," *North-South* (April–May 1993): p. 64.

57. Peter Passell commented: "To judge by the press reviews, Mexico's economic reformers did everything right. Why then did the peso collapse?" in Peter Passell, "Mexico's Lessons: Don't Depend on the Kindness of Foreign Investors," *New York Times* (January 12, 1995): p. D2. For another interesting and insightful piece about Mexico and the international export community on Mexico and officialdom see Paul B. Carroll and Thomas T. Vogel, Jr., "Peso Surprise: How Mexico's Crisis Ambushed Top Minds In Officialdom, Finance," *Wall Street Journal* (July 6, 1995): p. A1 and A4.

58. Chris Whalen, "Economic Outlook: Low Growth and Inflation, Rising Unemployment, External Deficits, and Foreign Debt," *The Mexican Report* (February 19, 1993): p. 2.

59. Jonathan Heath, "The Devaluation of the Mexican Peso in 1994: Economic Policy and Institutions," *Policy Papers on the Americas* (June 1, 1995): p. 19. See also the report of an independent task force, *Lessons of the Mexican Peso Crisis* (New York: Council on Foreign Relations, 1996).

60. Geri Smith with Stanley Reed, "Pulling the Banks from the Rubble," *Business Week* (June 12, 1995): p. 48.

61. Michael Adler, "Mexico's Sovereign Risk of Default in 1996 is Low But Market Risks are on the Rise" *Latin America*, eds. Donaldson, Lufkin and Jenrette (March 27, 1996): p. 1.

62. Passell, "Mexico's Lesson," p. D2.

63. Mexico's political assassinations and questions raised by the subsequent investigations remain an unfinished story. For a preliminary take on these events and their broader Mexican political context, see Andres Oppenheimer, *Bordering on Chaos* (Boston, Mass.: Little, Brown & Co., 1996).

64. The significance of Mexico's crisis assigned by U.S. policymakers has been evident by the high-level attention these matters receive in Washington as well as the intense interest (if not always complete and accurate picture) U.S. government agencies have placed on Mexican affairs. As an example, see Donald E. Schulz, *Mexico in Crisis* (Carlisle Barracks, Pa.: U.S. Army War College, 1995). Few details of the U.S.-Mexican strategic relationship are publicly acknowledged. One recent attempt is eds., John Bailey and Sergio Aguayo, *Strategy and Security in U.S.-Mexican Relations Beyond the Cold War* (La Jolla, CA.: Center for U.S.-Mexican Studies, 1996).

65. Peter H. Smith, *Labyrinths of Power: Political Recruitment in Twentieth-Century Mexico* (Princeton, N.J.: Princeton University Press, 1979), p. 3.

66. Sidney Weintraub and M. Delal Baer, "The Interplay Between Economic and Political Opening: The Sequence in Mexico," *The Washington Quarterly* (Spring 1992): p. 187.

67. Ruiz, *Triumphs and Tragedy*, p. 412.

68. Ibid., p. 480.

69. Heath, "Devaluation," p. 18.

70. Maxfield, *Governing Capital*, p. 165.

71. Santiago Levy, "Poverty in Mexico," *Banamex Review of the Economic Situation in Mexico* (April 1993): p. 144.

72. Nora Lustig notes of the cuts in social spending: "Social spending, comprising primarily expenditures on education and health, contracted by 33.1 percent between 1983 and 1988." *Mexico*, p. 79.

73. OECD, *Economic Survey: Mexico*, p. 113.

7

Brazil: Curiously Problematic

Fernando Henrique Cardoso won the presidential elections in October 1994. His victory and assumption of office on 1 January 1995 extended the chain of civilian-elected presidents of Brazil to three since the military's exit from power in 1985. While it could be argued that elective civilian government has been consolidated, the economy over which the new president presided continued to be disappointing and at the very least represented an ongoing challenge.

It is worth remembering that in 1983 most impartial observers felt Brazil, more than any other Latin American country, would be the first to escape from the debt crisis. Early evidence seemed to give credibility to this optimism. In 1984, exports rose to $27 billion, $7 billion higher than in 1980. The $13 billion trade balance that resulted was, at the time, regarded as the first swallow of the post-debt crisis summer. With real GDP recovering in the second half of 1984 and into 1985 at an annual rate of around 8 percent, close to Brazil's postwar average growth rate, it was widely assumed that the largest South American country had attained that economic state of grace known as "export-led growth." The fact that private savings in 1984 reached a creditable 25 percent of GDP, just about the highest ratio ever, lent succor to this impression.

The progress made in 1984 proved illusory. The country went on in the second half of the 1980s to suffer hyperinflation and economic and political ignominy. Several "shock plans" sought to tackle the seemingly ceaseless proclivity for inflation. As table 7.1 shows, Brazil failed and it failed badly until 1995 in comparison with its Latin American peers. However, in the mid-1990s under the Cardoso administration, prospects improved. The Real Plan, introduced by Cardoso as finance minister during the previous Franco administration, gradually reduced inflation and began to restore some hope for the future.

TABLE 7.1
Annual Inflation

	1986	1987	1988	1989	1990	1991	1992	1993	1994	1995
Argentina	82	131	343	3081	2315	172	25	11	3.9	1.6
Brazil	59	225	685	1320	2739	414	991	2103	1080	20
Chile	17	20	15	17	26	22	15	12.7	11.4	8.9
Mexico	106	132	114	20	27	23	15.5	9.8	7.0	52.2
Venezuela	13	28	29	84.5	41	34	31.4	38.1	70.8	57.0

Source: International Monetary Fund, May 1995.

To what extent does this inflation problem reflect the broader external debt problem? Brazil's external debt reduction package with its creditors under the auspices of the Brady Plan came about only in 1994 after almost three years of negotiations. Considering the lengthy process of coming to debt relief, it would indeed be tempting to "explain" the high inflation experience as having a strong causal connection with Brazil's external indebtedness. It is true that Argentina, Mexico and other countries in the region have all attained debt relief from their creditors and have all registered lower rates of inflation than Brazil. It is also true that Brazil has an important structural disadvantage over countries like Mexico, Venezuela, and Chile as the public sector in those countries is able to record a positive balance-of-payment on the current account. Thus, exports of oil by state-owned PEMEX in Mexico and PDVSA in Venezuela, and exports of copper by Chile's publicly owned copper enterprise CODELCO broadly match or exceed the public sector's outward external payments, the largest of which is interest service on the public sector external debt.

By contrast, Brazil's public sector has more foreign exchange commitments than it has revenues and therefore runs a deficit in its balance-of-payments current account. Thus, if the Brazilian public sector services its debt, it has to buy foreign exchange from the private sector to do so. This expands the monetary base, as domestic currency is swapped for foreign exchange. The resulting monetary growth will, *ceteris paribus*, accelerate inflation. Hence Brazil's calls in the 1980s for debt relief were couched in terms of the pursuit of domestic price stability as well as in terms of balance-of-payments constraints.[1]

While this argument carries conceptual weight, the plain fact is that in the 1980s and the 1990s, external resource transfers by the public sector in Brazil declined, yet inflation accelerated. International interest rates, although rising again in the latter part of the 1980s, resumed their downward movement in the early 1990s (before rising again in 1994). More importantly, Brazil has not, for most part of the period (until after the 1994 agreement), serviced its debt at the contractual rate. In 1987, the country declared a moratorium on its commercial bank debt and only repaid the $4 billion plus arrears it had amassed by the end of 1988 by obliging the banks to lend an equivalent amount in new money. In mid-1989, Brazil again stopped paying the banks and, when interest payments resumed, Brazil only paid 30 percent of the contractual interest payments due—a form of unilateral debt relief.

Thus, inflation accelerated despite a lowering of debt- service payments. As this chapter will argue, Brazil's external debt problem is a relatively minor one. The root cause of Brazil's present economic malaise was built up during several decades of military governments (1964–85), followed by the signal failure of civilian and democratically elected governments to tackle the on-going crisis in the public sector's domestic finances, along with the very late realization that supply-side reforms are essential to economic modernization. The history of Brazil in the postwar period has been that of a country that pursued "wrong" policies well, and "right" policies badly. As a result of the relative success with which it pursued wrong policies, devising mechanisms to overcome the negative consequences of those policies served to delay the identification and implementation of right policies. The Cardoso administration is clearly challenged by this legacy and how it is adopting and pursuing the right policies will determine how Brazil enters the next century.

Brazil Before the Second World War

Brazil is not a stranger to debt crises.[2] In 1889, when Portuguese-speaking Brazil declared itself a republic, the country's external debt stood at 33 million British pounds. This was the legacy of excessive spending during the period of empire which had followed independence from Portugal in 1822. The Baring crisis of 1890—when the continued default of the Argentine government led to a financial crisis and takeover by the Bank of England and the joint stock banks of the liabilities of Baring Brothers—and a collapse of commodity prices, halted international lending to Brazil. In 1898, a rescheduling ensued whereby Brazil committed to increase taxes and bring order to its public finances. A further restructuring occurred in 1916.

Following the First World War, Brazil had surprisingly easy access to embryonic U.S. capital markets. As a result, another debt crisis occurred in 1930. The resulting restructuring did not solve Brazil's problems, especially since the world depression led to a collapse of Brazil's export prices. In 1934, Brazil unilaterally scaled back its debt-service payments and in 1937, under the leadership of the dictator Getulio Vargas, all debt-service payments were suspended. Only in 1940 was partial debt-service resumed, and then on a reduced contractual amount. Brazil's external situation was properly formalized in 1943, when its debt was consolidated and stretched over forty to sixty years, with bond holders given a choice of options. By 1946, nearly 80 percent of bond holders had accepted the exchange offer. At this time, Brazil's external debt stood at $600 million, down from its peak of $1 billion in the early 1930s.[3]

Structurally, Brazil's economy was dominated in the prewar years by a small range of agricultural exports, notably coffee. Although industries were heavily protected during this period, this did not mean that Brazil was an entirely closed economy. As Mario Henrique Simonson observed, both exports and imports were around 23 percent of GDP in the early 1920s: in fact industries were protected "not as a matter of economic strategy, but to raise revenue through import duties."[4] In doing this, the government made a strategic mistake: it relied too little on export taxes. Consequently, the monopoly profits that arose from restricting the supply of coffee in order to keep its international price up accrued to the coffee producers, not to the government. Overdependence on coffee exports resulted.

Brazil's overdependence on coffee was soon demonstrated. At the end of the 1920s, nearly three-quarters of export revenues were from coffee and very little diversification occurred.[5] When coffee prices collapsed in the Great Depression (1929), the government was obliged to devalue, burn huge stocks of coffee to try to stem the price collapse, and introduce import controls. These controls mark the commencement of a thirty-five year period of inward-looking growth policy. They were reinforced by the economic nationalism of President Getúlio

Vargas (1930–45 and 1951–54), who was determined to industrialize and extend the role of the state in the economy.

In his first term at the helm of his country, Vargas created a number of state organizations that would have a hand in the country's economic life for the next several decades: the Brazilian Coffee Institute (IBC) was established to handle all coffee matters for the country, and the Instituto do Açuçar e do Alcool (IAA) (Institute of Sugar and Alcohol) was created to do the same for the sugar industry from production to final marketing. In fact, under the 1937 constitution, which provided the legal foundation for the corporatist "Estado Novo" or New State, mines, sources of energy (such as the oil industry), banks, and insurance companies were nationalized, and basic and essential industries were to be regulated by law.[6] Simply stated, Vargas laid down the foundations for all the subsequent expansion of the state as an entrepreneur, including such companies still in operation—Petrobrás, Electrobrás, the steel corporations (several of them, starting with Companhia Siderurgica Nacional), the mining company Vale do Rio Doce, all of which would later reproduce themselves into many other companies.[7]

While coffee's central role to the economy was not abandoned under Vargas, cotton exports were promoted and import-substitution was introduced. The shift to import-substitution was the result of a catastrophic reduction in imports, first caused by the global nature of the Depression and then by the Second World War. Faced with a loss of critical imports for the economy, Vargas adopted policies that encouraged local industry by exchange controls, tax incentives, and import quotas. At the same time, duties were lowered on imported machinery and raw materials.

Vargas's political ascendancy, first as elected president in 1930 and then as dictator in 1937, also reflected an important political realignment: the revolution of 1930 and subsequent election signified the end of the coffee oligarchy-dominated political system that lasted from 1889 to 1930. Described as the "bourgeois" revolution, 1930 represented a victory for the urban bourgeois groups which favored industrialization and the modernization of Brazil's economic, political, and social structures.[8] This meant Vargas transformed the relationship between federal and state authority—the former was greatly strengthened by gaining control over a number of areas, including education, labor, and external financing.[9]

Vargas ruled Brazil until 1945, when he surrendered power to an interim government headed by Eurico Dutra. Although the Estado Novo was over, it is important to stress that the foundations for a strong and pervasive state had been established. Brazil's strongman, however, returned as president in 1950 and serving from 1951 to 1954, when he abruptly ended his second time in power with a bullet to the heart because of widespread allegations of corruption in his government. Despite problems with inflation, which was on the rise, Vargas's two terms in office were periods of reasonably strong growth for the country. The average annual growth rate between 1930 and 1945 was 4.4 percent and 6.2 percent for the years 1951–1954. As Paulo Rabello de Castro and Marcio Ronci noted: "these are good records, particularly if we bear in mind that during his first period he had to maneuver the economy through a world recession, a civil war, and then, a world war."[10]

Prelude to Military Government

Following Vargas's death, new elections were eventually held and Juscelino Kubitschek became president (1956–60). Under Kubitschek, economic policy concentrated on infrastructural improvements to eliminate distribution bottlenecks and incentives were given to a number of industrial sectors, such as automobiles, chemicals, heavy mechanics, metallurgy, and shipbuilding. A new capital, Brasília, was carved out of the country's vast heartland. To stimulate foreign investment, Kubitschek also modernized the investment code. However, the policy of industrialization, started under Vargas, continued, with the domestic sector protected behind a wall of heavy customs duties and encouraged by currency-exchange incentives and large public investments. The overwhelmingly positive sense of advancement in Brazil was bolstered by an average economic growth in the 1956–60 years of 8 percent, with an increase in nominal wages of 26 percent, which stayed ahead of inflation. Kubitschek's fast-paced vision of Brazil, "50 years in five," produced advances, but simultaneously augmented the size of the public sector.

Brazil's political economy of state-capitalism and patrimonial democracy reached a temporary cul-de-sac in the 1960s. The country was traumatized by political unrest, which became more pronounced under the erratic leadership of Jânio da Silva Quadros, who won the 1960 elections and resigned after only six months. He was followed by his vice president, João Goulart, in September 1961. The new chief executive was regarded by the right and military as a dangerous demagogue and radical, a perception enhanced by the fact that he was in China on a trade mission when Quadros resigned. In many respects, Goulart was not so much of a radical as he was patronage-oriented and favored a rather paternalistic populism largely devoid of ideological content.[11]

To curb Goulart's power, the Congress had passed a constitutional amendment converting the country's presidential system into a parliamentary one, albeit with a president who would share power with a council of ministers named by him, but drawn from and responsible to the legislature. Goulart soon found himself confronted by parliamentary obstruction to most of his bills. Moreover, the economy soured, a situation that did little to improve the president's position vis-à-vis the country's powerful conservative groups.

Although Goulart was able to return the country back to a presidential system in a national plebiscite, the import—substitution-dominated economy floundered. Indeed, average annual economic growth slowed in this period to 5.3 percent, while inflation shot up. Most importantly, the populist-oriented Goulart government, as noted by de Castro and Ronci, "did not know enough about the limits of the fiscal budget and the exchange reserves."[12] A proposed land reform program fueled growing discontent with Goulart among the political and economic elite, while his intervention in internal military affairs helped stimulate the military, fearful of the spread of communism, into action. In 1964, the Brazilian military ousted Goulart in a largely bloodless coup. Brazil came under a long period of military rule.

The Brazilian armed forces had a particular view of the world that they soon imprinted on their nation. Concerned that the lack of economic development was a major factor in why revolutions occur, the armed forces had developed a considerable cadre of soldiers and civilian allies who attended the Escola Superior de Guerra (School of Higher Military Studies) which had strong views on economic policy.[13] This policy line included no or little political dissension, anticommunism, and a concentration on the economic policy that included favorable treatment of foreign capital.

The military regime's first minister of planning, Roberto Campos, created a program for attracting foreign capital by incentives that included the unhindered repatriation of profits, reduced taxes, and a special type of exchange for the payment of external financing in case of devaluation. Additionally, efforts were made to reign in inflation and correct the distortions inherited from state intervention in the economy. These efforts were supported by a reduction in government expenditures, the elimination of subsidies and wage controls.

Under the military presidencies of General Humberto de Alcencar Castelo Branco (the first military president [1964–67] and a student of the Escola Superior), Marshal Artur da Costa e Silva (1967–69), and General Emílio Garrastazu Médici (1969–74), the economy underwent a partial move away from the import- substitution model to a more open system, stressing the importance of exports. By 1970, the denationalization of certain sectors of the economy had resulted in a return of large foreign firms. The automobile sector, for example, was dominated by Volkswagen, Ford, and General Motors. At the same time, the large state sector was not dismantled. It was felt that the public sector, heavy in areas of raw material processing and public utilities, would instead offer inexpensive energy, raw materials, and steel to foreign firms. Additionally, the military did not put itself in a position where it was forced to release thousands of workers—a certain ingredient for political unrest.

In the early 1970s, the Brazilian economy went into overdrive. The long-promised miracle had occurred—Brazil as the country of the future was proving true. The country's economic growth rates, averaging 10 percent in the 1970–73 period, were the highest in the world. While the economic engine roared, other events buoyed the Brazilian spirit—winning the World Cup Soccer championship in 1970 and victories in other sporting events. Brazil appeared to be on the verge of moving up the development ladder into the ranks of industrialized countries.

Problems, however, lurked beneath the surface. The oil price increases that came in 1973–74 were a major shock to the economy, given its dependency on imported energy. Finance Minister Delfim Netto escaped a currency devaluation when he handed the stewardship of the economy over to President Ernesto Geisel's finance minister, Mario Henrique Simonsen. Although strong growth continued until 1979, the Brazilian currency was overvalued and sectors of the economy were becoming increasingly noncompetitive with international firms. The government turned to an ambitious investment program to expand the state enterprises, especially in the energy sector (the construction of power plants, oil mining and exploration, and the production of alcohol as an alternative fuel) to reduce the dependence on foreign oil. The Geisel government (1974–79) also embarked upon another round of import-substitution in the areas of heavy engineering, fertilizers, and metallurgy of nonferrous metals.

The growth of the state sector and an overvalued currency were part of a growing economic crisis that would in a few years crash upon Brazil. Largescale projects had to be paid for somewhere—the government's deficit as a percentage of GDP expanded from 1.4 percent in 1974 to 13.1 percent in 1979.[14] Attempts at this reform to close the growing fiscal gap were thwarted by vested interests. Consequently, the public sector's needs were financed by external borrowing and, increasingly, the inflation rate. Brazil's external debt rose from $5.1 billion in 1970 to $60.4 billion in 1979, while inflation rose from 15 percent a year in 1973 to 40 percent in 1979.[15] Widespread indexation, including that of wages, exacerbated the inflationary process.

When the Figueiredo administration assumed office in 1979 it was confronted with a growing list of headaches. External debt servicing accounted for more and more of the country's export revenues; oil prices were rising due to instability in Iran; and international interest rates were soon to shoot upwards. Adding to the disequilibrium, the Geisel administration had exited without implementing a currency devaluation. One of the first acts of the Figueiredo administration in December 1979 was to introduce adjustment measures in an effort to reduce inflationary pressures and install some equilibrium into the economy. A 30 percent devaluation was a major plank of the government's program which also included eliminating a number of tax exemptions, increasing tariffs of public services, and reducing withholding tax on interest paid abroad from 12.5 percent to 1.5 percent to stimulate further borrowing from international markets.[16] This latter decision proved to be a monumental mistake.

Although real GDP growth expanded by close to 8 percent in 1980, inflation continued to move upward to 110 percent (up from 77 percent in 1979). Monetary policy was tightened in 1981 to brake inflationary expansion, but the worsening of the international recession (which was bad for Brazilian exports), rise in international interest rates, and a burgeoning public deficit militated against a sound economic recovery. For the first time in many years, the economy in 1981 actually contracted by 4.4 percent and the recession continued into

1982. Brazil entered 1983 pummelled by high inflation and stagnating industrial production. Inevitably, the debt crisis hit Brazil. By that time, the structural imbalances of the country's interventionist model inherited from Vargas and moderated from time to time by liberal economic managers were starkly obvious. This economic crisis was passed on from the military governments to civilian governments that returned in 1985. The export-led recovery of 1984–85 failed to turn the corner for the Brazilian economy and pull it out of the debt crisis. Many analysts initially regarded the debt crisis as a short-term liquidity crunch; it now appeared to be a longer-term problem, reflecting structural disequilibrium in Brazil.

The Troubled Tenure of the Poet

José Sarney was never meant to be president and the lead act in Brazil's return to civilian leadership. The unexpected death of president-elect Tancredo Neves in 1985, however, thrust Sarney, a poet and politician by profession, into the presidency. A number of daunting political challenges faced the new president: the need to create a viable relationship between the executive and legislative branches of government; the necessity of drafting and implementing a new constitutional framework suitable for a complex society, with large social inequalities; and the interest in reshaping the party system.[17]

Complicating matters, the Brazil Sarney inherited from the military governments had slipped into a recession. The Sarney government's response to the deteriorating economic situation was to launch a radical stabilization program, the Plan Cruzado in February 1986. Under the guidance of Finance Minister Dilson Funaro, the Plan Cruzado was designed to halt triple-digit inflation through a freeze on wages, prices, and rents. The economy was to be deindexed and public finances were to be balanced. Moreover, the country's monetary unit, the cruzeiro, was replaced by a new monetary unit, the cruzado.

The Plan Cruzado initially appeared to work. Inflation dropped steeply in March and April, and the Sarney administration gave the appearance of being in command. The economy began to grow. This was helpful to progovernment forces in the November 1986 state and Congressional elections. However, by 1987, the Plan Cruzado was a failure and the old demon of inflation returned to plague the government. International reserves began to disappear. In these circumstances,

Sarney not surprisingly tried to blame the external debt for the country's problems. In a policy change, the Sarney government declared a debt moratorium. To a background of contentious relations with Brazil's external creditors, Funaro bowed out and was replaced at the Ministry of Finance by Bresser Pereira. In June 1987, Pereira launched a new stabilization program, referred to as the Bresser Plan. The key elements of the new program were once again wage and price freezes, while external debt was held accountable for the problems in Brazil.

Pereira's lack of strong political support ultimately undermined his ability to stick to the shock program. Like the Cruzado Plan, underlying the failure was the inability to contain the fiscal deficit. Efforts to control the public sector deficit and reach a deal with commercial banks both failed. By 1988, Pereira left and Mailson da Nobrega become the third finance minister under President Sarney. The Summer 1989 Plan (launched in January that year to correspond with the summer season in South America) followed a well-trodden path—wages and prices were frozen and war was declared on the fiscal deficit.

The Sarney government's inability to effectively deal with the twin problems of high inflation and external debt gave the appearance of a nation adrift. Clearly, the president became an isolated political figure, lacking determination, credibility, and political support in the Congress. In the last days of the administration, inflation was out of control. The Sarney government's reputation was, moreover, tarnished by a number of scandals.

A major factor in the failure of the Sarney administration's economic policies was the inability to address the issue of excessive state intervention in the economy. External debt was a problem; but more a symptom than a cause. The cause of Brazil's economic woes was that the majority of state corporations were not cost-efficient, characterized by low productivity, poor quality of goods and services, and usually ran at high costs (due to high labor costs and mismanagement). Another critical factor in all of this was that the central bank covered the public sector deficit by printing money. Because the central bank lacked autonomy from the government, it was unable to pursue an independent monetary policy to fight inflation. As Eliana A. Cardoso and Daniel Dantas noted: "Brazil has not 'adjusted' to the debt crisis. Instead, the Brazilian government has 'accommodated' the disappearance of external sources of finance by printing money and by creating domestic debt."[18]

A legacy that the Sarney period was to pass on to the next government was the 1988 Constitution. The 1988 constituent assembly bequeathed the nation a constitution that reflected militant nationalism, was in many respects antiforeign capital, and provided the state governments with considerable authority over their economic affairs. A number of bizarre provisions were included, such as the prescription of high real-interest rates. Resenting Sarney's desire to persuade provincial governments to extend his term of office until 1990, the constitution determined that some 50 percent of the federal tax revenue would go automatically to provincial governments. Without any question the 1988 Constitution, while providing a foundation for broad participatory democracy, left the country with a detrimental legacy of few domestic spending controls and an antiforeign investment code.

Brazil's confused political arena, weak political parties, and Sarney's unpopularity provided Fernando Collor, the charismatic young governor of a Northeastern state, an opportunity to run an outsider's campaign in the 1989 elections. Collor's campaign hit a responsive chord by promising to sweep out the "maharajahs" of corruption and to "kick" Brazil into the First World.[19] Out of a field of nine candidates, he came first, setting the stage for the second round against leftist Luís Ignácio "Lula" da Silva of the Workers' Party (PT). The symbolic clash between right (Collor) and left (da Silva) in the presidential joust was heightened on the international front by the fall of the Soviet Union and the demise of the Eastern bloc. Winning 53 percent of the second round vote, Collor appeared as a man with a mission, ready and able to jolt Brazil out of its lethargy and bring it into the late twentieth century.

Collor—The Man on Horseback

The Collor government that entered office on 15 March 1990 faced a very troubled economic environment. Although Brazil enjoyed 3.6 percent real GDP growth in 1989, economic activity had begun to slow in the later part of the year and by early 1990 the chill of recession was being felt. While economic activity slowed and then stagnated, inflation shot upwards—in 1988 it had registered 682 percent; by the end of 1989 it was 1,287 percent and on the rise. As an Inter-American Development Bank study reported of the situation: "Not only had growth halted but also public confidence was deeply eroded by the repeated failures of previous governments to correct the interrelated problems of runaway inflation and an unmanageable fiscal deficit."[20]

The Collor government's reform program sought to halt Brazil's slide and modernize the economy. The ultimate goal was to create an open, export-driven economy, capable of international competition. The so-called Collor Plan, according to the same Inter-American Development Bank report, was "undoubtedly the most ambitious stabilization and adjustment program in Brazil's history."[21]

The Collor Plan aimed to reduce liquidity as a precondition to lowering inflation, while bringing the fiscal deficit under control. Most bank deposits were frozen and government internal debt was unilaterally renegotiated. Public-sector debt reduction was to be achieved by increasing taxes, reducing tax evasion (a major problem), and drastically cutting the public sector's size, largely through privatization. The economic modernization program also entailed gradually opening the economy to outside competition in most sectors through deregulation, cuts in import duties, and modifications in exchange rate policy. As Marcílio Marques Moreira, Collor's second finance minister, noted: "From right to left across the political spectrum, Brazil's economic thinkers concur on the need to integrate the country competitively into the world economy and to abandon the old state-driven, debt-financed, import-substitution model."[22]

The Collor government also began negotiations with the International Monetary Fund in August 1990 and with the commercial banks in October 1990. By July 1992, lengthy negotiations with the commercial banks resulted in a Brady debt-reduction plan for a little over $40 billion of the country's total $120 billion external debt. However, completion of the bank debt deal was slowed by the political crisis that hit the country in 1992 as well as by the government's inability to rein in inflation and meet deficit targets favored by the IMF.

"Collorgate"

The Collor Plan to transform Brazil's economy and make it into a Latin American powerhouse ran into problems within months of the new president's inauguration. His move to half inflation by freezing $80 billion in bank deposits and financial equity incurred considerable opposition, while his scant party representation in the Congress weakened his ability to push reforms through the legislative process. At the same time, the government's privatization program lurched forward, fighting court battles and vocal union opposition. The privatization of VASP, the state of Sao Paulo's airline, was filled with irregularities, raising questions about the lack of transparency in the sale. Lacking political support in the Congress, facing a deepening recession and unable to move his reforms along, Collor was increasingly isolated. By early 1992, he was floundering, politically and economically.

The Collor presidency began to unravel in early 1992 when rumors surfaced about corruption surrounding the chief executive. Allegations were made that the president's lavish lifestyle (especially his wife's purchasing binges overseas) was not within his means and dependent on "other" sources. Although rumors abounded about political corruption, it was not until May 1992 that the president's position was strongly challenged. In a family feud gone public, Collor's brother Pedro, claimed the president was accepting funds from Paulo César Farias, who had helped Collor's 1986 gubernatorial campaign and was chief fundraiser in 1989. It was claimed that Farias was the chief bribe-taker and heavily involved in influence peddling. Ken Serbin provides a scope of Farias activities: "Farias, who admitted before Congress that he had violated electoral laws in 1989, implanted a network of extortionists and influence peddlers throughout the government to collect millions in kickbacks on official contracts. Ignoring the traditions of Brazilian corruption, which accepted 10 percent as a reasonable cut, Farias piped $130 million through false bank accounts, distributed $32.3 million to people within the government, and paid for the multimillion dollar renovation of Collor's private residence."[23] All told, the amount of money supposed to be grossed by Farias and Collor was estimated at $2 billion.[24] Beyond those problematic areas, the Collor administration was also linked to bid-rigging, while the president's wife was alleged to have abused public power and have profligate spending habits.

It was initially assumed that the scandal allegations would amount to little and that Collor would weather the storm. As one investment bank noted in early June 1992: "The recent allegations against President Collar are politically damaging, but in our opinion, they probably will not lead to a major Government crisis."[25] Answering the arguments tendered to support this thesis was that the departure of Collor would hand the presidency to Itamar Franco, the vice president, and that the nation's political elites would not allow such a weak personality to assume the office. Collor's position, however, was seriously undermined by the corruption allegations. When the pressure to oust the president began in earnest later in June 1992, a number of important bills for the modernization program were still in the Congress—tax reforms, privatization of the port system, and intellectual property rights and patents.

As pressure against Collor mounted, he sought to ensure his survival by turning to state governments, especially in the north. This was done by increasing state expenditures. Although Economy Minister Moreira provided a degree of stability on the financial front, the tensions between the embattled president and his growing opposition clearly detracted from other affairs of the nation. Collor's chances for survival diminished considerably on 26 August 1992 when the Congressional Investigating Committee approved the corruption report implicating the president by a sixteen to five vote. This was followed on 1 September 1992 by the Brazilian Bar Association and Press Association formally asking Congress to impeach Collor.

Growing public support for ousting Collor was finally heard in Brasilia. In September 1992, Brazil's 503–member Chamber of Deputies voted 441 to 38 with 24 abstaining to bring impeachment charges against President Collar. Although Collor vowed to fight on, he effectively lost political power on 2 October 1992, when Vice President Itamar Franco became acting president pending either the clearance of Collor's name or his impeachment or resignation (whichever came first).

Collor's fall from power indicated that Brazil's political system could function in a constitutional form, upholding the rule of law when it came to abuses by the country's leadership. Equally significant, the succession of Itamar Franco to the presidency occurred without mishap. However, there was also a downside: the situation had evolved where a vice president once again assumed the national leadership—a vice president whom many never thought would become the country's chief executive due to his lack of national prominence. Initial comparisons of Franco to Sarney in the Brazilian media were not flattering.

The Uncertain Tenure of Itamar Franco

Itamar Franco's presidency began on 2 October 1992, the same day that Collor officially left the chief executive's seat. The new national leader faced high inflation, a recession, and questions about his ability and commitment to the modernization of the economy. In financial circles the sentiment was that Collor had the right ideas, but was corrupt; Franco was honest, but was clueless on economic matters.

Franco inherited a sounder economic situation from Collor than Collor had from Sarney. Although inflation was high, it had stabilized in the 22–25 percent range for a period of ten months. Most prices had been freed, tariffs on public services had been adjusted to inflation; economic reform was underway via tariff reductions; privatization had been started as eighteen state-owned companies had been sold; and a number of decrees and bureaucratic procedures were streamlined. Significantly, Brazil had negotiated an economic program with the IMF early in 1992 followed by an external-debt deal with the Paris Club (for official debt) and the commercial banks.

While a degree of momentum had been achieved on the economic front, the political agenda facing the new president was heavy—the 23 April 1993 referendum would determine whether Brazil voted to maintain the presidential system or if it opted for a parliamentary one. In October 1993, the nation's legislative body converted into a constituent assembly to revise the 1988 Constitution. If the presidential system survived, Franco would preside over the 1994 presidential elections for which campaigning began in mid-1993. All of this meant that the Franco presidency assumed office at a time of tremendous uncertainty. As Roberto Teixeira da Costa noted in November 1993: "it is fair to estimate that very little space is going to be left President Franco to be a very effective and aggressive president during his interim mandate."[26]

Franco's first months in office were tentative, which further gave the appearance of drift, opening him to harsh criticism. As one Brazilian observer pinioned in December 1992: "The Itamar government has displayed an alarming lack of leadership definition and coordination as well as an increasingly clear, populist, statist, and national orientation."[27] Franco received particular criticism for the emergency tax-reform bill that was advanced late in 1991. Although the proposed bill would create four new taxes with the objective of augmenting state revenues to an amount equal to 4 percent of GDP, it was argued that the bill ignored the expense side of the fiscal equation.[28]

Franco's cautiousness continued through December 1992, when it was certain that Collor would not be returning due to his resignation only days before a critical vote in the Senate on impeachment. As

Brazil entered 1993, the government refused to make any major departures in policy. Friction with Finance Minister Gustavo Krause resulted in his exit and replacement on 19 January 1993 by Planning Minister Paulo Haddad. As it stood, the mainstays of the Franco economic program included continued avoidance of any shock plans that included price and wages freezes; reconciliation of continued monetary restraint with gradual reduction of real interest rates through fiscal reforms and reduction of the internal debt (much of it state- as opposed to federal- government generated); and modification of the privatization program that created a "new money" requirement, liberalized foreign participation, and clarified treatment of the "strategic" segments of the state sector.

Political stability eluded the Franco administration. Despite his efforts to create a broad-based governing coalition, the president was confronted with problems in keeping a finance minister. Haddad lasted two months, being replaced by Eliseu Resende, who was replaced two months later (in May) by Fernando Cardoso, the former foreign minister. Haddad's resignation was because of strong differences over appointments to the Banco Central and Banco do Brasil, while Resende's position was undercut by questions of corruption. This revolving-door nature of the Finance Ministry did little to create an atmosphere of confidence in the Franco government's ability to tackle economic woes. Although Cardoso was widely respected, he was the sixth economy minister since 1990 and the fourth since President Franco took office in October 1992.

Cardoso's appointment indicated that the Franco government was moving to the political center. At the time Cardoso assumed the finance ministry, Franco also forced the resignation of another minister, Luiza Erundina, from the leftist PT (she was in the cabinet against the expressed wishes of her party). Franco's gambit to create a strong centrist coalition, coordinated by Cardoso represented an effort to avoid another round of ministerial musical chairs that the government could ill-afford, especially with an increasingly restless military.

Cardoso's tenure as finance minister gained in importance through the summer of 1993. In June 1993, Cardoso's economic program, the Real Plan was launched with three phases: (1) fiscal reform, a major part of which was the introduction of a social emergency fund to shift spending from the Federal Government to the state and local governments; (2) the introduction of the Real Unit of Value (URV), designed to bring Brazil's complicated system of indexation in line with a single price adjustment mechanism; and (3) the final phase, the conversion of the URV into a new currency, the *real*. The *real* was backed by dollar reserves and issued at a rough parity with the U.S. dollar. By 29 March 1994, the day that Cardoso resigned as finance minister to run for the presidency, the verdict was still out as to the success of the plan.

The 1994 Elections: Wither Brazil?

Cardoso's campaign for the presidency was strongly challenged by Ignacio da Silva, also known as Lula, the leader of the Workers' Party (PT). Unlike most Brazilian parties, the PT has an ideology (populisitic-socialistic), a relatively disciplined party machine, grass roots operations, and ties to powerful unions. Most significantly, it promised to uproot the old elitist political game, best symbolized by the presidencies of Sarney and Collor. Once regarded as a radical leftist party, the PT in the 1994 campaign appeared to have become somewhat more pragmatic in its drive to power. It gave its blessing to a major overhaul of the public sector. Da Silva's 31 million votes in 1989 for the presidency indicated that he had the potential to win the presidency, despite internal party disputes. Da Silva led in many opinion polls during the campaign.

What made da Silva's presidential bid more credible in 1994 was the fact that many Brazilian voters were disillusioned. Ronald Schneider noted of the 1990 elections, which had some degree of relevance in 1994: "Indeed, Collor's greatest support came from the broad base of the Brazilian social pyramid, precisely those who according to class-based analyses should have mobilized in support for a Socialist or at least Social Democratic candidate rather than an outspoken advocate of giving free-enterprise capitalism a real chance to show what it could do in Brazil."[29] It was possible that this broad base felt their trust betrayed by Collor and would be attracted to his opposite in 1990—da Silva.

A possible PT victory in the 1994 general and presidential elections represented a looming political quandary. If da Silva and the PT won in a highly polarized election, would the more social democratic wing of the party emerge, providing a pragmatic set of policies and stave off a possible military intervention? Or would the PT seek to implement a radical economic program to reduce the country's poverty and violence that would also represent another push for greater state intervention in the economy? Would factional fighting within the PT bring down the government into gridlock? Although da Silva and the PT initially might have appeared as an alternative to the scandals and corruption of the Collor period, public opinion in the final months of the campaign gradually ebbed away from the leftist alternative and embraced Cardoso. The deficit in the opinion polls that initially placed Cardoso only at 20 percent to da Silva's 40 percent shifted and by mid-August a Gallup poll gave the former finance minister 37.5 percent of the potential vote to the PT leader's 27.6 percent.

Cardoso entered the 1994 campaign with a reputation as an honest man and someone who could put Brazil back on track, but without Collor's dash. As foreign minister and then finance minister, he had demonstrated a pragmatic sense and the Real Plan was working in controlling inflation—a major headache for most Brazilians. During the campaign a book, *Hands to Work: A Program of Government*, was published under his authorship, which posited Brazil's need for modernizing market-oriented reforms that would lead the country into a competitive position within the newly transformed global environment.[30] Cardoso indicated that for a new Brazil to emerge changes would have to be introduced in the constitution, privatization would have to be accelerated, and firmer measures would be required to manage the budget. He also indicated the need to balance such efforts with necessary social services, and uplift the nation's infrastructure. As William Perry noted of the last: "a very ambitious program of infrastructural renewal is envisaged that cannot be financed by the government. Thus, domestic capital must be mobilized, foreign capital attracted, and the resources of international lending institutions significantly tapped."[31] Together with such envisaged measures as further trade liberalization, reform of the tax system, better intellectual property laws, and a substantial reduction in protectionism in certain key sectors (such as mining, telecommunications, and informatics), Cardoso's message was one of change, based on his track record of being a steady, thoughtful reformer—a clear difference with the flamboyant Collor.

Cardoso easily won the first round of the national election on 3 October 1994 with more than 50 percent, enough to guarantee no recourse to a second round. Da Silva came in second in a crowded field of six other weak candidates. A second round of voting was held on 15 November 1994 for those contests which were not conclusive in the first round. The final tally in this contest bode well for the incoming president—out of eighteen governships at stake, Cardoso's Partido Socialista Democratica Brasil (PSDB) won six, his alliance partners, the Partido Frente Liberal (PFL) won two, and the PTB won one governship. The large centrist party, which formed part of the opposition in the Congress, the PMDB, won nine governships.

Cardoso's victory was significant on two levels. First, it reflected that the democratic experiment in Brazil is still continuing. The transfer of power from President Franco to President Cardoso was peaceful, making it the third such transferal since the military left the center of the political stage in 1986. Secondly, it indicated that the desire to reform Brazil was not dead and buried with the tarnished Collor presidency. Itamar Franco, despite his many critics, had not let the reform movement entirely lapse—after all, Cardoso had been Franco's finance minister and there was a considerable effort to make the transfer of power simple. Additionally, the appeal of Lula and populist alternatives ultimately proved ephemeral. At the end of the day, most Brazilians proved that they were more interested in electing a leader willing and able to end the long slugfest with inflation, and putting the country back to work.

President Cardoso's challenge to modernize the Brazilian economy is enormous. While the Brazilian leader clearly has a vision of where he would like to take his nation, he faces considerable challenges, ranging from the atomization of party politics in the legislative body which complicates any moves on the reform front, to extreme poverty in the country's large cities and countryside. To tackle these problems, the new president appointed a strong team.

The need to change and the ability to introduce change are two different things in Brazil. The Cardoso administration's efforts to reshape Brazil ran into trouble in the first months. While there was a pressing need to move beyond the Real Plan's stabilization of the economy, the reform process ran into Brasilia's legislative inertia. The rapid-fire pace of reform expected in January and February failed to materialize. Increasingly, it appeared that Cardoso was floundering in his bid to pass constitutional amendments that would overhaul the nearly bankrupt social security system and allow private investment in industries, including oil and telecommunications.

Cardoso's reform effort, however, was to benefit initially from an unexpected quarter: the 48,000 workers at Petrobrás, the state-owned oil company. On 3 May 1995, the oilworkers went on strike for higher wages. Cardoso refused to back down and soon the government and oil workers union were locked in a struggle that had far wider implications. The president's refusal to give in soon gained him a wave of support that he had been lacking prior. As people formed gas lines, and the industry found itself inconvenienced, the fact that oilworkers on average made $2,300 a month, more than six times the national average, became public. Any earlier sympathy for the oilworkers vanished. As Norton Ribeiro de Frietas, Jr., an economist for the Italian-Brazilian Chamber of Commerce noted: "This is working in his [Cardoso's] favor. The people and Congress are steamed at the strikers."[32]

The strike ended in June 1995 and Cardoso emerged victorious. His economic reform was also making strides as the Chamber of Deputies voted for amendments that would end monopolies in telecommunications, gas, and coastal shipping. Petrobrás's monopoly went on the bloc, when the Chamber of Deputies voted in June 1995 to end the state oil monopoly, first adopted in 1953. At the same time, Cardoso's efforts to bring the economy further under control were showing results—inflation was down from 45 percent monthly in July 1994 to a year-end rate of 20 percent in 1995 and foreign exchange reserves reached a high of $49.7 billion at the end of 1995.[33] At the same time, the government made progress in unifying several indexes and freezing some prices. The push in the years ahead is to dismantle the wage and price indexes that "have made Brazilian inflation a self-fulfilling prophecy" and kept away foreign investors.[34] Fiscal reform will also be a key task.

The Political Quandary

One of the most significant challenges confronting the Cardoso administration is political in nature. Collor's fall because of corruption, the problematic tenure of Itamar Franco, and the inability of the Brazilian government to develop a strong consensus about the economic situation reflect the serious political quandary Latin America's largest state faces on the edge of the twenty-first century. While Collor's ouster reflected an important victory of the rule of law—central to any democracy—it also reflected serious flaws in the political system.

Brazil's democracy is characterized by weak political parties, strong political personalities, and a considerable amount of backroom wheeling and dealing that is far from the public eye. The crucial component of consensus on economic matters continues as a lacuna in Brazil, especially when contrasted to Chile, Colombia, and Argentina.

Political scientist Riordan Roett has argued that Brazil is a patrimonial society, bolstered by the existence of a centralized, bureaucratic state. That state has allowed the continuation of the influence of the Brazilian elites. Roett noted: "Regardless of the time period, politics in Brazil have been dominated by a relatively small group of individuals who have been able to manipulate the mass of the population and define the goals of the state in their terms. The elite nature of the political system has been reinforced by the traditional and hierarchical nature of Brazilian political culture."[35]

Although Roett's analysis was made in 1972, it still has a degree of validity and raises serious questions about Brazil's ability to emerge from its current environment. Collor's plan to modernize Brazil incurred considerable opposition from the country's institutional elites, in particular from labor, elements of the business community, and the bureaucracy in the state enterprises. His impeachment did not address the country's economic woes, while Franco's administration was clearly transitional and marked by uncertainty. Brazil's economy continued along a recessionary track, inflation remained high, and the private sector, which has a number of dynamic companies, is shackled by state controls and the overall negative investment environment. While prospects are relatively positive under Cardoso, opposition clearly remains to economic reform on everything from privatization to opening up sectors of the economy to foreign investment. As Orestes Quércia, the former governor of Sao Paulo, stated regarding Cardoso's 1995 efforts to end state monopolies and promote privatization: "This government is promoting the breaking of monopolies in an irresponsible way, with the goal of selling the nation's patrimony for small change."[36]

Another dimension of the political problems facing any leader seeking to take Brazil into the twenty-first century is the spread of poverty, and the increase of violence against those with wealth. As one analyst noted: "In urban centers, criminals stage kidnappings for ransom, vigilante death squads murder street children, young girls work as prostitutes—and such diseases as AIDS and cholera silently spread."[37] Parts of big cities, such as Rio de Janeiro and Sao Paulo, are increasingly out of control of local authorities. Social discontent with the elitist system and a political leadership seemingly out of touch with, or insensitive to, the sufferings of a large segment of the population represent the potential for severe problems in the short and mid-terms.

Another political quandary facing Brazil is how to deal with political corruption and make democratic institutions work. As veteran Brazilianist Alfred Stepan noted: "Democracy is about fair elections, but it is also about rule of law."[38] The Congress followed the only constitutional course available in the case of Collor by pursuing impeachment, an action that enjoyed considerable public and media support. However, while this clearly enhanced the legitimacy of Brazil's democratic institutions, Brazil's political elite continue to have questionable accountability in the public eye. One year into Collor's terms, a poll indicated that 80 percent of the population believed that laws applied only to the poor and that the powerful were above the law.[39] The public perception has improved on this account, but perhaps only marginally and for the short term. Corruption, unfortunately, remains an element in the Brazilian polity.

Surviving into the Next Century

It would be very misleading to present a bleak future for Brazil. The country clearly has considerable economic strengths and a growing number of Brazilian firms have a global reach. In the areas of aerospace, mining, agriculture, and construction, Brazil boasts competitiveness in international markets. Souza Cruz, for example, is the world's largest exporter of tobacco leaf, supplying more than forty countries. Other Brazilian commercial giants include Aracruz Celulose, White Martins, and Banco Brasileiro de Descontos.

One of Brazil's best-known companies is the Companhia Vale do Rio Doce (CVRD). It is the world's largest producer and exporter of iron as well as the owner of large railroad, port, and shipping operations. Other activities of CVRD include mining sizeable amounts of aluminum, gold, and other minerals, and producing significant pulp, paper, and forestry products. Originally established in 1942 under agreements with the United States and United Kingdom in the Allied war effort, CVRD, though state-owned, has evolved into a highly competitive company. As a 1993 *Euromoney* survey on leading Latin American companies noted: "although government-controlled, CVRD confounds the usual received notions of a lumbering state enterprise. It is a well-managed, profitable and financially strong organization."[40]

CVRD's strengths rest on its broad-based diversification, vertical integration, and its strategic alliances with international partners. Within Brazil, CVRD is based in Minas Gerais and a new site in Para, Carajas, in the north. The Carajas site cost $3.7 billion to develop and has given the company iron ore reserves that are estimated to last for 500 years.[41] CVRD's international activities commenced in the 1960s when it began long-term sales contracts with Japanese steel mills. In the 1990s, CVRD's major customers are those major steel producers that lack iron ore reserves—Japan, Germany, South Korea, Taiwan, and China (China has low-grade, but not high-grade iron reserves).

CVRD's efforts to be competitive on the international stage is evident in its decision to participate in three joint-venture iron ore pelletizing companies, its acquisition of a steel plant in California in partnership with Cassock Steel of Japan, and other joint ventures to produce bauxite, aluminum, manganese, and certain alloys.[42] CVRD also expanded into Argentina when, in late 1992, it bought five percent of Cymose, Argentina's major steel company. The *raison d'être* for such overseas ventures is diversification and gaining a piece of higher value-added downstream business. Equally important and critical to maintaining an international competitive edge, such strategic alliances provide access to new markets, technology, and expertise. Under the Cardoso administration, this company, with a net worth of around $9 billion, is preparing to be privatized.

Grupo Odebrecht is another major Brazilian company, involved in engineering, heavy construction contracting, and petrochemicals. In the late 1980s and early 1990s, despite the adverse economic conditions at home, Grupo Odebrecht expanded its business to seventeen countries. In 1992, it posted sales of $5.6 billion. Grupo Odebrecht was established in the 1920s in Recife, eventually moving its headquarters to Salvador in 1926, the capital of Bahia. Enjoying contracts from both the government and private sector, Grupo Odebrecht expanded and in 1954 was officially incorporated as Norberto Odebrecht Constructora Ltda. In the 1960s, it become a major player in Brazil's markets and in the next two decades, Odebrecht expanded its operations outside of the country. By the early 1990s, Grupo Odebrecht presided over a broad range of activities beyond engineering—chemicals, oil drilling, electronics, and mining. One of the company's subsidiaries, SLP Engineering of the United Kingdom, even manufactures modules for offshore oil and natural gas platforms in the North Sea.

Grupo Odebrecht demonstrates that Brazilian companies can be competitive in international markets. In the 1990s, its firms are building airports and highways as well as metro systems and hydroelectric dams. Operations are in South America, Africa, Asia, Europe, and the United States, with offices in California, Florida, London, Lisbon, Singapore, and India. In the United States, Odebrecht has received contracts for Miami's Metromover Rail System and Route 56 Freeway in San Diego County.

Brazil's private sector is large and plays a critical role in maintaining the country's economic momentum. However, if Brazil is to survive to the next century as a viable economic entity, changes are necessary. Without a movement to fiscal responsibility, a reduction in inflation, addressing some of the social needs, and greater accountability in government, Brazil's passage into the next century will be problematic. The Cardoso administration has indicated that it regards many of these as problems, and measures are underway to rectify the situation, though the challenges remain significant.

Conclusion

Brazil remains "the country of the future." This large and resource-rich nation remains a powerful economic factor in the Americas, but its ongoing economic disequilibrium still weakens Brasilia's ability to consolidate a more active and positive regional role, let alone provide a better standard of living for the majority of its citizens. Brazil's inability to restructure its economy and deal with its social and political problems offers an uncertain scenario for the future. In fact, the assessment of Ronald Schneider that "during the first half of the 1990s Brazil will likely experience a variety of 'crises'" was not only accurate, but perhaps could be extended through the entire decade.[43] Brazil remains a victim of its own structural inefficiencies and the debilitating inability of its political elites to address the critical problems facing the nation. The Cardoso administration has been viewed as a turning point, and indeed it may be so, yet the challenges remain considerable. Brazil's full potential is in the next century.

Notes

1. See Government of Brazil, *Plano de Controle Macroeconômico*, Ministério da Fazenda, July 1987, p. 11 provides a development of the thesis that the external debt burden generates inflation.
2. A useful synopsis of Brazil's earliest debt crises can be found in Rudiger Dornbusch and Elaine Cardoso, *Brazilian Debt: A Requiem for Muddling Through* Discussion Paper No. 243 (London: Centre for Economic Policy Research, June 1988).
3. Ibid., p. 8.
4. Mario Henrique Simonsen, "Brazil," in *The Open Economy*, eds. Rudiger Dornbusch and F. Leslie C.H. Helmers (London: Oxford University Press, 1988), p. 285.
5. Ibid., p. 286.
6. Paulo Rabello de Castro and Marcio Ronci, "Sixty Years of Populism in Brazil," in *The Macroeconomics of Populism in Latin America*, eds. Rudiger Dornbusch and Sebastian Edwards (Chicago and London: The University of Chicago Press, 1991), p. 154.
7. Ibid., p. 157.
8. Benjamin Keen, *A History of Latin America* (Boston, Mass.: Houghton Mifflin Company, 1992), p. 347.
9. Thomas E. Skidmore, *Politics in Brazil: 1930–1964: An Experiment in Democracy* (London: Oxford University Press, 1967), p. 33.
10. De Castro and Ronci, "Sixty Years of Populism," p. 156.
11. Ronald M. Schneider, *The Political System of Brazil: Emergence of a "Modernizing" Authoritarian Regime* (New York: Columbia University Press, 1991), p. 83.
12. De Castro and Ronci, "Sixty Years of Populism," p. 160.
13. For more details on the Escola Superior de Guerra, see Alfred Stepan, *The Military in Politics: Changing Patterns in Brazil* (Princeton, N.J.: Princeton University Press, 1971), pp. 172–87.
14. See Maria Silvia Bastos Marques, "Aceleração inflacionária no Brasil: 1978–1983," *Revista Brasileira de Economia* 39, no. 4 (1985): p. 361.
15. World Bank, *World Debt Tables: External Debt of Developing Countries, Volume III. Country Tables, 1970–79* (Washington, D.C.: World Bank, 1989), p. 46.
16. De Castro and Ronci, "Sixty Years of Populism," p. 163.
17. Ronald M. Schneider, *"Order and Progress": A Political History of Brazil* (Boulder, Colo.: Westview Press, 1991), p. 306.
18. Eliana A. Cardoso and Daniel Dantas, "Brazil," in *Latin American Adjustment*, ed. John Williamson (Washington, D.C.: Institute for International Economics, 1990), p. 129.
19. Ken Serbin, "Collor's Impeachment and the Struggle for Change," *North-South Focus: Brazil*, vol. II, no. 2 (1993): p. 2.
20. Inter-American Development Bank, *Economic and Social Progress in Latin America 1991 Report* (Washington, D.C.: Inter-American Development Bank, 1991), p. 51.
21. Ibid.
22. Marcílio Marques Moreira, "The Brazilian Quandary Revisited," *In the Shadow of the Debt: Emerging Issues in Latin America* (New York: The Twentieth Century Fund, 1992), p. 140.
23. Ibid., p. 3.
24. Ibid.

25. Salomon Brothers, *Emerging Markets Biweekly* (June 5, 1992): p. 3.
26. Roberto Teixeiro da Costa, *Newsletter* (November 13, 1992): p. 11.
27. Blooker Associates, "Itamar: The First 60 Days," Blooker Associates, (Sao Paulo) (December 3, 1992): p. 1.
28. Ibid.
29. Schneider, *"Order and Progress,"* p. 346.
30. William Perry, "The 1994 Brazilian Election, Second Round Results," report #4 *CSIS Western Hemisphere Election Study Series* (January 12, 1995): p. 5.
31. Ibid.
32. Quoted in Ian Katz, "Brazil: This Could Just Be the Strike Cardoso Needed," *Businessweek* (June 12, 1995): p. 23.
33. International Monetary Fund, *International Financial Statistics, March 1996* (Washington, D.C.: International Monetary Fund, 1996) p. 129.
34. Matt Moffett, "Brazil Aims to Break Inflation's Bedrock," *Wall Street Journal* (June 29, 1995): p. A12.
35. Riordan Roett, *Brazil: Politics in a Patrimonial Society* (Boston, Mass.: Allyn and Bacon, Inc., 1972), p. 26.
36. Quoted from James Brooke, "Brazil's President Prevailing Despite Disruptive Oil Strike," *New York Times*, (June 2, 1995): p. A10.
37. Serbin, "Collor's Impeachment," p. 4.
38. Alfred Stepan, "The Brazilian Impeachment and Beyond," *Camoes Center Quarterly*, vol. 4, nos. 3 and 4, (Autumn and Winter 1992–93): p. 40.
39. Ibid.
40. "CVRD—an Eco-friendly Industrial Giant," *Euromoney* (May 1993): p. 122.
41. Ibid., p. 123.
42. Ibid.
43. Schneider, *"Order and Progress,"* p. 385.

8

A Road with Many Detours: Venezuela

In the dark hours just past midnight on 4 February 1992 a number of middle-level army officers and their troops gathered in Caracas and other Venezuelan cities. With the hardened resolve of men committed to the task of changing history, the rebels embarked on a mission to kill their country's elected president, Carlos Andrés Pérez, and install a military government guided by vague ideals that evoked the name of Simon Bolivar, the country's nineteenth-century liberator. By the end of the day, after an assassination attempt on the president, several battles between loyalist and rebel troops, and a number of dead and wounded, the coup attempt fizzled. Senior officers rallied loyal units to the government, the major conspirators were captured, and an uneasy calm settled on Venezuela. After months of rumors, public skittishness, and capital flight, another violent coup attempt erupted on 27 November 1992, when air force units sought to overthrow the government. Although quickly suppressed, the presidential palace was bombed and a large, unknown number of people were killed in the fighting.

Venezuela's coup attempts in 1992 sent shock waves throughout the Americas. What surprised many analysts was the bloody intention of the coup leaders to terminate the Pérez presidency. Equally unsettling was widespread public sentiment for the coup. The mood inside Venezuela had been uneasy since the February 1989 riots, provoked by the Pérez government's structural adjustment program. Public discontent with corruption in government, an erosion in the standard of living for many Venezuelans, and the perception of a growing discrepancy between the privileged few and disadvantaged many contributed to apathy over two coup attempts that could have ended a period of democratic government commencing in 1958.

Examining Venezuela in the mid-1990s suggests—at least for now—the absence of a clear-cut fast-forward option for Venezuela. While Chile, Argentina, and possibly Colombia are on their way to reaching the next level of development, Venezuela teeters on the edge. Although privatization has been launched and a broadening of elective offices has been implemented, serious questions linger about the extent of societal consensus over the direction of economic policy and the nature of political responsibility exercised by national leaders. Despite the durability of the political system to survive authoritarian challenges, the danger of economic failure, and ossification of the political system under the influence of personal greed, party politics and corruption remain critical challenges in the 1990s.

Venezuela evolved from the colonial period led by an upper class largely of European descent. While it attracted new waves of European settlers, much of the native population was either eliminated or became small peripheral groups in society. Venezuela also had a small segment of its population of African descent, especially in Caribbean coastal areas where slaves were brought to work on sugarcane plantations or mines. Venezuela, like neighboring Colombia, was part of the great liberation struggle against Spanish rule, with independence from Madrid coming to Colombia in 1819 and Venezuela in 1810. Simon Bolivar played an important role in the fight against Spain, and Venezuela was initially part of a confederation that included present-day Colombia, Ecuador, and Panama. That confederation collapsed by 1830 with Colombia and Venezuela going their own ways.

The Modern Venezuelan Economy: Oil King

Venezuela's modern national period commenced under the leadership of one of Bolivar's generals, José Antonio Páez. A number of strongmen or *caudillos* followed him, establishing a political economy that survived until the late 1920s. The early Venezuelan economy was agricultural and poor, dominated by tobacco, cacao, sugar, and indigo exports. The economy's agricultural orientation created a small ruling class of large land owners who controlled exports, accepted the state's protection, and, in turn, supported the various *caudillos*. The last included such individuals as Antonio Guzmàn Blanco (also known as

"The Illustrious American"), Cipriano Castro (who had the ill-fortune of incurring the wrath of a debt-collecting Anglo-German naval squadron in 1902), and Juan Vincente Gómez.

Venezuela's fortunes changed radically in the 1920s during the Gómez regime when modern oil exploration took off. Venezuela had long been aware of its oil resources, but it was only with the world shift to petroleum as a primary source of fuel in the early 1900s that demand increased sufficiently to begin largescale exploration and exploitation. By 1928, Dutch Shell, Standard Oil, and Gulf controlled close to 90 percent of the market, a situation reflected by the Maracaibo Basin being opened to commercial oil production. Venezuela would never be the same. As one observer noted: "The profits were enormous. Gómez and his supporters became extremely rich, but the flood of money also benefitted the country as a whole. A chronic debtor nation, Venezuela became solvent, and its currency, the bolivar, long a source of jokes, became a respected coin in international markets."[1]

Venezuela's changed circumstances had an impact on the country's political economy. The new inflow of wealth greatly allowed Gómez to centralize power, create a strong national army, and end banditry. The Venezuelan leader ruled with an iron hand, establishing and maintaining one of Latin America's more memorable dictatorships.[2] At the same time, Venezuela went from being one of Latin America's more backward economies and underdeveloped societies into one of the most cosmopolitan societies and industrialized economies. Ultimately, the old political structure presided over by Gómez buckled under the strain. While the old guard of large land-owners was increasingly marginalized, little of the oil wealth trickled down to the middle and working classes. It is important to underscore that Venezuela was changing, but the transformations benefited only a small group at the top. The agricultural sector, in particular, underwent a profound downturn: usually resistant to modernization efforts, the oil industry soon lured many of its workers away, reducing its supply of available labor. Moreover, imports of foreign foodstuffs were now affordable.

The modernization process rippling through Venezuelan society also created a middle class aware of the inequalities inherent in the Gómez regime. Venezuelan professionals and would-be entrepreneurs were angered and frustrated by what they perceived as foreign economic domination and the regime's inclination toward monopoly, nepotism, and corruption.[3] Discontent emerged in the universities in 1928, reflecting the birth of an anti-Gómez movement. Although the dictator lasted until 17 December 1935, when he died due to ill health, the authoritarian structure he created was not destined to survive him for long. In the 1936–46 period, a democratic movement emerged to challenge the autocrats. Of particular importance was Rómulo Betancourt. Although Betancourt's work as one of Venezuela's great democratic figures was temporarily overshadowed by the rule of Marcos Pérez Jiménez from 1948 to 1958, the foundations were laid for a "democratic" future.

It was in the 1930s and 1940s that Venezuela's future political elite was forged. The forerunners of what were to become Betancourt's Acción Democrática or Democratic Action (AD) and its long-time rival, the Comité Pro-Elecciones Independientes (COPEI) or the Christian Socialist Party, emerged in this period. Both parties advocated a democratic plank—elections, freedom of expression, and a more egalitarian view that the state existed for the benefit of the citizens, not a small clique who surrounded the president. In terms of economic policy, the state was to play a central role. In many respects, AD's early ideology can be described as socialist, a factor that initially incurred the mistrust of the business sector.

AD was legally recognized in 1941 and participated in a three year transitional regime before it was outlawed in 1948 after a military coup. During the Jiménez dictatorship, AD was an active member of the opposition and reemerged in 1958, with a broad base of support and a more moderate political philosophy that was more accepted in the business community.

Venezuela's other major party, COPEI, emerged in 1946 under the leadership of Rafael Caldera, who sought and failed to achieve the presidency in the 1947 elections. Although COPEI gained seats in the Chamber of Deputies and the Senate in that same election, it soon found itself in the opposition with the 1948 coup. The party's program was based on the social doctrines of the Catholic Church, which it sought to raise the country's standard of living.

Both AD and COPEI survived the Jiménez dictatorship to become the country's major parties. Through the 1960s and 1970s, Venezuela evolved as a two-party political system, alternating AD and COPEI presidents. Radical Marxist groups, inspired by the Cuban Revolution, were profoundly disappointed by this development, and in the 1960s briefly challenged the government through guerrilla warfare. However, by the late 1960s the guerrilla movement ebbed and a number of former Marxist rebels founded the Movimiento al Socialismo or MAS, sometimes referred to as Venezuela's second and a half party.[4]

The Statist Political Culture

Oil became the fountain of Venezuelan wealth in the twentieth century. From its wellsprings came a modern industrial economy, linked to the outside world through oil pipelines, tankers, and contracts with multinational firms. While oil provided Venezuela a source of wealth not shared by many nations, it also created a number of problems that continue to confound the country on the edge of the twenty-first century. In particular, the heavy reliance on oil established a pattern of development in which the state became the great purveyor of employment, financial well-being and, through those two, political power.

Robert Bottome, the president of Veneconomía, a Caracas-based economic consulting firm, has likened Venezuela's oil wealth and its political-economic role as analogous to a wheel with the state at the hub. Oil wealth was the property of the state because of the basic legal premise handed down from colonial times in much of Latin America that subsoil wealth does not belong to the surface property holder but to the Crown and, with independence, the national government.[5] With the central government at the hub, willing and able to distribute hydrocarbon revenues to other sectors of society, Venezuelans came to expect the state to provide economic growth and largesse. At the same time, the state's role as the supreme interlocutor meant that direct communication between individual sectors became almost nonexistent: each sector negotiated separately with the central government, seeking tariff protection or credit, and wage hikes. For the state's favor, business accepted a high degree of control and regulation, while labor accepted that its ability to strike was curtailed.

The evolution-of-the-wheel principle had a political dimension: although nominally a democracy, Venezuela's political system was in fact controlled by a relatively small national elite consisting of the bureaucracy, large business concerns, labor union chiefs, and the political parties. The wheel system worked well as long as oil prices remained relatively high and the country maintained its access to international capital markets. Although it would be difficult to argue that the Venezuelan political system was similar to Mexico's one—party-dominated system, the ability of the national elite to dominate in both major political parties cannot be dismissed. Moreover, the nature of the two major political parties in Venezuela had become increasingly bureaucratic and unresponsive to public demands. In a sense, Venezuela's initially strong participatory thrust was blunted by democratic centralism that rendered AD and COPEI incapable of adjusting to changed economic circumstances.[6]

The wheel system also provided the means to buy off the military and labor, and provide better health care and education to the population than in most Latin American countries. Despite the skewed nature of national income distribution, life expectancy increased from under fifty years in the 1920s to over seventy in the 1990s; the average Venezuelan is four to six inches taller than his or her parents; and illiteracy was reduced.[7] Furthermore, the country's oil wealth allowed successive governments to maintain artificially low prices on everything from milk and medicine to *arepas* (cornmeal buns). As one observer noted of the subsidized nature of the economy: "In financial terms, Venezuela was living in a dream world."[8]

The Venezuelan Constitution of 1961 upheld the statist development model. Carlos Ball, a Venezuelan journalist, commented of that document: "It is conceptually closer to the constitution of the old Soviet Union than to the U.S. Constitution."[9] Ball noted that a number of articles in the constitution offer gracious gifts of the state pertaining to education, health care, vacations, housing and employment. For example, Article 86 provides for paid vacations and holidays; the state will strive toward a shorter working day "and convenient measures will be implemented for the better use of free time."[10] Another example is Article 98, which sanctions the state's economic planning and regulation as well as controlling the distribution of wealth.

The combination of oil wealth, good intentions, and a statist development philosophy resulted in a welfare state that was eventually beyond the country's means. The massive upward surge in oil prices in 1973 and 1974 reinforced the tendency to look to the welfare state for guidance, an attitude that would be hard to change. Carlos Andrés Pérez's AD government, newly elected in 1973, benefitted from this windfall, especially after 1975 when the oil industry was nationalized. Exports shot up from $3.15 billion in 1972 to $11.1 billion in 1974, while foreign exchange reserves expanded from a little over a billion dollars to $5.4 billion in the same period.[11]

The massive infusion of capital into Venezuela resulted in reinforcing the wheel system as the two major political parties, AD and COPEI, held the power to decide the allocation of that capital. This situation also reinforced the tendency of state dominance in the economy which was reflected by overregulation. In 1970, state-owned enterprises accounted for 4 percent of industrial value added; by 1986 they were 42 percent, concentrated in petroleum refining, nonferrous metals, iron and steel, and chemical and petrochemical products.[12] State dominance of the economy was not limited to those sectors—the government monopolized telecommunications, shipping and port handling, and postal services. By the close of the 1980s, there were nearly 125 commercially oriented state-owned enterprises, many of which were dependent on government transfers to survive.[13]

While many state-owned firms were poorly run, accountability of national funds was lacking: a number of poorly conceived megaprojects were launched and corrupt politicians and their cohorts dipped into the public till. The enormous amount of wealth, however, made siphoning public funds less noticeable. Although there was some public outrage about corrupt practices, Venezuelans appeared to have reached a new stage of development in which they would soon become part of the industrialized club of nations.

The heavy demands for capital could not be met by oil revenues. In the 1970s the first Pérez administration, therefore, turned to foreign borrowing. Venezuela's total external debt grew from $1.78 billion in 1974 to $23.9 billion in 1979, Pérez's last year as president.[14] By 1983, when Venezuela's external debt peaked at $38.2 billion, the country was no longer able to live beyond its means and was soon forced to reschedule its external debt, which meant a greatly reduced access to outside capital.

Although the means by which to maintain the wheel system were greatly diminished in the 1980s, especially after oil prices fell drastically in 1986, opponents of change remained well-entrenched and able to slow any meaningful structural adjustments. This was painfully evident during Jaime Lusinchi's term as president from 1984 to early 1989. Coming into office with a comfortable level of reserves and high hopes, Lusinchi failed to adjust to new international circumstances. Instead of reducing the state's role in the economy and cutting costs, Lusinchi embarked upon an inflationary program that sought to spend Venezuela out of its recession. The oil price downturn, deepening corruption in the government, and failure of public spending to jumpstart the economy left the country adrift by 1988. Although 5.8 percent economic growth was achieved in 1988, inflation reached an unheard of 84 percent and the public sector deficit ballooned to 10 percent of gross domestic product.[15] Moreover, the very public affair of the president with his mistress, Blanca de Ibañez, and charges that she was exercising undue political authority in Miraflores Palace left many Venezuelans disillusioned with the political system.[16] The wheel had not only slowed, but was in the process of breaking down.

The 4 December 1988 elections were fought against a background of growing economic crisis. By election time it was evident that the economy was cooling. More worrisome was the widening deficit in the current account balance-of-payments, which would ultimately end the year at $5.8 billion, depleting the country's foreign exchange reserves and adding pressure on the government to seek a new round of external debt rescheduling with its commercial banks. Another sour note was growing concern that Colombian drug money was entering the nation and influencing political affairs—during the course of the campaign there were periodic allegations that funds were received from *narcotraficantes* seeking influence and access to power.[17]

The permeating sense of pessimism in Venezuela benefitted Pérez, who was able to project the image of a senior statesman already tested by national leadership. With assistance from local and North American public relations firms, he was able to tap a desire that he would restore the heady days of the 1970s when oil prices were high. COPEI's candidate, Eduardo Fernández, fought an uphill battle against Pérez's popular personality. His campaign was complicated by internal COPEI intrigue: former president Rafael Caldera, the party's founder, sought to gain his party's nomination as presidential candidate. Although Fernández defeated Caldera's gambit, the COPEI campaign failed to diminish Pérez's lead.

The country's smaller, less popular parties, such as the Movimiento al Socialismo and CAUSA R, were unable to break the dominance of the two major parties. Venezuela went to the polls on 4 December 1988 with the awareness that Carlos Andres Pérez was to return. He did not disappoint the country—Pérez won 54.6 percent of the vote, while Fernández received 41.7 percent. Disillusion with the major parties, however, was evident: seeking an alternative to AD and COPEI, voters gave the minor parties a record high of 38 seats in the Chamber of Deputies, 19 of which were on the united left ballot of MAS. AD as a party was the big loser because its plurality of 43 percent was well under its 56 percent showing in the 1983 elections. AD's failure to win an outright majority meant that the incoming president was forced to deal with members of other parties in Congress to pass his soon-to-be announced economic reform program.

The Return of Carlos Andres Pérez

The return of Carlos Andrés Pérez to the presidency in February 1989 brought high expectations for many Venezuelans. The Lushinchi years had, after all, ended on a sour note of political and economic scandals. Pérez was expected to return the country to a more prosperous path. Indeed, during the campaign he indicated that his administration would continue the state's largesse. The reality, however, was much different. The incoming president had decided to break with the past in a radical fashion. In 1989, the new Pérez administration initiated a series of reforms that sought to shift economic activity from government control to free markets, restructure a costly and inefficient public sector, and break the power of the political cliques that had been the major beneficiaries of state capitalism since the 1970s.[18] Pérez's program included eliminating price controls, freeing interest rates to market forces, scrapping exchange controls, reducing protectionist trade restrictions, and reorganizing or privatizing state companies and government services. Trade liberalization was bolstered by Venezuela's joining the GATT in 1989.

Despite a difficult year in 1989, with a steep economic contraction of 8.3 percent and antireform riots in February of that year, the government stuck to its policy. The economy responded in 1990, growing 5.3 percent with the nonoil sector expanding by 3.7 percent. Higher oil prices also helped: despite a large increase in government spending, the public sector generated a surplus of 1 percent of GDP.[19] Equally significant, inflation fell to 36.5 percent. On the external side, Venezuela achieved record exports of $17.4 billion, the current account was in a surplus of $8.2 billion, and the central bank's gross external reserves ended the year at $11.6 billion. Adding to the positive news was Venezuela's successful conclusion of a Brady Plan restructuring of its $21 billion commercial bank debt, which together with the economic reforms, tentatively restored the country's access to international capital markets.

Newfound confidence in Venezuela as a place for foreign investment was evident in 1991 when the government moved forward with
privatizing the national telephone company, the Compañía Anonima
Nacional de Teléfonos de Venezuela (CANTV). Bidding for the 40
percent controlling interest in CANTV was competitive, going at $4.7
billion on 19 November 1991 to a consortium led by GTE Corporation
and including AT&T Company, Telefônica de España, Venezuela's
Banco Mercantil and Electridad de Caracas. Under the agreement,
GTE gained control of 40 percent of the company with employees
holding 11 percent and the government retaining a 49 percent share.
Additionally, GTE was required to install some 300,000 new lines
annually—necessitating a yearly $600 million over the next 10 years—
and to double the level of service by 1997.[20]

What was encouraging about the privatization was the caliber of the
bidders. Other parties interested in purchasing ownership of CANTV
included a rival consortium headed by Bell Atlantic and Bell Canada,
with minor partners Italcable, Japan's NPP, and local investors Banco
Provincial, Finalven, and Organización Cisneros. Other companies
making bids were Ameritech, Southwestern Bell, U.S. West, PTT
Telecom Holanda, Cable & Wireless, France Telecom, and Detecom
Alemania.

CANTV was not the only company to be privatized. By the end of
1991, six other major holdings, including the national airline, VIASA,
joined the ranks of the private sector. Altogether these transactions
yielded roughly $2.4 billion in cash proceeds.[21] That was not all: the
Pérez administration also liquidated the national ports agency,
privatized cargo handling, and transferred responsibility for adminis-
tering the ports to new regional port authorities. The administration
also initiated major restructuring programs, encompassing various degrees of privatization in a number of other public enterprises: INAVI
(housing), IPOSTEL (postal service), INOS (water and sewerage),
CADAFE (electricity), SIDOR (steel), IMAU (trash collection), and
VTV (television).[22]

The economic reform package's radical nature established battle
lines between the reformers, a small group of government technocrats
and part of the private sector, vis-à-vis what has been referred to as
"vested interests." The latter have been identified as businessmen who
enjoyed the state's protection from foreign competition, long-time bureaucrats, labor leaders, and party officials, all of whom felt threatened

by a more open economic and political system. The difficult economic circumstances in which Venezuela found itself in 1989, when the economy contracted by 8.6 percent did not help matters, especially as opponents of reform were able to play on a reform program that had the support of the two organizations that often served as demons to developing countries, the International Monetary Fund and the World Bank.

The deep recession in 1989, characterized by high unemployment and rising prices on many daily necessities helped stimulate the February 1989 riots, during which Caracas and a number of major cities were briefly convulsed with rioting and a police crackdown. More than 300 people died in the riots according to official figures, leaving a number of Venezuelans to question the path their country had embarked upon. Despite periodic disturbances in 1990 and 1991, it appeared that the reform process was becoming rooted in Venezuela's political economy. However, discontent remained. Vested interests continued to hinder reforms, and the general public remained bewildered with the process that reshaped the economy around them, but left many of the same old groups in privileged positions. Public discontent was also heard within the lower ranks of the army.

The February 1992 Coup Attempt

The attempted military *putsch* by the Bolivarian Military Movement was short-lived and bloody. It was also a major shock to many who had come to take democracy for granted in Venezuela. Caracas, Maracay, and Valencia were the stages for this unexpected drama. The coup leaders announced that the revolt sought to "rescue the Venezuelan people, hurt so much by politicians, demagoguery, and bureaucracy."[23] President Pérez narrowly escaped certain death at the hands of the mutineers not once, but twice. Despite the murderous turn of events, the military rebellion was put down in about 12 hours. Five military units were involved: a paratroop battalion, an infantry battalion, an armored brigade, and two artillery units. In all, around 130 officers and 1,000 troops took part. The leader of the coup, Lt. Colonel Hugo Chávez, and a number of other officers were arrested. Lower ranks were not arrested as they were deemed to have been merely following the orders of their officers.

This crisis was a close call, and had the insurgents been luckier or better organized, it might have succeeded. President Pérez survived because of the loyalty of senior officers and other units of the army, the national guard, air force, and police. Without their support, Venezuela would have been transformed from being one of Latin America's more enduring democracies to a military regime with a hazy ideological base.

What caused the coup attempt? The mid-ranking and junior military officers involved were driven by the following: dissatisfaction with low military wages and poor housing conditions for military personnel; fears that the government was about to cede territory to neighboring Colombia in a border dispute; perceptions of widespread government, labor union, and judicial corruption; and adverse social consequences of the government's economic program, especially the 33 percent decline in living standards in the first three years of the Pérez administration.[24] Other reasons included rising crime, reduced personnel security, greater activity by extremist and subversive groups, and the need to make the main political institutions more responsive to the population.

Although all these factors were significant, corruption was probably one of the most problematic causes of the coup. While corruption in a time of plenty can be more easily tolerated, corruption in a time of austerity and belt-tightening by the majority is not tolerable. This was clearly an element in the Venezuelan *putsch*. As Ruth Caprile, an authority on corruption in Venezuela, noted: "In the 1960s, corruption was a form of redistribution of wealth, and was good in its way. But it has now become a strictly monetary transaction and is now concentrating wealth in the political class."[25] Additionally, in 1991 the president's chief of security was forced to resign over allegations of taking kickbacks, and the head of military intelligence and close friend, General Herminio Fuenmayor, resigned after one of his luxury cars was confiscated during a cocaine bust.

Unpunished, but well-known corruption among the nation's elite stimulated growing public disillusionment with Venezuela's political system and was a key factor in provoking the MBR-200 into action. In a prison interview, Lt. Colonel Chávez, the leader of the February coup attempt, stated: "If the ruling class continues to cling to its privileges, if it is incapable of understanding the evolution of the Venezuelan political process and stubbornly resists needed changes, inevitably Venezuelan society will once again exercise the right to rebel, as provided for in Article 200 of our Constitution."[26]

The seriousness of corruption in Venezuela should not be understated, especially as discontent with it drove a number of junior officers to seek the violent overthrow of the government. Other commentators, such as Robert Bottome and U.S. scholar Mark Falcoff, indicated the significance of the corruption factor in the coup attempt and how it threatens Venezuela's political and economic future.[27] Most Venezuelans frankly admit that this is one of their country's biggest problems and a root cause of widespread disgust with the nation's political leadership.

Fast-Forward or Reverse?: To the November Coup and Pérez's Fall

In the aftermath of the February 1992 coup, Venezuela underwent a period of deep soul-searching and political factions did considerable jostling for position. There was speculation that Pérez would not last to the end of his term. Although the situation remained tense, the country's economic performance continued to be solid. The economy actually grew by 8.5 percent in the first half of 1992, led by strong private sector performance.[28] Moreover, about one-third of the capital that foreign investors withdrew from Venezuela after the coup returned by June 1992.[29]

It was realized that if Pérez was to make significant new reforms and leave behind an important legacy of transforming Venezuela from a highly regulated and paternalistic state dependent on the fluctuating fortunes of oil, to a more diversified economy and more affluent society enjoyed by a wider range of citizenry, much was left to be accomplished. The coup attempt was a reflection of a society demanding more extensive reforms to deepen the democratic process and eliminate the privileges of vested interests in the party system and bureaucracy. As the independent governor of Carabobo, Henrique Salas Romer, noted in September 1992: "We're experiencing a civil war which is coming from below and pushing upwards for change, against political parties of Leninist structure and organization which are fighting back from above to hold off the reforms voters are demanding."[30] The coup attempt also signalled to the government that further socioeconomic reform had to take into consideration a number of factors that were previously given scant attention—the military, anticorruption measures, social aspects of the economic program, rising crime, and institutional reform. Without addressing these areas the Pérez government risked another coup attempt or a failed economic program.

Efforts were made to meet military grievances, introduce new anti-corruption measures, and modify the government's economic program to take into consideration higher social spending. In the aftermath of the coup in March 1992, the government softened the reform process by launching a $140 million social investment fund; a temporary price freeze on oil, electricity, and basic foodstuffs; and a 30 percent increase in the minimum wage. Although elements of this process were in motion prior to the coup attempt, the process was hastened after. Prior to the February coup, in January 1992 a social megaproject was proposed to congress, involving nearly $4 billion of additional expenditure on housing, education, transportation, and income support.

Despite these measures to reduce social tensions in Venezuela and diminish the possibility of another coup attempt, the large number of disturbances and strikes, including strikes by the police force, prolonged the harried atmosphere that preceded the coup attempt, especially in the urban areas. Frequent student demonstrations stretched police resources and led to complaints of inadequate police protection of property, in response to which the government decreed an early end to the summer term in the universities. At the same time, the Interior Ministry increased the number of personnel investigating the activities of far left groups including "Bandera Roja" (Red Flag) and "Tercer Camino" (Third Path).

Efforts to maintain control of political tensions failed on 27 November 1992 when a second coup attempt rocked the nation.[31] Although President Pérez's government survived, rebel units of the air force, navy, national guard, and a few police briefly gained control of Libertador Air Force Base in Maracay, 100 kilometers from Caracas, and the Francisco Miranda Air Field in eastern Caracas. They also launched attacks on the presidential palace by fighter jets. At the same time, soldiers stormed the country's television and radio stations, while a number of loyalist intelligence officers were gunned down.

Unlike the February 1992 coup led by mid-level and junior army officers, this attempt was undertaken by high-ranking navy and air force officers. On the other hand, both crises underscored similar problem areas: discontent with corruption, the political system's seeming lack of responsiveness, and the Pérez government's inability to politically justify the tough economic reform program. Although there was no mass uprising to support the coup, a number of Venezuelans took advantage of the temporary breakdown of law and order to loot shopping malls and stores. Sporadic sniper fire added to the confusion.

President Pérez appeared on television on Sunday November 29, stating that he would not resign over the coup attempt, arguing that to do so would "precipitate chaos and tragedy in Venezuela."[32] He also indicated that the 6 December 1992 state and local elections would take place as scheduled. While the president remained in office, the air force coup attempt ultimately resulted in the arrest of about 500 officers and 800 soldiers, and over 200 people were killed.

The implication of the air force coup was that the Pérez administration remained under considerable pressure to resign and the government to reverse the economic reform process. The president himself had become hugely unpopular and isolated with little influence in Congress. Although the president enjoyed a brief surge in the opinion polls for handling the November 27 coup, many Venezuelans remained cynical about the political system. Another equally significant implication was that while many Venezuelans questioned the legitimacy of the political system, the face of the coup as presented on television in the early hours of November 27—three unshaven and armed men of the leftist group Red Flag—demonstrated that the alternatives could be worse. In fact, many Venezuelans articulated that had another tape of well-groomed air force generals been shown on television, reflecting a sense of righteousness and anticorruption, the situation might have been different.[33]

With two coup attempts in Venezuela one of the most pressing projects for the government was to reform the country's political institutions. In February 1992, President Pérez established an eight-man, nonpolitical consultive council to advise on the correct response to the crisis. Apart from advocating an anticorruption campaign and several other steps, the council recommended an overhaul of the constitution, an obviously difficult process considering the entrenched nature of interest groups and their links to the country's political establishment.

Despite poor prospects for constitutional reform, the higher-than-expected voter turnout for the 6 December 1992 elections reflected that some faith continued to reside in the political system. At stake were 22 state governorships, 282 mayors, 2,116 municipal councilmen, and 2,284 parish junta members. This was the first time people voted at the municipal level and only the second time for governors and mayors. Prior to the November 1992 coup attempt, it was believed that there would be a massive voter no-show because they were disgruntled with the political system. After the November coup, voter registration and the distribution of identification cards (necessary to vote) gained considerable momentum. On 6 December 1992, over 50 percent of the voting population turned out to cast a ballot, most of which went against the ruling AD party which lost a number of governorships. At the same time, COPEI could not claim a great victory; a number of gains were made by Causa R, a party viewed for a while as a Venezuelan parallel to Ross Perot in the United States.

Riots, two coup attempts, and public dissatisfaction with the political system as well as the harsh impact of austerity measures on the population must be considered in scrutinizing Venezuela's inability to maintain the fast-forward mode in the early 1990s. Clearly elements of Venezuelan society were supportive of the reform process and believed that without structural adjustment and concomitant liberalization their country could not compete in international markets. However, they remained a minority and the reform process did not survive the Pérez administration. As Carlos Guervón, a professor of International Relations and Negotiations at the School of International Studies and International Economy at the Central University of Venezuela, Caracas noted: "Despite the success of the Pérez government's macroeconomic programs and the ameliorative effects of these compensatory social welfare measures, opposition has been widespread. The government has not managed to form a coalition that can consolidate support for its ambitious reform program, not even among parts of the private sector that have been complaining for years about excessive state intervention."[34]

Venezuela's reform process and political situation took an unexpected turn for the worse on 21 May 1993, when Pérez was peacefully suspended from office. This followed a Supreme Court decision to indict the president on corruption charges and the Senate's approval of the court's ruling. The core of the issue was over a $17 million secret state account authorized by Congress for use by the chief executive. Although Pérez's ouster was a shock, the country's institutions peacefully transferred power to Congressional president Octavio Lepage to act on an interim capacity as chief executive while an interim president was selected by the Congress. In early June, both major parties reached consensus of the elderly senator Ramon J. Valasquez, who served as president to the end of Pérez's term (February 1994).

Caldera's Return

With Pérez's exit, the candidates for the 1993 elections and party leaders assumed greater significance. Two of the major opposition figures, Eduardo Fernández, head of the COPEI and one-time presidential contender, and former COPEI president Rafael Caldera, had radically different views on the future direction of their country. Fernández was supportive of the reform process and indicated that if Venezuela was to compete in international markets, it must change, which meant continuing economic reforms. However, Fernández decided not to compete for the presidency, leaving the COPEI candidacy to the state of Zulia's governor, Oswaldo Alvarez Paz, whose views were close to the party's leader. Ironically, Alvarez Paz represented the greatest potential to carry on the process of economic reform started by Pérez.

The eventual winner, the seventy-seven-year-old Rafael Caldera, consistently opposed the reform process and for most of 1992 rated high in opinion polls as the most popular political figure in the country. However, he decided not run as COPEI's candidate and opted to run as an independent with a loose leftist-oriented alliance with MAS. As a candidate he indicated that he would undo much of the reform process. As one study noted: "The same tack was taken by Rafael Caldera, who centered his winning campaign on his reputation for honesty and on offering voters what opinion polls indicated they wanted: a rollback of market reforms and the reassurance that painful economic measures were not really needed."[35] In this, he had much in common with another major presidential candidate, the Causa R governor of Bolivar, Andrés Valásquez. Although Causa R lacked strong representation throughout the country, it made gains in the 6 December 1992 elections, capturing the mayoral seat of Caracas.

The last major candidate was the ruling AD's former Caracas mayor Claudio Fermin, who indicated that he would not change any national policies that were working well. Fermin's chances of victory, however, were not great because of the ruling party's unpopularity related to corruption and the country's difficult times.

Venezuela's elections were hard-fought and Caldera emerged as a victor with only 33 percent of the popular vote, his two nearest competitors placing a few percentage points behind him. Part of his message that appeared to have a resonant chord was his promise to improve the conditions of the country's poor. Although his leftist-alliance parties fared poorly in Congressional contests, Caldera assumed the national leadership in February 1994 in a relatively strong position due to the perception in many quarters that he would soon end Venezuela's drift.

A New Descent

Taking office in February 1994, the Caldera administration inherited an economy already in a downturn. What would complicate the situation was that while determined to roll-back many of the Carlos Andres Pérez administration's reforms, the new government was initially devoid of any ideas of how to deal with the economy. Real GDP contracted in 1993 and 1994. Inflation was high, around 70.5 percent on an annual basis in December 1994, and a banking crisis was soon to explode with a potential cost of $10 billion. Furthermore, reluctance to implement appropriate policies resulted in the resignation of the central bank president Ruth de Krivoy and several members of the governing board in late April 1994. Worse was soon to follow with a run on the country's currency in international markets and a rapid loss of foreign-exchange reserves, resulting in foreign-exchange controls. On top of all this, the budget deficit continued to widen, helping to fuel inflation. Reflecting these trends, the two major international rating agencies, Moody's and Standard & Poor's, downgraded Venezuela's external debt.

More interventionist than its predecessor and appearing to be desirous of redistributing national wealth, the Caldera administration early in its tenure in 1994 announced a $588 million package of subsidies to the poor (supposedly coming from a new tax on bank transactions).[36] Key funding areas included education, health, and job creation—all necessary to the country's development and certainly badly needed. However, with an already sinking economy, the timing of such a package was questionable. At the same time, Caldera refused to address other critical areas requiring tough decisions, such as tackling inflation which continued to run high in 1995 (around 57 percent at year end), controlling the budget deficit (10.3 percent of GDP at the end of 1995), or moving in any meaningful fashion in the area of privatization.

By early 1996, the Caldera administration's track record included almost continuous switching of top economic officials, an unsuccessful bank bailout (which will take years to recover from), imposed price and foreign-exchange controls, and an ongoing recession. Most of the country's banks were taken over by the government due to a liquidity crisis. Along the way to stemming a capital outflow, civil guarantees were suspended and the police were given the power to detain people without warrants, to enter homes without warrants, and to seize property without compensation.[37] Caldera also overrode Congress on the issue of suspending civil guarantees, leaving the presidency the dominant political force presiding over a troubled economy.

Carlos Ball, a Venezuelan journalist, in a June 1995 opinion piece in the *Wall Street Journal*, noted that Latin Americans "learned some tough economic lessons in the 1980s as the bills for years of ill-conceived statist policies came due."[38] He noted that the change in economic thinking in the region affected the economic notions that: exchange controls create more problems than they solve; price controls serve only as temporary stops against inflation and soon result in even higher inflation, causing economic distortions, shortages, and corruption; and future expansion and stability depend on economic liberalization, the attraction of long-term foreign capital and the allowance of market forces to determine investment priorities. Of his home country and the rest of Latin America's shift to economic reform, Ball commented: "Unfortunately, there is one exception—one country going with full sails in the opposite direction: Venezuela. Its government is using discredited economic formulas and annual oil revenues of $12.5 billion to undo free-market reforms that are now modernizing the rest of the region."[39] Ball also indicated that the government's antibusiness approach and its policies were contributing to an unemployment rate of 17 percent and the massive expansion of the informal sector, which accounts for 50 percent of the working population.

In a belated recognition of Venezuela's economic predicament, in April 1996 the Caldera government announced significant policy changes: lifting of exchange controls, higher sales taxes, raising of gasoline prices, and an economic restructuring program worked out with the IMF, the World Bank, and the Inter-American Development Bank. Yet, the credibility of the program remained linked to a politically weak government and to an international community numbed by years of dysfunctional Venezuelan actions.[40]

Is There Life Beyond Oil?

There is no question that in the last decade of the twentieth century Venezuela remains overly dependent on oil for its revenues, a lesson that the Caldera administration appeared to be only reluctantly willing to acknowledge. The country's export base needs to be broadened if the economy is to be buffered from changes in international hydrocarbon prices. Educational reform is also critical. Venezuela spends 3 percent of GDP and about 40 percent of the educational budget on higher education, which is greater than any other Latin American nation. But, as the World Bank noted: "the economic returns to higher education are lower than those of primary or secondary education."[41] This translates into 80 percent literacy, but a population not entirely prepared to handle the demands of an information-based global economy.

The question for Venezuela is whether the political will exists to stay the course in making difficult decisions and restructuring the economy. Under the Pérez administration, the answer was yes. However, under the Caldera government the answer was for too long no. This means the tough task of tackling the awkward and difficult problems of corruption and political reform are not likely to put the onus on the political elite to lead as opposed to exploit the situation.

Although Venezuela remains dependent on hydrocarbons and the political situation in the late-1990s appears to be in a muddle, there is a gradual attempt to develop other sectors. This should not be overstated, but one area being explored in the 1990s is bananas. Robert Bottome noted: "Venezuela has a very considerable untapped potential in tropical fruits and vegetables."[42] In the past this sector was neglected because of high transportation costs, leaving the country's banana crop to grow wild or to feed pigs. In the early 1990s, however, a local company Frutera del Lago became active in cultivating bananas in western Venezuela and exporting them. In 1991, estimated export earnings for bananas were $18.2 million, a long distance behind Ecuador's $716 million, Colombia's $419 million, and Costa Rica's $400 million.[43] However, export earnings are expected to rise to $80 million by 1996, reflecting a small, yet significant effort to diversify the country's export base and compete in international markets.

While Frutera del Lago is symbolic of a smaller entrepreneurial endeavor, not all Venezuelan firms are ready and able to compete.

This takes time and is dependent upon the national environment. A process of change is gradually beginning to plug the private sectors more into the international economy—something that is not always appreciated as some businessmen in Venezuela prefer to operate behind tariff and nontariff trade barriers. It would be erroneous to say that everyone favors this path. Elements of society, usually labor unions and well-protected businesses, are lukewarm at best and outright hostile at worst to the idea of nontariff trade barriers.

Another positive factor for Venezuela is the development of a free-trade zone with neighboring Colombia. Trade has steadily expanded in the 1990s between the two countries in an atmosphere of falling import restrictions. Initial trepidations came from a number of sectors in both countries, such as the automobile sector, metal-mechanic, and iron and steel industries in Colombia, and sugar producers in Venezuela. The move to freer trade, however, did not result in systemic economic shock along the borders, large numbers of businesses did not go bankrupt, and multitudes of Colombians and Venezuelans were not thrown on the street as newly unemployed victims of a trade agreement. In fact, freer trade along the Colombian-Venezuelan border stood at $360 million in 1989—by 1992 that number had reached a little over $1 billion and projections are for up to $4 billion by the year 2000.[44]

Conclusion

Venezuela has the potential to graduate to fast-forward status. However, that potential is not being reached in the 1990s due to the rebirth of a hazy and personalized shift to populism under Caldera, a lack of consensus on economic policy, and failure to diversify away from an ongoing dependence on oil. Part of Venezuela's dilemma is that the participation in the economy and polity are limited and controlled by deals made among factional potentates in the national elite. The perception is likely to be reinforced that government serves as a conduit for a privileged few, including the corrupt, against the interests of the many. If Venezuela fails to change its course before the turn of the century—despite a significant resource basis and human capital—it will become part of a second tier of troubled Latin American states.

Notes

1.   Iêda Siqueira Wiarda, "Venezuela: The Politics of Democratic Developmentalism,"

in *Latin American Politics and Development*, eds. Howard J. Wiarda and Harvey F. Kline, (Boulder, Colo.: Westview Press, 1985), p. 303.

2. Venezuelan historian Guillermo Morón noted of the period under Gómez: "Gómez ruled for twenty-seven years before he died, on December 17, 1935, to be buried with lavish honors. His period produced social loosening and moral deformation in the generations who had to live through it. The ideas of political liberty and civic integrity lacked all meaning since public feeling was blunted. Any voice which made a criticism was silenced; the gaol or exile were Gómez's 'peace'." *A History of Venezuela* (London: Allen and Unwin, Ltd., 1964), pp. 189–92.

3. Benjamin Keen, *A History of Latin America* (Boston, Mass. Houghton Mifflin Company, 1992), p. 486.

4. For a lengthy discussion of the emergence and genesis of MAS see Steve Ellner, *Venezuela's Movimiento al Socialismo: From Guerrilla Defeat to Innovative Politics* (Durnham, N.C.: Duke University Press, 1988).

5. Robert Bottome, "Venezuela: The Struggle for Reform," *In the Shadow of the Debt: Emerging Issues in Latin America* (New York: The Twentieth Century Fund Press, 1992), p. 62.

6. See John D. Martz, "Party Elites and Leadership in Colombia and Venezuela," *Journal of Latin American Studies*, vol. 24, part I (February 1992): p. 117.

7. Ibid., p. 64.

8. Norman Peagram, "Waking from a Dream State," *Euromoney* (September 1991): p. 202.

9. Carlos Ball, "Seeds of Venezuelan Revolt Found in Statist System," *Wall Street Journal* (February 7, 1992): p. A15.

10. Ibid.

11. International Monetary Fund, *International Financial Statistics Yearbook 1987* (Washington, D.C.: International Monetary Fund, 1987), pp. 710–13.

12. World Bank, *Venezuela and the World Bank: Preparing for the Future* (Washington, D.C.: World Bank, 1992), pp. 11–12.

13. Ibid., p. 12.

14. World Bank, *World Debt Tables, External Debt of Developing Countries, Volume III. Country Tables, 1970–79* (Washington, D.C.: World Bank, 1989), p. 232.

15. Inter-American Development Bank, *Economic and Social Progress in Latin America: 1991 Report* (Washington, D.C.: Inter-American Development Bank, 1991), p. 174.

16. Lusinchi's affair with his mistress, now wife, was highly damaging to the creditability of Venezuela's political system. As Carlos Guerón noted: "The marital and extramarital affairs of the president (a ferocious divorce suit and a flagrant affair between the president and his private secretary, upon which he bestowed extraordinary political and economic power to administer public favors, contracts, and the granting of preferential dollars) emerged simultaneously with serious problems concerning the financing of state expenditures, the drying up of private investment, and capital flight." Carlos Guerón, "Introduction," in *Venezuela in the Wake of Radical Reform* ed. Joseph S. Tulchin with Gary Bland, (Boulder, Colo.: Lynne Reinner, 1993), p. 5.

17. John D. Martz, "Venezuela," in *Latin America and Caribbean Contemporary Record, Volume VII: 1987–88* eds. James M. Malloy and Eduardo A. Gamarra (New York: Holmes and Meier, 1990), p. B199. Also see Melchor Miralles, "Dinero Negro, Beneficio Blanco," *Elite* (Caracas) (January 1, 1990): pp. 34–37; and "Cartel de Medellín Opera en Venezuela," *Ultimas Noticias* (January 19, 1990): p. 25.

18. Bottome, "Venezuela," p. 59. A superb analysis of Venezuela's reform efforts, including its political implications lies in Moisés Naim's, *Paper Tigers and Minotaurs: The Politics of Venezuela's Economic Reforms* (Washington, D.C.: Carnegie Endowment, 1993).
19. Peagram, "Waking from a Dream State," p. 202.
20. Larry Luxner, "GTE wins Venezuelan telephone bid," *The Times of the Americas* (November 27, 1991): p. B1.
21. Ibid., p. 12.
22. Ibid.
23. Quoted in Douglas Farah, "Venezuelan Mutineers Drew Wide Backing," *Washington Post* (February 6, 1992): p. A18.
24. Paul Luke, "Venezuela: Edging Back from the Brink," *Developing Country Research* (July 27, 1992): p. 3.
25. Quoted in Farah, "Venezuelan Mutineers," p. 18.
26. José Vicente Rangel interviewed Commander Hugo Chavez Frias, leader of the 4 February coup attempt, at the Yare prison; (date of interview not given) *El Nacional* (Caracas) (August 30, 1992): p. D2; and *FBIS-LAT-92* (September 21, 1992): p. 41.
27. Bottome, "Venezuela,"; and Mark Falcoff, "Venezuela's Crisis—and Ours," *Latin American Outlook* (September 1992): .
28. Joe Mann, "Caracas Posts 8.5% Growth," *Financial Times* (September 7, 1992) p. 3.
29. "Cash Returning To Venezuela," *Wall Street Journal* (June 11, 1992): p. A10.
30. Quoted from John Sweeney, "Working Against Political and Electoral Reform," *VenEconomy* (September 1992): p. 2.
31. For details of the second coup attempt see the December 14, 1992 issue of the Venezuelan weekly news magazine *Zeta*. Also see Joseph Mann, "Pérez Refuses To Resign Over Venezuela Revolt," *Financial Times* (November 30, 1992): p. 4.
32. Ibid., Perez.
33. This assessment is based on a number of interviews with Venezuelans the week after the coup attempt in December 1992 by Scott B. MacDonald.
34. Carlos Guerón, "Introduction," p. 8.
35. "Epilogue," in *Lessons of the Venezuelan Experience* eds. Louis W. Goodman, Johanna Mendelson Forman, Moisés Naím, Joseph S. Tulchin, and Gary Bland (Baltimore: The Johns Hopkins University, 1995), pp. 400–01.
36. Matt Moffett, "Venezuela's Crusade Against Hoarders Affirms the Obvious: The Economy Is Shot," *Wall Street Journal* (July 13, 1994): p. 12.
37. James Brooke, "New Leader Is Squeezing Venezuelas," *New York Times* (September 4, 1994): p. 18.
38. Carlos Ball, "Venezuela Keeps Swimming Against the Tide," *Wall Street Journal* (June 2, 1995): p. A9.
39. Ibid.
40. Diana Jean Scheno, "Venezuela Joins the Latin Trend to Free Markets," *New York Times* (April 27, 1996): pp. 37–39.
41. World Bank, *Venezuela*, pp. 18–19.
42. Robert Bottome, "Bananas: A Traditional Product; Now a Non-Traditional Export," *VenEconomy* (November 1992): pp. 18–21.
43. Ibid., p. 20.
44. Figures given at the 13th Annual Assembly of the Colombian National Federation of Businesses by the organization's president Sabas Pretelt de la Vega in April 1993.

9

Echoes in Peru

For most of the 1980s and into the early 1990s, the sound of Latin America's reform process was a distant rumble for Peru. While neighboring countries, such as Bolivia and Chile, reconstructed their economic ships, Peru sank into the depths of political turmoil and self-induced financial strangulation, compounded by a withering away of the state. The quirkish leadership of Alan García (1985–90), Sendero Luminoso's (Shining Path) bloody insurgency, the urban terrorism of the Marxist Tupac Amaru guerrillas, the spread of narcoterrorism and drug-related corruption, and economic depression brought Peru in the 1980s to the brink of anarchy and nihilism, a Hobbesian "state of reduce" in which life for many Peruvians was nasty, brutish, and short. The government of Alberto Fujimori, which entered office in July 1990, inherited a bankrupt national treasury, an economy in a depression, and a state losing presence over growing parts of the country as Sendero Luminoso and drug traffickers assumed greater control.

The advent of the Fujimori administration, however, brought a number of surprises, the most significant of which was his government's implementation of a far-reaching economic-stabilization program, followed by structural adjustment. Out of the disaster of hyperinflation, depression, and an almost total isolation from international creditors, the reform program was launched in August 1990, gradually bearing fruit. Inflation, which stood at 7,650 at the end of 1990, fell to 23.7 percent at the end of 1994.[1] Economic activity shifted from a steep recessionary track in the 1988–92 period to a renewal of strong expansion in 1993 and 1994. Peru's 12.9 percent real GDP expansion in 1994 made it the fastest growing economy in Latin America (as well as one of the fastest in the world), while forecasts keep it in the league of growth economies. At the same time, foreign exchange reserves increased from $511 million in 1988 to a healthy $7.1 billion in April 1995, while foreign direct investment, according to the International Monetary Fund, went from a dismal outflow of $89 million in 1984 to an inflow of $349 million in 1993. Yet, the outlook remains cloudy; 1995 forecasts for continued high economic growth were not quite met and an overheating economy was instead the cause of growing concern. Rising inflation and a growing current account deficit were pressuring Peru's free-market policies by 1996.[2]

Yet, despite all the dramatic gains of the Fujimori administration, Peru continues to face daunting challenges. The strong economic growth spurt in the 1993–95 period followed a 25 percent contraction in the 1988–92 period. Grinding poverty still exists and much of the mid-1990s economic turnaround has not trickled down to the vast majority of the population. As one commentator noted: "unless more is done in the area of social policy, income disparities will continue to widen, sewing the seeds for future social unrest."[3]

This chapter examines whether Peru's reform process will take root in the face of such challenges as potential social unrest. Peru's history in the 1990s reflects the difficult path to change the country's economy. In 1992, economic reform measures initiated by the Fujimori administration were potentially threatened by an aggressive return to the political fray by former president Alan García, who maintained a strong influence through his APRA party in Congress and the judiciary, which García had largely appointed. The frustration facing Fujimori with what he perceived as a corrupt and ineffectual political system led him to dissolve Congress and sack most of the Supreme Court in the April *autogolpe*. While these measures were not unpopular, the deterioration that followed in the security situation meant that Fujimori's standing waned. It was recouped, however, when the mystical leader of the Sendero Luminoso, Abimael Guzman, was arrested in September 1992, along with the bulk of the movement's leadership. There followed a sweeping victory for candidates supporting Fujimori (with 38 percent of the vote) in the 22 November 1992 elections for a constituent assembly, charged with reforming Peru's constitution. Although Fujimori won reelection in April 1995 (after Congress amended the constitution) and considerable positive strides have been taken, Peru remains a long distance from economic equilibrium.

A Background of a Two-Tiered Society

It has been said that Peru is a colonial society, much as it was under Spanish rule, with political and economic power in the hands of the local white and mestizo elite and labor supplied by the Indian masses. Although this is a broad generalization, there is some merit to this view in terms of the country's power structure in the 1990s. Peru is a society riven by various distinctions—between the European and mestizo elite, and the Indian lower classes; between urban and rural communities; and increasingly between those who live under the Peruvian state and those who still live under Sendero Luminoso's revolutionary banners. It is also important to add that the ruling classes did not form a monolithic group. They have often been given to intense rivalry, based on personal differences, ideology, and regional interests. In a sense, the past still shapes the present and future in Peru. As Tina Rosenberg noted: "The conquistadors established a society of patron and serf that evolved into the apartheid-like class differences, feudal economic patterns, corruption, and violence of present-day Peru."[4]

The importance of understanding the historical trap that Peru has fallen into was noted by Peruvian economist Felipe Ortiz de Zevallos, who detected six major and reoccurring tendencies in his country's development in the nineteenth and twentieth centuries. The first tendency in Peru's history was the "constant struggle[s] between the numerous and very distinct economic and social groups in Peruvian society that result in dramatic policy shifts."[5] The failure of one group to gain long-term ascendancy meant that national consensus was never fully developed in Peru as it was in neighboring Chile. This is not to argue that there is no Peruvian nationalism, but that a consensus was and is lacking about how to define the Peruvian nation. Clearly the European-descended family in Lima and Trujillo has a different perception about Peru, the Peruvian state and being a Peruvian citizen than their counterparts in a remote Indian village in the mountains around Cuzco or Arequipa. As Alain Hertoghe and Alain Labrousse noted: "Republican Peru has not given birth to a real nation, with its own proper identity, like Mexico after the revolution of 1910–1919. If, in the case of Mexico, the statues of the conquistador Cortez have been struck down, in Lima Francisco Pizarro dominates the central square from the top of his horse."[6] The presence of these rivalries in a political system that bears most of the traits of a patrician state, where the state's role has been defined in terms of its ability to *deliver* welfare, rather than create the conditions for the *creation* of welfare, has meant "recurrent internal conflicts on decisions regarding budgetary allocations and the prices of consumer goods."[7]

The second tendency in Peruvian history was a dependency on export commodities and an expectation of "a steady stream of income from what are essentially natural resource windfalls."[8] This was the case with guano, nitrates, copper, fishmeal, oil, and natural gas. When international markets for these goods increased, Peru's economy boomed; when global prices fell, Peru's economy usually went bust. For example, the age of guano took place in the mid-1800s and lasted until 1875, when supplies were almost exhausted in Peru. During most of the period from the 1840s to the Vienna Stock Market crash of 1873, Peru was able to borrow heavily based on projected future wealth generated by guano exports. Capital poured into the country, helping to develop railroads and other elements of the national infrastructure, not to mention into the pockets of the upper class. When prices plummeted, however, Peru's economy contracted drastically and by 1 January 1876 Lima officially defaulted on its international loan obligations.

Failure of a national consensus left little ground for agreement on the necessary policies to broaden the foundations of the economy and to diversify exports and markets. The almost "happy-go-lucky" approach to export-based development would leave Peru open time and again to booms and busts. It also detracted from concentration on developing any type of coherent fiscal policy, creating internal conditions in which tax evasion by both businesses and individuals was a societal norm while tax exemptions came to be expected by those with connections in the political elite.

The third tendency in Peru's history was the erratic shift in exchange-rate policies. Ortiz de Zevallos noted: "Uncertainty about terms of trade has been the rule rather than the exception because the prices for Peruvian exports have always tended to remain highly volatile while import prices have moved steadily upwards."[9] An added factor is that Peru has often been too optimistic about export price projections.

The fourth tendency is the heavy preponderance of military spending as part of the national budget. Peru, since independence, has had nine military confrontations with five nations on its borders, most recently in the 1990s with Ecuador. Peru's armed forces have also functioned as a key element in holding intact the center's political power; in fact, it has more than once ruled the country, the most recent period from 1968–80. During that time, the armed forces sought to reform Peru on many fronts. While internal differences and a lack of skilled labor undermined many of its state expansion initiatives, the armed forces government maintained a high level of spending for itself. Although it relinquished power to the electoral process in 1980, the Peruvian military continues to carry considerable behind-the-scenes influence, especially as the Sendero Luminoso has remained an ongoing national security threat. At the same time, defense spending—at times reaching 25 percent of the budget—has detracted from other sectors of the economy and arguably weakened initiatives to create national consensus.

The fifth tendency is that the state, through its bureaucracy and subsidies, has grown with every new administration, in particular since the 1960s. This has been because the budget was usually seen as a pork barrel for vested interests, and decisions about investment in new projects were based on political rather than economic criteria.[10] While this was largely true through the mid-1980s, it can be argued that the state began to contract by the late 1980s because of a sharp fall in revenues. As Richard Webb noted in 1991: "The tax base, the public sector's access to credit, and the polity are changing faster than the state itself. The government's food supply is running out, and more and more it is being outmaneuvered and even outmuscled by private citizens."[11] The state in some form, however, remains a central feature to the country's political landscape—albeit its nature may be changing in the 1990s.

The sixth tendency is related to external debt, which is critical to understanding the disastrous 1980s and early 1990s. Considering the various boom and bust cycles Peru has undergone, the inefficient local mechanisms for capital generation and pork barrel mentality of budget formulation, international credit became an indispensable item. Ortiz de Zevallos sadly commented: "The economy centers on borrowing whenever international credit is available, heavily mortgaging the future, particularly to foreign banks, which have been inconsistent regarding Peru's longer-term credit requirements."[12]

Despite these recurrent tendencies, Peru appeared in the 1950s and 1960s on the path of progressive economic development. In fact, World Bank data reveal that Peru's real GDP expanded by a strong 5.4 percent in the 1960–70 period, a more dynamic pace than in Argentina or Chile.[13] The 1970s, however, were to be a period when Peru's government rotated policies that would be replayed in the next two decades with disastrous results. In particular, the military government adopted an inward-looking import-substitution strategy during 1971–75. While this period initially witnessed dynamic growth of 5.3 percent, the foundations were made of clay. The downside to this growth was an increasingly overvalued exchange rate, declining exports, and an acceleration of imports. Unable to raise funds locally on its own underdeveloped capital markets, Peru turned to external borrowing. The end result of these policies was a current account balance-of-payments crisis and ultimately an inability (as in the past) to meet external debt repayments. During the 1976–80 period, the economy floundered, elements of the import-substitution model were abandoned, and annual GDP growth slowed to 1.7 percent.

Peru was also affected by other trends in the 1970s that have continuity in the crisis in the 1990s. Population growth remained high throughout the decade (2.7 percent from 1965–80 according to the World Bank), which helped stimulate the movement of large numbers of people from the countryside to Lima. While Peru's growing population was more urbanized, public-sector employment was created to mop up the numbers. At the same time, the gross inefficiencies of Peru's legal economy stimulated the development of a black market that was to emerge as a parallel economy almost half the size of GDP.[14] In this matrix of population growth, urbanization, expanded state employment, and parallel economy emergence, Lima became the beacon of peasants from the sierra, who had been adversely affected by an unrealistic exchange rate and direct subsidies for food importers.[15] Despite the implementation of orthodox stabilization reforms in the 1976–78 period, these patterns became well-established. Even the technocratic programs that marked the second Belaunde administration from 1980 to 1985 failed to rein in government expenses or create a more stable economic environment.

By the Belaunde administration's end in mid-1985 Peru's downward socioeconomic spiral was plumbing new depths. The number of state-owned enterprises mushroomed from fewer than 30 in 1968 to more than 200 by 1985. Accounting for around 20 percent of the GDP, these state firms were largely inefficient, noncompetitive, politically controlled, and were run at a loss. While the bloated public sector provided some basis for employment, it was not productive. Thus, in the early 1980s, Peru's macroeconomic conditions were deteriorating. In 1983, the real GDP contracted by 12 percent and inflation shot up to 125 percent, then a historic high. That year was also notable for terrible rains in the north and a severe drought in the south (partially caused by El Niño, a ten- to fifteen-year-cycled climatic disaster caused by the warm current off the Peruvian coast). Although there was a moderate recovery in 1984 and 1985, inflation rose sharply. By mid-1985, government finances were slipping further out of control, and an acute balance-of-payments problem marked the external sector. One last negative factor was that the Belaùnde administration was revealed to be exceedingly corrupt, with implications that members of the government were involved in the illicit drug trade and other criminal acts.

Enter Alan García

In times of great crisis and uncertainty, people often look to a savior to ride in on a white horse. On 28 June 1985, when Alan García was sworn in as president of Peru, he appeared to be the hero that the country needed to pull it back from the brink of economic collapse, political bankruptcy, and revolutionary terror.

Who was this new leader, only in his mid-thirties, who promised to bring Peru out of its crisis? The son of an accountant and a schoolteacher, his parents were both politically active as members of the center-left American Popular Revolutionary Alliance (APRA). His father was in fact a close associate to APRA founder Victor Raúl Haya de la Torre, suggestive of a degree of political activism which landed him in prison. The Garcia family's political involvement clearly influenced the younger man's views of the world and Peru's place in that world.

Haya de la Torre founded APRA in 1924 in Mexico, where he was living in exile. His idea was to create a mass-based party that would address the problems facing Latin America as a whole. A five-point program encompassed Haya de la Torre's program, elements of which were evident in García's thinking and speeches. These points were that: (1) the party would be antiimperialist; (2) political unity in Latin America was the ultimate goal; (3) lands and industries would be nationalized; (4) the Panama Canal would be internationalized; and (5) there would be solidarity with all oppressed classes and peoples of the world.[16] While these views were perceived as revolutionary by elements of Peru's upper class, APRA's ideology also rejected the Soviet approach and, in time, offered a reformist alternative in Peru's politics. By the end of the 1960s, APRA had become part of the political establishment with Haya de la Torre presiding over the party's fortunes. The close relationship between the APRA leader and the Garcías' clearly shaped the future leader's views on where he wanted to take his country.

García went on to earn a law degree at Lima's San Marcos University and later, on APRA-paid scholarships, studied political science in Madrid and the Sorbonne. In 1978 he returned home to Peru and was made the party's organization secretary. By 1980, García won a seat in Congress, which gave him national prominence and helped him launch his bid for the presidency in 1985. Ortiz de Zevallos provided one view of the man who came to lead Peru: "As a politician, he is unpredictable, a complex mixture of rational statesman and emotional revolutionary. His popular charisma is as powerful as Perón's was in Argentina or Castro's has been in Cuba. He clearly sees himself as Peru's messiah . . . ."[17]

The initial perception was that the new president, a youthful 36 years of age, came into office with considerable energy necessary to tackle the crisis that he inherited. García sought to preside over a nationalist, consumer-led "heterodox" economic-recovery program. This encompassed a unilateral decision that Peru would limit interest payments to no more than 10 percent of the country's export earnings as interest; freeze prices and exchange rates; raise wages; lower taxes; create public employment programs; and reduce domestic interest rates. These measures sought to stimulate demand and maximize the use of substantial idle capacity present in the economy.[18]

García's APRA government initially made a favorable impression with the majority of Peruvians. The message was simple: the nation's leader was placing his people's welfare above the external creditors in wealthy developed countries. Instead of seeking to make payments on what was then $13 billion external debt, García pumped those funds back into Peru. His popularity ratings were as high as 90 percent in his first months of office. Huge crowds, numbering in the thousands, flocked to the presidential palace to hear their national leader launch tirades from the balcony against the IMF, World Bank, and other international credit institutions.

The return to import-substitution and the 10 percent solution on debt repayments brought a dynamic, yet short-lived boom. From an anemic 2.4 percent real GDP growth in 1985, the Peruvian economy dramatically leaped forward in 1986 by 11.3 percent and 7.8 percent in 1987.[19] The main beneficiaries were the manufacturing, construction and agricultural sectors. At the same time, inflation dropped from 163 percent in 1985 to 78 percent in 1986 and rising marginally in 1987 to 86 percent. In terms of domestic politics, one of the big successes for García's APRA government was the 14.4 percent increase in real wages in 1986 and 8.7 percent in 1987. His ability to protect and augment real wages was even commended at the time by the United Nations.

In the making of the 1986–87 boom, García planted the seeds of his party's loss at the polls in 1990. First, the APRA government isolated Peru in the international creditor community as only a few countries have done (Sudan, Zaire, and Liberia are recent examples). While delighting in snubbing the international banks, García took his country one step further into isolation by announcing in 1986 that he refused to deal with the IMF. Consequently, arrears on both multilateral and commercial bank debt increased through the years of the García administration from $804 million in 1985 to $3.4 billion in 1989.[20] While Chile and Mexico wrestled with structural adjustment programs and sought to reenter international capital markets, Peru went the opposite direction. García's calls to create a debtors' cartel and for other countries to adopt his 10 percent solution won him little if any support among other Latin American nations. Throughout the García period, Peru's external debt mounted due to arrears: by 1989, Peru owed close to $20 billion and had no means to bridge the arrears gap.

The second destructive seed García sowed was his domestic economic program. The boom went bust by 1988, but even before that the business community found itself at odds with the APRA government over the nationalization of Peru's banks in July 1987. However, 1988 was the year of reckoning on the economic front. The state's fiscal resources were pushed to the limit by two years of massive deficit spending. Simply stated, the state-fed pipeline of funds began to sputter, while Peru was hurt by a decline in imported inputs due to a shrinking base of foreign-exchange reserves. These factors had an impact on the manufacturing, mining, and construction sectors, reflected by a 9 percent economic contraction. The mining sector was also effected by labor disputes and oil production decreased as wells ran dry. Without new capital investment, which the state lacked, the internationally linked parts of the Peruvian economy faced considerable problems. Real wages also contracted by a devastating 23 percent, while hyperinflation brought prices on the consumer price index up to 668 percent by the end of 1988. This situation did little to maintain Garcia's standings in the popularity polls.

García and the Sendero Luminoso

The ability of the García administration to implement and maintain policies was greatly undermined by its failure to make inroads against the Sendero Luminoso. Not surprisingly, the Sendero Luminoso emerged as a major national security threat during the García government: high expectations and the charismatic personality of the young president had promised much—too much. The APRA government could not deliver, even by taking an unorthodox path of snubbing the forces of international capitalism like the IMF. Part of the problem was the seeming inability of the APRA government to form a consensus about whether to go down the path of democratic reform or radical confrontation with opposing forces, especially the Sendero Luminoso. The outcome of this internal debate was a profound incoherence in policymaking and a lack of serious results.[21] APRA did propose a dialogue with Sendero Luminoso in the 1985 campaign and following García's election, but Sendero rejected it out of hand. This situation was compounded by a lack of skilled personnel within APRA and García's autocratic style and volatile personality.

The Peruvian public's high expectations were ultimately replaced by frustration and considerable distrust of traditional political parties and their leaders. Sendero Luminoso remained out beyond the traditional political game, refusing to come in from the cold, and maintaining a bizarre credibility among some political constituencies in and outside Peru.

What is the Sendero Luminoso? This radical Maoist group's origins can be traced to 1964 when the Peruvian Communist Party (PCP) held its fourth conference in Lima. At that meeting, members of the pro-Chinese faction split from the pro-Soviet main body to form a new Maoist party. One of the key players in the Maoist camp was Abimael

Guzmán, then a philosophy professor at San Cristobal de Huamanga University and leader of the PCP committee in the department of Ayacucho. Strongly influenced by the writings of veteran socialist José Carlos Mariategui (1894–1930), the fundamental thrust of the Maoist-PCP was rejecting peaceful coexistence that the Soviets opted for and embracing the Maoist maxim: Power grows out of the barrel of a gun. As Eugenio Chang-Rodriquez noted: "It firmly believed that revolutionaries must not await the spontaneous development of sub-jective conditions for revolution; on the contrary, it advanced the idea that true revolutionaries ought to create, develop, and organize the conditions."[22]

Peru's Maoists thought that the Chinese Communist Party's strat-egy of creating a peoples' war in the countryside and surrounding the cities was the correct path and applicable to Peru's conditions. Ac-cordingly, the ranks of guerrilla fighters were to be filled with peas-ants, who would work in an alliance with the workers. The short-lived Movement of the Revolutionary Left (MIR) in the mid-1960s, which was a violent offshoot of APRA, indicated that under certain circum-stances the Maoist strategy could work. Although the MIR was en-tirely crushed by 1966, it was, in varying ways, an inspiration for what was to become the Sendero Luminoso—an alliance between the Quechua-speaking peasants, white and mestizo segments of the popu-lation, and from a tactical perspective, a locus of operations in central Peru. These points were not lost on Guzmán and his closest cadres, who in 1970 broke with Peru's official Maoist Communist Party. While the older party maintained links to the Chinese Communist Party, the nascent Sendero Luminoso channelled its activities through several subsidiary labor and student organizations in southern Peru.

Sendero cadres were active in the 1970–75 period in the recruit-ment and training of peasants in revolutionary violence in the rural region around Ayacucho, while converts were sought in the ranks of teachers, students, and the lower classes in urban areas. According to Chang-Rodriguez, four major points were advocated by Sendero Luminoso: (1) that Peru was both semifeudal and semicolonial; (2) the bourgeoisie was bureaucratic; (3) that the revolutionary war was to proceed from the countryside to the city; and (4) that the country was living in a revolutionary situation.[23]

The 1975–80 period was marked by a withdrawal from university politics and a greater effort at recruitment among the lower class. Part of the appeal to the lower class was aimed at the poverty-stricken

Indian communities—much of Sendero's message was couched in terms of Indian mysticism. Sendero's ranks were also swelled by former MIR members and members of another revolutionary group, the Vanguardia Politico-Militar. By 1980, on the eve of the country's first national elections since the military came to power in a bloodless coup in 1968, Sendero Luminoso felt the time had come to begin its war of liberation. The first blow came on 17 May 1980 when *Senderistas* descended upon the village of Chuschi in Ayacucho department and burned ballot boxes and election materials as well as hanged dogs in Lima. By the end of 1980, as the newly installed civilian administration of President Belaunde took the reins of power, Sendero's attacks intensified and graduated to the assassination of public officials. By December 1982, the Belaunde administration was forced to declare a state of emergency in five provinces of the department of Ayacucho and send in the military.

The most sensational Sendero attack came in March 1982 when several hundred revolutionaries occupied the departmental capital of Ayacucho. Although the occupation was brief, Sendero Luminoso assaulted the headquarters of the Republican Guard, the building of the Peruvian Investigative Police (PIP), and the headquarters of the Civil Guard. They also captured a considerable amount of weapons and military-related equipment, which were taken with them when an orderly retreat was made. Sendero Luminoso was no longer a small gang of intellectuals with violent tendencies, but a full-scale revolutionary movement capable of taking cities.

In the 1980–85 period Sendero Luminoso's campaign intensified. *Senderistas* were responsible for dynamiting power lines and bridges, and assaults on police stations, barracks, and banks, and representatives of the Peruvian state. Although Ayacucho remained the main zone of operation, Sendero Luminoso forces penetrated Indian communities in the north. This included the coca-producing zone in the Upper Huallaga river valley, where Sendero Luminoso insurgents came into conflict with Colombian and Peruvian *narcotraficante* middlemen and the government's antinarcotics police. Sendero cadres were able to take the side of local coca growers and sought to cut the middlemen out of the trade. At the same time, Sendero helped defeat efforts by the antinarcotics police to uproot coca production and disrupt the peasants' source of livelihood.

By 1985, when García became president, Sendero Luminoso was a major challenge to government authority in a number of areas. In fact, it was actively creating a state within a state with an inner core of white and mestizo middle-class intellectuals, who headed an army of young men and women, many with little formal education, but all well-versed in the Senderist credo. While García sought to portray himself as a radical populist leader, seemingly always on the campaign trail, the Sendero Luminoso ideologically flanked him on the left and militarily eroded his control over parts of the country.

Sendero Luminoso, for their part, greeted APRA's April 1985 electoral victory with an assassination spree of the party's mayors and leaders. Although both APRA and García had expressed an interest in a dialogue with Sendero, García responded in his inauguration speech by promising to be implacable against terrorism. At the same time, he sought to take the moral high ground, noting that it was not necessary to combat barbarism with barbarism. Yet, by 1986, the García government was forced to decree a curfew in metropolitan Lima from 1:00 a.m. to 5:00 a.m., and military responses to Sendero Luminoso attacks became increasingly brutal, leading to claims of human rights' abuses.

For García, Sendero Luminoso represented an intractable problem. The president wished to be the man of the people, the savior of Peru, maintaining high standards for human rights, pursuing populist economic policies, and a nonaligned foreign policy. García's liberal-populist credentials were dealt a tough blow in June 1986 when security forces killed an estimated 300 rioting Sendero Luminoso inmates at Lima's jails. Not surprisingly, therefore, by the end of García's term, Sendero Luminoso was a far greater threat to the nation than when he had accepted the presidential sash, largely due to the government's induced economic crisis of historic proportions.

King Coca

Another problem with which the García government was forced to contend with was the international drug trade. In 1980, cocaine was in the process of becoming a multibillion dollar industry, stretching from the coca fields in the Bolivian and Peruvian Andes through refineries in Colombia and north to the lucrative North American markets through Caribbean, Central American, and Mexican transit points. Although Peru was not an exporter of cocaine, it played an important part in the trade as a major source of coca. In 1987, the second year of the García administration, Peru's coca leaf production was estimated between 98,000–121,000 metric tons.[24]

Peru's modern coca industry began in the remote Amazon area in the late 1960s, gaining considerable momentum in the 1970s and early 1980s. Colombian middlemen operating with Cubans in the United States represented the first wave of buyers. This situation changed only moderately in the late 1970s when the Colombians bought for their own organizations in the United States; the Peruvians continued to produce coca and maintained small-scale refining capabilities. The increased demand in the 1980s, however, pushed Peru's industry to produce more and, as drug enforcement measures impinged on refining operations in Colombia, an increasing number of laboratories were moved into the remote border areas of Peru.

The Belaunde government was half-hearted in its attempt to deal with the cocaine trade, and members of the armed forces and police were rumored to be involved. The United States, however, pressured the Belaunde administration to adopt a more rigorous stance on the issue. Beginning in 1982, the U.S. helped finance enforcement as well as crop-eradication and crop-substitution programs. Unfortunately these efforts backfired when the local economy suffered a decline, creating a discontented class of narcopeasants. The military, intent on defeating Sendero Luminoso, was not keen on allowing the narcotics police to make inroads on coca production, which helped generate even more peasant discontent with the central government.

Narcotics policy took a new turn under the García administration—or so it seemed. As the president stated in his inaugural address in July 1985: "A historical scourge threatens our country—the drug traffic, whose temptation to quick riches corrodes consciences and destroys institutions. Our country and others cannot be identified internationally as exporters of poison."[25] In a later state of union address in July 1988, García returned to the drug trade and hinted at the connection between Sendero Luminoso with "their homicidal ideology" and the drug trade: "But there is one very real and objective fact that must be considered separately from the original causes of terrorism. That is the existence of armed gangs—agents of annihilation that have become the armed branch of totalitarianism and drug trafficking in Peru. Criminal totalitarianism joining forces with drug trafficking can claim no ethical motivations."[26]

The García administration initially appeared to make inroads against the drug trade. The armed forces and police were purged of corrupt elements (at least the most noticeable), and significant quantities of coca paste were seized. A number of laboratories were destroyed and illegal airstrips were bombed. However, despite what appeared to be a promising start, the García government's antidrug policy soon became mired in the rest of the country's problems—the collapsing economy, declining capacity of the military, poor or at least testy relations with the United States (a key force in the war on drugs), and the terrorism of Sendero Luminoso and the Tupac Amaru. By the end of the García government in 1990, Peru was the world's leading producer of coca, with an estimated 121,300 hectares of licit and illicit cultivation.[27] Moreover, the Apurinac area was recognized as a second major production region with greater potential than the Upper Huagalla Valley. As one U.S. government report summarized the situation:

> [The government's] control efforts for most of 1990 were impeded by a variety of problems and changes in the political and economic landscape of Peru. The downward spiral of the Peruvian economy continued for the remainder of the administration of Alan García. As a consequence, many public sector responsibilities of the GOP were undermined, including the ability to field effective police and military forces against both traffickers and insurgents. The economic problems were accompanied by growing instability in rural areas, and intensified guerrilla attacks on civilian authorities, public facilities, police and military outposts. . . . President García took no steps to improve the effectiveness of Peruvian counter-narcotics operations in the closing months of his administration.[28]

It was no secret in Peru that the illicit drug trade had helped to keep the economy alive but had also caused many problems—such as keeping the new Sol currency high and discouraging legal exports. Estimates of the amount of drug money returning to Peru ranged from $1–1.5 billion, huge sums especially when compared to the shrinkage of the licit economy through the last years of the 1980s and into 1990.

The Ship of State Sails On—Barely

By the end of his term in 1990, García was a defeated figure, his administration hopelessly unable to stem the tide of Sendero Luminoso's insurgency or contain urban terrorism. The economy was spinning out of control: Peru's inflation rate was more than 7,000 percent and the economy contracted by 11.3 percent in 1989. When the Cambio 90 government of Alberto Fujimori entered office on 28 July 1990 following its electoral victories in April and June, it found the country's international reserves virtually nonexistent.

Fujimori's victory was initially regarded as a watershed for Peruvian democracy—the *autogolpe* was still a distant event. It underlined the people's desire for democracy: the majority of Peruvians preferred to cast their ballots than join ranks with Sendero Luminoso. The mere fact that Alberto Fujimori became the third successive elected civilian head of state in Peru since 1980, in a country with a long history of military intervention and suffering acute security problems, was testimony to this. However, the problems facing Fujimori were, and are, enormous. Despite the areas of progress detailed later in this chapter, the way ahead for Peru is extremely difficult.

Fujimori came into office after defeating the writer turned conservative politician Mario Vargas Llosa. He was, in fact, a surprise winner. A broad range of people, including Peru's political elite, expected Vargas Llosa to win. Vargas Llosa was perceived as the type of leader Peru needed to enact change—dynamic, not tainted by corruption, technocratic, and with a stated preference for market economics. Compared to Fujimori, the son of Japanese immigrants, businessman, and to most appearances a populist, Vargas Llosa's campaign presented a sweeping market-oriented strategy to reform the country's economy.

What tilted the scales of victory to Fujimori was that despite Vargas Llosa's marked ideological differences with the outgoing García administration, his campaign represented political continuity. This was because old-time politicians, largely from the white European elites, eventually rallied around the white politician. In this sense, Vargas Llosa's campaign became "too white," which helped Fujimori gain the vote of the majority of Peru's Indian and mestizo population—critical in winning the election—as exemplified in his campaign slogan, "Un Peruvano como tu," a Peruvian like you. In the end, Vargas Llosa's campaign also lacked deep convictions about the tough road ahead, leading for example to disputes about economic policies within the candidate's own constituency.

Although Fujimori had said little about economic policy as a candidate, his new administration was initially forced into concentrating on reducing hyperinflation and making quiet feelers to the IMF, World Bank, and creditor countries about coming in from the cold of financial isolation. In August 1990, he launched an economic "shock" program that sought to eliminate subsidies, reduce the size of the bureaucracy, initiate trade reform, and eventually reform taxes and privatize state-owned companies.

In 1991, the government began to gain a certain sense of momentum: a tough tight-money policy resulted in inflation falling to 139 percent for the year; talks with the international creditor community were proceeding and a program for eliminating arrears with the IMF, the World Bank, and Inter-American Development Bank was established; and the economy expanded by 2.7 percent after several years of contraction. In September 1991, the IMF gave its blessing to a stabilization program. Equally significant, Peru's net international reserves had grown to $1 billion by November 1991.

As part of the return to the world financial community and economic reform, the Fujimori government embarked upon fiscal consolidation, initially through better tax collection. The tax administration authority in Peru, SUNAT, began in 1990 and was the scene of reform measures: the bureaucracy was halved; all tax officials were required to sit for examinations; wages were competitive with the private sector; and new computers and software were donated by the Inter-American Development Bank. SUNAT gained the ability to hunt down tax evaders by cross-referencing four different types of expenditure—new cars, property, yachts, and foreign holidays.

The significance of improving government collection of revenues is critical, considering the public sector's reduced access to credit in recent decades. As one source noted: "Tax collections as a percentage of GDP had fallen from 20 percent in the late 1970s to 13.5 percent in 1985 and 4 percent last year [1990]. The government has managed to double that within a year (to almost $300 million a month), but only by relying on high, stop-gap fuel and energy taxes—damaging the poor and industry alike."[29] Hence, efforts to tap the parallel economy as well as better collection of the taxes already on the books were steps in the right direction, especially as other reforms were meant to reduce the bureaucratic obstacles to both domestic and foreign businesses. To indicate the seriousness of the effort, SUNAT took the unprecedented step of enforcing the temporary closure orders on six leading Lima businesses in November 1991. Moreover, one of the programs run by SUNAT was a campaign of tax and customs inspectors swooping down on the black marketeers. In one raid in November 1991, SUNAT netted the government some $10 million in black-market goods.

Additional tax reforms were introduced in 1993, furthering the process of fiscal consolidation. Stronger economic growth and increased privatization proceeds contributed to an increase in government finances. The result of such policies was that by 1994 and 1995, Peru had a healthy fiscal surpluses—in 1990 the government deficit as a percentage of GDP was 6.5 percent; in 1994, it shifted into a surplus of 3.5 percent.[30]

Fujimori's approach has been to undo decades of protectionism and state intervention in the economy. In 1991, he issued around 130 decrees under special powers granted by Congress to the executive branch for 150 days to promote private investment, create employment, and combat the Sendero Luminoso and Tupac Amaru. Some seventy economic decrees ended state monopolies in nearly every sector, created favorable terms for foreign and national investment in those sectors, and liberalized labor laws considered the most protective in the world.[31] Peru's conservative newspaper, *Expreso*, in a mid-November 1991 editorial commented of the decrees: "What is certain is that Peru has a new legal framework which has brought down, like the Berlin Wall shaken by a Peruvian-style *perestroika*, several decades of statism and populism which left only poverty, white elephants, and rhetoric."[32]

Efforts to transform Peru's statist economy into a private- sector—driven economy included the gradual termination of the state's monopoly over Peru's ports, electric, and water companies, railways, and postal service as well as its control over airport services and regulation of public transport. Telecommunications was added in November 1991 to the list. By early December, approximately 126 emergency decrees were forwarded to the Congress for passage into law.

The sweeping nature of Fujimori's reforms has also incurred considerable resistance. In December 1991, after a majority of legislators announced plans to eliminate or modify some of the 126 emergency decrees, the presidency and the congress became openly and bitterly confrontational. The president called for a plebiscite proposing a single term for congressmen and new elections for at least one-third of congress. At the same time, Fujimori announced that drug lords might have pressured congress to annul a presidential decree that cracked down on money laundering. In response, Congress passed a motion noting that the comments had "morally discredited" the president.

Congress's disinclination to passively accept sweeping reforms was related to one proposal to reduce the body's 240 members and merge the two chambers. Another area of congressional concern centered on proposals that would give the president and the military wider powers in fighting Sendero Luminoso. Along these lines, almost all political parties in Peru, except Fujimori's Cambio 16, signed a document stating that there was apprehension that "the decrees on pacification will bring about a change in the constitutional order that affect citizens' basic rights, restrict the freedom of popularly elected representatives and militarize the country."[33]

Although the battlelines were drawn about reforming the country in 1991, a struggle that carried over into 1992, the struggle became a national debate. A poll by the public opinion polling firm Apoyo noted in November 1991 that 72 percent of those surveyed supported the reform decrees. This reflected a growing awareness that without change of some sort, Peru would increasingly be unable to deal with the rapidly changing world beyond its borders. Industry Minister Victor Joy Way stated on a trip to Asia in late 1991: "Peru is no longer an island. Internationalization of the world economy is so rapid that if one does not adjust . . . it will further our situation of backwardness."[34]

The Road to the *Autogolpe*

Fujimori's reform of Peru was not without its opponents. Through 1991 and into early 1992 tensions mounted between those favoring the status quo, protected interests who felt threatened by the new Peru, and those who regarded Fujimori as autocratic and as a danger to the country's democratic institutions. At the same time, the chief executive felt increasingly frustrated and embattled. As the battle lines hardened, political corruption resurfaced as an issue and soon became part of the struggle.

The Belaunde administration was well-known for its corruption, which was a factor in the complete defeat of the right in the 1985 elections. The García administration added to the growing loss of confidence in the government by the citizenry. The most evident example of this was the alleged charges of embezzlement on the part of former president Alan García. In October 1991, Congress stripped him of his parliamentary immunity he enjoyed as a senator-for-life after it found him guilty of enriching himself by more than $400,000 during a decade as a public servant. Although the Peruvian Supreme Court, named by García, decided not to open court proceedings against him, finding "no grounds to charge with a crime," García remained the first former president in Peru's history to be stripped of his parliamentary immunity due to charges of corruption. It was restored, however, after the Supreme Court decision.

Other members of the APRA government were also linked to corruption. In the Bank of Credit and Commerce International (BCCI) scandal that had implications around the world, Peru's financial establishment was not exempt. In November 1991, seven former BCCI officials were charged with corruption linked to bribe-taking by former Peruvian officials, the former Central Bank president, Leonel Figueroa, and former Central Bank general manager, Hector Neyra. The BCCI seven and their government partners were allegedly involved in helping to create accounts in the Panama City branch of Swiss Bank into which $3.6 million in bribes were deposited for which BCCI received deposits of up to $270 million in Peru's reserves in the 1986–87 period.

The accumulation of corruption cases pointing to the former APRA government did little to enhance public confidence in Peru's political institutions. There was already little respect for Congress and its resistance to passage of the Fujimori reform decrees further alienated large segments of the population with the parliamentary form of government. Claims from the Sendero Luminoso that the formal political system was morally bankrupt appear to have more than a ring of truth in them.

The corruption factor and the anti-García sentiment of Fujimori were clearly elements in what motivated the April 1992 *autogolpe*.[35] The other factor was that Fujimori became convinced that the political system, especially Congress and the Supreme Court, were stacked against him and unless changed, would guarantee the failure of economic reform. García had just been reelected secretary of APRA and announced a plan of militant opposition to Fujimori. García's antics, in particular public denunciations of the structural reform process and declarations that he would reverse the government's programs if reelected national leader, made Fujimori increasingly determined to stay the course, but with an eye to some means of neutralizing his opposition. Moreover, the Peruvian leader was certain that he had the support of the majority of his countrymen. This was reflected by his statement in January 1992: "I do not have a majority in Congress; however, there exists a complete endorsement by the population of the structural changes that we wish to advance."[36]

In the late hours of 5 April and early hours of 6 April 1992 the "Fuji-coup" took place.[37] The military swung into action, closing Congress, and the majority of Supreme Court judges were fired. Fujimori announced his intention to restructure the political system and continue with economic reforms. On 13 May 1992 in an interview with the Peruvian press he stated: "There is no going back to 4 April. We need to reform the Constitution. There is a consensus of sorts on this issue in political circles."[38] Despite widespread international condemnation, the coup was largely popular within Peru. Many Peruvians were weary of congressional antics and hoped that a stronger presidency would be able to cope with the developmental problems and the Sendero Luminoso.

The Fujimori coup posed tough questions for Peru. The president stated that he would not relinquish power until the end of his term in 1995. At the same time, he recognized the international unpopularity of his action and sought to keep his diplomatic options open, particularly with the Organization of American States which condemned the action. Although the reform process continued, the political dimension hung over the country making any clear idea about the future difficult.

Serious Challenges

Fujimori's political gamble continued with the election of a congress in 1992 and a new constitution in 1993, which was approved overwhelmingly in a national referendum. One of the most significant changes in the constitution was an amendment allowing the president to run in back-to-back elections. With a more supportive congress and a new law, Fujimori tested his popularity for a second time with the Peruvian voters on 9 April 1995. Campaigning on his track record of having tamed hyperinflation and terrorism, and overcoming a bizarre effort by his estranged wife to run against him, Fujimori and his Cambio 90 alliance won an overwhelming victory, precluding any second round vote and giving him a clear working majority in Congress. Fujimori attained 64 percent of the vote, placing him well ahead of the second place finisher, former United Nations secretary general Javier Pérez de Cuellar. Fujimori's reelection, the reshaping of the economy, and a relative degree of political stability have helped return foreign investment to Peru and provide some hope among the population that better times are not far in the future.

Although the security threat has been greatly diminished, it has not been entirely eradicated. One offshoot of the long struggle against the Sendero Luminoso and other violent forces has been to assign to the Peruvian armed forces and civilian security institutions a powerful role in the political life of the nation. The Sendero Luminoso has not been the only group using violence to achieve its ends. The Movimiento Revolucionario Tupac Amaru (MRTA) has been, according to journalist Elizabeth Farnsworth, "a smaller, more conventional Marxist guerrilla organization," which has "also carried out bombings, assassinations, and kidnappings in Lima and has competed with Sendero for territory in the Huallaga Valley."[39] Although MRTA suffered a number of reversals in the early 1990s (including the capture of its leader, Victor Polay Campos, in July 1992), a rump movement continues to pose a minor security threat. Towards the end of the García government, elements of APRA formed their own armed bands to counter both Sendero and Tupac Amaru attacks.

The major area of militarization derives from the civil war in the rural regions, where small indian communities are forced to take sides with either the Sendero or the state. Peru's security forces have been known to be indiscriminate in using violence against "suspects," which has led to the Andean country getting poor grades in human rights score boards. At the same time, Sendero assaults against villages with state-backed militia have been equally bloody. In 1991, Fujimori's proposals to give the military powers to commandeer all property and mobilize people and institutions in regions subject to terrorist attacks, and to allow the national intelligence service to extract information it needs from public and private sources, made many in Congress apprehensive of a turn back to military government. As Luis Alva Castro, APRA's general secretary, commented of Fujimori's move: "His aim is militarization, civilian dictatorship, or even a coup."[40]

There has also been discussion about Fujimori's reliance on the military and the national intelligence service (SIN). The military is active in building roads and distributing food in shanty towns and inaccessible rural regions as well as conducting regular security missions. At the same time, SIN's role in Peruvian society has expanded under Fujimori. As journalist Sally Bowen noted: "The SIN, as the intelligence service is known, has been expanded into probably the most efficient of its kind in Latin America. One of its roles is continually to check on the president's popularity in the remotest corners of Peru."[41]

The issue of Peru's civil-military relations was highlighted in November 1992 with an "attempted" coup as well as in April 1993. In the former case, there was discontent with Fujimori's reliance on a cashiered captain as his main military advisor in the palace. In the 1993 case, army tanks rolled through the streets around Lima in protest of a congressional inquiry concerning the killings of nine students and a professor from the Enrique Guzmán University. The students were suspected of being Sendero Luminoso members and it was alleged in a document secretly provided to Congress that the army executed the group. Congress's investigation hit a raw nerve in the Peruvian military: there was a feeling that some disappearances and extrajudicial killings were necessary in the war against Sendero Luminoso and that no one had the right to challenge the integrity and dignity of the army.[42] Although the tanks returned to their barracks, it underscored the fragility of Peru's democratic experiment and hinted at the relative ease with which a military coup could happen. It also raised serious questions about Fujimori's control over the military.

The Sendero Luminoso remains a factor in Peru's future prospects and perhaps can be regarded as a continuing obstacle to meaningful socioeconomic reform. If allowed to deteriorate, such a situation has had the prospects of becoming what Hertoghe and Labrousse call, "the Khmer Rouge in the Andes."[43] Like their counterparts in Indochina, the Sendero Luminoso are highly xenophobic, antiimperialistic and place a strong emphasis on maintaining ideological purity. Operating with a totality of the correctness of their way, they allow no dissent and represent a dark future for Peru. The major obstacle to their assumption of power is that the majority of Peruvians still prefer the experiment with democracy to totalitarianism. Yet, the public's faith in institutions that are supposed to represent their demands is not always high, despite the recent economic turnaround.

The capture of Sendero leader Guzmán in Lima in September 1992, however, was a severe blow to the movement—perhaps a mortal blow in the long run. Many analysts of Peru, such as David Scott Palmer, feel that Guzmán's capture marks the end of the old Sendero Luminoso, if not the end of political violence in the country. If this is, indeed, the case, prospects for Peru might become more encouraging. The level of violence in 1994 through early 1996 did, in fact, decline, though Sendero Luminoso attacks still persist.

Finally, Peru has also had to deal with long-standing and more conventional border security disputes—most recently in February 1995 with Ecuador. Coinciding with Fujimori's reelection campaign, he won some praise from his military for his determined and high-profile leadership of this border dispute dating back to the 1940s. Yet, it also high-lighted the tension inherent in a situation where the government is determined to limit military expenditures yet is also faced with continuing reminders from its defense establishment of the need for a modern and effective national security. The internal dispute over weapon upgrades has been made more acute by the dispute with Ecuador, and is further complicated by government attempts to distance the armed forces from the counter-narcotics effort. The balance between insurgency, drug war, and conventional military needs remain unresolved issues in Peru's portfolio of civil-military relations.

While ham-fisted attempts to smash revolutionary activities have led to battlefield victories, and on the down-side, human rights' concerns, a weak national socioeconomic consensus has meant that a considerable part of the population remains marginalized. Many in the highlands live in Peru, but do not participate as citizens. Their standard of living is much lower than that of metropolitan Lima and the concerns of the national elite appear distant at best. Probably more than half of Peru's 24 million people live in poverty. Tina Rosenberg captures the broad nature of the problem and all its interrelated dimensions:

> In the Peruvian highlands, people turn against the government and toward Sendero Luminoso in part because the rebels' idea—razing the state and starting over—seems perfectly rational. The state has brought nothing but trouble to highland Indians. Rural families in the department of Ayacucho live as their ancestors did centuries ago. One in a hundred rural families has electricity and running water. Nearly half the department's adults, including city dwellers, are illiterate. Doctors, health clinics, schoolteachers, and paved roads all are scarce resources. Life expectancy in the highlands is 20 years shorter than in the capital, Lima.[44]

Another dimension of a split society and lack of national consensus is demographic pressure. Already unable to support a population of 24 million, the growth rate is expected (according to the World Bank) to decrease slightly from a pace of 2.3 percent in the 1980–89 period to 2.1 percent from 1989 to 2000.[45] By the year 2000, Peru's population is projected to be at 27 million and by 2025, a stunning 37 million. In 1989, women of child-bearing age as a percentage of all women in Peru amounted to 50 percent. Additionally, the fertility rate among

Peruvian women is 3.5 children, compared with 3.1 children for Latin American women and 2 children for women in the United States. The rate changes, however, when taking education into consideration, with the rate shifting to 1.7 children per woman for those with at least some college education and 2.8 for all of those who live in urban areas; compared to a rate of 6.2 children for rural Peruvian women who have little or no education.[46] As President Fujimori stated in his second inaugural address: "If we speak of the future we have to speak of planning, of controlling the birth rate."[47]

Considering the lack of employment opportunities, the probability of ongoing civil strife, and the difficulty the national elite has in closing ranks to form a consensus, Peru's marginal population remains an obstacle to more rapid development. It will remain for the foreseeable future as a major factor in the country's political and economic development and will have to be taken into consideration by the country's neighbors and trading partners.

One other potential challenge for Peru is the dual nature of integration with international finance markets. Mexico's peso crisis in December 1994 revealed that while international capital inflows from foreign investors can be a great bonus to the economy, they can be equally dangerous as they are fickle and can be pulled out of the country within a very short period of time. Peru had built up its foreign exchange reserves to over $7 billion in 1995, but it is facing pressure from a widening current-account deficit, much as was the case of Mexico. From a $1.82 billion surplus in 1993, the current-account balance-of-payments shifted to a deficit in 1994 of $2.26 billion. Peru's foreign debt was high, around $23 billion at the end of 1994, and Peru clearly needs to reach a settlement on favorable terms with its commercial bank creditors. Consequently, Peru's advances remain sensitive to developments and arrangements within international capital markets.

Conclusion

On 28 July 1995, President Fujimori was sworn into office for his second term. Taking the oath of office under intense security, he promised to maintain policies that transformed the economy over the last five years. Turning fifty-seven years old the same day that he started his second term, the question of time is critical for Peru's future development. Fujimori's efforts to reshape his nation into a viable, market-oriented economy capable of providing a better life for its citizenry requires a tremendous balancing act of maintaining the support of the public and the military, holding the old-line politicians, (such as García) at bay, and defeating the Sendero Luminoso, while demonstrating economic gains.

Sustaining the reform process is key. As the privatization program moves into a faster pace, foreign direct investment is expected to exceed the last several years. Investment commitments have been made by a number of British, Chinese, and U.S. companies in the mining, iron, and oil sectors. Privatizing the state mining and mineral firms, Centramin, Mineroperu, and Tintaya, parts of the telecommunications sectors, and a part of the electricity sector and other companies (such as Cementos Lima) are ultimately expected to exceed $3 billion in government revenues. While reducing costs to the government, returning these enterprises to private sector control is hoped to create a more efficient economy, capable of better serving the public. Peru's oil sector, in dire need of capital for upgrading equipment, could make a greater contribution to the country's external accounts if efficiency were improved.[48]

The government program is ambitious and seeks to accomplish much in a hurry. There are reservations about doing too much, too quickly—the country risk factor could cause privatization to be done at fire sale prices. If foreign investment fails to materialize in the next few years, will the domestic economy have enough stimulus to grow? If the privatization program and overall economic management fail to deliver and gains against inflation slip, Fujimori's economic gamble may reopen the door which has been closing to Sendero Luminoso.

The political agenda is also influenced by the time factor. Fujimori has won his second term; in the next few years he must demonstrate that having tamed hyperinflation and revitalized a moribund economy, he can spread the national wealth in the form of an improving standard of living and jobs. At the same time, his autocratic fashion of addressing Peru's problems must also undergo a transformation to a more democratic mode. Peru's economic and political conditions are not the same as when Fujimori first assumed the presidential sash—gone is the socioeconomic chaos that required a strong hand. Peruvians are more apt to measure the future role of the president in the lens of the recent relative stability. Failure to rebuild Peru's democratic institutions and to regain lost ground in social standards can re-open the door to radical forces. Peru has come a long distance since the 1980s, and the 1990s are a highly pivotal period in the country's drive toward the fast-forward mode. Much remains to be done.

Notes

1. International Monetary Fund, May 1995, p. 138.
2. International Monetary Fund, *International Financial Statistics, October 1991* (Washington, D.C.: International Monetary Fund, October 1991), p. 428; and International Monetary Fund, *International Financial Statistics, July 1995* (Washington, D.C.: International Monetary Fund, July 1995), p. 451; "Peru," *Financial Times Survey* (March 7, 1996).
3. "BankWatch," *Peru: BankWatch Sovereign Risk* (June 1995): p. 1.
4. Tina Rosenberg, "Beyond Elections," *Foreign Policy* no. 84 (Fall 1991): p. 80.
5. Felipe Ortiz de Zevallos, *The Peruvian Puzzle* (New York: Priority Press, 1989), p. 2.
6. Alain Hertoghe and Alain Labrousse, *Le Sentier lumineux du Pérou: Un nouvel integrisme dans le tiers monde* (Paris: Editions la Decouverte, 1989): p. 161.
7. Ibid., p. 2.
8. Ibid.
9. Ibid., p. 2.
10. Ibid.
11. Richard Webb, "Prologue," in *Peru's Path to Recovery: A Plan for Economic Stabilization and Growth* eds. Carlos E. Paredes and Jeffrey D. Sachs (Washington, D.C.: The Brookings Institute, 1991), p. i.
12. Ortiz de Zevallos, *The Peruvian Puzzle*, p. 2.
13. World Bank, *World Development Report 1980* (Washington, D.C.: World Bank, 1980), p. 112.
14. For a complete study on the informal sector in Peru, see Hernando de Soto, *El Otro Sendero: la revolución informal* (Buenos Aires, Editorial Subamericana, 1987). This was translated into English as *The Other Sendero*.
15. Ibid., p. 37.
16. See Victor Raul Haya de la Torre, *El antiimperilismo y el APRA* 4th edition (Lima: Imprenta Editorial Amanta, 1972).
17. Ortiz de Zevallos, *The Peruvian Puzzle*, p. 19.
18. Elizabeth Farnsworth, "Peru: A Nation in Crisis," *World Policy Journal*, vol. V, no. 4 (Fall 1988): p. 726.
19. Inter-American Development Bank, *Economic and Social Progress in Latin America 1989 Report* (Washington, D.C.: Inter-American Development Bank, 1989), p. 412.
20. World Bank, *World Debt Tables 1990–91: External Debt in Developing Countries, Vol. 2 Country Tables* (Washington, D.C.: World Bank, 1991), p. 290.
21. Carol Graham, "Peru's APRA Party in Power: Impossible Revolution," *Journal of Interamerican Studies and World Affairs* vol. 32, no. 3 (Fall 1990): pp. 106–07.
22. Eugenio Chang-Rodriguez, "Origin and Diffusion of the Shining Path in Peru," in *APRA and the Democratic Challenge in Peru* eds. Eugenio Chang-Rodriguez and Ronald G. Hellman (New York: The Bildner Center for Western Hemisphere Studies, 1988), p. 68.
23. Ibid., pp. 70–71.

24. Department of State, International Narcotics Matters, *International Narcotics Control Strategy Report, March 1988* (Washington, D.C.: Department of State, March 1988), p.
25. Alan García, *Three Speakers for History* (Lima, 1985).
26. Excerpts from Alan Garcia's state of the union address given July 28, 1988, quoted in *World Policy Journal* (Fall 1988): p. 748.
27. United States Department of State, Bureau of International Narcotics Matters, *International Narcotics Control Strategy Report, March 1991* (Washington, D.C.: Department of State, 1991), p. 114.
28. Ibid., 114–15.
29. Sally Bowen, "Peru Collects Taxes at Point of a Cannon," *Financial Times* (December 10, 1991): p. 6.
30. "Peru", *BankWatch*, June 1995, p. 2.
31. Mary Powers, "Peru Modernizing Its Economy by Decree," *Reuter* (November 28, 1991).
32. Ibid.
33. Ibid.
34. Ibid.
35. David Scott Palmer offers a summary of reasons for the *autogolpe*. They include Fujimori's lack of political experience and consequent frustration with the need to negotiate with a congress controlled by opposition parties. He also felt pressure from the military; was forced to act to impede the investigation when his wife blew the cover of a family scandal; and was incensed that former president Alan García, whom he blames for creating Peru's mess, had not only escaped being charged with corruption in courts he staffed, but was going to challenge Fujimori in the next elections. See David Scott Palmer, "Peru, the Drug Business, and Shining Path," *Journal of Interamerican Studies and World Affairs*, vol. 34, no. 3 (Fall 1992): p. 84.
36. "Fujimori: un liderazgo firme," *Vision* (Mexico City) (January 15, 1992): p. 12.
37. For a full description of the coup see Carlos Alcelay, "El harakiri de Fujimori," *Cambio 16* (April 13, 1992): pp. 6–9.
38. "Fujimori Interviewed on Government Policy, Reform," (Lima, in Spanish) *La Republica* (May 2, 1992): p. ; *FBIS* (May 13, 1992): p. 32.
39. Farnsworth, "Peru," p. 728.
40. Quoted from "Peru: Looking to authority," *The Economist* (November 23, 1991): p. 52.
41. Sally Bowen, "Firm Hand on the Popular Pulse," *Financial Times* (May 10, 1995): p. 12; Sally Bowen, "Cosy Accord Feels the Chill," *Financial Times* (March 7, 1996): p. 5.
42. Nathaniel C. Nash, "Army Deploys Tanks in Peru," *New York Times* (April 26, 1993): p. A11.
43. Hertoghe and Labrousse, *Le Sentier lumineux du Pérou*, p. 215. The brutality and social complexity of the Shining Path movement appears in Mario Vargas Llosa's most recent novel, *Death in the Andes* (New York: Farrar, Straus & Giroux, 1995).
44. Rosenberg, "Beyond Elections," p. 83.
45. World Bank, *World Development Report 1991*, p. 256.
46. Calvin Sims, "President's Call for Birth Control Is Dividing Peru," *New York Times* (August 12, 1995): p. 3.
47. Ibid.

48. Sally Bowen, "Peru Lays Out the Welcome Mat," *Financial Times* (March 25, 1993): p. 7; Sally Bowen, "Sell-Offs Strike Mother Lode," Financial Times (March 7, 1996): p.6.

10

Albanian End-Game or Democratic Transition? Cuba Reaches the Twenty-First Century

For most of Albania's existence as a sovereign state the somber figure of Enver Hoxha dominated all aspects of national life. Although independence was initially achieved in 1912, it was not until after World War II that Albania became better known internationally as an oddity. Hoxha was a hardline Stalinist who, after coming to power in the wake of a bloody civil war in 1944, proceeded to isolate his country from most of the world, including the United States, Western Europe, Yugoslavia, the Soviet Union (after Stalin), and after a period of close ties, even the People's Republic of China. At his death at the age of 76 in 1985, he left behind a country on the verge of economic and political collapse. Albania is still recovering from Hoxha's long reign.

Albania had become a sad joke of an inflexible Stalinist approach to development. Compared to the rest of Europe, Albania was the most backward in terms of its standard of living and industrial output. By 1991, the government acknowledged after elections that it could not control the downward spiral of the economy or the outflow of its people to neighboring countries, especially Italy. As the number of refugees sailing into Italian ports swelled in the summer of 1991, the Albanian government asked Rome to help restore some form of control over the situation. Soon Italian navy ships were helping to patrol Albanian waters, Italian soldiers were active in the distribution of food in the interior, Italian police were training their Albanian counterparts, and Italian economic and food assistance poured in to aid the country's 3 million inhabitants. The great irony in all this was that Italy, one of

Albania's former colonial masters and long denounced by Hoxha, was invited in by the Albanian government to avert a complete collapse of order.

Ninety miles south of the United States sits the island of Cuba, ruled by Fidel Castro and a small clique of loyal followers. Cuba in the early 1990s assumed many of the characteristics of Albania, in particular the refusal to depart from the strictures of "communism." Without changes in economic policy, Cuba was threatened of being rapidly left behind by history. One dimension of the downturn in the Caribbean nation's fortunes was that in 1991, as fuel was rationed, Cuba imported 600,000 bicycles for transportation use and major roadways linking the nation became the domain of ox carts. Statistically, Cuba's economic decline was marked by a GDP which contracted by 34.3 percent from 1989 to 1994.[1]

No analysis of hemispheric affairs is complete without an assessment of Cuba's future in the wake of more than three decades of Fidel Castro's rule. Assessing those prospects in the 1990s and beyond is shaped as much by Castro's own policy adjustments as by changes in the post-cold war order. Almost frozen in place since the early 1960s, Cuba's relationship to the rest of the region—and to the United States in particular—is now in fact changing. The ensuing policy questions will continue to absorb considerable interest in Washington and other capitals as well as in corporate boardrooms. Likewise, the debate over the eventual outcome of the Cuban situation will be fueled by competing political pressures in the United States (in particular, anti-Castro hardliners within the Cuban American community, liberal critics, and by a whole cast of constituencies in between) and diplomatic tensions abroad.

For its part, the Castro regime has adjusted to these difficult circumstances by devising a course that derives from the recent Chinese and Vietnamese experiences. Yet, allowing economic market reforms while seeking to maintain Community Party dominance in Cuba might be too little, too late, for both Cubans and Castro's critics overseas. What is certain is that the resolution of the Cuban issue will free the hemisphere from the last vestiges of the cold war era. Aside from its symbolic value, the political and economic impact of Cuba's reintroduction into the Latin American and Caribbean system is a significant marker.

Before Castro

Cuba was one of the oldest Spanish colonies that Madrid maintained long after it lost sway over the rest of the once expansive Latin American empire. The sugar industry became significant in the 1860s, but production was partially disrupted by war between local independence forces and the Spanish government. The off-again—on-again nature of this civil war was ultimately interrupted by the Spanish-American War of 1898. Spain exited Cuba and the United States entered, first with occupation and later with the Platt Amendment of 1902 that constitutionally permitted U.S. intervention. Although Cuba gained independence in 1902, U.S. influence was preponderant, both politically and economically. The Platt Amendment was not abrogated until 1934, which made Cuba a virtual U.S. protectorate and under its terms allowed the northern country to establish a naval base at Guantanamo Bay (which it still maintains). These aspects of U.S. dominance over Cuba remained a central feature through the early years of the nascent republic, occasionally being a flashpoint for Cuban nationalists as in the 1933 revolution that toppled the Machado regime.

The various Cuban governments that came to office through the 1900s to the 1950s were aware of U.S. power hovering in the background and would later be perceived as too pliant to the northern country's economic interests. At the same time, Cuba's political development was problematic: its nationalism was stunted; the political class was generally corrupt and more keen on rhetoric than creating a civic culture that would promote and support constitutional and democratic government; and political violence had become part of the game in student politics, labor-management relations, and between the political parties. Moreover, poverty in the countryside was widespread.

Despite the decay of Cuba's political class, when Fidel Castro came to power on January 1, 1959 the island state was one of the most developed countries in Latin America. Cuba's sugar industry was a world power and its tourist sector was a mecca to North Americans. Moreover, Cuba in the 1950s was more highly capitalized than any other Latin American nation and a higher percentage of the country's population had been brought into the money economy than in any other Latin American state.[2] Cuba in the 1950s was ranked fourth in

Latin America with respect to general economic and social development.[3]

Investigating the mythos of propaganda about the dismal nature of economic life in pre-Castro Cuba, Boris Goldenberg provided an interesting comparison of Cuba's level of development with the rest of its Latin neighbors. Cuba ranked number one in railways (about one mile of railway per four square miles) and television sets per capita; second in energy consumption, and private cars per capita; and third in radios, persons not employed in agriculture, life expectancy at birth, and university students per capita.[4] Out of the twenty Latin American republics, Cuba's annual income per capita (1956–58) was fifth. Cuba was also a world leader in the production and export of sugar. On an overall basis, Cuba fared relatively well compared with the rest of Latin America and in many areas was a leader, a factor that provided Castro with a base of national wealth upon which to build his socialist edifice.

Cuba's major market was the United States, which in the 1955–57 period accounted for roughly 80 percent of Cuban sugar exports. The United States was also the main trade partner in terms of imports, while the trade sector was the domain of large U.S.- and Cuban-owned trading companies.

Considering the concentration on sugar it is no surprise that the majority of the work force was rural. By 1953, only 13 percent of Cuba's population lived in urban areas with Havana as the primary city with a population of 1.2 million.[5] One report noted of the Cuban work force that "living levels of the farmers, agricultural laborers, industrial workers, storekeepers, and others, are higher all along the lines than for corresponding groups in other tropical countries and in nearly all other Latin American countries.[6] Despite the comparative standing of Cuba's rural population, poverty clearly existed in Cuba prior to 1959, especially in the countryside. As Goldenberg commented:

> The average peasant lacked knowledge, credit, adequate instruments, and tools. He was usually in debt to local traders and was exploited by middlemen. There was still in 1958 a shortage of roads, of schools, of doctors, of piped water. Housing conditions were very poor: according to the official census of 1953, 75 percent of all rural dwellings had no other floors but the naked earth, 80.9 percent had no electric light, 85 percent no running water, and 54.1 percent no lavatory.[7]

Hence, the pre-Castro Cuban economy was capitalist, export-oriented and heavily dependent on the sugar industry. While the country's overall economic rankings were high by Latin American standards, the country had considerable pockets of poverty or near-poverty. Additionally, a significant discrepancy existed between the urban and rural working classes, and the Cuban upper class was well-removed from both groups.

Ownership of the Cuban economy in the pre-Castro era was in a state of change. Since Cuban independence in 1902, U.S. commercial interests had dominated much of the economy, including control of public utilities, banks, the telephone system, and, of course, the sugar plantations. U.S. control also extended into the large oil refineries and elements of the mining industry. Yet, in the 1940s and 1950s a process of "Cubanization" was underway. The railways slipped out of U.S. control as did a number of banks. One of the most significant developments was in the sugar industry: in 1939, 56 sugar factories were Cuban owned, producing 22.4 percent of the country's sugar; the corresponding figures for 1958 were 121 (out of 161) and 62.1 percent.[8] Another important figure to consider was that in 1933 U.S. companies owned 5.7 million acres of sugar plantations; by 1958 it was only 1.9 million.[9]

While the Cuban economy Castro inherited was heavily dependent on sugar and tied to the U.S., ownership trends were clearly moving in the direction of the local capitalist upper class. However, the political situation hit a new low in the period immediately prior to the revolution's triumph. While Batista was initially able to restore order from the political gangsterism of the late 1940s and early 1950s, the old order's legitimacy was badly eroded. Fulgencio Batista's bloodless coup in 1952 was a reflection of the political decay of a failed political order. British historian Lord Hugh Thomas commented: "The coup came at a moment when the country had been rendered quite dizzy— first by a cycle of sporadic political gangsterism . . . and second, by the evident corruption under and by two popularly elected Cuban presidents, Ramón Grau San Martin and Carlos Prío. These two clever, amusing, self-serving men did more to damage the good name of democracy (in all Latin America) than even England's Henry Fox."[10]

The Batista period, which lasted until 1958, was marked by an upswing in the corruption of the state. Key leaders of the old political gangsterism either left the island or became part of the Batista regime and it appeared that everyone was taking bribes or seeking to take a slice of the economic cake. By mid-decade a new round of political violence rocked the island as an antidictatorship opposition emerged. One of the more notable manifestations of the new opposition was Fidel Castro's first attempt to take power in the Monacada Barracks attack in 1956. Political moderates in Cuba were once again overshadowed by men with guns, and by 1958 Castro and the 26th of July Movement (M-26) were well on their way to defeating Batista.

The last days of Batista were marked by a regime made of straw, devoid of legitimacy and abandoned by a completely disenchanted middle class. In contrast, Castro and the M-26 offered to remake Cuba along the lines of liberal democracy and to stamp out corruption. Aided by his charisma and the misplaced hopes of Cuban liberals, Castro became the leader of a broad-based coalition of forces that had one common denominator—the removal of Batista from power. Beyond that Castro and M-26 had a clear idea of where they wanted to take Cuba—a factor that was carefully concealed from the other groups.

Castro as Socialist Caudillo

Fidel Castro and his close cohorts in the 26th of July Movement, including his brother Raul and revolutionary comrade Ernesto "Che" Guevara, moved quickly to consolidate their "revolution within a revolution": the revolution that ousted Batista turned to remaking Cuba's socioeconomic system. This meant that the *fidelistas* and their increasingly close allies, the Cuban Communists, would seek to transform Cuba from a dependent capitalist state into a socialist economy. In the 1959–61 period, therefore, the role of the state was rapidly expanded into all spheres of Cuban life, especially in the economy. While Committees for the Defense of the Revolution (CDRs) were created in every neighborhood, private enterprises were nationalized and their duties assumed by the revolutionary state. Local opposition was shunted aside, with its members either opting for exile in the United States and elsewhere in Latin America or face imprisonment in revolutionary Cuba.

The leftist bent of the new Cuban government and the nationalization of U.S. companies also contributed to the eventual deterioration of ties between Washington, D.C. and Havana. The imposition of a trade embargo in 1960 (in response to the nationalization of U.S. firms), the abortive Bay of Pigs invasion in 1961 and the Cuban Missile Crisis in 1962 reflected the abrupt severing and mutual hostility of

U.S.-Cuban relations. This situation was further fueled by Castro's turn to the Soviet Union for military and economic assistance which helped sustain the regime against both foreign attempts at destabilization and local efforts to launch a guerrilla war against the new revolutionary state.

Castro's approach to consolidation of power was the gradual absorption of groups on the left, including the Communists and Socialists, into what was to eventually become the loosely-organized and *fidelista*-dominated Cuban Communist Party (Partido Communista Cubano or PCC). Although Fidel was resistant to institutionalizing the revolution and for a period in the mid to late 1960s sought to take Cuba along a Maoist-Guevarist track of radical collectivization, the limits of the country's dependence on the Soviet Union and domestic economic failures forced the socialist strongman or *caudillo* to relinquish a certain degree of power to others. Raul, as a key figure in the armed forces, gained influence as did some of the more pragmatic Communists. At the same time, ultimate power remained in the hands of Fidel. This was reflected by the two purges of leading old-line pro-Soviet Communists, like Anibal Escalante and other members of the so-called microfaction in 1962 and 1968. Moreover, the Cuban military, security apparatus, and those elements of society that benefitted from the policy of creating a socialized economy, remained faithful.

Castro's vision for a new Cuba was built around his desire to: (1) break his country's economic dependence on the United States; (2) transform the structure of the economy from its capitalist base to a completely socialized entity, setting in motion self-sustained and stable growth; and in the process of achieving the two previous points, (3) to achieve the social objectives of more equal distribution of the national wealth, less unemployment, price stability of essential consumer goods, and improved social services. Armed with a substantial infusion of Soviet financial aid (eventually between $4–5 billion annually), military equipment, and advisors, the Castro government massively expanded social services in the 1960s and 1970s. At the same time, the almost complete elimination of the private sector gave the new inflated state sector the means to provide full employment for the island-state's population. Together with artificial job creation, the Cuban worker no longer came to fear unemployment and was provided a new wide range of social services. The *fidelista* wheel of fortune even swung around to subsidizing the prices of consumer goods, while the

Soviet Union bought Cuba's sugar at an agreed upon price (usually above the international market price) and supplied it with most of its oil at a lower-than-market price. The Cubans then resold part of the Soviet oil at market prices.

The leading sector of the Cuban economy remained sugar. Sugar, however, presented certain ideological problems for Castro and Guevara, the early managers of the revolutionary economy. Tad Szulc noted: "Though sugar had always been Cuba's mainstay, the revolutionary chiefs developed during 1959 and 1960 the daring notion that the island should end forthwith its dependence on it—presumably because it was a bitter reminder of the American-dominated 'colonial' past."[11] Because of this view, planting was reduced beginning in 1959 and sugar harvests were allowed to drop in the 1962–64 period. However, socialist ideology ran aground Cuba's economic realities: by 1965 the Castro government, under increasing pressure from the Soviet Union, returned in a big way to sugar. In 1968, sugar became central to Castro's efforts to revitalize what he perceived as sagging revolutionary fervor on the part of the population. In a Cuban-made copy of China's then unfolding cultural revolution, Castro turned to sugar as a catalyst to stimulate the peoples' spirit in order to lift his country's production up to the 10 million ton mark. That mark was missed, and overconcentration on sugar hurt other sectors of the economy and generated widespread discontent.

After the excesses of the late 1960s and early 1970s, sugar production settled into a lower, yet more steady production mode. Other crops were encouraged, partially to mitigate public disgruntlement with food supply. This was supplemented in the late 1970s and early 1980s by allowing farmers, for the first time since the introduction of rationing in the 1960s, to privately sell whatever surplus they produced. Small markets sprang up throughout Cuba and analysts felt that more smallscale "capitalist" reforms would follow considering the success of these measures.

By the mid-1980s Castro had been in power for over twenty years and was now greying and overweight.[12] His promises of socioeconomic egalitarianism, an improved living standard, and new pride of nationalism were partially fulfilled. Cuba enjoyed an economic spurt of growth in the 1980–85 period due to strong and improving human resources, considerable investment, and improving labor productivity, stimulated by partly concealed but unsustainable levels of economic assistance from the Soviet Union and a build up of convertible-currency debt prior to 1982. Along these lines, the Cuban revolution recorded several achievements: (1) a highly egalitarian redistribution of income that eliminated almost all malnutrition especially among children; (2) a national health care program that was superior to others in the developing world; (3) the almost complete elimination of illiteracy and establishment of a highly developed multilevel educational system; and (4) development of a relatively well-disciplined and motivated population with a strong sense of national identification.[13]

These successes came at a frightful cost and were balanced by failures. Economist and long-time Cuba watcher, Carmelo Mesa-Lago noted in 1985: "the state has failed to reach most economic goals such as self-sustained and stable growth, sufficient capital accumulation and its efficient use, export promotion, and diversification of trade partners. In spite of the enormous state power and the colossal Soviet aid, the Cuban leadership has been unable to significantly change the island's economic structure after 25 years of socialism."[14] Cuba's economic policies throughout the revolutionary period up until the mid-1980s lacked consistency and, according to Mesa-Lago, were guided by the concept of "trading off equity for growth." While Cuba's economic managers could provide an improved lifestyle for the majority of the population, productive growth was made a secondary concern and the tab for revolutionary experimentation was picked up by the Soviets and, to a lesser extent, foreign bankers from Canada, Japan, and Europe as well as from official creditors in Europe and Latin America.

The *fidelista* wheel of fortune rolled around to a number of major failures in the mid- and late 1980s. These included: (1) a heavy dependency on Soviet economic aid ($4–5 billion annually) to meet minimal investment and consumption needs; (2) real economic growth remained only just ahead of population growth; (3) continued dependence on sugar for development of the domestic economy and foreign trade resulting in stop-and-go progress closely tied to volatile swings in world prices; (4) an increasingly inefficient bureaucracy and poor labor productivity due to a lack of incentives; (5) a heavy dependence on trade with Soviet bloc countries; and (6) a near complete reliance on a single energy source, Soviet oil (which accounted for around 98 percent of Cuba's oil and three-fourths of its total energy needs in the early 1980s).[15] Additionally, the brief spring of allowing small farmers' markets ended in the mid-1980s due to ideological concerns that a new class of capitalists was emerging.

Many of the problems Cuba had managed to stave off in the 1970s came home to roost in the 1980s. The major problem was that the inability of the Cuban economy to pay for itself led to a heavy and unsustainable dependence on outside sources of capital. As these sources dried up, first the Western commercial banks and then the Eastern bloc, Cuba found itself locked into a financial crunch of considerable magnitude. The story of Cuba's financial crunch has its beginnings in the 1970s and has continued to the present.

The maintenance of an artificial economy and the heavy costs of conducting "wars of liberation" in Angola and Ethiopia in the 1970s ultimately created a financial crunch at home. As the rest of Latin America wrestled with the external debt problem throughout the 1980s, Cuba was not exempt. Large garrisons of Cuban troops in Africa, a slump in sugar prices, and inefficiencies at home contributed to a growing plethora of problems. Initially, the massive inflow of Soviet assistance allowed the economy to continue along without any efforts at reform, but problems grew, hindering Cuba's ability to make payments on its commercial bank loans that it had taken out in the 1970s. To well-known banks, like the Royal Bank of Canada, Crédit Lyonnais, and the Bank of Tokyo, Cuba had been attractive because it was supported (at least in theory) by the Soviet Union. Moreover, Cuba was one market where U.S. commercial banks offered no competition because of prohibitions on lending to the Castro regime. Poland's forced rescheduling of its hard currency debt in 1980 indicated that the Soviet Union and its dominance of the Eastern bloc did not extend to guaranteeing the external credit obligations of its client states. By 1982, Cuba's total external debt stood at $10 billion of which $2.6 billion was owed to European, Canadian, Arab, and Japanese commercial banks.[16]

Despite the accumulation of a comparatively large external debt, Cuba managed to steer through the early 1980s without too many complications. However, by 1986 circumstances had changed. Cuba joined the queue of nations seeking a rescheduling as a shortage of foreign currency caused the Castro regime to suspend most debt-service payments to Western creditors. At that time, Cuba's commercial bank debt was estimated at $2.1 billion, while its debt to the Soviet Union and Eastern bloc countries ranged between $10–25 billion.[17]

This also meant that Cuba was forced to venture to the Paris Club to seek a rescheduling on its official debt.

Although the Castro regime was able to contain much of the growing economic crisis through the mid-1980s, the dismal turn of events was more than apparent by 1989. Many of the hard-fought gains achieved by Cuba in the social benefits area were quietly and relentlessly being eaten away by a contraction of fiscal resources. Muted discontent abounded at the differences between the privileged nomenklatura surrounding the state and the "masses" despite Castro's efforts to maintain a sense of revolutionary momentum. Simply stated, the state elite had better access to a dwindling supply of consumer goods and essentials. However, discontent even simmered within the main pillar of the *fidelista* regime—the armed forces. Overall, Cuba's international image as a dramatic example of radical change was fading.[18]

Frustrated veterans of the African wars increasingly looked to a younger generation of Cuban war heros, such as General Arnaldo Ochoa Sanchez. Apparently apprehensive that a younger leader could emerge to challenge the old-line *fidelista* order, a series of show trials in July 1989 convicted the popular General Ochoa and a handful of other high-ranking officers in the defense and security services of involvement in the illicit drug trade. Noriega's Panama and the necessity of smuggling U.S.-embargoed high technology goods into Cuba had opened the door to trading in cocaine, allowing the Caribbean state to be used as a transit point between South and North America, and the probable participation of Cuban officials in drug-money laundering schemes.[19] While considerable anecdotal evidence points to the involvement of Fidel and others of his close circle with Colombia's Medellín cartel and Panama's General Manuel Noriega, the Cuban government felt comfortable with trying and executing by firing squad a number of popular senior officers for these crimes. The message was clear—Castro was here to stay and opposition to the *fidelista* state would not be tolerated. The Ochoa execution was followed by a purge of some two hundred people from the government and state-security apparatus.

While the political situation was marked by a clamping down on potential sources of opposition to the regime, problems emerged in the economy's major growth engine, the sugar sector. Ranking among the leading producers and exporters for generations, the sugar industry had become one of the most mechanized parts of the Cuban economy and was largely self-sufficient. Cuba's trade agreements with Eastern bloc countries created a guaranteed market through most of the 1980s. However, Cuba was unable to produce enough sugar under these agreements and was forced to buy sugar on the international market to compensate for deficiencies. The result was noted by economists Jose F. Alonso and Peter J. Buzzanell: "While they reportedly had some early success in buying low and selling high, Cubazucar, the country's export marketing organization, has, trade sources also believe, suffered considerable losses of hard currencies as the market turned against them."[20] While this hurt Cuba's overall foreign currency position, the industry was also hindered by downtime at the mills; the lack of up-to-date maintenance at the mills due to a lack of currency to purchase new imported equipment; and by a scarcity of new land to expand production into, regarded as necessary for the country to remain in the league of major global producers. Fittingly, Alonso and Buzzanell conclude: "It is not conceivable, given the present world scenario, that Cuba's economy could manage to survive beyond the turn of the century unless it is radically restructured."[21]

Cuba entered the post-cold war era in search of new trade agreements with its old Eastern European trade partners. Cuba approached the Islamic Republic of Iran to barter sugar for oil. The sugar sector was affected by the energy crunch: the 1991–92 sugar crop was estimated to be smaller than the previous crop due to shortages in fuel and agricultural chemicals. The fuel shortage also hit other sectors of the island and reflected the dismal economic conditions. As Cuba entered the new year in 1992, the government introduced a plan to reduce national electricity consumption by 12 percent, after an earlier 10 percent reduction in 1991. Cuba had to either sell its sugar for hard currency or to barter for oil in order to keep the island from being pitched into darkness for most of the year.

Shaping a New End-Game

On the front page of the December 27, 1991 *Christian Science Monitor* a photo represented the dimensions of Cuba's Albanian end-game. The caption below the photo was descriptive: "Cuba's Surrealistic Roads Do Not Lead Home for Holidays: On Six-Lane Highway in central Cuba, a horse cart is king of the road as fuel shortages take toll."[22] In December 1991, nearly half of the country's fleet of buses were off the road; train services had been cut by 20 percent; and there were 25 percent fewer domestic flights from the beginning of the year.[23] Earlier in 1991, Castro also announced that Cuba would import bicycles from the People's Republic of China as another way of saving energy. According to a December 14, 1991 article in the state newspaper *Granma*, Cuba received some 600,000 bicycles and had contracted for more. In a bizarre sidenote, one of the growing safety problems in Havana in early 1992 was fatal bicycle accidents.

Cuba entered the realm of the unreal in the early 1990s—or as economist A.R.M. Ritter noted: "Cuba has entered the decade of the 1990s in a state of profound existential crisis. Cuba had become a curiosity from the 1960s rather than the wave of the future, as it once perceived itself." Ritter accurately noted that Cuba is reaching the end of the twentieth century "locked in a situation of political and economic paralysis."[24] Although still quite adept at tactical political responses, strategically, Cuba's leadership has ossified, having considerable difficulty in acknowledging that the world has changed. In late 1989, while the last facades of the old communist order were about to crumble in Romania and the rest of the Eastern bloc was busy implementing market economics, the first secretary of Cuba's Interest Section in Washington summarized his government's future blueprint: "the only discussion we want is how to improve socialism." Six years later, in a session sponsored by the Inter-American Dialogue, the head of the Cuban Interest Section highlighted the importance of limited market reforms, but noted the inapplicability of most democratic political reforms.[25]

Despite the pace of change in the former Soviet Union, which commenced in 1986 with *glasnost* and *perestroika*, Cuba clings to the ideology of the past. While the Soviet Union loosened controls over Central and Eastern Europe, withdrawing troops, agreeing to German reunification, and dismantling the vestiges of the command economy, Cuba remains steadfast to the dictates of Marxism-Leninism-Fidelism. However, the decentralization of economic decision-making in what is now Russia, the emergence of a private sector, and the Russian's own growing economic and political problems has had an impact on Cuba. Accustomed to dealing with one ministry, the Cubans have found many new parties for deal-making in Moscow. Moreover, the decline in dependability of the old Soviet Union as a trade partner was felt by reduced exports to Cuba and increased demands that the Latin American country's payments be made in hard currency.

Cuba's resistance to global transformations is both remarkable and problematic in defining the outlines of a successful future. At the congress of the Cuban Communist Party in October 1991 Castro stated that: "To speak of the collapse of the Soviet Union is to speak of the possibility of the sun not rising."[26] Yet, on 1 January 1992, the sun did not rise for Castro as the Soviet Union ceased to exist and a new Commonwealth of Independent States (CIS) succeeded the former superpower. But the difficulties of Russia's reform process, or China's continued resistance to political change, have given the Cuban government what may be a false sense of hope. Cuba in the 1990s runs the distinct danger of becoming a living socialist museum, with a society waiting for the inevitable end of El Commandante.

Pulling Off an Eleventh Hour Transformation

The game afoot in other Latin American countries includes a package of technology, financial and industrial infrastructure, and an acceptance that foreign investment and technology transfer can play a positive role in the creation of a better society. While Argentina, Chile, Colombia, Mexico, Venezuela, and even Peru have come to accept this developmental package, Cuba remains apart, its leadership refusing to abandon its rigid ideological stance. Cuba increasingly lacks the essential hardware for a world that is rapidly marketizing. It has no local capital markets, its banking system lacks sophistication and, with the demise of its socialist allies in Europe, it is cut off from key sources of technology and energy. And the more Cuba is isolated, the more its educational base falls behind, potentially condemning the next generation of Cubans to technological backwardness and hence economic underdevelopment. The old dictum that underdevelopment is a state of mind clearly has the potential to become true for a computer-illiterate Cuban society.

Briefly consider Cuba's financial sector. There are no stock markets or interbank markets, the insurance industry is a state monopoly, and Automated Teller Machines (ATMs) are as distant as the moon to the Cuban consumer. All banks on the island were nationalized in October 1960 and absorbed by the central bank, the Banco Nacional de Cuba (BNC). The BNC functioned as a monobank until 1983 when the Banco Popular de Ahorro, a state savings bank, and in 1984 the Banco

Financiero Internacional, an independent state-owned international commercial bank were created. While these two new institutions supplemented the operations of the central bank, the BNC retained its far-reaching responsibilities of controlling monetary policy—issuing and redeeming currency, being a banker to all state entities, and managing investment in the economy. Under this system, the state has virtually complete control over the economy and financial intermediation. The Banco Popular de Ahorro, for instance, manages citizens' personal accounts, while all state companies involved in trade must work through either the Banco Nacional or the Banco Financiero Internacional.

These large financial behemoths, however, have become obstacles to economic growth. The Banco Popular, for instance, pays only a limited amount of interest, because it wishes to discourage large accumulations of private capital. Hence, there are few incentives to save. Private sector capital in Cuba is almost nonexistent, making prospects for conversion to a market economy more difficult.

Without competition, banking services in Cuba are of poor quality and the financial system is heavily bureaucratic. Transactions to facilitate trade through the central bank became notoriously slow in the early 1980s. In fact, the Banco Financiero Internacional was created to provide a speedier and more flexible alternative to the sluggish BNC bureaucracy. The Banco Financiero Internacional was also given authority to trade in precious metals and Eurodollars on the London markets.

Cuba's financial sector has been ill-prepared for the 1990s with the exception of the small staff at the Banco Financiero Internacional. In general, the financial sector's rank and file lack an understanding of what are becoming widely accepted Western accounting principles. They have no concept of customer service, and both the banking and insurance sectors are bureaucratically bloated. The idea of competition is alien and the technological structure necessary to support a more sophisticated financial system does not exist. While other developing countries in Latin America, Africa, Asia, and Eastern Europe receive technical assistance from the Washington-based International Finance Corporation (IFC) or from other countries Cuba demonstrates no interest in moving from the status quo.

Another area where Cuba lags behind is in technology. Using Soviet technology, Cuba was the first Caribbean nation to begin construction of a nuclear plant, but a hard currency crunch and the dissolution of the Soviet Union have hindered its completion. In other areas, such as biomedical technology, Cuba's investments in the 1980s and promotion of commercial potential have appeared to be much exaggerated.

The severe shortage of capital since the late 1980s has also hurt Cuba's other efforts at developing a more sophisticated and diversified economy. Investments in communications have fallen and the country's telephone network has declined in performance. For example, a fire in November 1988 caused extensive damage to the main exchange and it was not until August 1990 that the system's repairs were completed. In 1992, Cuba managed to attract the Italian telephone company, Entel, to assist an overhaul of the phone system, a challenging and long-term job to say the least. Over the years, a succession of other communications industry deals, with Argentine, Mexican, and other sources of technical expertise and capital, have attracted attention without so far significantly changing the overall state of Cuban communications. Moreover, it can be argued that these technologies represent a double-edged sword for a regime bent on limiting the expansion of individual political expression as well as private enterprise.

Tourism is expected to emerge as one of the major components of the Cuban economy in the years to come, probably bypassing sugar as an earner of foreign exchange on a sustained basis. At the same time, other sectors of the economy are helping to broaden the range of exports. Cuba's higher growth after 1994 was largely due to increased production in oil, nickel, electricity, steel, cement, vegetables, and other products. Growth could be more significant, but has been hurt by the fall-off in sugar production. Tourism and other sectors of the economy have, therefore, grown in importance.

Cuba's laws concerning foreign investment and the activities of multinational companies are also obstacles to development. Currently there are no foreign multinational corporations in Cuba that have a majority-owned presence; only joint ventures are allowed (mainly in the mining and tourism sectors). Even then, most cases are restricted to 49 percent ownership. Recognized by the Cuban government as a necessary generator of hard currency income, tourism operates under looser considerations. The foreign firm is allowed to appoint its own executives, define production and sales plans, fix prices, export and import directly, and select and fire personnel. The joint-venture firm is also exempted from import duties, and tax on net profits is limited to a maximum 30 percent. In one of the more open dimensions of Cuba's foreign tourist sector, unhindered movement of hard currency is guaranteed. While by Cuban standards these are generous terms and have attracted German, French, and Canadian companies, they do not stand up well against bigger and more welcoming markets elsewhere in Latin America (and for that matter the developing world). Moreover, they have failed to open Cuba to a wider range of technology.

Castro's efforts to develop the tourist sector with capitalism has a social component that is clearly significant. In a sense, the emphasis on tourism, the exclusion of Cubans from tourist facilities (except as paid help), and the intense competition for the few well-paying jobs (by Cuban standards), is creating an apartheid society orbiting one sector of the economy. More importantly, as Cubans observed the success of the capitalist-oriented tourist sector in picking up hard currency, serious questions arose as to why the same medicine could not be applied to the rest of the economy. As veteran U.S. journalist Andres Oppenheimer observed: "Castro's attempt to save communism with a dose of capitalism was a losing proposition. There was no way to keep his isolated enclaves of free enterprise from spilling over to the rest of the economy. As growing numbers of Cubans flocked to tourism-related industries and added to a soaring black market of goods and services, the capitalist way was spreading like wildfire in Cuba."[27] To many Cubans, the inconsistency between capitalist reality in the tourist sector and socialist reality in the rest of the economy offer two increasingly clear-cut options for the country's future over which the figure of Castro hovers.

Cuba in the 1990s and beyond faces difficult choices, the most significant of which for Fidel Castro and his close supporters is how to enhance economic development while maintaining control over the political system. The market-Leninist approaches adopted in China since 1978 and Vietnam since 1986 have an appeal to Castro from the perspective of those governments' ability to preside over rapid economic growth and improving standards of living, coupled by ongoing political control. Yet, both China and Vietnam have made considerable changes in their economies, including reforming their trade regimes, promoting foreign direct investment, and allowing dynamic private sectors to emerge. Both Beijing and Hanoi have restored relations with the United States. Although China and Vietnam have considerable problems, billions of dollars of foreign direct investment have poured into their respective economies, helping to rebuild the infrastructure with electric power plants, upgrading ports and railway systems, and building roads. In comparison, Cuba has a long distance to travel. The remarks of Eliana Cardoso and Ann Helwege in 1992 remain applicable today: "Foreign investors wait in the wings. How much money they bring in depends on whether the government can provide secure property rights, reliable infrastructure, stable exchange rates, and cooperative trade relations with other countries."[28]

In September 1995, the Cuban parliament passed, unanimously, a new investment law. The new law specifies that foreigners are permitted to own 100 percent of their enterprises—and, on long lease, the land they stand on; the right to repatriate profits is guaranteed; the government is allowed to create duty-free zones; and foreigners will be able to establish assembly plants based on the Mexican *maquiladora* model, to manufacture for export.[29] Three sectors were excluded from the purview of the new law: health, education, and defense. In recent years, the Cuban government has also relaxed regulations regarding individual U.S. dollar holdings and transfers. Designed to soak into the U.S. economy remittances from exiles abroad, as well as come to grips with an enlarged underground dollar economy, these developments have been pushing the economic envelope of what may be politically acceptable for what remains a Marxist-Leninist regime.

Despite the changes in the law and a gradual increase in the number of joint ventures, foreign investors have not flooded into the Caribbean nation-state. Internationale Nederlanden Groep NV (ING), the Dutch financial firm, for a while opened a banking representative office, and some Spanish investments have appeared in the real estate and construction sector; some mining companies (and particularly visible Canadian investments) have entered the island. However, outside of the tourist sector, Cuba is not as attractive as other potential sites. The foreign-investment law theoretically opens up most sectors of the economy to foreign investment with the exceptions of defense, health, and education. In reality, the Cuban government has also indicated that foreign investors need not apply for retailing, gasoline distribution, and retail banking operations. Consequently, Cuba's take of foreign investment, either committed or delivered in the late 1990–95 period has been $736.9 million, compared to the billions of dollars that have gone into Latin America's economies over the same period.[30]

The U.S. Card

A sizeable U.S.-based Cuban exile community is waiting for Castro's finale. Through the 1988–91 period, considerable excitement was generated by the collapse of the old Communist order in Eastern Europe and the Soviet Union. The perception of many was that Fidel was next. Consequently, governing plans of all sorts are ready and waiting for that magic moment when the socialist *caudillo* exits the scene. While many eye the political arena, others already have plans for the economy. Large U.S. firms are eyeing a return to Cuba for operations.

However, Castro is not gone and the waiting continues. The same waiting strategy guides the U.S. policy, which was energized by the Cuban Democracy Act of 1992 (also known as the Torricelli law), which precludes resumption of official U.S.-Cuban relations until there are democratic and free elections in a post-Castro Cuba. More recently, the Cuban Liberty and Democracy Solidarity (LIBERTAD) Act of 1996 (also known as the Helms-Burton law) places further pressure on the U.S.-Cuba relationship—most notably by heightening the risk of doing business in Cuba by third-country investors, and allowing cases to be tried in U.S. courts against foreign parties utilizing property nationalized or confiscated under the Castro regime. But perhaps its most noteworthy feature was that it codified in law the U.S. embargo against Cuba dating back to the 1960s. Any future decision involving consideration of a lifting of the embargo would now involve Congressional oversight rather than customary Executive Branch action.

The Castro government constantly has used the United States as its reactionary bogeyman in the creation of a strong sense of nationalism and support for the regime. Indeed, one of the chief objectives of Castro as a young revolutionary chieftain was to destroy the traditional and geographically logical linkages to the northern giant. To some Cuban intellectuals, the United States had stolen their country's independence which local nationalist forces were on the verge of capturing when Washington intervened and defeated the old colonial master, Spain. The U.S. occupation (1898–1902) which stabilized the country after a bitter civil war, created a situation of dependency in which U.S. political influence and capital quickly came to dominate. This showed evidence of declining in the 1940s and 1950s with the process of "Cubanization."

Castro has artificially terminated his country's dependence on the U.S. despite natural and traditional affinities between the two countries. There is no doubt that the U.S. embargo on Cuba, which commenced in the early 1960s and has continued through to the present, has done considerable damage to the Cuban economy. Although not capable of causing an economic collapse, the U.S. embargo decidedly weakened the country's development, forcing it to develop ties outside of the hemisphere to sustain its independence vis-à-vis the Yankee giant.

By the early 1990s, Cuba had reached a stage of international isolation and developmental implosion. As many of the gains of past decades suffered the fate of being reversed, the future for the Cuban nation appeared bleak. Now, the Eastern bloc partners are gone, it has few real friends in the world, and has virtually no access to international credit that it desperately needs. While the newly independent states of the former Soviet Union join the World Bank and International Monetary Fund, and its Latin neighbors embark upon regional trade integration, Cuba remains barely afloat and heading backward. Eventually, with Castro or without, Cuba will have to rejoin the international community, which will ultimately mean a profound change in the relationship with the United States.[31]

An expanding body of opinion is arguing that the socialist shibboleths of command economics will have to be discarded, and the "U.S. card" could be of assistance in finding the path. The United States is a traditional and logical trade partner. Moreover, if the Cuban economy is to diversify and expand its tourist sector (especially as a source of hard currency income), the United States could be expected to become its major market as it was in the past. Currently, other North Americans, the Canadians, are Cuba's major source of tourists. Considering the vastly larger population of the United States, the potential for Cuba is considerable.

The debate as to how and when Havana and Washington can initiate a productive dialogue is politically charged. However, if Cuba and the United States could agree on a democratization agenda (which is difficult for Castro to envision without placing his own authority in question), and perhaps generally define the settlement of outstanding U.S. expropriation cases (valued at $5.2 billion by the U.S. Foreign Claims Settlement Commission), the way might be open for a more productive relationship. The 1996 Helms-Burton law outlines in considerable detail a process by which this could evolve (support for "civil society" institutional building, for example), although the political and economic costs needed to sustain this in the U.S. policy environment might be messy.

Even with political preconditions (a path toward democracy) this would provide Cuba an opportunity to rejoin the international economy and open doors to membership in the Inter-American Development Bank, the World Bank, and the International Monetary Fund. This, in turn, would allow Cuba to apply for badly needed economic and technical assistance.[32] Also, the U.S. tie would probably carry with it opportunities for Cuban preferential access to regional markets, using combinations of the Caribbean Basin Initiative (CBI), NAFTA, and other trade arrangements. Although sugar is one of the most politicized agricultural goods in the United States, it is also conceivable that market space (no doubt at the expense of other countries exporting to the United States) would be made, hence helping Cuba's foreign exchange outlook. Additionally, the end of the trade embargo would allow goods made with Cuban sugar in third countries, like Canada, to be exported to the United States.

Another component in these calculations is the role of the Cuban exile community. In popular perceptions, this has tended to be oversimplified, focusing either on South Florida's considerable political and financial influence, or ephasizing the likely tensions between those who stayed in Cuba and those who left. The reality is that successive waves of emigres have come to the United States, learned new skills, and became wealthy and self-employed. Although it is not expected that all Cubans living in the United States will flock back to Cuba once Castro quits the scene—indeed most surveys indicate that Cuban-Americans plan to visit but few plan to relocate permanently—some will return with both expertise and capital to help plug their homeland into the new economic order. As futurists Marvin Cetron and Owen Davies commented: "When Castro's reign is at last over, those emigres will form a resource that will give Cuba a powerful advantage over other nations trying to repair their crippled economies. . . . Many are rich. And many of them look upon their homeland as West Germans once viewed East Germany, as a brother nation to be given all possible help in building new lives once their repression ends."[33]

A last component brings out the fact that the United States is the only nation that is likely to help Cuba rise from a complete economic collapse. Russia and other members of the CIS have articulated little interest in paying for Castro's failed "socialism-in-the-sun" brand of economics and the newly invigorated European Community has concerns closer to home—the rise of Islamic fundamentalism in North Africa, Eastern Europe's economic reforms, and the breakup of Yugoslavia. Japan is more concerned with its trade relations with the United States and investment in what is emerging as a Yen bloc of nations in East and Southeast Asia. The People's Republic of China has similar concerns: trade with the United States is not worth incurring Washington's displeasure over flirtations with Castro. Cuba, therefore, is stuck with the United States; Cetron and Davies note the obvious: "The United States is the only country in the world with both the economic power to help feed Cuba's people and enough interest in the island to bother doing so."[34]

Ironically, the hinge of Cuba's effective use of a "U.S. card" is Fidel Castro. Drastic economic imperatives are forcing Castro's hand toward a series of measured economic reforms aimed initially at the foreign investment community. A revised legal framework was implemented in the fall of 1995 with that in mind. However, while Castro may make Cuba a bit more attractive to foreign investors, he faces pressure from a younger cadre of loyalists concerned with the nation's political isolation and chronic economic crisis. But the regime cannot go too far without undermining its own foundations, or more specifically, Castro's personal political control. Likewise, Cuba's interest in opening to the international community should not be overstated. The strictures of the economy are such that investment-grade opportunities remain limited through the mid-term. It is also certain that the Cuban government's overtures to the international business community are in part tactical, and are at times undercut by Castro's own flamboyant statements about socialism's historical correctness.

Another element in this equation lies in U.S. domestic politics and legislative initiatives. The debate in the United States has evolved since the early 1960s. Cuba's regional isolation, the end of the cold war, and the country's economic demise initially generated a sense of impending change. This was premature. Yet, as marginal as Cuban policy may be to U.S. national interests, there has been growing interest in a post-Castro political and economic environment. An activist Cuban American exile community has laid out its gambit, namely

Fidel Castro's unconditional demise. This position resonates across a broader ideological spectrum than is often assumed and explains in part the difficulty U.S. policy makers have in engaging Cuba on other terms.

However, what developed in recent years is a new constituency of proponents with no love lost for the Cuban government but with a concern for the dead-end nature of the current Cuban agenda. This eclectic group—from business interests to moderate policymakers (and a wider international community)—argues that the way to change Cuba is to engage Castro in a dialogue that will ultimately alter Cuban policies, and bring to the fore a more pragmatic generation of Cuban leadership that will eventually thrust Castro aside.

Naturally, U.S. hardliners regard this with suspicion since this dialogue with the Cubans appears open-ended and overlaps with the agenda supported by constituencies (and foreign governments) whose concerns are not directed at Castro but at simply maintaining the dialogue with the Cuban government in the hopes of short term political or economic advantages. To make matters more complicated, the Castro regime's own actions—the February 1996 shoot-down of two unarmed Cuban exile piloted planes being one spectacular example—have only buttressed convincingly those suspicions of much of Havana's policies.

It is in this context that U.S. legislative initiatives, such as the Cuban Democracy Act of 1992, gained both Democratic and Republican support. A further tightening of U.S. policy toward the Castro regime subsequently emerged with the Cuban Liberty and Democratic Solidarity Act (also known by its sponsors' names, Jesse Helms (R-NC) and Dan Burton (R-IN)). As noted earlier, this set in motion a debate that U.S. policy was not only overextending its bounds by creating further irritants with Washington's allies, but was pursuing a counterproductive policy strategy. In this unfinished chapter of U.S.-Latin American relations, the Helms-Burton Bill was voted by the U.S. Congress in March 1996, placing further anchors for U.S. policy makers.

Conclusion

Cuba has considerable potential for a dynamic future. As *Fortune* magazine noted in April 1992: "Among the country's attractions: a cheap labor force, fertile land, and a large entrepreneurial class in exile."[35] The revolution has provided one of Latin America's better educational and health care systems and Cuba's cities lack the depressed slums found around other Latin American cities, like São Paulo or Mexico City. The danger in the 1990s is that Castro's resistance to change could well make all of Cuba a slum. Putting aside political considerations, it can be argued that all of the achievements painstakingly gained since 1959 run the risk of being negated by a leader who refuses to provide a flexible, pragmatic approach to national development. Moreover, the limited economic reforms undertaken in 1994–95 could prove to be transitory. While Cuba is becoming an ossified society, held in check by a *fidelista* security apparatus, the rest of Latin America advances. One has to concur with the assessment of Ritter: "In the long run, there appears to be no reasonable alternative to a substantially marketized, mixed-ownership, and externally-oriented economic system."[36] The critical question here is how long is the "long-run"? The difficulty of that question has already generated a cottage industry of analysts attempting to gage Castro's demise and Cuba's future.[37]

Castro has proven himself a political survivor. He is aware that his base of support has shrunk. A new generation of Cubans have known only the socialist *caudillo* and nothing of the pre-Castro period. They are also aware of the world beyond their borders through both radio and television (as with Radio Martí or with the world coming *to* Cuba, such as the notion of a Papal visit). Through these communication mediums, they have been provided another image of reality which encompasses a wide choice of food and consumer goods, and no long lines. Yet the longer Cuba's younger generation remains in a closed society, the more unsettling will be the shocks that will come when the Castro regime passes from the scene.

Notes

1. Pascal Fletcher, "Cubans See—Or Hope For—Recovery," *Financial Times* (July 18, 1995): p. 4.
2. H.C. Wallach, *Monetary Problems of an Export Economy: Cuban Experience 1914–1947* (Cambridge: Harvard University Press, 1950), p. 6; and William Anderson, *Foreign Agriculture* (Washington, D.C.: U.S. department of Agriculture, March 1961).
3. Boris Goldenberg, *The Cuban Revolution and Latin America* (New York: Frederick A. Praeger Publishers, 1965), p. 121.
4. Ibid., pp. 120–21.

5. Derek R. Hall, "Cuba," in *Urbanization, Planning and Development in the Caribbean*, ed. Robert B. Potter (London: Mansell Publishing Limited, 1989), p. 84.
6. Ibid., p. 123.
7. Ibid., pp. 125–26.
8. See *Anuario Azucarero 1959* (Havana, 1960).
9. Ibid.
10. Hugh Thomas, "Cuba: The United States and Batista, 1952–1958," in *Cuban Communism* sixth edition, ed. Irving Louis Horowitz (New Brunswick, N.J.: Transaction Books, 1984), pp. 4–5.
11. Tad Szulc, *Fidel: A Critical Portrait* (New York: William Morrow and Company, 1986), p. 536.
12. For an overall assessment of the revolution's track-record, see Hugh S. Thomas, Georges A. Fauriol, and Juan Carlos Weiss *The Cuban Revolution, 25 Years Later* (Boulder, Colo.: Westview Press, 1984).
13. Lawrence H. Theriot, "Cuba Faces the Economic Realities of the 1980s," in *Cuban Communism* sixth edition, ed. Irving Louis Horowitz (New Brunswick, N.J.: Transaction Books, 1984), pp. 217–18.
14. Carmelo Mesa-Lago, "Cuba's Centrally Planned Economy: An Equity Tradeoff for Growth," in *Cuban Communism* sixth edition, ed. Irving Louis Horowitz (New Brunswick, N.J.: Transaction Books, 1984), p. 180.
15. Theriot, "Cuba," p. 218.
16. See U.S. Congress's Joint Economic Committee, *Cuba Faces the Economic Realities of the 1980s* (Washington, D.C.: U.S. Government Printing Office, 1982).
17. "Cuba," *ABECOR Country Report* (July 1990): p. 2.
18. For an original essay, see Juan M. del Aguila, "Perceptions of Cuba in the 1980s," in *Cuba: The International Dimension*, eds. Georges A. Fauriol and Eva Loser (New Brunswick, N.J.: Transaction Publishers, 1990), pp. 405–439.
19. Andres Oppenheimer, *Castro's Final Hour: The Secret Story Behind the Coming Downfall of Communist Cuba* (New York: Simon and Schuster, 1992), see part 1.
20. Jose F. Alonzo and Peter J. Buzzanell, "Cuba's Sugar Economy: Recent Performance and Challenges for the 1990s," in *The Politics of the Caribbean Basin Sugar Trade*, eds. Scott B. MacDonald and Georges F. Fauriol (New York: Praeger, 1991), p. 62.
21. Ibid., p. 67.
22. *Christian Science Monitor* (December 27, 1991), p. 1 (photo).
23. Ibid.
24. A.R.M. Ritter, "The Cuban Economy in the 1990s: External Challenges and Policy Imperatives," *Journal of Interamerican Studies and World Affairs* vol. 32, no. 3 (Fall 1990): p. 117.
25. Quoted from Louis M. Smith, "Cuba Intends To Stay the Course on Socialism, Says Diplomat," *The Times of the Americas* (November 1, 1989): p. 16. The Inter-American Dialogue session was held in Washington, D.C., on February 14, 1996.
26. Quoted in "Cuba: Holding On," *The Economist* (October 19, 1991): p. 18.
27. Oppenheimer, *Castro's Final Hour*, p. 421.
28. Eliana Cardoso and Ann Helwege, *Cuba After Communism* (Cambridge, Mass.: The MIT Press, 1992), p. 100.
29. "Castro Takes One More Step Toward Capitalism," *The Economist* (September 9, 1995): p. 45.
30. Jose de Cordoba, "Cuba's Business Law Puts Off Foreigners," *Wall Street Journal* (October 10, 1995): p. A16.
31. A creative assessment of Cuba's economic realities and post-Castro regime ap-

pears in Ernest H. Preeg with Jonathan D. Levine, *Cuba and the New Caribbean Economic Order* (Washington, D.C.: Center for Strategic and International Studies, 1993).

32. As Eliana Cardoso and Ann Helwege commented: "This is the best way to help the Cuban government phase in reforms and stabilization. Technical assistance, as with the Soviet Union, is badly needed and can start immediately." Cardoso and Helwege, *Cuba*, pp. 113–14.

33. Marvin Cetron and Owen Davies, *Crystal Globe: The Haves and Have-Nots of the New World Order* (New York: St. Martin's Press, 1991), p. 113.

34. Ibid., p. 114. See also Preeg, *Cuba and the New Caribbean Economic Order* for an analysis of a post-Castro Cuba's sources of external funding.

35. Joshua Mendes, "Ready to Dance on Castro's Grave," *Fortune* (April 6, 1992): p. 16.

36. Ritter, "Cuban Economy," p. 144.

37. Among many, this includes Florida International University's massive multi-authored study, *Cuba in Transition: New Challenges for U.S. Policy* (Miami: Florida International University, a project of the Cuban Research Institute, Latin American Caribbean Center, 1993). See also Rand's efforts in this area, most notably studies by Edward Gonzalez, *Cuba, Clearing Perilous Waters?* (Santa Monica: Rand, MR-673-OSD, 1996); Gonzalez (and David Ronfeldt) *Storm Warnings for Cuba* (MR-452-OSD, 1994); and, Gonzalez and Ronfeldt *Cuba Adrift in a Postcommunist World* (R-4231-USDP, 1992).

11

Outlook for the Fast-Forward Process

The central questions facing observers of the Latin American environment revolve around the following determination: is the region's reform process for real? Are U.S. policymakers conceptualizing a hemispheric future that takes this process into full account? The short answer to this basket of issues, touched upon throughout this book, is affirmative. There is in fact something resembling a regional consensus, as well as a timetable in the area of hemispheric trade and economic integration derived from the 1994 Miami Summit. If there is uncertainty, it may lie in the United States' abilities to sustain these regional initiatives against occasionally strong domestic political opposition. A second danger lies in the possible "fatigue" that will undermine Latin American governments' commitments to maintain economic and political reforms in the face of domestic opposition.

The argument against the notion that the fast-forward process can be reversed supposes that the Latin American reforms are becoming increasingly institutionalized. Indeed, some of the changes are probably here to stay. As Moisés Naim noted in the aftermath of Mexico's 1994–95 peso crisis: "The Latin American boom of the early 1990s was not just another financial bubble that finally burst once fickle portfolio investors lost interest in the region. The reforms induced important changes, many of them irreversible."[1]

For the industrialized countries, especially the United States, it is important to understand the implications of a changing Latin America. Granted, specific problems exist, including criminally and politically motivated violence and uneven socioeconomic levels of performance. But what is different from past cycles of boom and bust is that simul-

257

taneously a number of Latin American countries are making important economic and political reforms while similar processes are evident around the world. The early part of the twenty-first century will show that Latin America's fast-forward mode of development, if successful, will be a major influence on U.S. policy; and if not successful, its reversal will be a blow to U.S. strategic interests in the post-cold war era.

Although tensions in U.S.-Latin American relations are not likely in the short term, there are issues that in varying ways have the potential to slow down or even derail the fast-forward path. These issues include a breakdown in the democratization process, expansion of the illicit drug trade, trade wars over fair-market access, intellectual property rights and related issues, and arguments over the salience of environmental issues.[2] These concerns must be addressed with a background of a violent and somewhat unstructured new international order that can augment the dangers and enhance the chances for failure. Considering the history of Latin American nations, their relations with the industrialized club of nations (best symbolized by the OECD), and the quest for new guidelines in international affairs, considerable thought must be given to the tone and content of dialogue. Clearly, changes in the international context of U.S.-Latin American relations makes this even more pressing on the edge of the twenty-first century.

One can perhaps argue that in the 1990s, policymakers in North and South America lack the relative comfort of the frame of reference that was provided by the cold war. Without the so-called danger of pro-Soviet Communist revolutionaries, where will the new dangers occur? Do the Latin American relationships with the United States and other industrialized nations shift only to an agenda driven by economic issues—market access to Latin American countries and conversely, Latin access to U.S., European, and Asian markets? Will economic integration in the Americas create new patterns of power between those in the American trading network and those outside of it? Or will relations between Latin America and the United States return to that akin to the 1960s and 1970s, driven by notions of unevenness, economic dominance, and political distrust that led to confrontation in a number of areas? What in fact frames the relationship?

In his early 1990s assessment of the hemispheric environment, Robert Pastor suggested that Latin America and the Caribbean have represented a policy "whirlpool" for the United States. The director of

Latin American and Caribbean Affairs on the National Security Council from 1977 to 1981, Pastor contends that U.S.-Latin American/Caribbean relations follow a distinctive historical pattern. The United States, with interests around the world, sits just beyond the whirlpool of policy issues represented by the lands to the south. That whirlpool, according to Pastor, "draws the United States into its center, where it spins us in perilous eddies and then, just as suddenly, releases us to drift to the rim, where we forget the region and deal with other matters."[3] Recent examples of this situation are the U.S. interventions in Grenada and Panama, involvement in the affairs of Nicaragua and El Salvador, and, overall, the U.S.-Mexican relationship. In each case, with the possible exception of the last, the issues that brought an intensification of relations eventually faded.

The downside of Pastor's line of argument is that it appears to connote a somewhat helpless vision both of U.S. options as well as the policies of other nations in the region. More seriously, perhaps, "whirlpool" defines a forced relationship with the United States' geographically close neighbors but implies an inability to develop a strategically significant vision of the rest of Latin America. What is clearly accurate is that the United States has faded in and out of hemispheric policy, leaving much of the region to assume occasionally not only disinterest, but also tension, and conflict with Washington. Complacency toward Latin America and Caribbean affairs is an Achilles heel of U.S. foreign policy, shaped in part by the Eurocentric vision (and now a competing Asia-centric vision) of the traditional core of the policy establishment in Washington.

The arguments presented in these chapters propose a different vision of hemispheric policy—one that is latent in the present relationship. The United States remains the most influential force in the Americas, for better or worse. Therefore, one strategic argument of "fast-forward" is that recent Latin American trends in part have been stimulated by U.S. initiatives—and at minimum, U.S. responsiveness. In practice, if there is a whirlpool, it is often *when* the United States acts. As messy as the Central American crises of the late 1970s and 1980s were, ultimately, it was the United States that shaped the terms of the debate (this should not be confused with suggesting that Washington achieved what it set out to do). Likewise, it is the ability of U.S. policy to project a new vision of regional trading relationships and liberal economic reforms (President Bush's 1990 Enterprise for the Americas Initiative) that further galvanized a new hemispheric momentum in the 1990s.[4]

The corollary argument of "fast-forward" is particularly relevant to the situation the hemisphere faces into the early part of the twenty-first century. This alludes to the sense of *positive* dynamism that cuts across Latin America's political and economic experience. Without taking anything away from the indigenous roots of this dynamism, the very success of the Latin American revival has in part been predicated on linking the notions of success at both ends of the hemisphere. This is not the gushing sound made famous by Ross Perot as U.S. jobs moved to Mexico; rather, what this is all about is the roar of activity and the popular applause that will accompany the realization that Latin America needs the United States to sustain the "fast forward" process, and simultaneously, the United States needs a vibrant hemisphere to strengthen its own fast track. More broadly, the success of these strategies is individually linked to a continued strengthening of Latin American ties with Europe and the Pacific Basin, and U.S. geoeconomic post-cold war policies that link the vitality of the domestic economy with a substantial U.S. global role. These visions will coexist uneasily, and occasionally clash, with protectionist sentiments throughout the hemisphere and isolationist elements in the United States.

The Post-Cold War System: Coming to Terms

The idea that the end of the Cold War was to usher in a new era of democratic governments, peaceful coexistence between nations, and an easy transition to a world of content capitalists is obviously erroneous. Contrary to Francis Fukuyama's extravagant argument that ideological debates are convincingly over, the "end of history" is not at hand.[5] While democratic governments (in the broadest of definitions) are in ascendance in the 1990s, many such experiments are fragile. Authoritarian forces continue to exist around the world, currently out of favor but no doubt waiting in the wings. While cooperation between nations does exist and should not be understated, tensions abound on such issues as ethnicity, religion, and regionalism. In a perhaps exaggerated way, the follow-on argument to Fukuyama appears to run counter to the "end of history." Global politics has entered a new phase, in which religion, history, language, and tradition are defining conflict and cooperation—what Samuel Huntington has proposed calling the "clash of civilizations."[6]

While many in the developing world, as in Latin America, find the economic reform process painful, they usually are not aware that a related process is underway in much of the industrialized club of countries. Futurist Alvin Toffler accurately assesses that the global system in the 1990s is the process of creating an entirely new system of wealth creation: "This new system for making wealth is totally dependent on the instant communication and dissemination of data, ideas, symbols, and symbolism. It is, as we will discover, a super-symbolic economy in the exact sense of that term."[7] This economic transformation moves past the deindustrialization or the hallowing process in which developed countries export their old-line manufacturing industries to offshore locations where labor is cheaper, and moves beyond mass production toward increasing customization. Now, according to Toffler, technology is causing a shift in jobs back to industrialized nations—but not necessarily with the same number of workers, and with new means of production. Simply stated, old methods of wealth generation are replaced by new.

For example, a hog breeder in Minnesota now uses an ultrasound machine to measure exactly how lean a hog is in a few minutes with little complications to either man or beast, or a metal processor in Cleveland learns how to wield laser light like a blacksmith's hammer to pound extra strength into steel.[8] As the flow of information, and access to the most updated technology revolutionizes life in the industrialized nations, it also uproots society as new winners and losers emerge. In the United States, Europe, and Asia economic structures are changing, adjusting to the new market conditions, which is proving to be a difficult, painful, and at times, politically unpopular process. The stakes, however, are high. As Barnaby J. Feder noted: "No enterprise is without its technological frontiers. Command of those frontiers has long been recognized as a key to competitive success, but the globalization of national economies has stepped up pressures on business leaders and policy makers alike to manage the invention and use of new technology more effectively."[9]

The words "structural adjustment" have a bad connotation in Latin America. They are usually associated with higher unemployment, economic shocks, widening the misery index, and in general, societal upheaval. Although the process of structural adjustment is regarded as a bane on Latin America, the reality is that it has also spread to the United States, Europe, and Asia. It could even be argued that structural adjustment was a factor in President George Bush's defeat to Democrat Bill Clinton in 1992. U.S. citizens found the economic transformation they were going through unsettling, especially after a period of strong growth in the 1980s, and the nation's leadership appeared out of touch with its citizenry.

If the question were asked to a U.S. citizen whether he or she regarded structural adjustment as a significant factor in their daily life, it is probable that you would get a blank look. The concept of structural adjustment as it is known in Latin America is not known in the United States. However, if questions were asked about changes in the work place, job security (or the lack therefore of), or whether U.S. products and workers can compete with foreign workers, the reaction would be different. As in Latin America, articulation is given to frustration about foreign competition, loss of jobs, and apprehension that the local factory will move offshore—to Southeast Asia, the Caribbean, Central America, or Mexico. For many North Americans (Canadians included) the future has become a fearful and uncertain place where entire sectors of the economy are jettisoned, new sectors rapidly emerge demanding new skills, and the middle-class standard of living comes under increasing strain. Ross Perot tapped into these concerns in the 1992 U.S. presidential elections, and Pat Buchanan enlarged on these fears in the 1996 race.

As hemispheric relations mature in the 1990s, Latin Americans should understand that the United States has a bad case of angst. The United States is in a period of self-examination and coming to terms with a wide range of problems that were papered over in the previous two decades. Briefly consider the following statistics for the United States in the early 1990s: 10 percent of the population is on food stamps; 20 percent of children live in poverty; 35 million people are without health insurance; one person is murdered every twenty-five minutes; the United States has the highest prison rate in the industrial world; and it has the lowest level of literacy among the advanced industrial nations.[10] As Jeffrey Garten noted of these figures: "Herein lies the problem not just for life at home but also for our international position—for in today's world, there is no separating domestic and foreign policy."[11]

While the United States must deal with nagging socioeconomic problems as well as a large budget deficit that hinders its ability to regain strong economic growth, the process of structural adjustment—

the shift from industrial society to the symbolic economy—is not unique to North America. Many of the same or similar problems confront the European Union (EU), Japan, Australia, New Zealand, and even the more advanced Asian economies of Singapore, Taiwan, South Korea, and Hong Kong. Even Asia's economic giant, Japan, has remained mired in low growth through much of the early and mid-1990s.

While the industrialized nations struggled with structural adjustment in the early 1990s, the very same countries were in the process of consolidating or expanding regional trade blocs. In the post-cold war order, this is a significant consideration. The EU reached the historic date of 1 January 1993, at which point it was officially a single market of 340 million people and since has expanded to include Austria, Finland, and Sweden; the United States, Mexico, and Canada created the North American Free Trade Area; and the Southeast Asian countries coalesced around the Association of Southeast Asian Nations (ASEAN). These trends reflect the process of trade integration, driven by lowering or completely dismantling tariff and nontariff barriers to regional trade. The process of regional integration in the Americas as exemplified by NAFTA, MERCOSUR, and the Andean Pact has a number of components and will be a difficult trend to reverse in the short term.

While trade blocs reform trade within the bloc, they also represent a potential threat that must be considered in the context of U.S.-Latin American relations. The United States will have to guard against protectionist tendencies that preclude any further extension of free-trade agreements within the Americas. This is not to argue that the U.S. economy should be left open to unfair trade practices, but that free-trade agreements should be carefully negotiated with those countries that are ready and able to follow such a course, such as Chile. For the United States, as the leading industrial country in the Americas, the task will be how to help Latin America help itself in reaching beyond the fast-forward stage to self-sustaining growth. The closure of markets will clearly not help—indeed it can undermine the region's current experiment with democratic capitalism and help usher back authoritarian solutions. This threat of closing markets is not limited to North America—a number of Latin American countries such as Chile, Colombia, and Mexico, have discovered the importance of trading and investment with Asian countries, such as Thailand, Singapore, Malaysia, and China.[12]

Another factor that has emerged in the post-cold war era that will certainly be an influence on U.S.-Latin American relations (as well as Euro-Latin American relations) is the volatility of international capital. Mexico's 1994–95 peso crisis exemplified how quickly funds can leave a country, due in part to technological advances that provide amazing mobility of capital. It also reflects the key word of "confidence." Mexico, for a number of reasons, some unique to itself and some evident elsewhere in Latin America, lost investor confidence and paid the consequences. Naim puts into context the combination of reform and capital markets: "The success in tackling inflation, the unprecedented growth in trade among neighboring countries, and euphoria of foreign investors obscured the drag on the region's economic prospects by high income disparities, low productivity, low international competitiveness and—most of all—ineffectual public institutions."[13] The first rounds of reform were tough and their success brought renewed confidence in the region, reflected by capital flows in emerging markets. However, the next round of reform is equally difficult, and thus far, incomplete. Mexico's 1994–95 troubles reflected a realization on the part of foreign investors that the reform process was incomplete and that considerable problems remained.

Mexico, in many regards, was a test of the evolving global capital market in which largescale investors can rapidly facilitate market entry and exit. For Latin America nations (and other developing countries seeking foreign capital) this means that confidence remains essential to external capital flows, and that confidence is based on sound macroeconomic policies. International capital markets expect and reward decisive action; conversely they penalize its absence. For investors (and policymakers dragged along with them) Mexico represented a need to have better knowledge of the actual conditions in Latin America, not what imagemakers wanted to portray.

Another factor in the post-cold war era is that the United States is less likely to be as active in intervening in Latin American affairs due to considerable challenges elsewhere around the world. Problem areas outside of the Americas include the Middle East, Asia, the Balkans, and the former Soviet Union. Outside of a violent political change in Cuba or the possibility of drug traffickers obtaining tactical nuclear weapons, the appetite for being sucked into a policy quagmire in Latin America and the Caribbean is not large. At the same time, a number of issues exist that will increasingly bind North and South America closer together.

The Strategic Dilemmas

In the 1990s, the strategic policy dilemma of the United States vis-à-vis the Western Hemisphere is to redefine what has been essentially a narrowly focused political and diplomatic interest. To oversimplify, perhaps, post-World War II U.S. policy has been dominated by the desire to prevent the emergence of leftist or communist regimes or to combat direct or indirect Soviet influence. Such scenarios have faded and have been replaced by a more ambiguous agenda of economic competitiveness, concerns over democratic governance, environmental concerns, and social development. There are indications in some regions of the world that nationalism is a potent force that is dividing an uncertain post-cold war era. In this context, what is the basis of U.S. involvement in the hemisphere?

Five Quick Snapshots

1. First, as obvious as this may be, Latin America remains in the unique position of being able to affect the fabric of U.S. (and, to a lesser extent, Canadian) society. There is a profound transnational economic and social interaction—sustained by an extraordinary process of migration that is expanding both Latin and West Indian influence in the United States as well as furthering the Americanization of Latin America and the Caribbean.

2. A second major feature to recall here is that, for all of the region's well-known problems, Latin America does represent, in very broad terms, a group of fairly sophisticated political and economic communities. It is grossly lacking in some areas—such as locally developed technology—but the potential is there for a cutting-edge industrial and consumer infrastructure. More significant, the region is increasingly interconnected with interests and actions elsewhere in the world. In fact, sustaining economic competitiveness is likely to remain the "make or break" challenge of most governments in the region.

3. The third major feature is related to democracy. Its reversal would be a blow to U.S. credibility worldwide, let alone lead to the weakening of the vigor of democratic governance in the Western Hemisphere. Although prospects for a return to military governments are dim in the late 1990s, failure to improve social conditions as well as the ongoing implementation of reforms by democratic governments could reopen

the door to nondemocratic solutions. It is also doubtful that nondemocratic governments would be in any better position to tackle the same socioeconomic challenges.

4. A fourth interest is related to what might be called hemispheric regionalism. In recent years, the attention focused on integration in Europe has shifted to the trends in the Western Hemisphere. The economic and political—and ultimately strategic—implications are potentially profound.

We are beginning to see a segmented region, with interaction among the United States, Canada, and Mexico acquiring a distinct dimension. Beyond NAFTA, the notion of a North American community somewhere over the next 20 years is not farfetched—despite the political debate (and economic resistance) this is triggering already within the three countries. The linkages of a revived Central American common market with North America seems possible. Similarly, how Caribbean integration efforts such as the Association of Carribean States (ACS) the Caribbean Community (CARICOM) and Organization of Eastern Caribbean States (OECS) come into play in this context therefore becomes a relevant question.

South American states have reinvigorated hopes for regional and subregional integration, primarily through MERCOSUR. By bringing together Brazil and Argentina, a powerful association of economic (and political) forces is being put in play. Whether it is a counterweight to NAFTA's vision of hemispheric free trade or simply a partner is as yet unclear. The viability of this debate is dependent on continued economic growth in the MERCOSUR group as well as further definition of U.S. regional trade policy. The outcome will define whether the 1994 Miami Summit objective of a free trade area from Canada to Tierra del Fuego by 2005 will come to pass.[14]

5. Finally, a security interest does remain. But the prevailing sense of conventional regional security of earlier decades has broken down under the weight of other considerations: illegal immigration and refugee flows; fears of terrorism; Latin American civil-military relations; and more recently, drug trafficking. Some might even add environmental crisis to the list.

The fundamental issue is the vision of the Western Hemisphere the United States wishes to pursue as developments elsewhere in the world redraw its international priorities. The fact of the matter is that the way the United States interacts with Latin America is part and parcel of a mosaic of local and international trends. A reconstructed world with one superpower, if it holds, will trigger a reapportionment of U.S. interests among an enlarged and unified Europe, an increasingly dynamic, yet complicated Pacific Basin arena, and Latin America. From a European perspective, Latin America is a concern, but clearly its place is subordinated by regions closer to home—North Africa, Russia, and the Balkans. The same is true in Japan, with Southeast Asia, China, and the Korean Peninsula.

As decision-makers in Latin America have slowly come to recognize, continued economic growth and support for political pluralism cannot be assured without full hemispheric participation in global affairs. Some in the United States will view these trends as leading toward the replacement of U.S. leadership with the emergence of alternative sources of power. The real issue for Washington will revolve around the search for policies that sustain cooperative leadership among multitiered regional and global relations.

In the new era of international relations, the relative importance of Latin America to the United States will continue to increase markedly—both directly and in terms of our global economic competitiveness. Concomitantly, the importance of Latin America may well proportionally decline for Europe and Japan, and the more developed Asian countries (such as South Korea and Singapore). However, that depends somewhat on U.S. policy considerations. U.S. interests would need to be forcefully redefined to accord the region the kind of priority which in the past the United States only assigned to East-West, European, East Asian, and Middle Eastern affairs. This is a strategic break from traditional post-world War II visions of global U.S. interests and requires creative thinking in Washington. A broad, integrated, long-term U.S. policy initiative must be carefully tailored to a considerable number of substantially different subregional economic, trade, and political circumstances.

The Political, Economic, and Security Agendas

1. Picture two different visions of Latin America's political future. The first is cast in the nasty afterglow of burning buildings controlled by various guerrilla groups and powerful criminal cartels. Democracy has failed and parts of Latin America have slipped out of control of central authorities, the only order that exists comes from a barrel of a gun.

The sky rains acid rain down on horridly eroded land, stripped of its soil due to relentless exploitation of rain forests and strip mining. There is no sense of compromise, no sense of the future, only a haunting Blade Runnerish perception that life is ugly and short. Relations with the United States and other more industrialized nations are bad—external debts remained unpaid, Latin American goods (excluding Mexico's) are excluded from the North American market, and in some cases, U.S. military intervention looms as a possibility. This is the Latin America of failed economic experiments of the state-oriented and neoliberal prescriptions: a world in which the underpinning political institutions and their international support systems have collapsed.

2. The other vision of Latin America is one in which problems still remain, but efforts are being made to rectify the imbalances of incomes and the inadequacies of political institutions in meeting the public's demands. In the international realm, a number of Latin American nations are actively involved in major issues and within the Western Hemisphere relations with North America are characterized by cooperation and a decreasing sense of dependency. Trade issues, not military intervention, dominate the agendas between Washington and Mexico City, Caracas, Buenos Aires, and Brasilia.

Considering these two visions of what the future may be, the bedrock objective of the United States in the political sphere will be completing the transition of the region to the practice of democratic government, consolidating and perfecting past gains, and helping local democracies to defend themselves against myriad challenges, one of the most pressing being social inequalities such as those that resulted in Chiapas. With respect to completing the process of regional democratization, Cuba will comprise the most difficult and dangerous case—although troubles can also be expected in nations such as Haiti, and perhaps again elsewhere in the Carribean and in Central America.

To consolidate and deepen the function of existing democratic governments, the United States will want to see (and local leaders will need to deliver) improved, sustained performance in the realms of economic and social policy, and the administration of justice. This will not prove to be an easy challenge. A substantial element of Latin America's population is poor. As one observer noted: "In Latin America, 46 percent of the population is poor. In 1994, one out of every five people in the region did not have the money to ensure an adequate daily diet."[15] This problem is compounded by a very uneven distribution of income and consumption. According to the World Bank, the top 20 percent of Brazil's society (in terms of per capita income) accounts for 67.5 percent of national consumption, with comparable ratios in Venezuela at 49.5 percent, and Chile at 60.4 percent.[16] Even though the strong growth spurt and lower inflation in the 1990s have contained the spread of poverty, the pace and duration of such advances have not been enough to make inroads on actual poverty reduction.[17] As Uwe Bott and Scott B. MacDonald noted in 1991 (and is still applicable to today): "Without social development, Latin America will not be able to compete economically in the world of the 1990s, especially considering the emphasis placed on the ability of a society to assimilate and use new technology. A poorly educated and malnourished population will not provide solid social foundations for a better future."[18]

To deliver improved, sustained performance in the realms of economic and social policy, and the administration of justice, institution building is another critical area of reform. Latin American governments must continue to reinvent themselves with the objective of providing better public service at lower costs. In Venezuela, for example, the failure to move ahead on institution building was reflected by the country's banking crisis in the mid-1990s. The banking sector was deregulated in a relatively quick period, but the reform of Venezuela's bank regulatory authorities lagged. Before regulatory authorities were well-established to help manage a safe and sound banking system (in particular in the determination of loan policies), a legacy of poor commercial lending practices, helped by an economic downturn, brought about a collapse of most of the country's banks.

Finally, the presently near-universal triumph of freely elected, civilian forms of government in the hemisphere will not permit Washington to adopt a complacent attitude with respect to challenges to their continued existence in the mid-term future. Guerrilla insurgency, populist radicalism, military reaction, criminal penetration or takeover, and, perhaps, new and more virulent forms of narcotrafficking will clearly threaten certain presently democratic governments—especially in the Central American, Caribbean, and Andean areas. Therefore, it will be a cardinal objective of U.S. policy to maintain the maximum number of functional democratic governments operating in the region—both to further American and hemispheric ideals, and for the very practical reasons that follow.

3. The United States, in foreign policy terms, will want to cultivate

as much local cooperation as possible in order to secure effective bilateral, subregional, and hemispheric treatment of common political, economic, security, and social problems. In addition, the weight of regional actors on such wider international issues as trade, the environment, and new forms of arms control—and in such global fora as the United Nations, WTO, and the World Bank—will be of increasing importance to the United States.

4. Economically, an increasingly competitive global environment (especially vis-à-vis the expanding EU, Japan, and the Asian tigers) will strongly impel the United States to continue to forge closer economic relations with the nations of this hemisphere. Washington will want to broaden and accelerate the pace of the effort originally outlined in President Bush's Enterprise for the Americas initiative and to a degree codified through the 1994 Miami Summit. That is to say, it will seek the continued reform of the economies of the region—and in practice, associate them more closely with the United States in terms of trade and investment. As is already the case, priority attention will be devoted to Mexico and then to the larger and more vibrant regional economies which are experiencing positive results from their reform programs. The purpose here will be to expand U.S. exports toward closing of its chronic trade deficit and forge what amount to joint production arrangements with these relatively lower-wage nations so that improved product lines can be competitively exported to third-country markets. In addition, of course, the United States will want the support of local governments on matters of international economic policy, especially with respect to trade—and at global fora like the World Trade Organization, the World Bank, and the International Monetary Fund. Also, in view of continuing instability in the Middle East, Washington will be seeking ways to expand and guarantee access to the substantial energy resources of this hemisphere.

5. In the security realm, the United States will endeavor to keep local conflict (internal and between regional nations) to a minimum, with special emphasis on protecting local democracies and U.S. citizens and society, as a whole, from adverse developments in the region. A relatively high priority will be accorded to enlisting hemispheric governments into updated regional and bilateral arrangements that effectively address a new agenda of common security problems on a far more multilateral basis than in times past. Regionally, this is most likely to gravitate toward attempts to redefine (more likely, revi-

talize) aging institutions (such as the OAS) and defense structures (1947 Rio Treaty) toward a new conflict resolution/peacekeeping regime. Meetings of the region's defense ministers (begun in 1995) vaguely allude to this process. More narrowly, in the absence of other major security considerations, concern for narcotics trafficking will continue to provide—uneasily—new missions for the region's law enforcement and military establishments.

Locally, the agenda will include complications engendered by the Castro regime, local guerrilla insurgencies, anarchy, terrorism, criminality, spill-overs of social problems across national lines, and bids by authoritarian elements of whatever complexion for power within regional states. And, on a wider level, it will involve some attention to arms sales and production, and questions of arms control in the new regional order that is currently emerging.

6. U.S. political, economic, and security interests in the region will be increasingly seen to comprise a seamless web—in which objectives in each of these areas reinforce the others. Political and security goals will be almost impossible to achieve unless economic aims are realized. And economic performance is important to controlling security problems and maintaining the type of democratic governments from which we can expect the most effective cooperation on a wide array of relevant foreign policy issues.

7. Finally, it will be progressively realized that the course of events in Latin America exercises an increasing impact on U.S. society. Especially with respect to such pressing issues as immigration and efforts to control drug trafficking—and the degree to which progress toward a hemispheric free-trade area helps U.S. economic competitiveness (while simultaneously causing disruptions in certain sectors)—developments in the region will affect the lives of the average American more directly than events in any other part of the world. Also, the rapid growth in the number of citizens and residents of Latin American origin will change U.S. society and come to play a growing domestic political role, particularly in states that are critical to the balance of political power within the United States.

Conclusion

Latin America has undergone considerable changes since the 1980s. Those changes are continuing, and will continue into the next century.

In a sense, the reform process of the early 1990s was the first round. Much has been made of the fact that Latin America's trade has been liberalized, state enterprises privatized, budgets balanced, exchange rates pegged, and strong economic growth recorded. Without a doubt, Latin America in the 1990s is a more prosperous and economically stronger region than it was in the 1980s.

The challenges that remain, both economic and political, are considerable: social inequalities, institution-building, increasing national savings ratios, education reforms, export expansion, labor reform, and infrastructure development. The fast-forward process is undergoing a second and perhaps more difficult round of reforms. If these challenges are not adequately addressed, the importance of the earlier process of reforms is considerably diminished. A critical foundation of Latin American and Caribbean development in the twenty-first century will have been lost.

We believe otherwise. The fast-forward process is in train. Its foundations, if shallow, are widening. A sense of mutual self-interest, commercial and political, is counteracting the anxieties generated by change and turmoil. Several large Latin American economies—Brazil, Mexico, Argentina—face historical opportunities. At a lower order of magnitude, the same applies to a second tier of Latin American and Caribbean states. There is no need, therefore, to minimize the strategic salience this represents for the United States; on the edge of the twenty-first century, a Latin American take-off is a significant possibility.

Notes

1. Moisés Naim, "Latin America the Morning After," *Foreign Affairs* (June/August 1995): p. 53. Naim's most thorough analysis of the region's reform process appears in *Paper Tigers and Minotaurs* (Washington, D.C.: Carnegie Endowment, 1993); see Jeffrey Sachs' "Introduction," which highlights the three interrelated challenges: a bankrupt state apparatus; the impact of the reform programs themselves, and; the salience of effective political management.
2. For example, neither U.S.-Cuban relations or the 1994 military operation in Haiti neatly fit the economic reform, trade policy and democratic polity foundations of the rest of hemispheric priorities. Yet, these two countries alone have consumed enormous U.S. foreign policy capital in recent years. For a broad view, see Michael Mandelbaum, "Foreign Policy as Social Work," *Foreign Affairs* (January/February 1996), vol. 75, no. 1, pp. 16–32. For a narrower, case-study perspective, see Georges A. Fauriol, ed. *Haitian Frustrations, Dilemmas for U.S. Policy* (Washington, D.C.: Center for Strategic and International Studies, 1995).
3. Robert A. Pastor, *Whirlpool: U.S. Foreign Policy Toward Latin America and the Caribbean* (Princeton: Princeton University Press, 1992), p. xi.

4. For an assessment of the transition of policy consideration from the troubled 1980s to a more visionary 1990s, see Georges A. Fauriol, "The Shadow of Latin American Affairs," *Foreign Affairs* vol. 69, no. 1., pp. 116–134.

5. Francis Fukuyama, *The End of History and the Last Man* (New York: The Free Press, 1992); and Fukuyama's more concise and readable, "The End of History," *The National Interest* (Summer 1989): pp. 3–18.

6. See Samuel P. Huntington, *Foreign Affairs* (Summer 1993) vol. 72, no. 3, pp. 22–49.

7. Alvin Toffler, *Powershift: Knowledge, Wealth, and Violence At the Edge of the 21st Century* (New York: Bantam Books, 1990), p. 23.

8. Barnaby J. Feder, "Managing the Technological Frontiers," *New York Times* (January 13, 1993): p. D1.

9. Ibid.

10. Jeffery Garten, "U.S. Needs New Approach to Keep Up," *Asian Wall Street Journal* (April 20, 1992): p. 14.

11. Ibid.

12. María Cristina Caballero, Antonio Martínez, Verónica Saez, and Román Orozco, "América por los mares del sur," *Cambio 16* (December 28, 1992): pp. 6–11.

13. Naím, "Latin America," p. 46.

14. See Georges A. Fauriol and Sidney Weintraub, "U.S. Policy, Brazil and the Southern Cone," *The Washington Quarterly* (Summer 1995), vol. 18, no. 3, pp. 123–134.

15. Naim, "Latin America the Morning After," p. 55.

16. World Bank, *World Development Report 1995* (New York: Oxford University Press, 1995), p. 221. The figures were for Brazil for 1989, Chile 1992, and Venezuela 1989.

17. Naim, "Latin America," p. 55.

18. Uwe Bott and Scott B. MacDonald, "Social Conditions in Latin America," in *Latin American Debt in the 1990s: Lessons from the Past and Forecasts for the Future*, eds. Scott B. MacDonald, Jane Hughes, and Uwe Bott, (New York: Praeger, 1991), p. 86. See also Nora Lustig's "Introduction," in Lustig, ed. *Coping With Austerity, Poverty and Inequality in Latin America* (Brookings, 1995), pp. 1–41.

Appendix

The Difficult Decade: The 1980s

Anyone working in, living, or studying Latin America cannot help but to have been saddened by the difficult decade of the 1980s. Heavy external debt burdens, the bankruptcy of the import-substitution strategies, and failed efforts at economic stabilization and structural adjustment left an air of pessimism about the future, drove away foreign investors, and stimulated flight capital. People and companies with substantial monetary holdings in Latin America had few reasons to leave their investments in countries that heavily taxed savings and, in general, regarded business firms as cash cows. While the investment environment worsened, social conditions spiralled downward as evidenced by deteriorating health care and educational standards. U.S. economist John Williamson best summarized Latin America's experience in the 1980s: "As the decade ended, the region remained mired in stagflation, burdened by foreign debt, disfigured by the world's most inegalitarian income distribution, and crippled by a continuing lack of confidence on the part of not only its foreign creditors but also its own entrepreneurs, manifested in low domestic investment and massive holdings of capital flight."[1]

How did Latin America fall into this state? Was the crisis in economic development equally onerous in each of the major countries? And, what were the political implications of the difficult decade on the region? These are the questions addressed here. Although the Latin American "debt crisis" has been covered in numerous publications, it is important to have a brief summary for the purposes of the rest of the book as it provides an important background to events now shaping Latin America.

275

A Brief Overview of the Debt Crisis

In most discussions about the debt crisis, there is considerable finger-pointing as to who is to blame. One theory is that the international
bankers from the United States, Canada, Europe, and Japan descended
upon the hapless Latins (and other equally defenseless "Third
Worlders") and forced loans upon them. What drove these "go-go"
capitalists was greed. Veteran journalist Anthony Sampson captured
the mood of this viewpoint in 1981 in describing the annual Washington, D.C. World Bank-International Monetary Fund conference held at
the Washington Sheraton Hotel:

> Through the main entrance more bankers are swarming in, whose roving eyes
> suggest a very practical purpose. . . . Here—there can be no doubt of it—they are
> searching out the world, lingering awkwardly by the elevators, dawdling by the
> newsstand, and then suddenly walking—almost running—too fast for dignity. Across
> there a pack of Japanese bankers—they seem to move in sixes—is converging on a
> finance minister. Along the corridor a grave-looking French banker, looking very
> *haute banque*, looks as if he is in full pursuit of new African prey. Many of them
> begin to look not so much like bankers as financial middle men, contact men, or—
> could it really be?—salesmen.[2]

While sentiment exists to fully burden the bankers and their ilk, the
reasons behind the many stabilization and structural adjustment programs, antiausterity riots and demonstrations, and bouts of
hyperinflation in Argentina, Bolivia, Brazil, and Peru are more complex. U.S. economist Rudiger Dornbusch noted that three factors gen-
eralized the debt problem: (1) poor management in the debtor countries; (2) the world macroeconomy took a singularly bad turn; and (3)
overlending.[3] We have already noted evidence of the latter à la
Sampson. In terms of addressing the former point, the economic policies implemented in the Latin America in the 1960s and 1970s, the
import-substitution model (ISM), in particular were key factors.

The import-substitution model had its roots at the close of the nineteenth century, but it was not until the 1930s, when Latin American
economies were severely disrupted by the world depression that the
region's heavy export orientation was seriously questioned. Because
Latin economies had been open to international trade and were largely
dependent on primary exports, they were highly vulnerable to rapid
price changes that often disrupted local economies with a high social
cost. Moreover, other areas around the world began to offer competi-

tion to Latin exports and breakthroughs in science created substitutes. As economist Jeannine Swift noted: "Africa and Asia, also via European investment, became suppliers of coffee, cacao, and rubber, and U.S. and European technological advances that economized on raw material usage further reduced the rate of demand growth. Synthetic nitrates began to displace guano, and synthetic rubber competed with natural rubber; sugar beets, though not as productive as cane, received protection through tariffs in the United States and Europe."[4] While these trends were discouraging to Latin export industries, the Second World War stimulated local industrial growth in the absence of many foreign goods that were previously imported. Latin thinking about economic development gradually changed from outward orientation, dominated by agricultural or primary goods, to inward orientation, fueled by domestic industrial production.

By the late 1950s and early 1960s, another concern emerged—rapid population growth rates. Latin America's economy was characterized by a lack of required dynamism, or stated in another fashion, the rate of industrial development was too slow to meet the growing social strain of population expansion. With the outward-looking development model, Latin America would continue to have an inequitable income distribution and lack social harmony.

A number of Latin economists, led by Argentine Raul Prebisch and the Economic Commission for Latin America (ECLA), perceived that the international system had shortchanged their countries in an ongoing deterioration in the terms of trade. According to Prebisch, there was a "tendency toward a foreign constraint on development resulting from the low-income elasticity of demand for imports of primary products by the centers compared with the high-income elasticity of demand at the periphery for manufacturers from the centers."[5] The solution was import-substituting industrialization. Why? Latin America, with its large pool of labor, lacked sufficient arable land for its growing population; hence industrialization, which would soak up excess labor. With a mobilization of national savings, local industry would ultimately produce many of the items that were imported, helping to adjust the balance-of-payments in a direction favorable to Latin America.

Another element of the import-substitution strategy included the protection of local industry from imports. This was intended to provide cover for infant domestic industrialists to learn their trade and establish their market presence. At the same time, part of the funding for industrialization was to be derived from higher taxes on agricultural production.

The state was given a star role in the nation's economic development as a facilitator, channeller and promoter. It was, after all, the state that was responsible for erecting higher tariffs, shrinking import quotas, and applying administrative controls. The entire process of successive backward integration inherent in the import-substitution strategy was guided by the state. In those sectors where local private industry was lacking, the state moved in to fill the gap with large state-owned enterprises. This came to include everything from oil production and railroads to aircraft and beer.

While the state's role was essential to bringing about economic recovery and then development without serious fluctuations, the import-substitution process was to be complemented by regional support. This regional support would bring together neighboring nations to form a common market that would allow the various national actors to develop protected trade links in certain selected and agreed-upon areas. Eventually, Latin economies would emerge on the world stage as largely self-sufficient, industrializing countries able to rub elbows with the older and more established core industrialized countries in North America and Europe.

Despite the good intentions of those favoring the import-substitution model in Latin America, the strategy was fundamentally flawed. Peruvian economist Daniel M. Schydlowsky has referred to it as the "Latin American prescription for economic disaster,"[6] hardly a flattering description. Part of the problem is that the protected industries required capital, especially in the early stages when they imported key industrial tools. This, of course, required foreign exchange, which often resulted in a drain on foreign-exchange reserves or, in the 1960s and 1970s, borrowing from international banks. Even when local industries began producing goods, their inferior quality often made them uncompetitive as foreign-exchange earners. Moreover, though they were forced upon the local market, many times they failed to win the heart of the consumer. And, in time, protectionism denied the local economy access to new technologies. This was because the multinational corporations that would have helped disseminate technology in Latin economies were not welcome partners. Hence, many foreign companies avoided the region altogether and were more selective in where they did business. Many of these businesses were attracted to northeast Asia (Korea, Hong Kong, and Taiwan) and Singapore and later to southeast Asia (Indonesia, Thailand, and Malaysia).

While Latin economies set themselves apart, import-substitution industrialization lacked flexibility. In Asia, and in particular South Korea and Singapore, the state played an active role in the economy, but maintained an outward-oriented approach and the flexibility to be able to make rapid changes based on market and technological transformations. In east Asia, the state often provided initial protection of infant industries, but once again forced those enterprises to be internationally competitive. While Latin American industry was locking itself into the domestic market where it was protected and able to continue with outdated production modes, East Asian industry was expanding into international markets where it was forced to compete as well as be exposed to new means of production which were taken home and improved upon. The Northeast Asian countries discarded many import-substitution mechanisms before they proved to be overly expensive and inefficient, in sharp contrast to the Latin American case.[7]

Another flaw in import-substitution was that industry was supposed to become the engine of growth. This meant that the industrial sector was expected to grow faster than the rest of the economy. As Schydlowsky noted: "industry needs imported raw materials to produce, and therefore the demand for imports will have to grow rapidly. But the supply of foreign exchange is provided by the primary sectors, which are growing more slowly—as they are intended to do. At some point, the growth in demand for imports is going to exceed the growth in the supply of exports, and a foreign exchange crisis will result."[8] This situation led to many highly protected, inefficient, and noncompetitive industries craving for imports of intermediate and capital goods, which in turn aggravated balance-of-payment deficits in developing countries. As Uwe Bott commented: "import substitution produced an environment of inwardness and state interventionism, still prevalent three decades later in many Latin American countries."[9]

It would not be accurate to cast all blame on the Latin implementation of the import-substitution strategy or, for that matter, debtor country mismanagement. Part of the problem, as Dornbusch noted, came from deteriorating conditions in the industrialized countries, especially after the first oil shock in 1973–74. As Arab oil-producing countries watched their exports net ever-growing profits, a new wave of investors hit the industrialized countries. Higher energy prices helped fuel inflation, and the inflow of "petro-dollars" into Western banks threatened additional monetary pressures. One solution was to discreetly urge commercial banks to lend to developing countries, especially those with large economies and in need of imported industrial inputs and capital goods, like Argentina, Brazil, and Mexico. This development coincided with the expansion of the Eurocurrency markets in the first part of the 1970s. The 1970–73 period was, as American Express economist Richard O'Brien noted, the "time the Eurocurrency markets were beginning to flex their muscles and banks were getting into the habit of looking for international lending possibilities."[10] Consequently, commercial banks overlended to many developing countries.

The following conditions prevailed when a number of macroeconomy shocks hit: a second oil price hike; rising inflation and recession in the industrialized nations; concomitant hikes in interest rates; and a fall in a number of commodity prices key to the export income of developing countries. Forced to pay more debt because of higher interest rates, developing countries also watched their means of payment shrink. The expansion of external debt, the inability to repay, and the ensuing economic and concomitant political crises brought Latin America from a period of growth in the 1960s and 1970s into a decade of contraction and stunted societal aspirations. The region was on the road to becoming economically irrelevant vis-à-vis the rest of the world, especially in the late 1980s. There were exceptions to this, but the majority of countries were hit by the same problems stemming from the bankruptcy of import- substitution strategies and a difficult international environment, compounded in the early 1980s by a recession in the industrialized countries and a substantial rise in interest rates.

The Lost Decade: The 1980s

The August 1982 external debt crisis began when Mexico indicated that it could not make its repayments. In what was much like a chain reaction, Mexico was soon followed by a host of other countries, like Argentina, Brazil, Nigeria, and the Philippines. Ultimately, most of Latin America, with the exception of Colombia, would undergo the process of debt rescheduling and losing access to international capital markets. Latin America's GDP fell 8.9 percent during the 1981–84 period alone, and inflation shot out of control throughout the region.[11]

One of the major problems that dogged Latin America during the 1980s was the difficulty creditor countries had in reconciling the conflicting interests of commercial banks, foreign policy, and manufacturing. This applied especially with the United States, Latin America's major creditor nation. The creditor countries initially "muddled" through the crisis, regarding it as a short-term balance-of-payments problem, which could be reversed through austerity and import compression. By mid-decade it was apparent that the nature of the problem was structural and long-term. This stimulated the first official U.S. effort at a debt policy, the Baker Plan, named after Secretary of Treasury James Baker III (1981–88). The plan recognized that sustained, export-driven economic expansion was required if Latin America was to grow out of its debt problem. At the same time, new capital was perceived as necessary from creditor governments, commercial banks, and multilateral institutions like the World Bank.

The Baker Plan, despite its good intentions, did not succeed in pulling Latin America out of the external debt problem. By 1989, Dornbusch critically concluded: "Baker's 'muddling' through remains the Reagan administration's strategy, a treadmill of pretense and make believe in which both debtors and creditors are falling behind."[12] Part of the problem was that commercial banks did not actively open the books to new loans in Latin America. In the commercial bankers' perception, there was no need to throw good money after bad. And, while the international banks dallied, many Latin governments balked at making what were going to be draconian and unpopular cuts in spending.

While the Baker Plan took considerable heat for its "failure" to address the problems and overreliance on the magic of the marketplace for solutions, the International Monetary Fund (IMF) and World Bank became important actors in the breaking drama. Teams of Fund and the World Bank experts visited Latin countries like country doctors, seeking to find what ailed the patient and then to prescribe the cure. The cure was usually a stabilization program, in which the balance-of-payments deficits would be brought under control through import compression and austerity in government spending. New funds were made available, but only if certain macroeconomic targets were made. This was referred to as "conditionality" under which Latin governments promised to meet these targets in order to unlock new IMF and World Bank loans.

Conditionality soon became a dirty word in many nationalistic circles because dictating terms was regarded as demeaning. For both the far left and the far right, it was another example of the industrialized countries dominating the developing world. On the other hand, many industrialized-country leaders and international bankers felt that conditionality was the only way to encourage Latin countries to make the necessary reforms. The reforms would be beneficial in creating strong and more diversified economies in the southern hemisphere that would be capable of meeting their external obligations. However, the mere fact that conditionality was a form of dictating by one party to another left bad feelings and led to a certain amount of resistance on the part of Latin leaders who did not want to became smeared as a toady or puppet of the IMF and the industrialized nations. Although the democratic order was able to maintain its hold over the region's political systems by the end of the decade, there was no shortage of politicians that offered simple solutions to complicated problems.

As most Latin governments implemented harsh stabilization programs, cuts were made in education, social and health care programs, and infrastructural improvement programs. Because of a noticeable decline in the quality of life, Latin populist politicians were able to portray the IMF and foreign bankers as the villains. Anti-IMF (and antiausterity) riots took place in Argentina, the Dominican Republic, Venezuela, and Brazil during the 1980s in protest of harsh conditions many poor people felt were imposed upon them unfairly. Resentment toward the outside world developed and sizeable elements of the Latin American population grew estranged with a capitalist world order that appeared to have forgotten them except to squeeze them dry of their last pesos, bolivars, cruzados, and Australs.

A number of countries witnessed real GDP contraction throughout the decade, as in the cases of Argentina and Bolivia. In other cases, abrupt, short, and steep shocks occurred such as the case of Chile in 1982, when the economy contracted by 14 percent. These experiences in Latin America were a dramatic difference from the high rate of real GDP growth that marked the two decades prior. Alejandro Orfila, secretary-general of the Organization of American States observed: "There is unanimous agreement that the region is going through the most dramatic and most serious period it has experienced since the great world crisis of the 1930s."[13]

One factor that contributed to the difficult nature of the times was flight capital. Considering the high-income concentration throughout Latin America, those hit the hardest, the working classes, had far less to buffer themselves from several years of economic contraction. At the same time, macroeconomic deterioration and hints of political instability created apprehension at the top of the income spectrum. The result was, as Pedro-Pablo Kuczynski noted: "A perception that the status quo is unstable tends to create pressures toward capital flight."[14] What this meant in terms of income per capita was an outflow of capital, often times clandestinely, from economies that were increasingly denied further access to international capital. As the money left the country, less capital was available for investment in the local economy, which in turn meant fewer jobs. Fewer jobs or hours meant less income and with that the social impact on the lowest rung of society was devastating.

TABLE A.1
Latin America's Real GDP Growth Rate
(in percentages)

	1965–80	*1980–90*
Argentina	3.4	-0.3
Bolivia	4.4	-0.9
Brazil	9.0	3.0
Chile	1.9	2.7
Colombia	5.7	3.5
Costa Rica	6.3	2.8
Cuba	NA	NA
Dominican Republic	8.0	2.4
Ecuador	8.8	1.9
El Salvador	4.3	0.6
Guatemala	5.9	0.4
Haiti	2.9	-0.5
Honduras	5.0	2.3
Mexico	6.5	0.7
Nicaragua	2.5	-1.6
Panama	5.5	0.5
Paraguay	7.0	2.2
Peru	3.9	0.4
Uruguay	2.4	0.1
Venezuela	3.7	1.0

(World Bank, *World Development Report 1991*)

To make matters worse, the total external debt of a majority of countries actually rose during the 1980–89 period. Argentina's total external debt rose from $27.2 billion in 1980 to $64.7 billion in 1989 and Brazil's from $71 billion to $111.3 billion over the same period. In a sense, Latin American countries once in the debt trap sank deeper. This was indeed a distressing factor for many Latin American governments, especially those that worked hard to meet the economic targets established by the IMF, the World Bank, and the commercial banks. Instead of the burden shrinking, it actually appeared to expand. This trend obviously played into the hands of those who favored radical approaches to the debt problem, such as a moratorium on interest and principal payments. Table A.2 provides an idea of how Latin America's external debt expanded in the 1980s.

TABLE A.2
Latin America's Total External Debt, 1980–1989
(in U.S.$ billions

	1980	1982	1986	1989
Argentina	27.2	43.6	52.5	64.7
Bolivia	2.7	3.3	5.6	4.4
Brazil	71.0	92.8	113.0	111.3
Chile	12.1	17.3	21.1	18.3
Colombia	6.9	10.3	15.4	16.9
Costa Rica	2.7	3.6	4.5	4.5
Cuba	NA	NA	NA	NA
Dominican Rep.	2.0	2.5	3.6	4.1
Ecuador	6.0	7.7	9.3	11.3
El Salvador	0.9	1.4	1.7	1.9
Guatemala	1.2	1.5	2.8	2.6
Haiti	0.3	0.5	0.7	0.8
Honduras	1.5	1.8	3.0	3.4
Mexico	57.4	86.0	100.9	95.6
Nicaragua	2.2	3.3	6.2	9.2
Panama	3.0	3.9	4.9	5.8
Paraguay	0.9	1.3	2.1	2.5
Peru	10.0	12.3	16.1	19.9
Uruguay	1.7	2.7	3.9	3.8
Venezuela	29.3	32.2	34.6	33.1

Source: World Bank, *World Debt Tables 1990–91: External Debt of Developing Countries, Vol. 2, Country Tables* (Washington, D.C.: The World Bank, 1990).

The response to the debt crisis in Latin America was largely reactive. What had appeared to be a long, steady surge of growth abruptly ended, leaving Latin governments to grapple with new problems. The options included compliance with largely distasteful orthodox IMF stabilization programs and, at the other end of the spectrum, rejection of othrodox programs. Peru sought to reject the othrodox path under

President Alan Garcia and increasingly found itself locked out of the house of international capital. Few Latin leaders and their governments had any desire to entirely close the door to the outside world by complete rejection of the harsh medicine the IMF doctors prescribed. The failure in most cases to find a way out of the debt crisis led to two contradictory views: one was that Latin leaders lacked the political will to bite the bullet and make the necessary adjustments and; two, that the developing world was being forced to pay to the benefit of the industrialized nations.

Most Latin governments sought to cooperate with the international creditor governments and the IMF, and implement stabilization programs. The main reason for this was that most Latin American governments were confronted by the need to reverse the real resource transfer and restore the flow of development capital into their countries. By taking the difficult decision of IMF stabilization programs, multinational funding was unlocked. Considering the lack of funding available from other sources, the IMF, World Bank, and Inter-American Development Bank funds became a lifeline of sorts. The IMF loans, in particular, were usually short-term and had to paid back quickly which contributed to an ironic flow of funds out of Latin America.

The widespread nature of the Latin American debt crisis also had a political impact. Despite the gloomy economic winter, the 1980s were remarkable for their political spring: the grip of military/authoritarian governments over most of Latin America loosened and elected governments became a majority. Argentina held successive elections in 1983 and 1989, with civilian president Raul Alfonsin passing the president's sash to Carlos Menem. Brazil held elections in 1985 and 1990, while in Chile General Pinochet relinquished control after a majority of his countrymen voted for his opponent Christian Democrat leader Patracio Aylwin in 1989. Even the long-lived Stroessner dictatorship in Paraguay came to an end in 1989, ultimately replaced by a popularly elected government. Only Cuba has remained as the major blatant holdout.

The reemergence of elective governments in the 1980s was all the more remarkable considering the severe nature of the economic crisis. The newly elected governments in most cases were expected to service the external debt, practice belt tightening, and respond to often times long pent-up social pressures. The resources at hand did not allow these new administrations to meet social expectations. In terms of income per capita, there is little doubt that it plummeted in most countries. While having an impact throughout Latin societies, the crisis hit the poorest the hardest. This was due to the fact that, as Jeffery A. Frieden noted, "they had the least reserves to cushion the impact of the worst depression in modern Latin American history."[15]

An example of the deterioration in social conditions as a result of the economic crisis is the return of health problems such as malnutrition, and diseases like cholera and malaria, which had been greatly reduced in the 1970s. On November 4, 1991 the ministries of El Salvador, Honduras, Guatemala, Nicaragua, and Costa Rica released a report that reflected the erosion of health standards through the 1980s and into the present. According to that report, some 120,000 Central American children under age five die each year of malnutrition and one-third of the region's population, or some 12.2 million persons, lack permanent access to health services.[16] It was noted: "The decrease in investment in the social sector has worsened the traditional insufficiencies in basic infrastructure and public services, and has increased the lack of adequate response to the essential needs of large sectors of the population and has worsened the existence of a social debt of vast proportions."[17] While Central America contended with a return of malaria and measles after a fifteen-year absence, South America was hit by a return of cholera and dengue fever in 1990 and 1991.

In the Fall 1990 issue of *Foreign Policy*, Jamaica's Prime Minister Michael Manley summarized the social impact of the debt crisis on social development:

> The debt crisis has also fueled the explosive growth of the drug trade; in Colombia wealthy and powerful drug cartels have undermined democratic government. When meeting subsistence needs legally seems impossible, the attractiveness of illegal alternatives, such as drug trafficking increases. Inadequate health services and malnutrition retard the development of millions of children around the world, preventing them from becoming productive members of society. Driven by poverty, rural residents abandon their lands and migrate to cities, placing incredible pressure on urban governments trying to provide basic services and frustrating national efforts to achieve self-sufficiency in food supplies.[18]

The lost decade can be measured partially in the fall of spending on central government expenditure. In Argentina, total central government spending on education stood at 20 percent in 1972: beginning in the early 1980s it spiralled downward, ending the decade in 1989 at 9.3 percent of total expenditure.[19] In the same period, the numbers fell from 8.3 to 4.2 percent in Brazil and from 23.6 percent to 15.6 percent in Peru. In terms of spending on housing, amenities, social security, and welfare, total central government expenditure from 1972 to 1989 also declined in Brazil, Chile, Peru, and Uruguay.

By the mid-1980s Latin America's new democracies were left with the difficult task of beating the very same debt crisis that had helped overthrow the region's authoritarian governments. While wanting to address their countries' social needs, the new leaderships often found the debt crisis a major impediment. Naturally this created tensions and, in some cases, bred ill-will between Latin America's new leaders and their creditors, many of whom were suspect as a result of lending to the former authoritarian regimes. These feelings were occasionally opened as in the case of President Alan Garcia's debt policy of paying only a small percentage of Peru's export earnings to its creditors. At the United Nations on September 23, 1985, Brazil's president Jose Sarney stated what many Latin leaders felt: "Brazil will not pay its foreign debt with recession, nor with unemployment, nor with hunger."[20]

The Danger of Becoming Irrelevant

As Latin American countries grappled to contain the shock waves of the debt crisis, another danger quietly advanced on the region—the danger of becoming irrelevant to the emerging new world order. Though it was difficult to detect at the beginning of the 1980s, the global economy was continuing an accelerated process of transformation from what futurist Alvin Toffler has called "smokestack civilization" to the informatic age. An earlier wave of economic growth was based upon mass, heavy-industrial production, which was symbolized by the smokestack. Steel, automobile, and manufactured goods dominated the world markets. According to Toffler, subtle changes in the structure of power related to technological innovations began to undermine the old smokestack order beginning in the 1950s. With each successive decade up to 2025, the pace of change will have accelerated in a "hinge period in which smokestack civilization, having dominated the earth for centuries, is finally replaced by another, far different one following a period of world-shaking power struggles."[21] The new "commanding heights" of the next wave are computers, telecommunications, electronics, information, and biotechnology.

In the early 1980s, these information-intensive "industries" took off in a mad dash of enhancements, minaturations, and mass-marketing. Suddenly, the "old industries" of steel-making and others were being bypassed by information goods, which required brain power, excellent communications and, above all, flexibility to deal with a rapidly changing marketplace.

The countries that prohibited the free movement of information or sought to control the flow of information were at a loss as evidenced by the Soviet Union, the People's Republic of China, and a number of Middle Eastern authoritarian states like Iraq and Saudi Arabia. In the Soviet case, despite pouring billions of rubles into defense, the creative synergies of the information age could not be harnessed in an information-controlled environment. The result was the political fragmentation of the Soviet Union, a deep economic crisis in 1989–92, and serious questions about whether the many parts that emerged from the former Soviet Union will become economically competitive. Other countries, like many in Latin America with import-substitution models and antimultinational corporation mentalities, found themselves outside of the information flow. While the United States, Japan, Canada, and the European Community moved ahead with new technology programs and breakthroughs, the technology base of Latin American economies became increasingly outmoded. As the world ended the 1980s, the emerging trend was the breakdown of the tensions between East and West, and North and South. There was an emergence of nations that would be in the "fast" group of information-industry breakthrough and implementation, and the "slow" group of countries that would resist change and look backward to the past for nonexistent answers.

The developing world also became a more competitive place in the 1980s as a number of Asian economies began a trajectory toward breakthroughs into a higher, more competitive level of development. While Latin American governments grappled with austerity, how to keep the military in the barracks, and ways to revitalize stagnating economies, Asian countries like Taiwan, South Korea, and Singapore became more integrated in the global capitalist system, pushing their way into the emerging fast group. Areas such as computers, computer chip production, robotics, and electronics increasingly defined the shape and scope of these flexible economies.

The Latin American response was slow. Hamstrung by socioeconomic problems that tugged creative energies in other directions, resistance to change and the impact of the outside (which in recent memory was not entirely positive) slowed the awareness of the colossal transformations sweeping the world. While the real GDP size and economic clout of countries like South Korea, Taiwan, and Singapore, and to a lesser extent, Indonesia, Malaysia, and Thailand advanced, the position of the three largest Latin American economies—Argentina, Brazil and Mexico—all slipped through the 1980s as demonstrated by table A.3.

TABLE A.3.
Real GDP Size and World Ranking

	1985	*1989*
Argentina	24th	31th
Brazil	8th	10th
Mexico	11th	14th

Source: World Bank, *World Development Report 1991*. This includes the Soviet Union in terms of calculated real GDP size.

Latin American countries came out of the 1980s running the risk of becoming economically irrelevant in the international economic system because of the external debt problem and local economic systems not capable of competing, with a few exceptions as we will see. On an overall regional basis, the nature of the dilemma was that Latin America's significance in the 1980–87 period, according to World Bank data, slipped from 13.6 percent in 1980 to around 4.8 percent in 1987, as reflected by the region's percentage of global real GDP.[22]

An additional element that has little quantitative measurement is the mentality about development of leadership elites in Latin America. Throughout the 1970s, Latin leaders concentrated on the modest reproduction of the standard of living of the industrialized countries in the upper part of the income pyramid. After the debt crisis hit full force in the 1980s, this goal gradually slipped out of grasp. The failed aspiration of creating a level of economic development comparable to the most advanced industrialized societies revealed a Latin resistance to assimilate the ever-increasing inflow of technological advances. Chilean economist Fernando Fajnzylber captured the nature of the challenge:

> The opening of the black box of technological progress is a task that transcends the industrial and business world, and forms part of a social attitude vis-a-vis the

incorporation of technological progress. This new attitude of social appreciation of creativity—that is, the pursuit of formulas that respond to internal deficiencies and potentialities—assumes a modification of the leadership from which flow the values and orientations diffused through society as a whole. It is difficult to imagine the linkage between a leadership influenced by a rent-seeking mentality and a society-wide diffusion of values in which the internal deficiencies and potentialities are converted into a conductor axis for socioeconomic transformation.[23]

The Political Revolution

By the beginning of the 1990s, many dark clouds still hung on the horizon. The world outside the region was changing and Latin Americans were left with the very real problem of discerning what they wanted for their future. The head of the Brazilian Export Association, Marcus Vinicius de Moraes, caught the dilemma for Latin America when he asked in 1990: "Where does a struggling Latin America fit into this scenario?"[24] That future offered two options: to maintain a rent-seeking mentality that seeks against the odds to uphold a societal order that is being swept away or to make difficult changes, scrap old shibboleths, and plug into a new world order based on flexible thinking.

If Latin America is to sustain this second path, another related issue will have to be considered—deepening and strengthening democratic institutions that have the flexibility required to make technological leaps. In many cases, constitutions in Latin America are ill-adapted to deal with the complexities of modern government or political pluralism. Instead of promoting government which is responsive to the demands of the citizens, many constitutions have produced legislative bodies that appear to be filled with self-seeking politicians capable of disrupting the implementation of government programs, while failing to address pressing socioeconomic issues. The colorful, yet sad image of congressmen gleefully punching each other in the national assembly (on more than one occasion) has done little to promote a positive image of the political elite and the seriousness of Latin American governance.

Until the election of President Cardoso, a good example of this was Brazil. The 1988 constitution stipulated that any external-debt settlement made with international commercial banks must pass the senate for approval; or that all the states in the nation have considerable autonomy over their finances. These two constitutional amendments made it exceedingly difficult for the Collor and Franco governments in the early 1990s to create a national consensus on the need to implement an economic program to bring inflation under control. As a Brazilian banker is reported to have sardonically noted in 1988 on the seeming failure of his nation's legislative bodies to take any decisive action on the country's many problems: "The Brazilian Congress is like Nero, happily playing the fiddle while the country burns."

It would be very misleading to portray the elective governments of Latin America in the 1980s all in negative terms. Despite considerable odds these governments struggled into the 1990s, seeking in many cases to deepen the democratic process. Moreover, the lost decade did not solely affect those states that experimented with some form of capitalism, be it free-market or mixed capitalist-statist. It also hit the sole "communist" country in the region, Cuba. Held up as a key force during the 1970s and early 1980s in advancing educational and health services for the majority of its population, the socialist dictatorship of Fidel Castro staggered into the 1990s. The gains in social services, much of it supplemented by Soviet largesse to the tone of roughly $4 billion annually, was slowly eroded by economic mismanagement and a heavy external debt to Western Europe, Japan, Canada, and the Soviet Union, now Russia. The contrast with the rest of the hemisphere became apparent by the early 1990s, in spite of the continuing fragility of the region's democratic experience. Some have argued that in terms of its geopolitical significance, the democratization of Latin America may be comparable to the fall of the Berlin Wall and the collapse of the USSR, ranking, one scholar noted: "among the great epochal transformations of the late twentieth century."[25] Even though this may be a premature assessment, the fact that Latin American politics were transformed in tandem with the profound economic crisis of the 1980s is in fact a significant development, with both policy and conceptual relevance.

While there was a sea change in the political scene, shifting from authoritarianism to more democratic governance, progress was also made on the economic front. Initially, this affected only the area of debt reduction. Beginning in the 1983–84 period, a number of commercial banks turned to trading Latin American debt on the secondary market. This market expanded throughout most of the decade from $2 billion in 1984 to $50 billion in 1988. The secondary market provided an escape for many regional banks to dump their Latin debt. At the same time, it generated a limited amount of net debt reduction.

Real advances, however, in debt reduction came from the U.S. government. In March 1989, the new secretary of the U.S. Treasury Department, Nicolas Brady, advanced what was soon known as the Brady Plan. The Baker Plan had largely failed, with the commercial banks largely abandoning the field and official sources filling in the gap for Latin America's capital needs. The new program was founded upon the idea that debt reduction was necessary to break out of the crisis: in those cases where structural adjustment and economic liberalization were taking place, debt reduction could be applied. Measures, such as privatization and debt-for-equity swap program, were regarded as positive macroeconomic steps. The debt reduction scheme was greatly strengthened by the support of funds provided by the World Bank, IMF, and Inter-American Development Bank. As David Mulford, former undersecretary for international affairs at the U.S. Treasury Department, commented: "These key principles built on the prior macroeconomics and structural reform approach and shifted the debt strategy from static management to dynamic resolution, significantly shrinking the stock of debt while providing a sustainable basis for new capital flows."[26]

The Brady Plan opened an important door for many Latin countries seeking to escape the burden of external debt. Debt-reduction agreements were signed with Mexico, Chile, Costa Rica, and Venezuela in the period after 1989 and negotiations were opened with Argentina and Brazil. By 1992, twelve of the sixteen major debtor nations (most of which are in Latin America) had reached debt-reduction refinancing agreements with their commercial banks, accounting for 92 percent, or around $240 billion, of their outstanding commercial bank debt with an expected $50 billion in actual debt reduction.[27] These agreements were the product of considerable economic reforms in Latin America as well as flexibility with the creditor nations and commercial banks.

Conclusion

Latin America in the 1980s underwent a period of economic collapse that brought about a considerable amount of finger-pointing as to who was to blame. With the substantial changes occurring in Central and Eastern Europe, the former Soviet Union and the Newly Industrializing Economies in Asia, Latin America as a region entered the last decade of the twentieth century with a substantial debt overhang and declining competitiveness. While the title of "lost decade" is appropriate for the impact on the social structure, ranging from education to health services, the 1980s served as a shock to the political system and set in motion a serious reevaluation of thinking about development and where Latin America fit in a transforming world system. Although the debt overhang existed as a problem, efforts were made to turn the situation around—through the Brady Plan, but also through the reformist path undertaken by a number of governments.

Notes

1. John Williamson, *The Progress of Policy Reform in Latin America* (Washington, D.C.: Institute for International Economics, January 1990), p. 30.
2. Anthony Sampson, *The Money Lenders: The People and Politics of the World Banking Crisis* (Harmondsworth, United Kingdom: Penguin Books, 1981), pp. 14–15.
3. Rudiger Dornbusch, "The Latin American Debt Problem: Anatomy and Solutions," in *Debt and Democracy in Latin America*, eds. Barbara Stallings and Robert Kaufman (Boulder, Colo.: Westview Press, 1989), pp. 7–9.
4. Jeannine Swift, *Economic Development in Latin America* (New York: St. Martin's Press, 1978), p. 56.
5. Quoted in Uwe Bott, "Central America and the Caribbean," in *The Global Debt Crisis: Forecasting for the Future*, eds. Scott B. MacDonald, Margie Lindsey and David L. Crum (London: Pinter Publishers, 1990), p. 43.
6. Daniel M. Schydlowsky, "The Tragedy of Lost Opportunity in Peru," in *Latin American Political Economy: Financial Crisis and Political Change*, eds. Jonathan Hartlyn and Samuel A. Morley (Boulder, Colo.: Westview Press, 1986), p. 218.
7. This point is made by Alejandro Foxley, *Latin American Experiments in Neo-Conservative Economics* (Berkeley, Cal.: University of California Press, 1983), p. 20. Also see A. Hirschman, "The Political Economy of Import-Substituting Industrialization in Latin America," in his *A Bias for Hope* (New Haven, Conn.: Yale University, 1971).
8. Schydlowsky, "Tragedy," p. 220.
9. Bott, "Central America," p. 43.
10. Richard O'Brien, "Introduction—a perspective on debt," in *The Global Debt Crisis: Forecasting for the Future*, eds. Scott B. MacDonald, Margie Lindsey and David L. Crum (London: Pinter Publishers, 1990), p. 1.
11. These figures are according to Stephany Griffith-Jones and Osvaldo Sunkel, *Debt and Development Crises: The End of an Illusion* (Oxford: Clareden Press, 1986).
12. Dornbusch, "Latin American Debt," p. 7.
13. Alejandro Orfila, Secretary-General of the OAS, *OAS Press*, January 12, 1984, quoted in "North-South Monitor", *Third World Quarterly* (April 1984), p. 475.
14. Pedro-Pablo Kuczynski, *Latin American Debt* (Baltimore, M.D.: The Johns Hopkins University Press, 1988), p. 27.
15. Jeffery Frieden, "Winners and Losers in the Latin American Debt Crisis: The Political Implications," in *Debt and Democracy in Latin America*, eds. Barbara Stallings and Robert Kaufman (Boulder, Colo.: Westview Press, 1989), p. 28.
16. Gustavo Palencia, "Central America: Poverty Hits Children Hardest," *The Times of the Americas* (November 13, 1991): p. 10.

17. Ibid.
18. Michael Manley, "Southern Needs," *Foreign Policy* no. 80 (Fall 1990): p. 46.
19. World Bank, *World Development Report 1991* (New York: Oxford University Press, 1991), p.
20. Quoted in Rosemary Thorp and Laurance Whitehead, "Review and Conclusions," in *Latin American Debt and the Adjustment Crisis*, eds. Rosemary Thorp and Laurance Whitehead (Pittsburgh, PA: University of Pittsburgh Press, 1985), p. 318.
21. Alvin Toffler, *Powershift: Knowledge, Wealth and Violence at the Edge of the 21st Century* (New York: Bantam Books, 1991), p. xix.
22. This figure was estimated from data extracted from the World Bank, *World Bank Development Report 1982* (New York: Oxford University Press, 1982), p. 114; and World Bank, *World Development Report 1989* (New York: Oxford University Press, 1989), p. 168. World Bank data did not include the Soviet Union, Bulgaria, East Germany, Vietnam, Mongolia, and Albania.
23. Fernando Fajnzylber, *Unavoidable Industrial Restructuring in Latin America* (Durham, N.C.: Duke University Press, 1990), p. 183.
24. Quoted in Mac Margolis, "Brazil's Bad Dreams," *Best of Business* (Spring 1990): p. 72.
25. Howard J. Wiarda, "Sustaining the Democratic Revolution," *The Washington Quarterly*, (Summer 1995), vol.18, no.3, pp. 91–92. The literature on the interplay between democracy and economics is becoming extensive; three good examples are Wiarda, *The Democratic Revolution in Latin America* (New York: Holmes and Meier, 1990); in a more theoretical vein, Ross E. Burkhark and Michael S. Lewis-Beck, "Comparative Democracy: The Economic Development Thesis," *American Political Science Review*, (December 1994), vol. 88, no. 4, pp. 903–10; and a 1990s perspective, Gustav Ranis, "Will Latin America Now Put a Stop to 'Stop-and-Go?'", *Journal of Interamerican Studies and World Affairs* (Summer/Fall 1996), vol. 38, no. 2/3, pp. 127–40.
26. David C. Mulford, "Moving Beyond the Latin Debt Crisis," *Wall Street Journal* (August 21, 1992): p. A7.
27. Ibid.

Bibliography

Adelman, Jeremy, "Socialism and Democracy in Argentina in the Age of the Second International." *Hispanic American Historical Review* 72, no. 2 (May 1992): .

Aguayo, Sergio and Bruce Bagley, eds. *En busca de la Seguridad Perdida: approximaciones a la seguridad Mexicana.* Mexico: Siglo Veintiuno Editores, 1990.

American Institute for Free Labor Development, AFL-CIO.

Foreign Investors: Oiling the Cuban Government Machine: A

Special Report. Washington, D.C.: American Institute for Free Labor Development, 1995.

Arriagada, Genero. *Pinochet: The Politics of Power.* Boston, Mass.: Unwin Hyman, 1988.

Aspe, Pedro, Andres Bianchi, and Domingo Cavallo. *Sea Changes in Latin America.* Washington, D.C.: Group of Thirty, 1992.

Atkins, G. Pope. *Latin America in the International Political System.* Boulder, Colo.: Westview Press, 1989.

———, ed. *South America into the 1990s.* Boulder, Colo.: Westview Press, 1990.

Attali, Jacques. *Lignes d'horizon.* Paris: Fayard, 1990.

Baer, M. Delal. "Profiles in Transition in Latin America and the Caribbean." *Annals* (March 1993): .

Baer, M. Delal, eds. *The NAFTA Debate: Grappling with Unconventional Trade Issues.* Boulder: Lynne Rienner, 1994.

Baer, Werner. *The Brazilian Economy: Growth and Development.* New York: Praeger, 1983.

Bagley, Bruce Michael and Sergio Aguayo Quezada, eds. *Mexico: In Search of Security.* Miami, Fl.: North-South Center, 1993.

Bailey, Norman A. "Venezuela and the United States: Putting Energy in the Enterprise." In *Lessons of the Venezuelan Experience*, edited by Louis W. Goodman, Johanna Mendelson Forman, Moisés Naim, Joseph S. Tulchin, and Gary Bland, 387–97. Baltimore, MD: The Johns Hopkins University Press, 1995.

Bailey, Norman and Richard Cohen. *The Mexican Time Bomb.* New York: Priority Press Publications, 1987.

Ball, Carlos. "Venezuela Keeps Swimming Against the Tide." *Wall Street Journal* (September 4, 1994): 9.

———. "Seeds of Venezuelan Revolt Found in Statist System." *Wall Street Journal* (February 7, 1992): A15.

Barber, Benjamin R. *Jihad vs. McWorld: How the Planet Is Both Falling Apart and Coming Together and What This Means for Democracy.* New York: Times Books, 1995.

Bassini, Emelio. "The Chile Fund." *Smith Barney: A Look at the ROC Taiwan Fund and the Chile Fund* (December 1991): .

Bazant, Jan. *Historia de la deuda exterior de Mexico (1823-1946).* Mexico City: El Colegio de Mexico, 1968.

Berry, Albert, Ronald G. Hellman, and Mauricio Solaún. *Politics of Compromise: Coalition Government in Colombia.* New Brunswick, N.J.: Transaction Publishers, 1980.

Betancourt, Ernesto. "Castro's Legacy." *Society* (July/August 1994): 66—72.

Bloomberg, "Mexico's Vitro Acquires Bolivian Glass Maker Vidrio Lux." *Bloomberg,* October 2, 1995.

Botero, Libardo, et al. *Neoliberalismo y subdesarrollo: un análsis crítico de la apertura económica.* Bogotá: Ancora, 1992.

Bott, Uwe and Scott B. MacDonald. "Social Conditions in Latin America." In *Latin American Debt in the 1990s,* edited by Scott B. MacDonald, Jane Hughes, and Uwe Bott, 75–88. New York: Praeger, 1991.

Bottome, Robert. "Venezuela: The Struggle for Reform." In *In the Shadow of the Debt: Emerging Issues in Latin America,* edited by, . New York: The Twentieth Century Fund Press, 1992.

Bouzas, Roberto. "Beyond Stabilization and Reform: The Argentine Economy in the 1990s." In *In the Shadow of the Debt: Emerging Issues in Latin America,* edited by, . New York: The Twentieth Century Fund Press, 1992.

Bowen, Sally. "Cosy Accord Feels the Chill." *Financial Times.* (March 7, 1996): 5.

———. "Sell-Offs Strike Mother Lode." *Financial Times.* (March 7, 1996): 6.

Brooke, James. "Colombia Becoming an Oil Power in Spite of Itself." *New York Times* (March 20, 1995): D2.

———. "New Leader Is Squeezing Venezuelans." *New York Times* (September 4, 1994): 18.

———. "Guerrillas Are Imperiling Colombia's Oil Bonanza." *New York Times* (November 10, 1992): A3.

Burkhart, Ross E. and Michael S. Lewis-Beck. "Comparative Democracy: The Economic Development Thesis." *American Political Science Review.* (December 1994): 903–10.

Calleo, David P. *Beyond American Hegemony: The Future of the Western Alliance.* New York: Basic Books, Inc., 1987.

———. *The Imperious Economy.* Cambridge, Mass: Harvard University Press, 1982.

Camp, Roderic Ai. "Political Liberalization: The Last Key to Economic Modernization in Mexico?" In *Political & Economic Liberalization in Mexico,* edited by Riordan Roett, 17–34. Boulder, Colo.: Lynne Rienner, 1993.

Camp, Roderic A., ed. *Mexico's Political Stability: The Next Five Years.* Boulder, Colo.: Westview Press, 1986.

———. "Mexico." In *Latin America and Caribbean Contemporary Record Vol. VII: 1987-1988,* edited by James M. Malloy and Eduardo, A. Gamarra. New York: Holmes and Meier Publishers, 1990.

Cardenas, Cuauhtemoc. "Mexico's Left Is Committed to Market Reform." *Wall Street Journal* (August 12, 1994): A11.

Cardoso, Eliana and Ann Helwege. *Latin America's Economy: Diversity, Trends, and Conflicts.* Boston, Mass.: The MIT Press, 1993.

———. *Cuba After Communism.* Cambridge, Mass.: The MIT Press, 1992.

Carothers, Thomas. *In the Name of Democracy: U.S. Policy Toward Latin America in the Reagan Years.* Berkeley: University of California Press, 1991.

Carroll, Paul B. and Thomas T. Vogel, Jr. "Peso Surprise: How Mexico's Crisis Ambushed Top Minds in Officialdom, Finance." *Wall Street Journal* (July 6, 1995): A1, A4.

Castaneda, Jorge G. *Utopia Unarmed: The Latin American Left After the Cold War.* New York: Alfred Knopf, 1993.

————. "Latin America and the End of the Cold War." *World Policy Journal* (Summer 1990): .

"Chile's Telecom Firms Prospect Latin Markets", *Latin American Information Services Americas Trade & Finance* (New York), September 1992.

Cline, William and Sidney Weintraub, eds. *Economic Stabilization in Developing Countries.* Washington, D.C.: Brookings Institution, 1981.

Cohen, Alvin and Frank Gunter, eds. *The Colombian Economy: Issues of Trade and Development.* Boulder, Colo.: Westview Press, 1992.

Constable, Pamela and Arturo Valenzuela. *A Nation of Enemies: Chile under Pinochet.* New York: W.W. Norton, 1991.

Consuegra-Barquin, Juan C. "Cuba's Residential Property Ownership Dilemma: A Human Rights Issue Under International Law." *Rutgers Law Review* vol. 46, no. 2 (Winter 1994): .

Cornelius, Wayne A. "NAFTA Costs Mexico More Job Losses Than U.S." *New York Times* (October 17, 1995): A24.

————. "Mexico's Delayed Democratization." *Foreign Policy* (Summer 1994): 53–71.

Corradi, Juan E. *The Fitful Society: Economy, Society, and Politics in Argentina.* Boulder, Colo.: Westview Press, 1985.

Crawford, Leslie. "Chile Squeezes Copper Company's Budget." *Financial Times* (January 8, 1993): 26.

DeCastro, Paulo Rabello and Marcio Ronci. "Sixty Years of Populism in Brazil." In *The Macroeconomics of Populism in Latin America*, edited by Rudiger Dornbusch and Sebastian Edwards, 151–74. Chicago: The University of Chicago Press, 1991.

del Aguila, Juan M. "Perceptions of Cuba in the 1980s." In *Cuba: The International Dimension*, edited by Georges A. Fauriol and Eva Loser. New Brunswick, N.J.: Transaction Publishers, 1990.

DePalma, Anthony. "One Revolution Is Enough in Mexico." *New York Times* (October 8, 1995): E14.

De Soto, Hernando. *El Otro Sendero.* Lima: Instituto Libertad y Democracia, 1989.

Dix, Robert H. *The Politics of Colombia.* New York: Praeger, 1987.

Dogas, John, et al. *Los caminos de la descentralización: diversidad y retos de la transformación municipal.* Bogotá: Departmento de Cienca Políca, Universidad de Los Andes, 1992.

Dornbusch, Rudiger. "Mexico's Economic Success Story: Lessons for Brazil." *Harvard International Review* (Fall 1991): .

Dornbusch, Rudiger and Sebastian Edwards, eds. *The Macroeconomics of Populism in Latin America.* Chicago: University of Chicago Press, 1991.

Drake, Paul W. and Ivan Jaksic, eds. *The Struggle for Democracy in Chile, 1982–1990.* Lincoln, Neb.: University of Nebraska Press, 1991.

Dunn, Timothy J. *The Militarization of the U.S.-Mexico Border, 1978–1992.* Austin: The Center for Mexican American Studies/The University of Texas, 1996.

The Economist, "Mexico: PRIsed Apart." *The Economist* (October 21, 1995): 42.

————. "Venezuela: Whoosh." *The Economist* (September 16, 1995): 54–5.

————. "Peru: The Last of the Brady Bunch." *The Economist* (September 16, 1995): 88–9.

————. "Emerging Market Indicators." *The Economist* (May 6, 1995): p.106.

————. "Argentina: Fighting Menem." *The Economist* (April 22, 1995): 42–3.

The Economist Intelligence Unit. *Chile 4th Quarter 1994.* (London), October 21, 1994.

Euromoney, "Just Waiting for the Signatures." *Euromoney Supplement* January 1992: 35.

Evans, Peter. *Dependent Development: The Alliance of Multinational, State and Local Capital in Brazil.* Princeton, N.J.: Princeton University Press, 1979.

Falcoff, Mark. "The Cuba In Our Mind." *The National Interest*

————. *Modern Chile, 1970–1989: A Critical History.* New Brunswick, N.J.: Transaction Books, 1989.

————. "Venezuela's Crisis—and Ours." *Latin American Outlook* (September 1992): .

Fallows, James. *Looking at the Sun: The Rise of the New East Asian Economic and Political System.* New York: Pantheon, 1994.

Fauriol, Georges A. and Eva Loser, eds. *Cuba: The International Dimension.* New Brunswick, N.J.: Transaction Publishers, 1990.

Fauriol, Georges A. and Sidney Weintraub. "U.S. Policy, Brazil and the Southern Cone." *The Washington Quarterly.* (Summer 1995): 123–34.

Fauriol, Georges A. *U.S.-Caribbean Relations into the 21st Century.* Washington, D.C.: Center for Strategic & International Studies, 1993.

————. "The Shadow of Latin American Affairs." *Foreign Affairs* vol. 69, no. 1 (1990): 116–34.

————. *The Third Century: U.S.-Latin American Policy Choices for the 1990s.* Washington, D.C.: Center for Strategic & International Studies, 1988.

————. ed., *Haitian Frustrations, Dilemmas for U.S. Policy.* Washington, D.C.: Center for Strategic & International Studies, 1995.

Feinberg, Richard E. "Latin America: Back on the Screen." *International Economic Insights* (July-August 1992): .

Ferrer, Aldo. *Living Within Our Means: An Examination of the Argentine Economic Crisis.* Boulder, Colo.: Westview Press, 1985.

Fidler, Stephen. "IMF Mixes Stiff Medicine for Venezuela." *Financial Times* (October 16, 1995): 7.

Financial Times, "Peru." *Financial Times Survey.* (March 7, 1996).

Fleischer, Lowell. *Colombian Elections, June 19, 1994: Post-Election Report.* CSIS Western Hemisphere Election Study Series, vol. XII, Study 10 (August 18, 1994) .

Fleischer, Lowell and Eduardo Lara. *Colombian Policy in the Mid-1990s.* Washington, D.C.: The Center for Strategic & International Studies, 1994.

Florida International University. *Cuba in Transition: New Challenges for U.S. Policy.* Miami: Florida International University, a project of the Cuban Research Institute, Latin American and Caribbean Center, 1993.

Foxley, Alejandro. *Latin American Experiments in Neoconservative Economics.* Berkeley: University of California Press, 1983.

Franco, Andrés. "Colombia's Test of Confidence." *North-South* (February-March 1994): 16–21.

Fraser, Damian. "Rothchild Group to Open Office in Mexico." *Financial Times* (April 30, 1993): 33.

Garreton, Manuel Antonio. *The Chilean Political Process.* Boston, Mass: Unwin Hyman, 1989.

Gómez, Hernando José. "Notas sobre el tamano del Narcotráfico y su impacto economico." *Revista Ecónomia Colombiana* (Bogotá), (February 1990): .

Gonzalez, Edward and David Ronfeldt. *Storm Warnings for Cuba.* Santa Monica: Rand, MR-452–OS, 1994.

————. *Cuba Adrift in a Postcommunist World.* Santa Monica: Rand, R-4231–USDP, 1992.

Gonzalez, Edward. *Cuba Under Castro: The Limits of Charisma.* Boston, Mass.: Houghton Mifflin Company, 1974.

————. *Cuba, Clearing Perilous Waters?* Santa Monica: Rand, MR-673–OSD, 1996.

Goodman, Louis W., Johanna Mendelson Forman, Moisés Naim, Joseph Tulchin, and Gary Bland, eds. *Lessons of the Venezuelan Experience.* Baltimore, MD: The Johns Hopkins University Press, 1995.

Graham, Carol. "Peru's APRA Party in Power: Impossible Revolution, Relinquished Reform." *Journal of Interamerican Studies and World Affairs* vol. 32, no. 3 (Fall 1990): 75–116.

Grayson, George W. *The North American Free Trade Agreement: Regional Community and the New World Order.* Lanham, MD: University Press of America, 1995.

Griffith-Jones, Stephany. *Chile to 1991: The End of an Era?* London: Economist Intelligence Unit, 1987.

Grosse, Robert. "Colombia's Black Market in Foreign Exchange." *World Development* (August 1992): 1193–207.

Guillermoprieto, Alma. "Letter from Mexico: Whodunnit?" *The New Yorker* (September 25, 1995): 44–53.

Hansen, Roger D. *The Politics of Mexican Development.* Baltimore, MD: The Johns Hopkins University Press, 1971.

Harrison, Lawrence E. *Underdevelopment is a State of Mind: The Latin American Case.* Lanham, MD: University Press of America, 1985.

Hartlyn, Jonathan and Samuel A. Morley, eds. *Latin American Political Economy: Financial Crisis and Political Change.* Boulder, Colo.: Westview Press, 1986.

Hartlyn, Jonathan, Lars Schoultz, and Augusto Varas, eds. *The United States and Latin America in the 1990s: beyond the Cold War.* Chapel Hill: The University of North Carolina Press, 1992.

Hausmann, Ricardo and Liliana Rojas-Suárez, eds. *Baking Crisis in Latin America.* Washington: Inter-American Development Bank, 1996.

Heath, Jonathan. *The Devaluation of the Mexican Peso in 1994: Economic Policy and Institutions.* CSIS Policy Papers on the Americas, vol. 6 (June 1, 1995).

Hertogne, Alain and Alain Labrousse. *Le Senteir Lumineux du Perou: un nouvel integrisme dans le tiers monde.* Paris: Editions Descouverses, 1989.

Hirst, Monica, ed. *Continuidad y cambio en las relaciones Amercia Latina-Estados Unidos.* Buenos Aires: Grupo Editor Latinamericano, 1987.

Horowitz, Irving Louis, ed. *Cuba Communism* Sixth and Seventh Editions. New Brunswick: Transaction Books, 1984, 1989.

Hughes, Jane. "Actors in the Latin American Debt Crisis I: The Domestic Actors." In *Latin American Debt in the 1990s: Lessons from the Past and Forecasts for the Future,* edited by Scott B. MacDonald, Jane Hughes, and Uwe Bott, 41–58. New York: Praeger, 1991.

Huntington, Samuel. "The Clash of Civilizations." *Foreign Affairs.* vol. 72, no. 3 (Summer 1993): 22–49.

James, Dilmus. "Mexico's Recent Science and Technological Planning: An Outsider Economist's Critique." *Journal of Interamerican Studies and World Affairs* (May 1980): 163–93.

Jessup, Jay and Maggie Jessup. *Doing Business in Mexico.* Rocklin, CA: Prima Publishing Company, 1993.

Jordan, David C. *Revolutionary Cuba and the End of the Cold War.* Lanham, MD: University Press of America, 1993.

Katz, Ian. "Brazil: This Could Just Be the Strike Cardoso Needed." *Businessweek* (June 12, 1995): 23.

Kalter, Eliot. "The Mexican Strategy to Achieve Sustainable Economic Growth." In *Mexico: The Strategy to Achieve Sustained Economic Growth,* edited by Claudio Loser and Eliot Kalter, . Washington, D.C.: International Monetary Fund, 1992.

Kaslow, Amy. "Mexico's Recovery Rides on Investor Confidence." *Christian Science Monitor* (October 18, 1995): 5.

Kaufman, Robert R. "Stabilization and Adjustment in Argentina, Brazil and Mexico." In *Economic Crisis and Policy Change: The Politics of Adjustment in the Third World,* edited by Joan M. Nelson. Princeton, N.J.: Princeton University Press, 1990.

Keen, Benjamin. *A History of Latin America.* Boston, Mass.: Houghton Mifflin Company, 1992.

Ketkar, Suhas, Walter Molano, and Dorothy Ellis. "Colombia: A Post-Inauguration Update." *CS First Boston Economist Department Update* (November 10, 1994): .

Kjonnerod, L. Erik, ed. *Evolving U.S. Strategy for Latin America and the Caribbean.* Washington, D.C.: National Defense University Press, 1992.

Kraft, Joseph. *The Mexican Rescue.* New York: Group of Thirty, 1984.

Kuttner, Robert. *The End of Laissez-Faire: National Purpose and the Global Economy after the Cold War.* New York: Alfred A. Knopf, 1991.

LDC Debt Report. "Bank Autonomy Plan Nudges Mexico Toward First World." *LDC Debt Report.* May 24, 1993: p.1.

LaFranchi, Howard. "Latin America's Longest Guerrilla War Tries a Short Cut." *Christian Science Monitor* (March 2, 1995): 7.

Lajous, Roberta, "Profile of Mexican Presidential Candidate Ernesto Zedillo." *North-South* (July-August 1994): 10–13.

Lambardi, John V. *Venezuela: The Search for Order, the Dream of Progress.* New York: Oxford University Press, 1982.

Larrain, Felipe and Marcelo Selowsky, eds. *The Public Sector and the Latin American Crisis.* San Francisco: ICS Press, 1991.

Latin American Investment Securities Limited, *Colombia: A Look at the Stock Market and Economy* (London) March 1992.

Lavin, J. *Chile: A Quiet Revolution.* Santiago: Empresa Editora Zig-Zag, 1988.

Lee, Rensselaer W. III. *The White Labyrinth: Cocaine and Political Power.* New Brunswick, N.J.: Transaction Publishers, 1989.

Lewis, Paul. *The Crisis in Argentine Capitalism.* Chapel Hill, N.C.: University of North Carolina Press, 1992.

Loser, Claudio and Eliot Kalter, eds. *Mexico: The Strategy to Achieve Sustained Economic Growth.* Washington, D.C.: International Monetary Fund, September 1992.

Lowenthal, Abraham F. *Partners in Conflict: The United States and Latin America.* Baltimore, MD: The Johns Hopkins University Press, 1987.

Lowenthal, Abraham F. and Gregory F. Treverton, eds. *Latin America in a New World.* Boulder: Westview Press, 1994.

Luke, Paul. "Venezuela: Edging Back from the Brink." *Developing Country Research Morgan Grenfell Debt Arbitrage and Trading* (London), July 27, 1992.

Lustig, Nora. *Mexico: The Remaking of an Economy.* Washington, D.C.: Brookings Institution, 1992.

———. "Introduction." in Lustig, ed. *Coping with Austerity, Poverty and Inequality in Latin America.* Washington, D.C.: Brookings, 1995.

MacDonald, Scott B. "Colombia." In *International Handbook on Drug Control*, edited by Scott B. MacDonald and Bruce Zagaris, 157–70. Westport, Conn.: Greenwood Press, 1992.

———. "The Latins Are Coming, The Latins Are Coming . . . to the U.S. Market." *North-South* (December 1993–January 1994): 37–40.

MacDonald, Scott B. and F. Joseph Demetrius. "The Caribbean Sugar Crisis: Consequences and Challenges." *Journal of Interamerican Studies and World Affairs* (Spring 1986): 35–58.

MacDonald, Scott B. and Georges A. Fauriol, eds. *The Politics of the Caribbean Sugar Trade.* New York: Praeger, 1991.

MacDonald, Scott B., Jane Hughes, and David Leith Crum. *New Tigers and Old Elephants: The Development Game in the 1990s and Beyond.* New Brunswick, N.J.: Transaction Press, 1995.

MacDonald, Scott B. *Dancing on a Volcano: The Latin American Drug Trade.* New York: Praeger, 1988.

———. *Mountain High, White Avalanche: Cocaine and Power in the Andean States and Panama.* New York: Praeger, 1989.

———, Margie Lindsay and David L. Crum, eds. *The Global Debt Crisis: Forecasting for the Future.* London: Pinter, 1990.

MacDonald, Scott B. and Paul Luke. "A Word to the Wise: Latin American Bond Issues." *LatinFinance* (May 1991): 43–46.

———. *The Argentine Economy in the 1990s: Out of the Rubble?* CSIS Policy Papers on the Americas vol. III, no. 1 (February 14, 1992).

MacDonald, Scott and Eric Mendelsohn. "Venezuela Faces Further Downgrades." *CS First Boston Corporate Strategist* (July 1994): 35–37.

MacDonald, Scott B. and Kathleen Stephonse. *Chile: A Country Profile, DLJ Credit Research.* February 1996.

Malán, Pedro and Regis Bonelli. "The Brazilian Economy in the Seventies: Old and New Developments." *World Development* 5, no. 1/2 (1977): .

Mandelbaum, Michael. "Foreign Policy as Social Work." *Foreign Affairs.* vol. 75, no. 1 (January/February, 1996): 16–32.

Mann, Joseph. "Venezuelan Opposition Picks Reformer." *Financial Times* (April 27, 1993): p. 7.

Martz, John D. "Party Elites and Leadership in Colombia and Venezuela." *Journal of Latin American Studies* (February 1992): .

———. "Venezuela." In *Latin America and Caribbean Contemporary Record, Volume VII: 1987–88*, edited by James M. Molloy and Eduardo A. Gamarra. New York: Holmes and Meier Publishers, 1990.

Maxfield, Sylvia. *Governing Capital: International Finance and Mexican Politics.* Ithaca, N.Y.: Cornell University Press, 1990.

McCartney, Scott and Jonathan Friedland. "Catching Up: Computer Sales Sizzle As Developing Nations Try to Shrink PC Gap." *Wall Street Journal* (June 24, 1995): 1.

McClintock, Cynthia and Abraham F. Lowenthal, eds. *The Peruvian Experiment Reconsidered.* Princeton, N.J.: Princeton University Press, 1983.

Mead, Gary. "Argentina Ending Oil Monopoly." *Financial Times* (July 12, 1990): 22.

Mesa-Lago, Carmelo. Cuba's Economic Recovery: How Good Are Those 1995 Predictions? *Cuba Brief* (Washington, D.C.: Freedom House, June 1995).

————, ed. *Cuba After the Cold War*. (Pittsburgh, PA: Pittsburgh University Press, 1993).

————. "Cuba's Centrally Planned Economy: An Equity Trade-Off for Growth." In *Latin American Political Economy: Financial Crisis and Political Change*, edited by Jonathan Hartlyn and Samuel A. Morley, 292–318. Boulder, Colo.: Westview Press, 1986.

Miller, Tom. *Trading with the Enemy: A Yankee Travels Through Castro's Cuba*. New York: Atheneum, 1992.

Millman, Gregory J. *The Vandals' Crown: How Rebel Currency Traders Overthrew the World's Central Banks*. New York: The Free Press, 1995.

Miralles, Melchor. "Dinero negro, Beneficio blanco." *Elite* (Caracas) (January 1, 1990): 34–37.

Moffett, Matt. "Venezuela's Crusade Against Hoarders Affirms the Obvious: The Economy Is Shot." *Wall Street Journal* (July 13, 1994): 12.

Molineu, Harold. *U.S. Policy Toward Latin America*. (Boulder, Colo.: Westview Press, 1990).

Montaner, Carlos Alberto. "The Cuban Revolution and Its Acolytes." *Society* (July/ August 1994): 73–79.

Moody's Investors Service. "Press Release: Anchor Glass SR Notes Cut to 'B2' from 'Ba3'." *Bloomberg* (September 27, 1995): .

Moreira, Marcilio Marques. *The Brazilian Quandary*. New York: Priority Press, 1986.

Morris, Felipe with Mark Dorfman, José Pedro Ortiz, and Maria Claudia Franco. "Latin America's Banking Systems in the 1980s: A Cross-Country Comparison." *World Bank Discussion Papers*, no. 81 (1990).

Naim, Moisés. "Latin America the Morning After." *Foreign Affairs* (June/August 1995): .

————. "Mexico's Larger Story." *Foreign Policy* (Summer 1995): 112–30.

————. *Paper Tigers & Minotaurs: The Politics of Venezuela's Economic Reforms*. Washington, D.C.: Carnegie Endowment for International Peace, 1993.

Nelson, Joan M. *Economic Crisis and Policy Choice: The Politics of Adjustment in the Third World*. Princeton, N.J.: Princeton University Press, 1990.

Newell G., Roberto and Luis Rubio F. *Mexico's Dilemma: The Political Origins of Economic Crisis*. (Boulder, Colo.: Westview Press, 1984).

Nye, Joseph S. "What New World Order?" *Foreign Affairs* (Spring 1992): .

Oppenheimer, Andres. "Three Scenarios for Zedillo." *North-South,* (July-August 1994): 14–17.

————. "Peru: On the Road to Full Democracy." *North-South* vol. 2, no. 3 (August-September 1992): 6–9.

————. *Castro's Final Hour: The Secret Story Behind the Coming Downfall of Communist Cuba*. New York: Simon and Schuster, 1992.

————. *Bordering on Chaos*. Boston: Little, Brown and Co., 1996.

Ortiz de Zevallos, Felipe. *The Peruvian Puzzle*. New York: Priority Press, 1989.

Palmer, David Scott. "Peru, the Drug Business, and Shining Path: Between Scylla and Charybdis?" *Journal of Interamerican Affairs and World Studies* vol. 34, no. 3 (Fall 1992): 65–88.

————, editor. *Shining Path of Peru*. New York: St. Martin's Press, 1992.

Passell, Peter. "Mexico's Lessons: Don't Depend on the Kindness of Foreign Investors." New York Times (January 12, 1995): D2.

Pfaff, William. *The Wrath of Nations: Civilization and the Furies of Nationalism*. New York: Simon and Schuster, 1993.

————. *Barbarian Sentiments: How the American Century Ends.* New York: Hill and Wang, 1989.

Purcell, Susan Kaufman. "Mexico's Political and Economic Reforms." *SAIS Review* (Winter-Spring 1995): 1–14.

Paredes, Carlos E. and Jeffery Sachs, eds. *Peru's Path to Recovery: A Plan for Economic Stabilization and Growth.* Washington, D.C.: Brookings Institution, 1991.

Pastor, Robert. *Whirlpool: U.S. Foreign Policy Toward Latin America and the Caribbean.* Princeton, N.J.: Princeton University Press, 1992.

Payne, Douglas W., Mark Falcoff, and Susan Kaufman Purcell. *Latin America: U.S. Policy after the Cold War.* New York: Americas Society, 1991.

Peagram, Norman. "Waking from a Dream State." *Euromoney* (September 1991):

Preeg, Ernest H. with Jonathan D. Levine. *Cuba and the New Caribbean Economic Order.* Washington, D.C.: CSIS Significant Issues Series, vol. XV, no. 2 1993.

Petras, James and Morris Morley. *U.S. Hegemon Under Seige: Class, Politics, and Development in Latin America.* New York: Verso, 1990.

Ranis, Gustav. "Will Latin America Now Put a Stop to 'Stop and Go'?" *Journal of Interamerican Studies and World Affairs.* vol. 38, no. 2/3 (Summer/Fall 1996): 127–40.

Report on the Independent Task Force, *Lessons of the Mexican Peso Crisis.* New York: Council on Foreign Relations, 1996.

Ritter, A.R.M. "The Cuban Economy in the 1990s: External Challenges and Policy Imperatives." *Journal of Interamerican Studies and World Affairs* vol. 32, no. 3 (Fall 1990): 117–50.

————. *The Economic Development of Revolutionary Cuba: Strategy and Performance.* New York: Praeger, 1974.

Rodriguez, Allen. "All That Glitters: Latin America's Stock Markets." *North South* (February-March 1994): 43–47.

Roett, Riordan. *Political & Economic Liberalization in Mexico* (Boulder, Colo.: Lynne Reiner, 1993).

————. *Brazil: Politics in a Patrimonial Society.* Boston, Mass.: Allyn and Bacon, Inc., 1972.

Rosenberg, Mark, ed. *The Changing Hemispheric Trade Environment: Opportunities and Obstacles.* Miami, Fl.: Florida International University, 1991.

Rosenberg, Tina. "Latin America's Magical Realism." *The Wilson Quarterly* (Autumn 1992): .

————. "Beyond Elections." *Foreign Policy* no. 84 (Fall 1991): 72–92.

Rubio, Luis. *Como va a Afectar a Mexico el Tratado de Libre Comercio?* Mexico: Fondo de Cultura Economica, 1992.

Rubio, Luis and Francisco Gil-Diaz. *A Mexican Response.* New York: Priority Press Publications, 1987.

Rufin, Jean-Christophe. *L'Empire et les nouveaux barbares.* Paris: Lattes, 1991.

Ruiz, Ramon Eduardo. *Triumphs and Tragedy: A History of the Mexican People.* New York: W.W. Norton and Company, 1992.

Sanders, Philip. "Foreign Investment in Chile Rises 16% to $1 Bln in First Qtr", *Bloomberg* (May 2, 1995): .

Scheno, Diana Jean. "Venezuela Joins the Latin Trend to Free Markets." *New York Times.* (April 27, 1996): 37–9.

Schneider, Ronald M. *"Order and Progress": A Political History.* Boulder, Colo.: Westview Press, 1991.

Schlossstein, Steven. *Asia's New Little Dragons: The Dynamic Emergence of Indonesia, Thailand, and Malaysia.* Chicago: Contemporary Books, 1991.

———. *The End of the American Century.* New York: Congdon & Weed, 1989.

Sigmund, Paul E. *The United States and Democracy in Chile.* Baltimore, MD: The Johns Hopkins University Press, 1993.

Skidmore, Thomas E. and Peter H. Smith. *Modern Latin America.* New York: Oxford University Press, 1989.

Skidmore, Thomas E. *Politics in Brazil: 1930–1964: An Experiment in Democracy.* London: Oxford University Press, 1967.

Skidmore, Thomas E. *The Politics of Military Rule in Brazil, 1964–85.* New York: Oxford University Press, 1988.

Smith, H. Peter. *Labyrinths of Power: Political Recruitment in Twentieth-Century Mexico.* Princeton, N.J.: University of Princeton Press, 1979.

Smith, Peter H. *Talons of the Eagle: dynamics of U.S.-Latin America Relations.* New York: Oxford University Press, 1996.

Smith, William C. "Neoliberal Economic Reforms and New Democracies in Latin America." *North-South Issues* (May 1992): .

———. *Authoritarianism and the Crisis of the Argentine Political Economy.* Stanford, Cal.: Stanford University Press, 1989.

Snow, Peter. "Argentina; Politics in a Conflictual Society." In *Latin American Politics and Development*, edited by Howard J. Wiarda and Harvey F. Kline, . Boulder, Colo.: Westview Press, 1990.

Stallings, Barbara and Robert Kaufman, eds. *Debt and Democracy in Latin America.* Boulder, Colo.: Westview Press, 1989.

Stepan, Alfred. "The Brazilian Impeachment and Beyond." *Camoes Center Quarterly*, (Autumn and Winter, 1992–1993): .

———. *State and Society: Peru in Comparative Perspective.* Princeton, N.J.: Princeton University Press, 1978.

Stoga, Alan. *Beyond Coexistence: The United States and Mexico.* CSIS Policy Papers on the Americas, vol. II, report no. 6 (May 10, 1991).

Strong, Simon. *Shining Path: Terror and Revolution in Peru.* New York: Times Books, 1992.

Thomas, Hugh S., Georges A. Fauriol and Juan Carlos Weiss. *The Cuban Revolution: 25 Years Later.* Boulder, Colo.: Westview Press, 1994.

Thomas, Hugh. *The Cuban Revolution.* New York: Harper & Row Publishers, 1977.

Thoumi, Francisco. "Why the Illegal Psychoactive Drugs Industry Grew in Colombia." *Journal of Interamerican Studies and World Affairs.* vol. 34, no. 3 (Fall 1992): 37–64.

Toffler, Alvin. *Powershift: Knowledge, Wealth and Violence at the Edge of the 21st Century.* New York: Bantam Books, 1991.

Treaster, Joseph B. "Arrest in Colombia Heartens U.S." *New York Times* (June 12, 1995): A8.

Truell, Peter and Larry Gurwin. *False Profits: The Inside Story of BCCI, the World's Most Corrupt Financial Empire.* New York: Houghton and Mifflin Company, 1992.

Truell, Peter. "Mexico Stands on Familiar Ground at Forefront of Foreign-Debt Crisis." *Wall Street Journal* (December 31, 1987) .

Tulchin, Joseph S., with Gary Bland. *Venezuela in the Wake of Radical Reform.* Washington, D.C.: Woodrow Wilson Center Current Studies on Latin America, 1993.

Urrutia, Miguel. "On the Absence of Economic Populism in Colombia." In *The Macroeconomics of Populism in Latin America*, edited by Rudiger Dornbusch and Sebastian Edwards, . Chicago: University of Chicago Press, 1991.

————. "Cost-Benefit Analysis of the Drug Trade for Colombia." Paper presented for the Project on Hemispheric Cooperation of Drug Abuse and Trafficking, April 1990, Woodrow Wilson Center, Washington, D.C. Mimeographed.

Valenzuela, Arturo. *The Breakdown of Democratic Regimes: Chile.* Baltimore, MD: The Johns Hopkins University Press, 1978.

Valenzuela, Arturo and Samuel Valenzuela, eds. *Military Rule in Chile: Dictatorship and Oppositions.* Baltimore, MD: The Johns Hopkins University Press, 1986.

Vargas Llosa, Mario. *Death in the Andes.* New York: Farrar, Straus & Giroux, 1995.

"Vitro and Corning Joining Forces", *El Financiero Internacional* (Mexico City), August 19, 1991: 3.

Weintraub, Sidney. *A Marriage of Convenience: Relations between Mexico and the United States.* New York: Oxford University Press, 1990.

Weintraub, Sidney. "The Economy of the Eve of Free Trade." *Current History: Mexico* (February 1993): 67–72.

Weintraub, Sidney. *NAFTA. What Comes Next?* Westport, Conn.: Praeger (The Washington Papers/166), 1994.

Weintraub, Sidney and M. Delal Baer. "The Interplay Between Economic and Political Opening: The Sequence in Mexico." *The Washington Quarterly* (Spring 1992): .

Whalen, Christopher. "Bordering on Repression." *Washington Post* (December 27, 1992): C1.

————. "Economic Outlook: Low Growth and Inflation, Rising Unemployment, External Deficits, and Foreign Debt." *The Mexican Report*, February 19, 1993: p.2.

Wiarda, Howard J. "Sustaining the Democratic Revolution." *The Washington Quarterly.* vol. 18, no. 3 (Summer 1995): 91–2.

————. *The Democratic Revolution in Latin America.* New York: Holmes and Meier Publishers, 1990.

Wiarda, Howard J. *Democracy and its Discontents: development, interdependence, and U.S. Policy in Latin America.* Lanham, MD: Rowman & Littlefield, 1995.

Wiarda, Howard J. and Harvey F. Kline, eds. *Latin American Politics and Development.* Boulder, Colo.: Westview Press, 1989.

Williamson, John, ed. *The Progress of Policy Reform in Latin America.* Washington, D.C.: Institute for International Economics, 1990.

YPF, *YPF Prospectus* (for the issuing of ADRs on the New York Stock Exchange), January 5, 1994.

Official Documents

Banco Central de Chile. *Statistical Synthesis of Chile, 1985–1989.* Santiago: Banco Central de Chile, 1990.

Banco de Mexico. *The Mexican Economy, 1993.* Mexico: Banco de Mexico, 1993.

Government of Brazil. *Plano de Controle Macroeconomic.* Ministero da Fazenda, July 1987.

Inter-American Development Bank. *Economic and Social Progress in Latin America 1987 Report.* Washington, D.C.: Inter-American Development Bank, 1987.

————. *Economic and Social Progress in Latin America 1989 Report.* Washington, D.C.: Inter-American Development Bank, 1989.

International Finance Corporation. *Emerging Markets Factbook 1991.* Washington, D.C.: International Finance Corporation, 1991.
International Monetary Fund. *International Financial Statistics Yearbook 1991.* Washington, D.C.: International Monetary Fund, 1991.
————. *International Financial Statistics, March 1996.* Washington, D.C.: International Monetary Fund, 1996.
Organization for Economic Cooperation and Development. *OECD Economic Survey: Mexico.* Paris: Organization for Economic Cooperation and Development, 1992.
U.S. Congress, Joint Economic Committee. *The Caribbean Basin: Economic and Security Issues.* (Washington, D.C.: U.S. Government Printing Office, 1993).
U.S. Department of State, Bureau of International Narcotics Matters. International Narcotics Control Strategy Report, March 1988. (Washington, D.C.: U.S. Department of State, March 1988).
U.S. Drug Enforcement Administration. Colombian Economic Reform: The Impact on Drug Money Laundering Within the Colombian Economy. (Washington, D.C.: Drug Enforcement Administration, September 1994).
World Bank. *World Development Report 1980.* Washington, D.C.: World Bank, 1980.
————. *World Debt Tables, External Debt of Developing Countries, Volume III. Country Tables, 1970–1979.* Washington, D.C.: World Bank, 1989.
————. *Argentina: Reforms for Price Stability and Growth.* Washington, D.C.: World Bank, 1990.
————. *Argentina: Reallocating Resources for the Improvement of Education.* Washington, D.C.: World Bank, 1991.
————. *Venezuela and the World Bank: Preparing for the Future.* Washington, D.C.: World Bank, 1992.
————. *World Development Report 1994.* Washington, D.C.: World Bank, 1994.
————. *World Development Report 1995.* Washington, D.C.: World Bank, 1995.

Index

Agriculture. *See also* Drug trade;
  Industry
  Argentina, 72–73
  Chile, 40, 41
  ejido farms (Mexico), 123, 129,
    145n41
  Latin America, 7–8
  Mexico, 114, 123, 128–30, 145n41
  Venezuela, 178, 196
Albania, 231–32
Alessandri, Arturo, 30
Alfonsín, Raúl, 67–69
Alfonso, José F., 242
Allende, Salvador, 32–34
American Popular Revolutionary
  Alliance (APRA) (Peru), 202, 207–
  13, 220
Andean Pact, 103–4, 263. *See also*
    Economic trade
Argentina. *See also* Latin America;
    Latin America, 1980s
  agriculture, 72–73
  Alfonsín administration, 67–69
  Austral Plan, 68
  authoritarianism, 64
  black deal, 78, 87n34
  Campora administration, 65
  Confederación General del Trabajo
    (CGT), 77–78
  constitution, 73
  corruption, 66, 79–80
  currency, 66, 70, 81–82
  democracy, 14, 59, 62–64, 68, 69,
    75, 76, 85n4

economic growth, 5, 6, 59–60
economic reform, 14, 20–21, 70–73
economic reform obstacles, 75–83
economic trade, 2, 55–56, 60, 66–
  67, 68–69, 72–73, 263, 266
fiscal policy, 80–81
foreign debt, 59, 66–67, 68, 82–83
foreign investment in, 1–2, 61
Front for a Country in Solidarity
  (FREPASO), 74
future economic assessment, 83–85
history, 60–63
human rights, 66
Illia administration, 64
import-substitution model, 66–67
inflation, 59, 66, 67, 68–69
International Monetary Fund (IMF),
  82–83
Menem administration, 59, 69–75
MERCOSUR, 55–56, 263, 266
militarism, 62–67, 78–79
Onganía administration, 64–65
Perón administration, 62, 63–64,
  65–66
politics, 14, 59, 60–67, 73–75, 85n4
privatization, 70–71
Radical Civic Union (UCR), 61–64,
  68, 73–75
socialism, 61–62, 85n4
standard of living, 7, 63, 75
stocks, 1–2
taxation, 72
terrorism, 66
unionization, 63, 65, 68, 76–78,
  87n34

307